"Sylvia and Brian are two of my favc
churched or under-churched, they sti
new book is perfect for scholars and new Bible readers alike, and for everyone in between. They rescue one of the most misused books of the Bible from the hands of colonizers and crusaders. And they help us listen with first-century ears to the anti-imperial love story of Romans."

—**Shane Claiborne**, author, activist, and cofounder of Red Letter Christians

"If you want to hear—and experience—Paul's letter to the Jewish and gentile Christ-followers in Rome as you never have, read this book. And re-read it. Study it in your church circles. Talk about it with your friends. Assign it in your courses. As with their earlier *Colossians Remixed*, Keesmaat and Walsh have once again interwoven close textual reading of the New Testament (they clearly *love* the Scriptures!) with its unabashedly Jewish roots and its explosive relationship to the Roman imperial context. Most importantly, they bring the message of Romans into dialogue with our lives today, as we struggle to be faithful to the good news of Messiah Jesus in our own imperial context."

—**J. Richard Middleton**, Northeastern Seminary
at Roberts Wesleyan College

"In 1918 Karl Barth published his commentary on Romans, which ignited a profound theological turn. A century later, Keesmaat and Walsh write into the headwinds of Trumpism, deepening social disparity, ecological crisis, and endless war. Building on recent scholarship, this brilliant study engages the original audience, who labored under the shadow of empire, in a way that brings its message to life for similarly struggling North American Christians. The authors employ a robust imagination, an interlocutor, and keen historical literacy to free Romans from its captivity to dogmatic and pietistic interpretations, restoring it to its social context (with all its disturbing parallels to our own). The result is a fresh and committed reading by two of our generation's best interpreters of Word and world. May it, too, inspire a turning!"

—**Ched Myers**, Bartimaeus Cooperative Ministries

"You (and I!) have never read Romans like this before. It has been weaponized by some and reduced to abstraction by others as has perhaps no other biblical book. Sylvia Keesmaat and Brian Walsh have disarmed such uses and returned it to the real, flesh-and-blood world. The sheer immensity of the gospel, announced as it is in the midst of the frightening, frustrating, groaning grind of actual life, is nothing short of exhilarating. The scholarship herein provides a deep foundation for an imagination that is even greater. Keesmaat and Walsh introduce to the hermeneutic process both a present-day interlocutor, who raises many of the questions and objections you may have yourself, and two residents of ancient Rome, who 'hear' the epistle as it is first read, granting us fresh access to the world we live in and how we are invested in it. The authors don't attempt to wrestle from the text (yet again) Paul's systematic theology of the gospel; instead, by rooting their exegesis firmly in history, the practical and revolutionary nature of the gospel is revealed. Here the empire of any era, including our own, is disarmed and its caesar cast down; its perverse values repudiated; and the liberating, home-making, salvific power of a greater Lord and King is revealed."

—**Greg Paul**, Sanctuary Toronto community member and author of *God in the Alley* and *Resurrecting Religion*

"In *Romans Disarmed*, Keesmaat and Walsh use an artistic mix of story, poetry, imaginative discourse, and solid biblical and social-cultural-historical background that allows the reader to understand the book of Romans from an alternative, and I believe more accurate, point of view. Paul's letter to the Romans was not written from an enlightenment-bound worldview and this book dislodges any such notions. I am grateful for the authors' skill in helping us all view the apostle Paul's world and ours through an unconventional and more preferable lens; one that has tremendous practical application for us today."

—**Randy S. Woodley**, author of *Shalom and the Community of Creation: An Indigenous Vision*

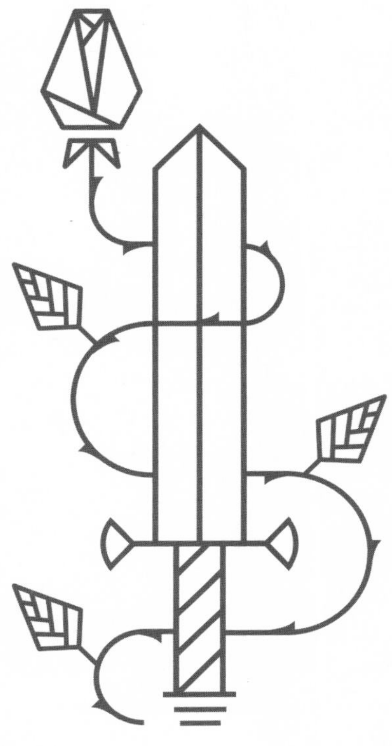

ROMANS DISARMED

RESISTING EMPIRE, DEMANDING JUSTICE

SYLVIA C. KEESMAAT AND BRIAN J. WALSH

BrazosPress
a division of Baker Publishing Group
Grand Rapids, Michigan

Published by Brazos Press
a division of Baker Publishing Group
PO Box 6287, Grand Rapids, MI 49516-6287
www.brazospress.com

Printed in the United States of America

Library of Congress Cataloging-in-Publication Data
Names: Keesmaat, Sylvia C., author. | Walsh, Brian J., 1953–, author.
Title: Romans disarmed : resisting empire, demanding justice / Sylvia C. Keesmaat and Brian J. Walsh.
Description: Grand Rapids: Brazos Press, 2019. | Includes bibliographical references and index.
Identifiers: LCCN 2018034282 | ISBN 9781587432842 (pbk.: alk. paper)
Subjects: LCSH: Bible. Romans—Criticism, interpretation, etc.
Classification: LCC BS2665.52 .K37 2019 | DDC 227/.106—dc23
LC record available at https://lccn.loc.gov/2018034282.

ISBN 978-1-58743-442-6 (casebound)

19 20 21 22 23 24 25 7 6 5 4 3 2 1

To the Sanctuary Community

a city of refuge in the heart of Toronto

Contents

Abbreviations

General

alt.	altered translation
BCE	before the Common Era
CE	Common Era
cf.	*confer*, compare
chap(s).	chapter(s)
ed.	edition, edited by, editor
e.g.	*exempli gratia*, for example
esp.	especially
et al.	*et alia*, and others
i.e.	*id est*, that is
LXX	Septuagint (Greek version of the Jewish Scriptures)
MT	Masoretic Text (Hebrew)
n.	note
no(s).	number(s)
p(p).	page(s)
repr.	reprint
rev.	revised
trans.	translated by, translation, translator
v(v).	verse(s)
vol(s).	volume(s)

Modern Scripture Versions

NIV	New International Version (2011)
NRSV	New Revised Standard Version (1989)
RSV	Revised Standard Version

Old Testament

Gen.	Genesis
Exod.	Exodus
Lev.	Leviticus
Num.	Numbers
Deut.	Deuteronomy
Josh.	Joshua
Judg.	Judges
Ruth	Ruth
1–2 Sam.	1–2 Samuel
1–2 Kings	1–2 Kings
1–2 Chron.	1–2 Chronicles
Ezra	Ezra
Neh.	Nehemiah
Esther	Esther
Job	Job
Ps./Pss.	Psalm/Psalms
Prov.	Proverbs
Eccles.	Ecclesiastes
Song	Song of Songs
Isa.	Isaiah
Jer.	Jeremiah
Lam.	Lamentations
Ezek.	Ezekiel
Dan.	Daniel
Hosea	Hosea
Joel	Joel
Amos	Amos
Obad.	Obadiah
Jon.	Jonah
Mic.	Micah
Nah.	Nahum

Hab.	Habakkuk
Zeph.	Zephaniah
Hag.	Haggai
Zech.	Zechariah
Mal.	Malachi

New Testament

Matt.	Matthew
Mark	Mark
Luke	Luke
John	John
Acts	Acts
Rom.	Romans
1–2 Cor.	1–2 Corinthians
Gal.	Galatians
Eph.	Ephesians
Phil.	Philippians
Col.	Colossians
1–2 Thess.	1–2 Thessalonians
1–2 Tim.	1–2 Timothy
Titus	Titus
Philem.	Philemon
Heb.	Hebrews
James	James
1–2 Pet.	1–2 Peter
1–3 John	1–3 John
Jude	Jude
Rev.	Revelation

Old Testament Apocrypha and Pseudepigrapha

1 En.	1 Enoch
1–4 Macc.	1–4 Maccabees
2 Bar.	2 Baruch
Sib. Or.	Sibylline Oracles
Sir.	Sirach
Wis.	Wisdom of Solomon

Preface

It is a sleepy, hot afternoon as we walk from the house down to the pasture to move the fences for the cows. It is so hot that the cows are congregating under the trees in the laneway, slowly chewing over their morning graze. The dogs walk slowly with their tongues out. Mosquitoes and deer flies buzz around our heads. We have forgotten that in six months we won't be able to walk down here without battling the snow in coats, hats, and boots. As we walk we talk about Romans: How would a slave have heard this letter? How would someone captured from Judea have heard it? What about someone who had lost their land? Would gender make a difference? It is a leisurely conversation, punctuated by brief comments about where the fence line should be today and how hard and dry the ground is getting. This daily walk to move the cattle is a little oasis. When we return to the house we will need to pick up one of our kids from work. The phone will ring. We will need to finish marking a thesis. There will be a sermon to be written, a pastoral conversation to be had. And we will be back into the busyness of life on a farm, with kids and interns.

In some ways this brief glimpse into our daily summer routine captures the dynamic of writing this book. The years that we have spent speaking, preaching, teaching, and writing about Romans have also been filled with farming, raising children, doing campus ministry, and mentoring interns and students. This has slowed our writing considerably and enriched it in many ways. We apologize to those who have been waiting many years for this book. As those who have read our previous book, *Colossians Remixed*, will know, we seek to ground our reading of Paul in the minutiae of daily life, both in the first century and today. Such a grounding takes time, not only to read the extensive literature on first-century Roman life and the Epistle to the Romans but also to explore the parallels in our own time to the issues that Paul was addressing. The result is, we hope, a book that firmly places the Bible in the messiness of daily life.

As you will see, we have attempted to provide an embodied reading of Romans in many ways: through the eyes of first-century hearers of the letter, by means of targum, and through dialogue with a present-day interlocutor. All of these genres are in service of making Romans come alive for our readers both as a vivid, challenging letter in the first century and as an engaging and compelling letter today.

Our reading of the Bible has been deeply shaped over the years by the work of our friends Ched Myers and Elaine Enns. Ched also invited Sylvia to teach the biblical component of a permaculture design course that had a deep impact on the writing of this book and on our lives. We thank Ched and Elaine for creating fruitfulness and healing at the margins for so many of us.

There are many other people without whom this book would not have been possible. At the top of the list are a number of our summer interns who not only came to learn about permaculture, organic gardening, and sustainable living but also insisted that their task was to make it possible for us to write. We would especially like to thank Justin Van Zee, Ben Stevenson, Imelda Lee, Robert Miller, Jamie Miller, Ben Lootens, and Claire Perttula. Without you guys telling us repeatedly, "We've got this; go inside and write!" this book wouldn't have been finished. We will have to wait for the resurrection to thank our friend and intern Adam Wood. Our ongoing sorrow over the tragic loss of Adam is never too far from the surface in this book.

In addition, there are those who made it possible for us to share this material with others by looking after the farm while we were away: Benjamin Groenewold and Tricia Van Dyk, Dave Krause, Eliot Abbey-Colborne, Carla Veldman, John Kirstein and Joanna Douglas (and Louis!), and Robert and Jamie Miller. We are deeply grateful that you were willing to take on the challenges of heating and cooking with a woodstove, negotiating how to live with only solar power, and dealing with animals and, occasionally, snow.

Various audiences in Australia, England, the United States, and Canada listened to and gave us feedback on various portions of the book, as did our students at the Institute for Christian Studies and Wycliffe College, as well as members of St. James Anglican Church, Fenelon Falls. The Wine Before Breakfast community that Brian pastors has been through the Epistle to the Romans three times in the past twelve years. Members of the Generous Space community listened to a number of chapters at their annual CampOut. Questions and challenges from many people in these places were woven together to become the voice of our interlocutor throughout the book. We thank you for prodding us to be clearer, giving us new insights, and making us change our minds on occasion. In a very real sense, this book was written for your pastoral needs, your struggles with the Bible and Paul, and your deep desire to walk with Jesus. Various student preachers at Wine Before Breakfast also deepened our insights into Romans. They are duly acknowledged in the footnotes!

In addition to our students, a number of other people read portions of this book and gave welcome feedback: Tom Wright, Aaron Holbrough, Lyds Keesmaat-Walsh, Beth Carlson-Malina, and Terry LeBlanc. Terry provided valuable Indigenous wisdom to us as we negotiated the slippery terrain of writing about Indigenous suffering from our place as part of the colonial majority. We hope that in spite of our own privilege we have been able to provide a helpful context for telling that story of suffering, and we urge our readers to hear that story directly from Indigenous teachers and storytellers themselves.

Byron Borger and Andrew Stephens-Rennie read the entire manuscript and provided detailed feedback that was profoundly insightful and improved the book considerably. Susan Spicer not only read the entire manuscript but was also a source of pastoral encouragement throughout this project.

Geoff Wichert, in a stroke of brilliance, came up with the title *Romans Disarmed*. This is a lovely double entendre on the way in which the letter to the Romans both disarms the violence of the first-century Roman Empire (and our imperial realities today) and the way in which the letter to the Romans needs to be disarmed itself, after centuries of being used theologically as an instrument of oppression and exclusion.

We are thankful not only for Geoff's ability to catch our intent so clearly but also for his support and presence as a colleague in campus ministry. We also thank Brian's other colleagues in campus ministry: Marcia Boniferro, Carol Scovil, Deb Whalen, Amanda Jagt, and Aileen Verdun. All of you enable us to see how the story that Paul tells might indeed be true.

We are grateful to Aileen Verdun for preparing the indexes. Her theological depth meant that the task was done with creativity and enthusiasm.

Our editor at Brazos, Bob Hosack, didn't give up on this project when it took so long. We have appreciated his patience. Melisa Blok provided astute editing that improved our writing in many places. Her comments and questions also helped us to discern where further clarity was needed. We are deeply grateful for her good work.

Serving as a Christian Reformed campus minister at the University of Toronto has proven to be a deeply hospitable calling for Brian's writing projects over the years. We are indebted to Classis Toronto of the CRC for supporting this work through sabbaticals and writing leaves. Andrew and Ericka Stephens-Rennie are alumni of this campus ministry, and they generously supported one of those writing leaves. Thank you, dear friends. The Priscilla and Stanford Reid Trust have been generous in their support of every one of Brian's writing projects for the past twenty years. We hope that this book bears good witness to the kind of culturally transformative faith that animated the Reid's lives.

Our children, especially the two youngest, have grown up with conversations about Romans swirling in the air. We thank Madeleine and Lyds for listening to lectures and talks about Romans over and over again as we dragged them around the world. And we thank Jubal and Sue for the joy they bring into our lives, and especially our grandson Oskar for making us get down on the floor to play with trains.

This book would not have taken the shape it did without our friends who are part of the Sanctuary Community in Toronto. Sanctuary is a diverse community of poor and rich; homeless and housed; settler and Indigenous; Black, white, and Asian; straight, gay, trans, and bi, all equally broken, all resting in grace. They are singing, dancing, eating, weeping, and laughing their way into the alternative community that Paul envisions. We can't name you all, but we want to mention a few who have influenced us deeply: Simon Beairsto, Greg Paul, Thea Prescod, and Rachel Tulloch. The Sanctuary Community gives us hope and makes it possible for us to carry on in these dark times. This book is dedicated, in lament and hope, to the entire Sanctuary Community.

Russet House Farm
The Feast of St. Mary Magdalene
2018

Visit http://empireremixed.com/romansdisarmed
to access a study guide
and additional resources for this book.

1

Reading Romans and Disarming Empire

Joy and Sorrow in the City of Refuge

It takes fewer than two bars for everyone to know what's up. Fewer than eight beats and anyone who hasn't been dancing joins the throng. Hands raised, feet moving, smiles of recognition, faces of joy.

There we were. Rich and poor, Indigenous, white, Black, and Asian, well-housed and homeless, straight, gay, trans, and bi, young and old, male and female, all dancing till kingdom come.

You see,

> There's a city across a river
> and it's shining from within.
> People are dancing on the ramparts
> beckoning to you, come on in,
> to the city of refuge.[1]

It's another night at Grace's. Another night of music and art at Sanctuary in Toronto.[2] Another night of celebration.

1. Red Rain, "City of Refuge," track 3 on *A Night at Grace's*, Red Rain, 2006. Used by permission.

2. Sanctuary is an amazingly inclusive church and ministry in the downtown core of Toronto, and Red Rain is, in effect, the rock band that founded this church. See www.sanctuarytoronto.ca.

It is the thirtieth anniversary of Red Rain, the rock and blues band that has always been at the heart of this inner-city church. And as the band launches into "City of Refuge," the Sanctuary Community dances with deep longing and enthusiastic joy, with faith and doubt, with tears of loss and hope, and with a confidence that *this* dance floor *is* a city of refuge, even as we long for the liberation of that other city, across the river, that's shining from within. This night *we* are dancing on the ramparts beckoning everyone to come on in to the city of refuge.

We didn't have to bribe the doorman to get into this party. We didn't have to be one of the beautiful people to get into this club. We didn't need to have a ticket or dress a certain way or know the right people. There were no reserved seats and no preferential treatment for certain folks. And on the dance floor, the only thing that got special attention was the enthusiasm of your dancing, there for all to enjoy.

The joy was palpable. As we belted out that chorus together about a city across a river that's shining from within, the shining seemed to come directly from us. There was light, liberation, and deep, deep joy on that dance floor.

But just a few feet from the dancing throng, something else was happening. Just on the edge of the dance floor, there was deep, deep grief. Frenchy had been the first guy on the floor that evening. There he was, all by himself, dancing and beckoning others to join him. Frenchy was grooving to the music, hands outstretched, embodying joy. And there he stayed throughout the first set and into the second.

Until something happened. We don't know what it was. Maybe a line in a song hit him hard. Maybe he just remembered something. But in the midst of his joy, sorrow surfaced. Frenchy sat on the sidelines and wept. Surrounded by friends who were holding him in their arms, Frenchy wept and wept and wept.

And somehow, though he could no longer dance, we all knew that he was still in the city of refuge. Whether he was on the dance floor in exuberant joy or collapsed in a chair in profound grief, this party, this community, this place remained a city of refuge for him. He was safe in his joy and safe in his sorrow.

When the apostle Paul describes the character of the Christian community living at the heart of the Roman Empire, he writes, "Rejoice with those who rejoice, weep with those who weep" (Rom. 12:15). Frenchy asked us to do both of those things that night at Sanctuary: join him on the dance floor, embracing the joy of life in music and liberating dance, and then sit with him, embracing him in his grief, loss, pain, and hurt.

While hope is born of joy, grief is the child of shattered hope. When the apostle offers his first doxology in the epistle to the Romans, he writes, "May the God of hope fill you with all joy and peace in believing, so that you may abound in hope by the power of the Holy Spirit" (15:13). This comes at the end of a passage calling the Roman Christians to be a community of radical welcome. Only in such expansive hospitality will the "gentiles" rejoice. Welcome begets joy and joy begets hope. "May the God of hope fill you with all joy and peace in believing *so that* you may abound in hope." We need joy, the apostle is intimating, if we are to have hope. And the joy on the dance floor that night—Frenchy's joy and everyone else's—proved Paul's point. While we were dancing together, even though we all knew of the hard evidence against joy in our city, in our own lives, and all around us, the joy of the dance filled us with hope nonetheless.

Until it didn't. At a certain point, the joy of music and dance could not be sustained and the sorrow took over. Frenchy and the rest of the community had good cause for sorrow, good cause for losing hope. So many had died in the past months. So many had been beaten down, bruised and abused by a life of poverty, alcoholism, disease, violence, drug abuse, and homelessness. So many had borne the scars, the festering wounds of racism, oppression, and cultural genocide. And so many of those who had been lost were Indigenous brothers and sisters.

Each death hurts, but there was one death that was still very close and raw in the community that night. Greg "Iggy" Spoon had died on March 17, 2015, one day short of his forty-seventh birthday.[3] This First Nations brother had seen some hard times. He was bruised and broken, acquainted with grief.[4] His life was plagued with alcoholism and other substance abuse, homelessness, violence, and trouble with the police. And yet Iggy was recognized in the Sanctuary Community as an artist, a teacher, and a friend. It was never easy with our brother Iggy, but something about this man made him a respected member of the community. When he was admitted into the intensive care unit in early March, the community set up a twenty-four-hour vigil. Iggy, who had spent so much of his life on the streets, was never alone. And when he died, he was surrounded by some twenty friends and family, so deeply was Iggy loved and honored. His memorial service was a standing-room-only event. Frenchy was Iggy's close friend.

This party, the thirtieth anniversary of Red Rain, happened with the pain of Iggy's death still fresh in everyone's hearts.[5] The release, two days earlier, of the

3. Greg Paul shares something of Iggy's story in his *Resurrecting Religion: Finding Our Way Back to the Good News* (Colorado Springs: NavPress, 2018), 173–79.

4. See Anna Bowen, "Cop Out," March 19, 2014, *This*, https://this.org/2014/03/19/mayjune-cover-story-cop-out/.

5. Since Iggy's passing, there have been other deaths in the First Nations community connected to Sanctuary, one from a massive heart attack and another from suicide. And Ramsey Whitefish, who mournfully sang a lament at Iggy's memorial service, was murdered.

report of Canada's Truth and Reconciliation Commission only deepened the sense of hurt and betrayal.[6] This prestigious body openly declared that Canada's policy of forceful removal of Indigenous children to place them in church-based residential schools amounted to nothing less than an act of cultural genocide. This was an important, yet deeply painful, truth. This wasn't a social "issue" for us. This was personal. This was about Iggy and Chris and James and Fred and so many other members of the community. This report described a shared grief in our midst.

You need a great capacity for joy if you are to sustain life in the midst of such sorrow. But any "joy" that averts its gaze from sorrow, any "joy" that will not embrace the grief and hurt at the heart of things, is cheap sentimentality at best, an emotional cover-up and lie at worst. And if you are going to look sorrow in the face, then you will need to name names. You will need to have the courage, audacity, and prophetic honesty to name the source of that pain, and to name the forces that will strip us of hope.

Our friends at Sanctuary understand this better than most. And so Red Rain introduced a new song that night. It is called "Iggy's Song." Slowing things down and moving the show to a place of quieter introspection, Red Rain front man and Sanctuary pastor Greg Paul spoke of joy and sorrow, of the Truth and Reconciliation Commission, and of Iggy. And then lead guitarist Dan Robins began to sing the song that he wrote, starting with the chorus:

> I saw you shaking your head
> I clearly heard what you said
> Another f***ing drunk Indian better off dead
> You don't know s*** about me[7]

Dan Robins isn't a man given to profanity. He's usually the guy with the innocent, though slightly off-the-wall, humor. But not tonight. Taking Iggy's voice, and the voice of so many of our other Indigenous friends, Dan named the attitude of dismissal and disgust that our friends face every day on the streets of Toronto and throughout the Americas. And he named the reality that shaped that attitude: "You don't know s*** about me."

6. Canada's Truth and Reconciliation Commission has now been transferred to the National Centre for Truth and Reconciliation (NCTR). The report of the Canadian Truth and Reconciliation Commission can be accessed at their archived website: http://www.trc.ca/websites/trcinstitution/index.php?p=890 or at http://nctr.ca/reports.php.

7. The publisher does not allow the rendering of certain expletives in print; hence we have emended the original lyrics.

The song proceeds to educate the hearer about "the crack and meth and Listerine / the cheap booze and weed and gasoline / the suicide and incest and fear you've never seen." This was Iggy's reality. But this brokenness didn't come from some inherent character fault in First Nations people. No, it has its roots in colonial oppression.

> Raped by the white man for hundreds of years
> The traders, the army, and the pioneers
> The government, police, and the church overseers
> You don't know s*** about me

You don't know about the despair and anguish of the reservations, the squalor of a system of neglect and broken promises. You have no idea of the rich spirituality that has been desecrated and bludgeoned to death.

> Abused since we were babies, no one heard our cries
> You're so quick to judge, so quick to despise
> My heart feels the hatred there in your eyes
> You don't know s*** about me[8]

The loud and boisterous crowd at Sanctuary was rendered silent. One community member, whose shouts of joy tend to pierce the air at these kinds of parties, came over to us to be held in her sadness and to ask for prayer.

Paul writes his epistle to the Romans from a place of "great sorrow and unceasing anguish" (9:2). We suspect that you can't really understand what Paul is up to in this ancient letter if you don't have some access to such a place. In his opening greetings Paul says that he has been "longing" to visit the Christian communities in Rome so that there might be some mutual encouragement (1:11–12). This isn't just a polite way to say that he's tried to get there but circumstances have prevented such a visit. No, there is a longing here that can be heard throughout the letter. Paul's desire for mutual encouragement is in the face of a deeply discouraging situation. There is a pathos to Paul's writing that gets lost when interpretation gets too focused on the nature of the theological argument that Paul is mounting. For example, it is no accident that when Paul uses the psalms of Israel in his writing of this letter, he tends to reach for psalms of lament.[9] Here, it would seem, the apostle finds a spiritual

8. Dan Robins, "Iggy's Song," unpublished. Used by permission.
9. E.g., Pss. 10; 18; 44; 71; 94; 110; and 143.

and emotional resonance with his own understanding of the gospel at the heart of the Roman Empire.

Indeed, for the apostle, this pathos, this longing, goes all the way down and all the way up. A bondage has taken hold of creation, and that is why all of creation "has been groaning in labor pains" (8:22), longing to be set free, aching for rebirth. And as creation groans, so also do we "groan inwardly while we wait for adoption, the redemption of our bodies" (8:23). There is a resonance here between the anguish of humanity and the anguish of creation that a person like Iggy would deeply understand. But the pathos that goes all the way down to the core of creation also goes all the way up to the heart of God. In concert with both human and nonhuman creation, the Spirit "intercedes with sighs too deep for words" (8:26). In the face of the violent, fruitless, and despairing bondage of creation and humanity, the Spirit adds her voice with wordless groans. Again, Iggy would get this.

Somehow we will have to find ourselves in the midst of this pathos, this sorrow and anguish, if we are going to understand Paul's letter to the Romans. We will need to find ourselves both on the dance floor in liberating joy and on the sidelines holding Frenchy, keeping vigil at Iggy's bedside, bearing witness to one more death, one more betrayal, one more deep, deep hurt, with tears running down our cheeks. Without standing in such places, we will miss the power of this epistle both in its ancient context and in a contemporary reading.

There is, however, nothing generic about hurt and betrayal. Sorrow and anguish are always located in real time and real places. This kind of pathos is specific to particular hurt and oppression. As both Dan Robins's song and the Truth and Reconciliation Commission's report attest, the wounds and scars of the First Nations people of Canada (and by extension all Indigenous peoples around the world) are rooted in a history of colonialism. Iggy was, among other things, a casualty of empire, and we do his memory a disservice if we do not name his pain in such a way.

In the face of such imperial hurt, Canada's Truth and Reconciliation Commission has called for a unilateral disarmament process. The empire of colonialism must be disarmed if there is to be justice, healing, and reconciliation with the First Nations.

Of course, empires never voluntarily disarm themselves, precisely because such disarmament would entail the dismantling of the empire itself, and that would be a betrayal of its own narrative of cultural superiority. The story of empire is always one of more cultural, economic, and military power, never less.

Indeed, from the perspective of empire, maintaining hegemony amounts to a moral imperative. The unfolding of history and the progress of civilization depend on the growth of the empire. From the center of empire, relinquishing such power voluntarily is unimaginable. From the margins, however, from the places at the edge of empire and especially among the casualties of empire, disarming the empire is both imaginable and crucial if there is to be hope. After hearing the stories of thousands of Indigenous Canadians and bearing witness to their pain and anguish, the Truth and Reconciliation Commission's call to repudiate the ideology of conquest, assimilation, and genocide amounts to a disarming of the foundations of a colonialist society.

What happens if we read Paul's letter to the Christian house churches in Rome as something akin to a call to disarm the empire? What happens if we read this letter written to the heart of the empire from the perspective of the margins of that empire? What happens if we read Romans at the edge of the dance floor, weeping with Frenchy? Or holding Iggy's hand as his broken body and broken heart lie dying in the intensive care unit? What happens if we bring that pathos, longing, and hurt to hearing Romans and then allow Paul's ancient letter to speak into our own context of twenty-first-century empire?

Romans, the Gospel, and Empire

Hang on a minute. I've got to interrupt you at this point. I'm not trying to be rude, but I have a whole load of questions about this project, and you've hardly even begun.

You don't think that you could wait until we have a little more on the table before you start raising your questions?

No. I simply can't keep reading without getting some stuff off my chest.

Then by all means, what's bothering you?

Well, as I was reading, I found myself on that dance floor with you that night. I could feel the joy of the community, and I've got to admit that my eyes started to well up as you told the stories of Frenchy and Iggy. And while I don't usually use the kind of harsh language that we meet in "Iggy's Song," I could see the painful truth of what Dan Robins wrote. So translating that hurt and grief into the apostle's "great sorrow and unceasing anguish" made sense to me, even if that is not the way I usually read the Bible. Sure, let's read Romans through the lens of this kind of sorrow and anguish and see what happens.

What has got me struggling is the idea of reading Romans from the margins. It all seems so pretentious. I mean, how can a couple of PhDs like you two even pretend to be writing from the margins? You guys personally and professionally are too successful and secure to be able to do that.

But it isn't just the question of how you can relate in any way to the margins. It's also the question of how the church could ever dare to speak from the margins, given its own important role in colonialism, its own comfortable position and support of empire.

And while I'm at it, let me also say that the church has used Paul's letter to the Romans as a weapon in its own internal wars and as a sword against anyone seen to be outside the so-called theology of the letter. How can we go about disarming any empire if we are appealing to a text that has been used in the arming of that empire?

Wow. You've jumped right into the most difficult questions.

First, you are right that we have no privileged access to the margins of the imperial world in which we find ourselves. Even if we strive in our life together and as a family to seek alternative ways of life that would subvert the empire, we are still, by virtue of education, economic class, race, and cultural power, people close to the center and far from the margins. And we make no claims to speak on behalf of those at the margins and certainly not on behalf of any First Nations brothers and sisters.

If we have any access to the margins, to the hurt and betrayal that was born in our brother Iggy's body and soul, then it can only be through deep listening and shared tears. With a deep spiritual intentionality we must weep with those who weep, even as we rejoice with those who rejoice.

Second, you are right about the church as well. How can the church, which has been so close to power, so close to wealth, privilege, and cultural legitimacy—indeed, so close to empire—ever speak from the margins? It is pretty hard to presume to be a church at the margins when we maintain all the vestiges of the center. How can the church be a force for disarming the empire when its bishops still wear imperial purple?

The good news, however, is that the church has itself been marginalized. Having aided and abetted empire during the period of conquest, and even having faithfully served as an agent of cultural genocide by colluding with the governing powers in the residential schools, the church now finds itself discarded as an irrelevant institution of a past era. We got in bed with the forces of modernity, and once they had had their way with us, we were sent back to the street, abused, confused, and of no further use. The end of "Christendom" is a profound blessing. It is true that the church did not engage in a process of unilateral cultural disarmament. No, that was left for history to accomplish. Or perhaps we could say that God brought an end to "Christendom" so that a church now stripped of its cultural power could be liberated from empire and take up its proper mission in the kingdom of God.

Part of our strategy in this book is to see how Paul addresses Christians living at the center of the Roman Empire in order to discern how the church might live at the margins of our own imperial reality.

Well, that prompts my third question. The letter to the Romans and disarming the empire? Romans as a counter-imperial epistle? Romans from the margins? Not only am I having a hard time seeing how this ancient theological treatise was a threat to the Roman Empire, let alone any other empire in history, but it seems to me that when Paul finally does address the empire in chapter 13, all that he can counsel is unquestioning obedience.

This is, of course, the central interpretive question. And really there are two questions here. First, is Paul writing a theological treatise in Romans, a systematic outline of his theology? Second, did this letter serve to legitimate or subvert the foundational myths, symbols, structures, and practices that characterized life at the center of the empire?

Let's begin with the first question. The sheer scope of this ancient document gives some credence to the notion that Paul is writing some sort of systematic theology here. But by those terms, the Corinthian correspondence is even larger than Romans, though no one thinks that those letters represent a systematic summation of Paul's understanding of the gospel.

Of course not. The letters to the Corinthians are clearly addressing particular crises in the community at that time.

Precisely. The Corinthian letters, like all of Paul's letters, are addressed to Christian communities in particular places.[10] Rather than writing to Christians in general in these letters, Paul directs his writing to a specific people and the circumstances that they face in their context. This is true of the letter to the Romans as well.

But if Paul had never met the Romans, would he have known enough about their context to address it?[11]

Imagine that you are writing a letter to someone you have never met who lives in Washington, DC, or New York City. You would still be able to address their context. You might ask if they have been to the Lincoln Memorial or if they

10. The only exception to this is, of course, Ephesians. But even Ephesians is a circular letter written to communities in a certain geographical area.

11. Much of this section is dependent on Sylvia C. Keesmaat, "Reading Romans in the Capital of Empire," in *Reading Paul's Letter to the Romans*, ed. Jerry L. Sumney (Atlanta: SBL Press, 2012), 47–64. They have been reworked here with permission of SBL Press.

have ever visited Ground Zero. You might even offer an opinion on an event that happened in one of these cities. In the ancient world, Rome had enormous stature. News traveled throughout the empire about the city, its architecture, and its rulers. In addition, what happened in Rome dictated the behavior of the rest of the empire. The story of Roman military power was circulated in art and on coins, portrayed in architecture, talked about, and retold in song. Roman law and societal structures shaped daily interactions throughout the empire.

That is all pretty general knowledge though.

You are right, but Paul and the churches in Rome had even stronger connections. Romans 16 shows that Paul personally knew quite a few of the leaders of the churches in Rome. He worked with some of them (Prisca and Aquila, v. 3); he was imprisoned with others (Andronicus and Junia, v. 7); others had provided support for him. These people would surely have conveyed to Paul a clear picture of what life in the capital was like.

Part of that picture would have been this: there is some evidence that in the year 49 CE the emperor Claudius ordered at least some of the Jews expelled from Rome. We don't know what effect, if any, this had on the new Christian communities in Rome, although we know that at least two leaders from one community were expelled. Those two were Prisca and Aquila, the courageous and creative missionary couple that Paul mentions in Romans 16. At the time Romans was written, they had only recently returned to Rome because they had been part of the forced deportation under Claudius.[12]

What we do know is that the attitude of the non-Jewish population toward Jews was generally not positive and that such tensions were likely to have been present in the earliest Christian communities as they developed.[13] This might be why Paul repeatedly emphasizes an ethos of mutual welcome (14:1; 15:7) that abstains from exclusionary judgment (14:3–4, 10, 13). He encourages the community to "pursue what makes for peace and for mutual upbuilding" (14:19). And just a moment after enjoining the community to greet one another with a holy kiss, Paul urges them "to keep an eye on those who cause dissensions and offenses" (16:17). He is preoccupied with fostering a community of welcome and unity precisely because that was not the reality in the house churches of Rome.

12. Acts 18:1–3 describes Paul meeting Aquila and Priscilla (Prisca) in Corinth because all the Jews had been ordered by Claudius to leave Rome. This text also tells us that all three of them were tentmakers (or, more accurately, awning makers).

13. So also Mark Nanos, who suggests that these were precisely the tensions that would have arisen in synagogues with growing gentile adherents. Mark Nanos, *The Mystery of Romans: The Jewish Context of Paul's Letters* (Minneapolis: Fortress, 1996), 384.

What's this got to do with the relationship between Jews and gentiles?

Everything. Both recent history and the long story of Jews in Rome told the tale of a despised and shameful people.[14] Not only were the Jews a constant irritant to Rome in that outpost of the empire called Judea; they were also held under suspicion when they lived in the city of Rome itself. So Christian or not, the non-Jewish inhabitants of the city knew that Jews were trouble. And Jews didn't have a very high opinion of gentiles either; gentiles were considered to be immoral idolaters in Jewish eyes. Now that Jews and gentiles were unexpectedly together in communities that followed Jesus, they had to learn to overcome their deep-seated prejudices about each other.

It is not surprising, then, that the conflict between Jewish and gentile Christians runs through the whole epistle. From Paul's early refrain that the gospel is the power of God for salvation "to the Jew first and also to the Greek" (1:16) to his critique of the gentiles' idolatrous ways of life (1:18–32), while insisting that Jews and gentiles share equal guilt before God (chap. 2), to the retelling of the Abraham and Adam stories (chaps. 4 and 5) to the anguished retelling of Israel's story (chaps. 9–11), and in countless other ways, Paul is struggling to shape a community of Christian unity at the very heart of the empire. And that is a crisis in Rome, not because some folks are arguing that gentile converts need to submit to the laws of the Torah (as is the issue in Galatians) but because there is a made-in-Rome tension between Jewish and gentile believers.

Let's say that I'm willing to accept that Paul's letter to the Romans is in fact addressing these kinds of tensions that have arisen from these historical events. That places this letter, like his other letters, in a real sociohistorical context. But Paul still seems to be writing something like a systematic theology to address these tensions. Now exactly how that works, I'm not sure, but it seems that "justification by faith" remains the heart of his argument in this letter. That sure sounds like theology, and from what I know of the history of the church, this is the very place where the church has used this ancient letter as a weapon.

Of course Paul is going to talk about justification by faith. What else would he do when the church as a whole is facing persecution and the Jewish believers have themselves come in for a significant amount of suffering? He needs to talk about justification because this is a crisis of justice.

What does justification have to do with justice? And I'm not sure I have ever noticed the word justice *occurring more than once in the letter to the Romans.*

14. The expulsion of the Jews from the city under Claudius was not the first time this had happened. Such a forced migration happened in 139 BCE and then again under Tiberius in 19 CE.

N. T. Wright has helpfully described justification as God's redemptive purpose of "setting to rights" that which has been wrong or restoring to right relationship that which has been broken. In these terms, justification has everything to do with justice. Justification is making things just, a reversal of injustice and a restoration of all relationships that have been deformed by injustice.[15]

We don't find the word *justice* in our translations of the letter to the Romans because the original Greek is usually translated as "righteousness." In Greek the word *dikaiosynē* is used to translate two Hebrew words, "righteousness" (*tsedaqah*) and "justice" (*mishpat*). The Greek word *dikaiosynē* therefore has both of those meanings. Since the word *righteousness* doesn't have much meaning in our culture (except when we call someone "self-righteous"), we will follow Costa Rican theologian Elsa Tamez and translate *dikaiosynē* as "justice" in order to retain the social, political, and cultural overtones of the Greek.[16] Just reread Romans replacing the word *justice* every time you read *righteousness* and see what happens.

Maybe I'll do that. But first, why would this suffering raise questions of God's justice?

How well do you know the Psalms? In Romans, Paul refers to Psalms 10, 18, 44, 71, 94, 110, and 143, all of which are psalms of lament. When these psalms cry out to God for justice, what are they looking for?

Usually for enemies to be crushed and defeated and for God's faithful people to be vindicated.

Exactly. In these psalms, God acts in justice and faithfulness when oppressors (often gentile) are defeated and God's people are rescued. This is what God's covenant faithfulness looks like. And this story is not that different from the story of Rome, where those blessed by the gods (the Romans) defeat the barbaric pagan hordes.

If these are the stories that surround you, then a group of Jews who have been expelled by the empire, even if they have been allowed to come back, look like the ones who have been abandoned by God. In fact, Paul spends Romans 9–11 arguing against precisely this point. According to Paul, God has *not* abandoned his people (11:1, 11–32). And you can imagine why he needed to make this argument. The very justice of God—that is, God's faithfulness to his people, to his promises—was at stake.

15. N. T. Wright, *Paul and the Faithfulness of God*, book 2 (Minneapolis: Fortress, 2013), 925. Also helpful is Wright's *Paul in Fresh Perspective* (Minneapolis: Fortress, 2005), 57.

16. Elsa Tamez, *The Amnesty of Grace: Justification by Faith from a Latin American Perspective*, trans. Sharon H. Ringe (Nashville: Abingdon, 1993).

So this community could be thinking that because the Jews are suffering, they are no longer chosen by God?

Precisely. In a situation of gentile boasting (11:17–24; 14:10) Paul is telling another story, one where suffering does not signify defeat. And in telling that story Paul is undermining parts of the story of Israel *and* the story of the Roman Empire.

How can you be sure that his intentions are so focused? What you have outlined here are themes of suffering and justice that can be found throughout Israel's Scriptures. They are much wider than the context of these Christians in Rome. Since Paul was dealing with a story much larger than the story of Rome, isn't it possible that he would not have been addressing the Roman Empire directly? Paul was writing about cosmic issues: death, sin, and the defeat of evil at the hands of Jesus. To say that he was addressing the Roman Empire would be to limit the cosmic scope of his vision and his writings.[17] *In other words, while the crisis in the community might be real, and even suffering at the hands of Rome might be in the background of this letter, doesn't Paul have bigger fish to fry than to worry about the Roman Empire specifically?*

That would be a compelling argument, except for one thing. Throughout the biblical story the people of Israel need to learn how to be faithful to the covenant God in their particular time and place. Moses does not warn the Israelites in Deuteronomy in merely abstract terms about choosing the path of death; rather, he names the idolatry of Canaan and the threat of acting like they are still in Egypt.[18] Similarly, the prophets do not call Israel to faithfulness merely by pointing out grand cosmic themes; rather, they root those themes in the specific unfaithful practices of Israel and Judah, with regard to *this* land and *these* people and *those* political alliances.[19]

Faithfulness to the covenant God is always embodied in particular historical situations and contexts. Conversely, the challenges to such faithfulness—the power of evil, death, or injustice (*adikia*, as Paul puts it)—are always embodied in particular narratives, particular idolatrous practices, particular symbols. There is no way to address the large themes without talking about what they look like in *this* place and with *this* people. Throughout all biblical literature, those places

17. This argument is found in John Barclay, *Pauline Churches and the Diaspora Jews* (Tübingen: Mohr Siebeck, 2011), chap. 19. N. T. Wright engages Barclay's argument in some depth in *Paul and the Faithfulness of God*, book 2, pp. 1307–19.

18. Deut. 4:3; 12:2–4, 29–31; 16:21–22; 17:16; 18:9–14; 24:17, 21; 29:16–18; cf. Lev. 19:36.

19. E.g., Isa. 5:8–10; Jer. 5:26–29; Hosea 5:13; 7:11–13; 8:1–10; Amos 2:6–8; 3:9–11; 4:1–3; 5:10–13; 6:4–8; 8:4–6; Mic. 2:1–2; 3:9–11.

invariably had the shape of empire. Walter Brueggemann is right: biblical faith is always shaped "in the shadow of empire."[20]

Say that I accept your argument that Paul would have been aware of the context of the churches in Rome. It is still not clear that he addressed the Roman Empire in this letter. I've never picked up on any "shadow of empire" in Romans. I mean, Paul doesn't mention the empire once, nor does he refer to any emperors, and he doesn't explicitly say anything about the imperial story.

That is correct. And yet the symbols, vocabulary, and structure of the empire underlie the world that he describes in Romans.

Why doesn't Paul just come out and say that he is challenging Caesar and the empire?

Paul doesn't need to make such an overt statement. It is similar to that old campaign where Christians said "Jesus: He's the Real Thing" as a cultural reference to the Coke campaign that proclaimed "Coke: It's the Real Thing." If they had spelled it out, "Jesus, not Coke, is the real thing," their assertion would have lost some of its power. But, more importantly, they didn't need to explain it; everyone knew what they meant.

I have no idea what you are talking about. Perhaps that isn't the best example.

Actually, it proves our point entirely. When we were young, everyone knew that this Christian slogan challenged an advertising claim. It didn't need to be spelled out. But now it does. In the same way, Paul's language in Romans didn't need to be spelled out at the time, because everyone understood his allusions to the empire. It is only now that we have to do the clumsy work of explaining the references.

So you are saying that because we are no longer living in the context of ancient Rome, we don't catch all the allusions?

That's right. Let's take a more current example. If in an election year someone were to go on a lecture tour titled "Jesus for President!," that phrase alone would convey a challenge to the story of American presidency.[21] Or if we had a

20. Walter Brueggemann, "Always in the Shadow of Empire," in *Texts That Linger, Words That Explode: Listening to Prophetic Voices*, ed. Patrick Miller (Minneapolis: Fortress, 2000). See also Richard A. Horsley, ed., *In the Shadow of Empire: Reclaiming the Bible as a History of Faithful Resistance* (Louisville: Westminster John Knox, 2008). Wes Howard-Brook offers an expansive reading of the whole Bible in terms of empire in *"Come Out, My People!": God's Call out of Empire in the Bible and Beyond* (Maryknoll, NY: Orbis, 2010). For our own situating of Paul's writings in the context of empire, see Brian J. Walsh and Sylvia C. Keesmaat, *Colossians Remixed: Subverting the Empire* (Downers Grove, IL: IVP Academic, 2004), esp. chaps. 3 and 4.

21. Shane Claiborne and Chris Haw did go on such a lecture tour with this title in 2008. Their book that accompanied the tour, *Jesus for President: Politics for Ordinary Radicals* (Grand Rapids: Zondervan, 2008), contrasts the gospel of Jesus with the "gospel" of both Rome and contemporary American culture.

bumper sticker that said "God Bless the Whole World. No Exceptions," it is likely that you would see this as a challenge to the more prevalent bumper sticker that says "God Bless America." Or if we had a slogan that said "Amish for Homeland Security," you would understand that we were saying something about the current militaristic nature of the Department of Homeland Security, and that we were suggesting a less violent alternative.[22] These examples make sense to us because we know the larger cultural context of the allusions. Paul didn't need to be more explicit because at the time his allusions made sense in terms of the wider cultural narrative. For us, however, two thousand years later, a little explanatory work is necessary.

I think an example from Romans would be helpful.

Well, let's consider the first four Greek words of the letter: "Paul, a slave of Messiah Jesus."[23] Just imagine how this would have sounded in the context of an empire governed by status and a culture governed by an honor/shame dynamic. Rather than introduce himself in language designed to increase his social standing, Paul deliberately uses a phrase that identifies him with those at the bottom of the social ladder.

Four words and the author has already given notice. Four words and the oppressive hierarchical structures of Rome are thrown on their heads. Paul has, in these mere four words, set the agenda for his most extensive letter of subversion.

Paul . . . a slave. Not Paul, a citizen of Rome. Not Paul, claiming to have the legitimacy that is afforded by the empire. Not Paul, enjoying his status as a citizen, a free man. No, Paul . . . a slave. Paul takes no refuge in such legitimacy but identifies himself with the lowest of the low.

And whose slave is he? Who is the master of the letter writer? To whose household does the author belong? "Paul, a slave of Messiah Jesus." Not a slave of any Roman citizen, not a slave of any Roman household, not a slave that bears ultimate allegiance to the emperor who is the father of the whole Roman household. Not Caesar Augustus but Messiah Jesus. Let the regime and all who have dismissed the Jews as a shameful race be put on notice. Paul writes as a slave of Jesus the Messiah. The household to which he belongs is the household of Jesus, a Jewish Messiah. And he now writes to the church at the center of the empire, the church

22. This last example is from the film *The Ordinary Radicals: A Conspiracy of Faith at the Margins of Empire*, directed by Jamie Moffett (Philadelphia: Jamie Moffett Media, 2008), DVD.

23. The word Paul uses here, *doulos*, is most accurately translated "slave," although many translations use "servant" instead. Although our English translation here is six words, there are only four words in the Greek.

sometimes close to the imperial household, sometimes oppressed by that household, and presumes to speak to this church with the authority of a slave of Jesus.

You find all that in those four words?

Yes, and the subversive nature of those four words is borne out in how he qualifies his own slavery to Jesus: "Paul, a slave of Messiah Jesus, called to be an apostle, set apart for the *gospel of God*, which he promised beforehand through his prophets in the holy Scriptures" (1:1–2 our translation).

Just as *slave* was a word that carried significant socioeconomic meaning, so also *gospel* was a politically loaded term. The word *gospel* (*euangelion*) often referred to the "good news" of an imperial military victory.[24] Paul not only uses this word; he also carefully qualifies it. We can better catch the sense if we translate "gospel of God" as "the proclamation of the triumph of God."[25] The implications are clear: Whose gospel has triumphed? The gospel of God, not Caesar. Paul is on dangerous political ground here. His language is seditious, and he's only two verses into his letter!

Rome, like all empires, has a gospel, but Paul wants to make sure that his readers understand from the outset that he is proclaiming the alternative gospel of Jesus, and here in the opening sentences of his magnificent letter he delights to say so over and over again.

"Paul, a slave of Messiah Jesus, called to be an apostle, set apart for the gospel of God"—not the gospel of Caesar. While Rome's gospel is from Nero, who has claim to the throne by being a descendent of Augustus, Paul proclaims a "gospel concerning his Son, who was descended from David according to the flesh" (1:3). In this rare reference to David, Paul wants to make clear that the gospel he proclaims is that of a Jewish Messiah, rooted in the Jewish royal line. These are the very Jews who have been a scapegoat and object of derision in the empire.

When a little later Paul says that he is eager "to proclaim the gospel to you also who are in Rome" (1:15), we ought not miss the audacity of this sentiment. Presuming to proclaim the gospel to those who are in Rome amounts to a radical reversal of the direction that these things go. Paul brings the gospel *to* Rome,

24. Neil Elliott, "Paul and the Politics of Empire," in *Paul and Politics: Ekklesia, Israel, Imperium, Interpretation*, ed. Richard Horsley (Harrisburg, PA: Trinity Press International, 2000), 24; Dieter Georgi, *Theocracy in Paul's Praxis and Theology*, trans. David E. Green (Minneapolis: Fortress, 1991), 83; N. T. Wright, "Gospel and Theology in Galatians," in *Gospel in Paul: Studies on Corinthians, Galatians, and Romans for Richard N. Longenecker*, ed. L. Ann Jervis and Peter Richardson (Sheffield: Sheffield Academic Press, 1994), 226–28.

25. This translation is from Neil Elliott, *The Arrogance of Nations: Reading Romans in the Shadow of Empire* (Minneapolis: Fortress, 2008), 152.

while Rome assumes that the only gospel to be proclaimed is generated by Rome and goes forth *from* Rome.

With such seditious audacity, it is no surprise that the apostle then boldly proclaims, "I am not ashamed of the gospel" (1:16). Even though he has clearly identified this gospel with those resisters to the empire who are deemed to be shameful, even though this is a gospel rooted in a story of a shameful people who have been vanquished by one empire after another, and even though this is a gospel of one who was put to shame on a cross in some far outpost of the empire, Paul is not ashamed. I am not ashamed of this gospel, he exclaims, because it is nothing less than "the power of God for salvation to everyone who has faith, to the Jew first and also to the Greek" (1:16). The gospel is nothing less than the *dynamis*, the dynamite of God that can blow the top off imperial notions of shame and the oppressive power that comes from the deceitful rhetoric of the imperial gospel.

In the face of an imperial gospel that proclaims that all salvation lies in Rome, and that identifies the emperor as both lord and savior, while bringing crosses, crippling taxes, agricultural exploitation, economic destruction, war, and violence wherever it goes, Paul brings a gospel of deep, transformative, creation-restoring salvation that turns the empire on its head. You have to realize that proclaiming Jesus, the Jewish Messiah, as Lord flies in the face of imperial ideology. This is seditious language because if Jesus is Lord, then Caesar is not. Moreover, this gospel reverses the order of the empire by coming to the Jew first and then to the gentile.

That's the power of the gospel. Gospel, gospel, gospel, gospel, gospel—five times Paul names the gospel. This is a gospel that proclaims that Jesus of Nazareth is Messiah and therefore Lord of all, not because he succeeded the previous emperor, not because he has a Roman imperial lineage, and not because he has successfully deposed or murdered his predecessor but because he rose from the dead (1:4). He was declared to be Son of God not because his father is now among the gods but because he has blown open the grave, broken an imperial seal that would have kept him there, and been established as Son of God through resurrection.

And now if there is any gospel left to be proclaimed from the heart of the empire, it is that a struggling group of Jesus followers have bent the knee to the Messiah, have named him as their Lord, have embraced a faith alternative to fidelity to the empire, and have an obedience in their lives that subverts imperial obedience.

That's the good news coming out of Rome these days. That's the gospel, Paul is saying, and that's the only gospel worth talking about.

You find all that in Paul's use of the word gospel?

Yes, and more! Why does Paul introduce himself as a slave of Jesus and not a citizen of the empire? Because the gospel that he proclaims overturns the order of the empire! Paul is not a citizen but a slave. And he says that as a slave of Messiah Jesus he is in debt "both to Greeks and to barbarians, both to the wise and to the foolish" (1:14).

This is socially revolutionary stuff! In an honor/shame society, in which everyone is indebted in one way or another to those above them in the social hierarchy, Paul says that as a slave of Christ, he is at the bottom of the social ladder, and therefore he is indebted to all above him. But he goes even further. He is not just indebted to the wise and the foolish, the educated elite and the illiterate masses; he is also indebted to both the Greeks and the barbarians. Speaking to the very heart of the empire, he says that he is indebted to those identified with the height of civilization, those whose myths and gods are at the foundation of the empire, *and* he is indebted to those on the margins of the empire, those who are so savage, so uncivilized, so primitive that they resist the empire and are in a constant war of terror against the empire.

Well, if Paul begins with phrases that undermine the imperial story, he moves pretty quickly to theology. The whole theme of the letter in Romans 1:16–17 is clearly about salvation, righteousness, and faith. It seems that he abandons imperial allusions in favor of the themes of biblical hope.

Not at all. Here we meet the most subversive language of all: "I am not ashamed of the gospel; it is the power of God for salvation to everyone who has faith, to the Jew first and also to the Greek. For in it the justice of God is revealed through faith for faith; as it is written, 'The one who is just will live by faith'" (1:16–17 NRSV alt.).

Again, you are translating what my Bible calls "righteousness" as "justice."

Good eye. Here is the first and most crucial place where it is important to translate *dikaiosynē* as "justice." We will have occasion to come back to these verses throughout this book, but it is important at this point to hear the imperial overtones, even as they are in dissonance with the overtones of Israel's Scriptures. This God of Israel is proclaimed as the one whose justice (*dikaiosynē*) is revealed through faith for faith (*ek pisteōs eis pistin*; 1:17). Justice and faith. With these two words, ringing with deep resonances with Israel's Scriptures, Paul challenges the imperial ideology at its core.

You see, if there is one thing that Rome prided itself on, it was Roman justice. And Roman justice was bestowed on the empire by the goddess Iustitia (*justice*; the Latin equivalent of the Greek *dikaiosynē*), who was closely identified with the reign of Augustus. Moreover, one of the lauded virtues of the Augustan reign was none other than *fides* (faith or faithfulness, which is the Latin equivalent of the Greek *pistis*).[26] Far from retreating into abstract theology, Paul here throws down the challenge that goes to the core of the empire's self-understanding. Where does the world meet justice and faith? In the imperial narrative of Caesar or in the story of Israel as reinterpreted in light of the story of Jesus? These programmatic verses, then, pick up the themes of the empire and powerfully reinterpret them in the context of another story, the story of the God of Israel, who has come to bring salvation through another Lord: Jesus. And as we will see, Paul draws deeply on that story, particularly those moments in Israel's Scriptures where the faithfulness of God is questioned in the face of oppression.

Come again? How does a theological assertion like "the righteous will live by faith" function as a counter-imperial rallying call?

Well, you could go back and see where Paul got the phrase. If you read Habakkuk 2, you will see that the words "but the righteous live by their faith" (Hab. 2:4) occur in an oracle that was decidedly in critique of an earlier empire, the Chaldeans. In fact, this is the immediate context of the line that Paul quotes:

> Look at the proud!
> Their spirit is not right in them,
> but the righteous live by their faith.
> Moreover, wealth is treacherous;
> the arrogant do not endure.
> They open their throats wide as Sheol;
> like Death they never have enough.
> They gather all nations for themselves,
> and collect all peoples as their own. (Hab. 2:4–5)

Looks like empire, acts like empire, has the arrogance of empire, has the insatiability of empire, and engages in the violent colonializing policies of empire. In the context of empire, Habakkuk receives a vision in which the righteous will live by faith.

26. N. T. Wright, "The Letter to the Romans: Introduction, Commentary, and Reflections," in *The New Interpreter's Bible*, vol. 10 (Nashville: Abingdon, 2002), 404. On *Iustitia*, the Latin equivalent of *dikē*, Wright refers to Ovid's *Black Sea Letters* 3.6.25 and *The Deeds of Divine Augustus* 34.

Paul reaches back to Habakkuk's vision of how to maintain faithfulness in the context of one empire in order to shape the imagination of the Christian community for a life of faithfulness in the capital city of another. And he even agrees with a core belief of the Roman Empire. Justice is indeed rooted in faithfulness. But he is asking, *which* justice, *whose* faithfulness, and faithfulness *to whom*? It is not Roman justice, nor is it Roman fidelity that has the power of salvation. No, this is the justice of God that he is talking about, a justice rooted in the covenantal faithfulness of this God revealed in the Jewish Messiah, Jesus. And the faithfulness of this God calls forth faithfulness in response so that the one who is just is the one who will live by faith.

So you are saying that all these words—slave, gospel, lord, debt, salvation, justice, faith—*carry certain kinds of meaning in the context of the Roman Empire and that Paul is deliberately using them in critique of that very empire.*

Well, let's nuance that just a bit. Yes, Paul is using these terms in a way that is on a collision course with the rhetoric of the empire. But it isn't simply a matter of Paul grabbing the discourse of Rome and reinscribing it with different meaning. Rather, most of these terms have similar meaning in both the rhetoric of Rome and the imagination of Israel. For example, it would be a mistake to say that Rome uses the language of salvation and the emperor as savior in "political" ways while Paul reinterprets that same language to refer to some sort of nonpolitical "spiritual" salvation. Again, the terms carry the same range of meaning for both Rome and Israel. Salvation is invariably political in the imagination of Israel, and salvation is effected when Israel's God destroys and defeats Israel's enemies.[27] So the semantic range of meaning is the same. The question is the actual content of that meaning. The issue isn't whether salvation has political meaning but who is the agent of that salvation.

Why does it matter? I've always read Romans as being about salvation. Heck, I've even helped people walk the "Roman road" to salvation.[28] *But there was nothing political about those conversions. People gave their lives to Jesus, not to a political agenda.*

Look, we're happy that folks have come to put their faith in Jesus, but there is a profound danger if the Scriptures are misinterpreted in the process. You see, whether Paul's letter to believers living at the heart of the empire subverts that

27. The references are extensive: Pss. 13; 18*; 25; 35*; 36*; 37; 68; 79; 118*; Isa. 25:6–12; 33:2–6; 46:12–13; 51:4–8; 52:7–12; 62:1–12 (* = psalms quoted by Paul in Romans).

28. There are numerous references to the "Roman road" as "a well-engineered path to salvation" on the internet. E.g., "The Roman Road," All About God, https://www.allaboutgod.com/the-roman-road.htm.

empire or not has everything to do with what kind of gospel people will hear and what kind of Lord they will give their lives to. Spiritual salvation devoid of radical liberation from the power of empire is too safe, too comfortable. This amounts to a piety that may be personally fulfilling and rewarding but is unfaithful to the radical call to submit to Jesus as Lord of all of life.

You may be right, but I'm still uncomfortable with all of this. What about sin? Isn't salvation about sin and forgiveness?

Almost as if he anticipated your question, Paul moves from talking about salvation, justice, and faithfulness to talking about sin and, if anything, he heightens his critique of the empire in the next few verses where he criticizes those who practice injustice.

"Injustice?" My Bible reads "wickedness." What are you guys up to here? Righteousness becomes justice, and somehow wickedness becomes injustice. Sure looks to me like you are imposing a political agenda on this text.

Maybe a better way to put it is that the translations we are used to are trying to *depoliticize* the text. You see, just as *dikaiosynē* can be accurately translated as "justice," so also the word usually translated as "wickedness" carries with it a similar reference to justice. The Greek word is *adikia*, which has the same root as *dikaiosynē* and literally means "without justice" (*a* = no; *dikē* = justice), hence our translation of *adikia* as "injustice." Of course, injustice is wicked, but we invite you to do the same interpretive experiment with reading "wickedness" as "injustice" as we suggested for reading "justice" wherever you meet the word "righteousness."

If you do that here at the end of the first chapter of Romans, you will see that ungodliness and injustice always go together (1:18). Such lives of injustice betray not enlightened but darkened minds (1:21). Such people may think that they are shaping a powerful civilization, but their thinking is futile (1:21). They are not wise but are fools (1:22). And while it may look, in the splendor of the imperial elite, that they have all the glory, the truth is that in their idolatry they have exchanged their glory for cheap, hollow, and empty images (1:23, 25).

Hear this in the context of Rome. Not only is justice at the heart of the Roman imperial imagination, but it was rooted in the blessings of the gods and specifically devotion to Iustitia. But Paul describes this world as one of ungodly injustice. Here is an empire that views itself as the apex of civilization, the height of human achievement and wisdom, but Paul dismisses it as futile and foolish. Here is a culture where the glory of Rome is manifest in its cities, monuments, architecture, roads, and temples, and Paul deconstructs the whole edifice as an idolatrous exchange of any real glory that humans might possess for cheap, disempowering imitations.

We will have cause to return to this passage on a number of occasions in this book, but just look at where all this injustice, foolishness, futility, and idolatry ends up. God gives them up "in the lusts of their hearts" to practices of degrading sexual immorality (1:24–27). Full of "every kind of injustice," they engage in covetousness, malice, murder, strife, deceit, slander, and insolence. They are inventors of evil, rebellious toward parents, heartless and ruthless. We have not rehearsed the whole list of vices in Romans 1:28–31, but you get the picture. And it would seem that anyone hearing this letter read in the city of Rome would have gotten the picture too. A picture that looks an awful lot like the imperial household! What we have here is a fairly accurate portrayal of the lives of the recent emperors, particularly Caligula. Others at that time described Caligula as cruel and malicious; he had family members murdered and engaged in outrageous and humiliating sexual predations, with both men and women. He had an incredible arrogance and divine pretensions.[29] The very empire that was supposed to be a manifestation of the goddess of justice was ruled by those who demonstrated the most rampant injustice.

I thought that these verses were standard Jewish diatribe against gentiles.

They may well share the rhetorical structure and tone of such diatribes,[30] but the all-too-clear reference to the imperial household would not likely have been lost on Paul's audience. Indeed, the overt critique of an idolatrous life at the end of Romans 1, read with the anti-imperial overtones of the whole chapter, makes the parody of the lives of the recent emperors complete.

The apostle is at it again. The clues are all there. This is a subversive letter, undermining the imperial imagination, disarming the imperial ideology, deflating imperial arrogance, dethroning the imperial lord, and upsetting imperial hierarchies.

And then what? Or maybe I could put the question this way: So what? What do I do with all of this? Reading Romans as a theological treatise on justification by faith

29. Referring to Caligula, Neil Elliott writes,

> It would be difficult to imagine a career that better illustrated the precise sequence that Paul describes:
>
> arrogant refusal to honor the divine creator;
> the turn to idolatry and worship of the creature;
> a descent into defiling sexual lust;
> and finally an expansive catalogue of cruelty and outrage. (*Arrogance of Nations*, 80)

30. Joseph A. Fitzmyer, *Romans: A New Translation with Introduction and Commentary*, Anchor Bible (New York: Doubleday, 1993), 272–74, who refers to Wis. 13:1–19; 14:22–31; 4 Macc. 1:26–27; 2:15.

didn't necessarily make the whole letter any easier for me to understand, but at least that reading of sin and salvation gave me a clear evangelistic agenda. It helped me to understand how I am saved by grace and not works. It gave me a moral vision that helped me to judge evil practices and know to avoid them in my own life. But what do I do with what you have just given me?

Or let's put this in your terms, not mine. What does any of this have to do with Iggy and Frenchy? How does this reading of Paul's letter relate to their lives or to a post-Christendom church? If Paul is engaging in a subversive exercise in the face of the Roman Empire, then what does that look like for people living in the early years of the twenty-first century?

"So what?" is probably the most important theological question that we can ask of an ancient biblical text like this one. Or maybe we could put the question this way: What would Paul's letter to the Romans look like if it were written in the last number of weeks rather than some two thousand years ago?

Yes, that would be a good way to put it.

Maybe one way to answer that would be to reach back to a rabbinic practice. The rabbis in the Jewish Diaspora throughout the Roman Empire used to engage in a reading of the biblical text that was somewhat different from our practices today. They would stand to read the Torah in the synagogues, but because most of their congregations did not understand Hebrew, the rabbis would have to translate as they read. And recognizing that the Torah needed to speak the word of God into the midst of the community's contemporary life, they updated the text, applying it to the changing context and employing the language of the community. The results of such an expansive interpretive exercise were called targums—extended paraphrases of the text.[31]

What happens if we do the same thing today? What happens if we take these opening paragraphs, paying close attention to the kinds of overtones to the empire that we have discerned here, and rewrite them speaking into our own sociohistorical context? What might the opening of this epistle sound like if Paul knew Iggy and Frenchy? If he had been at that party at Sanctuary? If he were writing in light of the geomilitary conflicts that we have seen since September 11, 2001? If he were paying attention to the economics of empire and the machinations around the collapse of 2008? If he knew of the rise of racism and nationalism in the last number of years?

To this kind of an imaginative exercise we now turn.

31. See Sylvia C. Keesmaat, *Paul and His Story: (Re)Interpreting the Exodus Tradition* (Sheffield: Sheffield Academic Press, 1999), 28–30.

Romans 1:1–25 Targum

Paul, a slave of Jesus the Messiah,
called to a ministry of authority
in a world that is suspicious of all authority.

Set apart in a world of bland consumerist sameness,
advocate of nothing less than the gospel of God,
the good news of God's radical kingdom.

This gospel, this kingdom proclamation,
is a story with a rich heritage.
It was promised by the Hebrew prophets
and it is the news of Jesus—the Son of God,
the one who embodied truth and reconciliation.

This Jesus is a descendent of the infamous King David
but was pronounced to be God's Son
by the explosive power of the Spirit
of all that is pure, all that is deeply right,
when he rose from the dead.

Jesus isn't the Son of God because he was elected
or because he has the most economic power
or because he commands great armies.
No, he is the Son of God because he defeated the power of death.

This is Jesus the Messiah.
This is Jesus whom I dare to call my Master, my Lord,
regardless of how politically incorrect that may appear.

It is through this Jesus, the messianic Master,
that I have met a grace that makes beauty out of ugly things,
the deepest of all gifts.

And it is through this gift of grace
that I am called to proclaim good news,
nothing less than faithful obedience,
in a self-serving and narcissistic culture.

I do all this subject to his name.
If I am to be branded,
then let me be branded with the name of Jesus.

He is my Master, not some corporate logo,
not any nationalist ideology,

not any economic system,
not any political party, social class, or ethnic identity.

And I invite others to bear the brand of Jesus,
including you, my friends, who are also called out of empire.
Here is your identity; here is your home.
You belong to Jesus!
Here is your ultimate loyalty and allegiance.

To all of you who live in the empire of global capitalism,
to all who bear its scars and wounds,
to you who are called out to be an alternative people:
Grace to you and peace from God our Father
and our Master, Jesus Christ.

Grace and peace.

Lord knows that we have seen little peace in our time,
and grace seems to be erased from our cultural life.
But you won't have one without the other,
and both are on offer from Jesus.

I am so thankful for all of you.
You see, while the mainstream media proclaims
the exploits of empire throughout the world,
there is another story being told from the heart of the empire.
Your story, your good news.

The news of your faithfulness
has been proclaimed throughout the world.

Your commitment to the poorest of the poor
who live within walking distance of the corridors of power;
your vigil at the side of those who have been broken by empire;
your passionate advocacy for justice
in the face of police brutality, homelessness, and neglect.

Your courage in standing up against the injustice
of trade agreements that serve the rich and exploit the poor;
your audacity in praying on the steps of the legislatures
where the political leaders hatch their conspiracies;
your deep commitment to the healing of this fragile planet;
your community gardens, intentional communities,
and parties that will hold the joy and the sorrow in tension with each other;

all of this is good news of liberation from captivity,
and it filters out to the very farthest reaches of the empire.

I tell you that the God whom I serve
in announcing the good news of his Son
bears witness to my constant prayers for you all.

And what I pray is that I might finally
get through the homeland security wall
in order to visit you.
The longer I have been delayed and blocked from coming to you,
the more severe has the ache in my heart become.

What I want is to come and bring you a measure of grace
that will give you the strength to go on against all the odds.
But to be honest, I'm looking for some encouragement too,
and I am sure that I will find it
in the midst of your community of welcome and discipleship.

You know, my friends,
I've been trying to come to you for years now.

This liberating revolution of Jesus is breaking out everywhere,
and I want to help it happen at the heart of the empire.
But there have been obstacles along the way.
Sometimes other urgent ministries came up,
and sometimes (as you know) the authorities have blocked my way.

But here's the thing.
I will not play by the rules of the empire.
I will not go along with their racial profiling,
their immoral surveillance tools,
their demonization of any and all who do not conform,
who would dare question the inherent goodness of the empire
and the story of progress that it proclaims.

Because I follow Jesus and proclaim his good news of redemptive love,
I am obligated, indeed I am indebted,
to the wealthy and the impoverished,
the educated elite and illiterate poor,
fine wine drinkers and crack addicts,
powerful politicians and my most dejected homeless neighbors,
security personnel and "terrorists,"
to Palestinians and Jews,

straight and queer,
black and white,
Indigenous and settler,
those who fit and those who don't.

And because I am indebted to all,
including those most excluded, shamed, and despised,
I am incredibly eager to come to you,
at the very heart of an exclusionary empire,
to proclaim the embracive good news of Jesus.

And here's the kicker, friends.
I will not be ashamed of this gospel.
I refuse to be ashamed of this gospel
because I will not submit myself to the empire's categories of shame.
I will not be ashamed of this gospel
even when it is perverted and employed for shameful purposes
by those who would make Christian faith the handmaiden of the empire.

I may be ashamed when the church colludes with the state
in the cause of cultural genocide.

I may be ashamed when the name of Jesus
is invoked to baptize ideologies of national security.

I may be ashamed when Christians
defend their right to bear arms.

I may be ashamed when Christians are mean spirited
regarding immigration policy,
youth crime,
homelessness, and drug addiction.

I may be ashamed when politicians invoke the name of Jesus
to justify wars that are based on lies and deception.

I may be ashamed when our highest leaders
confuse the promise of America with the hope of the kingdom of God.

And I am deeply ashamed when consumerism and greed
are embraced in the name of a gospel of abundance
that wears a thick veneer of Christian spirituality.

These are all shameful gospels,
but I will not be ashamed of the gospel of Jesus Christ.

I will not be ashamed of this gospel
because it is nothing less than the power of God
that sets us free from the oppressive regime of the empire.

It is the power of God for salvation,
for liberation from captivity:
real this-worldly salvation, not some heavenly life after death;
real salvation, not the empty gospel of "America is open for business"[32]
or "Make America Great Again!";
real salvation, not the facade of a militarily imposed "democracy";
real salvation, not the facile hope of consumptive fulfillment.

This is the salvation of God for everyone who is faithful to its call,
to the Jews first and then to the non-Jews.
To the shamed and excluded first,
and only then to the well-situated and secure.

Why am I not ashamed of this gospel?

Because in this good news about Jesus we meet the justice of God.
This is the restorative justice that heals the world.

You want an "infinite justice"?[33]
Then don't look to the violent justice of the empire,
but turn to the justice of God manifest in Jesus,
tortured in a CIA interrogation cell,
executed by imperial forces.

In this gospel we meet the infinite justice
of the Messiah subjecting himself
to the violence of the empire . . . unto death.

The good news of Jesus has an empire-overturning power
because in Jesus the embracing and forgiving power of God is revealed.

This power is revealed through God's faithfulness in Jesus Christ,
which then calls forth our faithfulness as subjects of his coming kingdom.

32. President Bush's word of salvation to the nation on the evening of September 11, 2001. "Text of Bush's Address," CNN, September 11, 2001, http://edition.cnn.com/2001/US/09/11/bush.speech.text/.

33. Recall that George W. Bush's first name for the military intervention that he launched after the 9/11 attacks was "Project Infinite Justice." He withdrew that name within days because of the outcry that the notion of "infinite justice" meted out by any nation-state in history is both pretentious and blasphemous. That the Bush White House could have ever approved such a name for a geomilitary intervention is nonetheless a telling testimony to its own imperial agenda.

That is why, in the shadow of an earlier empire,
the prophet Habakkuk wrote that
"the one who will be righteous will live by faith
. . . the one who will embody justice will live by faithfulness."

Righteousness, justice, faithfulness—all in the shadow of empire.
This is the fruit of the gospel that I long to proclaim in your midst.

So let's be clear about what is going on these days.

Let's not engage in cover-up with talk of market corrections
or market misbehavior.

Let's not try to salvage this leaky ship of fools
with deregulation and tax cuts for the very rich.

No, my friends, that's way too cheap
and doesn't begin to address the problem.

What's going on at the heart of the system of global capitalism
is nothing less than the wrath of God
being revealed against all ungodliness, all injustice, all greed,
all false gospels and the distorted lives they engender.

An empire of deceit, an economy of lies
can only be sustained by suppressing the truth of God
that is plain from the very nature of creation.

What part of the finite and gift character of creation
didn't they get when they adopted an ideology of infinite greed,
insatiable consumption, and an ever-expanding economy?

Doesn't the very nature of creation
bear witness to a God of abundance rooted in justice?
Doesn't the very goodness of creation
bear witness to the generosity of this God,
and our calling to image this God through loving and careful stewardship?

So here's the sad truth, my friends.
This empire of greed, this narrative of economic growth,
this whole house of cards is based on lies and deception.
This whole culture of consumption,
this whole empire of money, is based on self-willed ignorance.

Creation proclaims a better way
because creation bears witness to a God of grace.
But we have suppressed this truth, engaged in denial and cover-up.

Refusing to live a life of gratitude,
refusing to live a life of thanks to the God who called forth such a rich
creation,
refusing to honor this Creator God,
and embracing a culture of entitlement and ingratitude,
we abandoned the God of light and embraced the dark.

In all our complex theories,
in all our sophisticated and incomprehensible economic talk,
in all our high-sounding rhetoric on the campaign trail,
we became futile in our thinking;
we ended up with lots of talk but no sense:
theories that are empty,
vanity of vanities.

We thought that we were so wise.
We thought that we had it all figured out,
but the joke has been on us,
and we have been fools.

That's what happens when you get in bed with idols.
That's what happens when you don't image God in faithful justice.
That's what happens when you embrace graven images,
cheap imitations that look so good, look so powerful.
Idols will always fail you, will always come up short
because they are impotent.

Empty idols, empty minds.
Dumb idols, lives of foolishness.
Betrayal and disappointment.
Fear and terror.

Idolatry and empire,
they always go together.
And idols require sacrifice.
Child sacrifice, blood sacrifice.

The victims are there to be seen on the streets.
In the broken lives of the poor,
bodies and souls racked with pain.
In the empty opulence of the rich,
numbed-out with indifference.

Embrace the idol of economism,
believe its false promises of abundance,
allow your lives to be shaped by the greed of this idol,
and you will reap the bankruptcy of that false faith.
You'll be hooked on avarice,
caught up in an idolatry of ideology,
and your life will be reshaped in the image of that pitiful idol.

Embrace the idol of economism,
believe its false promises of wealth and power,
and you will find yourself facing no options.
Your life will be constricted and bound.
You will be stuck in a moment that you can't get out of.
You will awaken from your dream of economic freedom
to the nightmare of lost value,
international terrorism, and a despoiled planet.

My friends, we are not facing an economic crisis.
We are facing a spiritual crisis.
The issue isn't fundamentally the markets or trade agreements.
Nor can we scapegoat immigrants and refugees.
The issue is idolatry at the very root and foundation of our society,
at the very root and foundation of our way of life,
at the very root and foundation of our souls.

We are called to live in the truth.
We are called to raise children in the truth.
We are called to embody truth in our lives,
but we have traded in the truth for a lie.

Our imaginations have been taken captive.
We can hardly dream of a life outside the grip of idolatry.
We can scarcely imagine a life that isn't enslaved to consumption.
We can't even begin to get our heads around justice and righteousness.
Generosity and contentment are alien to us,
and an economics of enough is impossible to imagine, let alone live.

We have gotten into bed with idols
and not known the Lord.
We have bent the knee to idolatry
and not worshiped the Creator,
who is blessed forever. Amen.

Imagination and Faithful Reading

Well, that was quite the feat of imagination.

Thank you.

I'm not so sure I meant that as a compliment.

Oh. You don't like imagination?

I'm fine with imagination, but I get a little nervous when people get too imaginative in their interpretation of the Bible.

And what would count as too imaginative?

When the interpretation isn't clearly rooted in the meaning of the text in its ancient context and when its contemporary application seems forced, perhaps ideologically driven.

Fair enough. These are large interpretive questions. What meaning or meanings might this text have carried when it was first written, heard, and interpreted? And given the range of meanings that might justifiably be attributed to this text in its original composition and reception, what meanings might it bear today, and what are the criteria for evaluating any such contemporary interpretation?

Yes, that's a good way to put it. Your targum was a feat of imagination, and I chose my words carefully when I said that I'm "not so sure" that this is a compliment. I'm really not sure. Maybe it is a compliment. I found myself drawn into your imaginative construal of this section of Romans 1. The text did indeed "come alive" for me, even when I wasn't so sure that I agreed with the contemporary connections you were making. But I'm having a hard time figuring out what to do with something like this. How do I evaluate a targum, both in terms of how you rehear Paul's letter in the twenty-first century and in terms of how it would have been heard by those in Rome to whom the letter was first addressed?

These are great questions and they will accompany us throughout this book. We think there are three issues here: (1) how imagination works, (2) how we evaluate something like a targum, and (3) how we understand an ancient epistle like Romans in its original context. We suggest that the second and third issues are subspecies of the first. It is all about imagination. So we'll close this chapter with some brief comments about each question.

It is all about imagination. We will have occasion to return to the question of imagination later, but some comments are in order at this stage of the discussion. It has become commonplace today to say that we live in the age of the image. From the thousands of corporate images that we meet every day of our lives to the way in which products, organizations, politicians, churches, and corporations are "branded" to produce a certain feel or impression, the "image" is ubiquitous.[34] And, of course, the role of such images is precisely to shape our imagination. A particular product may do the same thing as another one, but the branding of the product captures the imagination of a certain demographic better than the other one does. There may be little substantive difference between two politicians or, for that matter, two churches, but loyalty will often be captured by the image that is portrayed.

While there is something to be said for evaluating late capitalism as a culture that privileges image over substance, there is, in fact, nothing unique about the power of image in shaping culture.[35] This is as old as the first drawings on cave walls by our earliest predecessors. James K. A. Smith stands in a long tradition of cultural understanding when he argues that humans are imaginative creatures "who live off the stuff of imagination: stories, pictures, images, and metaphors are the poetry of our embodied existence."[36] Charles Taylor is getting at the same thing with his notion of society shaped by an implicit "social imaginary" that is carried in "images, stories, legends." A social imaginary both informs us of "how things usually go" and gives us an idea of how things "ought to go."[37] Those who control the images control society precisely because they control the cultural imagination. And when Paul subverts dominant Roman images of lordship, slavery, salvation, justice, and faithfulness, he is engaging in a contest of imagination. Imagination is never neutral or generic. It is rooted in specific stories and metaphors imbued with particular meaning in contrast to, and often in conflict with, other stories and metaphors.

Walter Brueggemann has memorably said that "the key pathology of our time, which seduces us all, is the reduction of the imagination so that we are too numbed, satiated and co-opted to do serious imaginative work."[38] So the issue before us, and we believe the issue before Paul (though he wouldn't have put it this way), is not *too much* imagination but the *captivity* of the imagination.

34. Naomi Klein's *No Logo: Taking Aim at the Brand Bullies* (New York: Picador USA, 2000) remains a groundbreaking discussion of the role of image and branding in late capitalist society.

35. Chris Hedges makes the claim that the ethic of unfettered capitalism is a celebration of "image over substance." *The World as It Is: Dispatches on the Myth of Human Progress* (New York: Nation Books, 2013), 44.

36. James K. A. Smith, *Imagining the Kingdom: How Worship Works* (Grand Rapids: Baker Academic, 2013), 126.

37. Charles Taylor, *A Secular Age* (Cambridge, MA: Belknap, 2007), 172–73.

38. Walter Brueggemann, *Interpretation and Obedience* (Minneapolis: Fortress, 1991), 199.

Imperial stories and images are so ubiquitous and so powerful that it is hard to imagine life outside the confines of the imperial imagination.

Again, Smith is helpful. Noting that imagination is always contested, he argues that "the way to our hearts is through our imaginations, and the way to our imaginations is story, image, symbol, song."[39] But when most of our "stories, narratives, images, and sounds come from centralized, for-profit transnational corporations,"[40] any community that would seek to be liberated from such a dominant imperial imagination will need to sing new songs, embrace or reinterpret powerful symbols and images, and, most foundationally, tell an alternative story. This, we believe, is what Paul is up to in his epistle to the Romans—telling a new story for the formation of a Christian imagination, praxis, and community.

So when a targum like the one we offered in this chapter is described as a "feat of imagination," we take that as a compliment, not simply because it says something about our imaginative skills but more importantly because we think that a faithful interpretation of Paul's amazing letter needs to be directed at the imagination.[41] While not denying that there are important intellectual debates to be had in the interpretation of this letter, or even that the letter was itself something of an intellectual tour de force, we think that the imaginative point has often been lost in the intricacies of theological debate.

Now, more briefly, let's reflect for a moment on the second question. How do we evaluate something like a targum? In *Colossians Remixed* we wrote about the process of "double immersion" wherein we come to a contemporary interpretation of a biblical text by means of being deeply immersed in that text (within the context of the whole biblical narrative) while also being immersed deeply into our own world.[42] The meaning (or better, meanings) of a text is a living thing, found in the interplay or dance of fidelity and creativity. It is important to insist that interpretation be disciplined by the text at hand. Imagination is not a matter of doing whatever you want with a text but of engaging the text deeply as *this text* written in a particular time and context.

39. Smith, *Imagining the Kingdom*, 162.

40. Smith, *Imagining the Kingdom*, 162, citing Michael L. Budde, "Collecting Praise: Global Culture Industries," in *The Blackwell Companion to Christian Ethics*, ed. Stanley Hauerwas and Samuel Wells (Oxford: Blackwell, 2006), 124.

41. Of course, the reader knows that the interlocutor who has said that the targum was a "feat of imagination" is also a construct of our own imagination. But not a construction out of nothing. Everything that our interlocutor says in this book has resonances with real comments and questions that we have met over the years of lecturing and preaching on Paul's letter to the Romans.

42. Walsh and Keesmaat, *Colossians Remixed*, 136.

Fidelity of interpretation requires, at its foundation, a deep engagement and close reading of the particular text. But texts are not autonomous. Texts do not stand alone. Texts exist, indeed live, within traditions. The Epistle to the Romans can only be understood within the broader context of the Scriptures, stories, symbols, and metaphors of Israel. And so we need to hear, or perhaps "overhear," the echoes, allusions, and narratives of Israel if we are to understand a text written by a first-century Jewish Christian who was deeply schooled and shaped by the traditions of Israel.[43]

The first criterion, then, for evaluating an interpretation such as a targum has everything to do with imagination. Not only do we need to situate the text in the social imaginary of its author and readers (the "images, stories, legends" of the interpretive community) but that very act of situating the text is itself an imaginative endeavor.

Faithful interpretation, however, also requires an immersion into the cultural context of the contemporary reading community. This leads us to the second criterion. Romans is a historical text that spoke into a historical context. As we have seen, and as we will continue to explore in this book, we need to imaginatively construe the imperial context of the Christian assemblies in Rome if we are to attempt to hear the text in its own first-century context. But if this is a living text, a text that we believe continues to speak words of truth and vision through the ages, then we will need to hear this text *as if* it were written two weeks ago. That kind of reading requires creativity grounded in serious spiritual discernment of our present cultural (and imperial) context. That is why we will also need to continue with the kind of cultural analysis that we have already begun in the targum. We can't make a quick and cheap ideological jump from Paul's discussion of creation and idolatry in Romans 1:18–25 to a targum addressing the problems of globalized economics. This needs to be a careful and faithful interpretive move that has been called "dynamic analogy."[44]

Dynamic analogy is the imaginative attempt to discern dynamic equivalents in our own cultural context to those addressed in the ancient text. For example, if the text refers to idolatry distorting life and resulting in societal degeneration, then what might we discern to be the idols of *our* time, and what is the social brokenness that such idolatry reaps today? Or if the text refers to people who

43. Paradigmatic for our exegetical method is Richard B. Hays, *Echoes of Scripture in the Letters of Paul* (New Haven: Yale University Press, 1989).

44. See James A. Sanders, "Canonical Hermeneutics," in *From Sacred Story to Sacred Text: Canon as Paradigm* (Philadelphia: Fortress, 1987), 70.

are dismissed as shameful in its own imperial context, then who might be similarly dismissed and marginalized in our cultural context? Dynamic analogies do not make one-to-one static correspondences between the biblical text and the contemporary context. Rather, they are imaginative hunches that we hope are suggested by the biblical text. If we read our own world through biblical eyes, and specifically through the eyes of a text like Romans, then we hope to come up with interpretations that just might be Spirit led, thereby demonstrating the abiding power of not only the letter to the Romans but, more importantly, the gospel that the apostle here proclaims.

Such interpretation seeks to be faithful and creative, consistent and innovative, stable and adaptive. Creativity without fidelity ascends to an imagination without grounding or roots. Fidelity without creativity descends to an orthodoxy devoid of imagination and adaptable, life-giving power and vision.

I'm still stuck on how securely rooted all of this is. If I grant you the point that all interpretation is an act of imagination, how do I evaluate how faithful that imagination is?

Do you mean faithfulness to Jesus Christ? Faithfulness to the gospel? Because that would be a crucial question for any discussion of Romans. As we have already intimated in our earlier discussion, faithfulness is at the heart of this epistle: the faithfulness of Jesus Christ and our faithfulness in response to him.

I can see how those questions would be important for this discussion. But my question was slightly different. I'm asking about how I can know that the dynamic analogies that you are drawing are faithful to the text in its original context. I'm asking that third question about how this letter would have been heard in its original context.

Thanks for bringing us back to that question. Granted that any such reconstruction of how those Roman Christian assemblies would have heard this letter is itself an imaginative enterprise, can we ground that exercise historically?

Yes, that's the question.

We hope that the opening exposition of how Paul's language was deliberately provocative in the face of the empire might give an indication as to how this letter would have been heard.

But would gentiles and Jews have responded in the same way to Paul's insistence that the gospel is the power of God to everyone who has faith, to the Jew first and then to the gentile? How would slaves have heard Paul's self-identification as a "slave of Jesus Christ"? How would citizens and freedmen and women have heard it?

My question is, Does it matter whether you are a Jewish follower of Jesus or a gentile? Does it matter whether you are a slave or free, whether you are living in relative economic security or always at the edge of crippling poverty? Does it matter whether your belly was full or empty?

Of course it matters. Social, ethnic, economic, and cultural identities are key to how we interpret the world and, undoubtedly, to how we interpret texts.[45] And it is clear from even a cursory reading of Romans that Paul is attempting to mediate conflicting visions of life between Jews and gentiles in the Roman assemblies. But there is more going on than the Jew/gentile division in this letter. From the greetings at the end of the epistle it appears that Paul is addressing very diverse Christian assemblies who are situated in different geographical locations in the city and who represent varied economic and social positions.

Environmental philosopher David Orr proves helpful here. Orr argues that things like the built environment, landscapes, energy systems, modes of transportation, and economic transactions shape and instruct life in fundamental ways. These things "structure what we see, how we move, what we eat, our sense of time and space, how we relate to each other, our sense of security, and how we experience the particular places in which we live. Moreover, by their scale and power they structure how we think, often limiting our ability to imagine better alternatives."[46] Social, geographical, and economic locations (often linked to ethnic identity) shape how we think and how we imagine the world. So how would someone like a gentile slave woman hear Paul's letter when read in her assembly compared to, let's say, a Jewish tradesman? How would their relative senses of security shape their hearing of this letter? How would their freedom of movement, the neighborhood in which they lived, and their economic location influence what they would make of this letter? And if they ever had the chance to discuss the letter in each other's company, what would that conversation look like? Where would they disagree? What would be the points of tension or the points of joyous coming together?

So we now turn to another exercise of the imagination. To get more deeply into the question of historical fidelity, we need to introduce you to Iris and Nereus.

45. One of the first projects that demonstrated the importance of social location was Fernando F. Segovia and Mary Ann Tolbert, eds., *Reading from the Place*, vol. 1, *Social Location and Biblical Interpretation in the United States*, and vol. 2, *Social Location and Biblical Interpretation in Global Perspective* (Minneapolis: Fortress, 1995).

46. David Orr, *The Nature of Design: Ecology, Culture, and Human Intention* (Oxford: Oxford University Press, 2002), 31. Sandra R. Joshel and Lauren Hackworth Petersen's *The Material Life of Roman Slaves* (Cambridge: Cambridge University Press, 2014) explores these same dynamics in relation to the lives of slaves in the Roman Empire.

2

Kitchen Walls and Tenement Halls

Iris's Story[1]

At first I didn't know whether to believe it. When Quintus told me that a letter had come from Paul, *the* Paul, who was spoken of so glowingly by Prisca and Aquila, I was skeptical. Quintus lives with such hope that sometimes he imagines good news. But then, while at the market, I bumped into Alexandra, one of Prisca's slaves, and she said it was true: Paul sent a letter that had arrived yesterday, in the hands of a woman, Phoebe, a leader in the church in Cenchreae. She would share it with the community tonight.

Tonight. As much as I wanted to go and hear Paul's letter myself, I could not imagine being able to sneak out tonight. I don't have the freedom to come and go as I wish. Or freedom of any kind, really. Although occasionally I could arrange to trade my childcare duties with another slave for a chance to go to the market, I doubted whether I would be able to leave the household for a meeting that would take the whole evening. Alexandra knew my problem well. "If you aren't there," she said, "I'll remember all I can and come and tell you tomorrow. I'm sure that Prisca will give me leave to share the good news with you and the others." With that I had to be content.

1. We have taken the name Iris from graffiti in Pompeii that refers to Iris, an innkeeper's slave. She is described in Peter Oakes, *Reading Romans in Pompeii: Paul's Letter at Ground Level* (Minneapolis: Fortress, 2009), 33–37. We have borrowed only the name and not the persona of Iris, since the Iris referred to on the wall was probably a slave forced into prostitution by her master. However, there is overlap between the Iris mentioned on the wall and the Iris we have created.

When I became a follower of Jesus, I had known, of course, that it would not be easy to join the assembly at the house of Prisca and Aquila.[2] As the slave of a master who did not follow the Way, I could not easily slip away unnoticed. Slaves like Alexandra, with believing masters, were encouraged to meet with the assembly. I had to sneak out, if I went, and hope that my master, Narcissus, would not want my services while I was away. If he did, I would be whipped. Generally, this wasn't a risk I was willing to take.

That may have been just as well. Prisca and Aquila's workshop could only accommodate about thirty people, even if we did sit on the rolled-up cloth for the awnings. If all the believing slaves from my household attended at once, there would not be room for us all.[3] Thankfully, there were other members of the household of Narcissus who were followers of Jesus, and we were able to meet late at night, when most of the household was asleep.[4] That is where I would likely hear about this letter from Paul.

As the day progressed, it became clear that only one person from our household would be going to hear Paul's letter. My master was hosting a dinner party that night. The kitchen slaves would be preparing and serving food well into the night, the slave who normally cleaned the latrines would be cleaning up after the guests, and I would leave my duties of looking after Narcissus's wife and children to sexually satisfy the guests as well as our master. The children, of course, would attend some part of the feast.[5]

2. Paul refers in Rom. 16:5 to the *ekklēsia* that meets in the house of Prisca and Aquila. Rather than translating *ekklēsia* as "church," which has more recent organizational and institutional overtones, we use the term *assembly*. This is also a better translation of *synagogē*, a term usually translated as "synagogue," which has similar institutional overtones that are more fitting for a later historical period. *Assembly*, therefore, straddles the continuum between synagogue and church.

3. To be a "tentmaker" in the first century, as were Prisca and Aquila (and Paul), largely meant providing awnings for shade that were used on shop fronts and for the wealthy in the amphitheater. It is likely that Prisca and Aquila made linen tents or awnings that were used for protection from the sun during the games and also to cover atriums in private homes. Shopkeepers used linen tents for their market stands. Leather tents were used mainly by the military, who had their own skilled workmen. See Peter Lampe, *From Paul to Valentinus: Christians at Rome in the First Two Centuries*, trans. Michael Steinhauser (London: T&T Clark, 1987), 188–89, 192. Oakes, *Reading Romans in Pompeii*, 89–97, calculates that a typical house church in a craftworker's shop could accommodate about thirty people. Oakes's careful reconstruction is based on detailed and extremely helpful demographic work on house sizes in Pompeii, transposed into the setting of the city of Rome.

4. Paul greets those who belong to the family of Narcissus in Rom. 16:11.

5. On the presence of children at feasts, see Margaret Y. MacDonald, *The Power of Children: The Construction of Christian Families in the Greco-Roman World* (Waco: Baylor University Press, 2014), 19–22, 41–42.

As the day wore on, I remembered with longing the days when the master's sons were young. I had been wet nurse for both of them, and for the two years following each of their births no one was allowed to use me for sex. I was free to nurse the children and raise my own children alongside them.[6] Although I had two surviving children of my own, my role was primarily to raise my master's sons. Until recently I had taught all four of them. They particularly loved it when I told them the stories of Rome. Their favorite by far was the story of the great Aeneas, who fled the fallen Troy with his father and their household gods and his small son.[7] Maybe they loved it so much because of our trips to the Forum of Augustus, where they were able to see the impressive statue of Aeneas carrying his father and holding the hand of this son. Of course, they knew that the story of Aeneas came to its climax with Augustus, the *Pater Patriae*, the Father of the Fatherland, the direct descendent of Aeneas. Augustus in his triumphal chariot pulled by four powerful horses was the central figure in the Forum. When they looked up at his figure, the children were overawed, as much by the powerful beasts that did his bidding as by Augustus himself.[8] Who would not want to be part of such a wonderful story? For the story of Aeneas tells of the beginning of Rome, the great empire, fatherland of a great people whom the gods have ordained to rule the whole world, to bring justice and peace to all peoples. According to this story, our savior and lord, Caesar, is the one descended from the gods and through whom the gods rule. That is why we worship not only our household gods but also Venus, the mother of Aeneas, and Mars Ultor, the god of war, who gives Caesar victory. The story became even more impressive when we stood in the temple of Mars in the Forum and looked

6. On wet nurses and their influence, including as educators, see MacDonald, *Power of Children*, 40–41; Christian Laes, *Children in the Roman Empire: Outsiders Within* (Cambridge: Cambridge University Press, 2011), 72–77.

7. Virgil's account of Aeneas's escape from Troy is found in *The Aeneid*, book 1. This story not only was standard in education but also was frequently performed in the theater and was a common subject for wall paintings, decoration on household objects such as lamps, and graffiti. Thus this was a story known across the social classes. Nicholas Horsfall, "Virgil: His Life and Times," and "Virgil's Impact at Rome: The Non-literary Evidence," in *A Companion to the Study of Virgil* (Leiden: Brill, 1995), 1–25, 249–55.

8. This statue was found in the courtyard of the Augustan Forum. One passed it on the way to the temple of Mars Ultor, which contained the statue of Aeneas in an alcove on the northwest side. For a description of the Augustan Forum, see Mary Beard, John North, and Simon Price, *Religions of Rome* (Cambridge: Cambridge University Press, 1998), 1:199–200, 2:80–83. Not only were legal cases heard in the Forum but also generals were sent to war from there, the senate met there to discuss wars and campaigns, and returning generals brought the "symbols of their triumph" to it. It is unclear whether this referred to booty or the laurels of victory. Beard, North, and Price, *Religions of Rome*, 2:82–83.

up at the magnificent statues of both Venus and Mars towering far above our heads.[9]

Of course, we didn't have to go to the Forum to see these stories around us, though the Forum was the most magnificent place to tell them. Aeneas was on our lamps, and his story was depicted on the wall where Narcissus hosted his feasts. We had even, on occasion, heard the story powerfully recited at the theater. And we had seen the story of Aeneas offering a sacrifice depicted on the *Ara Pacis*, the Altar of Peace, demonstrating the piety that led not only to Roman victory but also to Roman abundance.[10] It was a story that the children wanted to be part of. A story of piety, faithfulness, and true virtue. A story of triumph and power. Sometimes even I began to think it might be true, even though it was not my story and the Romans were not my people.

That is the story I *used to* tell to the children in my care. But then one day Narcissus took my son and daughter with him to the marketplace and returned alone. I knew that I couldn't ask him what had happened to my children. I couldn't ask because I am a slave. Slaves don't have children. I had borne two bodies for Narcissus, to use as he wished, to sell as he wished.[11] I had no idea if they were in another household like this one or if they had been sold to the warehouses in Transtiberium to measure grain or if they had been taken to be slaves on a rural estate. Either way, they seemed so small, too small, for any of that! My son was only six and my daughter three.[12] How could a mother bear

9. According to Paul Zanker, *The Power of Images in the Age of Augustus*, trans. Alan Shapiro (Ann Arbor: University of Michigan Press, 1988), 193–96, the Forum of Augustus had the explicit function of educating the people in the new mythology of Aeneas, Venus, and Mars. Although this mythology was no longer "new" at the time that Paul wrote this letter, evidence from Pompeii demonstrates that the story of Aeneas was still the subject of inscription and artwork; see Mary Beard, *The Fires of Vesuvius: Pompeii Lost and Found* (Cambridge, MA: Belknap, 2008), 51–52, 59.

10. A description of the *Ara Pacis* can be found in Beard, North, and Price, *Religions of Rome*, 2:83–85. On how the images of abundance and military triumph on the altar are mutually reinforcing, see Zanker, *Power of Images*, 172–75.

11. On how the Greek word *sōma* (body) is used to describe slaves, see Jennifer A. Glancy, *Slavery in Early Christianity* (Oxford: Oxford University Press, 2002), 10–11.

12. On the splitting of slave families, see Carolyn Osiek, "Female Slaves, *Porneia*, and the Limits of Obedience," in *Early Christian Families in Context: An Interdisciplinary Dialogue*, ed. David L. Balch and Carolyn Osiek (Grand Rapids: Eerdmans, 2003), 258; Beryl Rawson, "Family Life among the Lower Classes at Rome in the First Two Centuries of the Empire," *Classical Philology* 61, no. 2 (April 1966): 71–83. On the types of work done by children, see Christian Laes, "Child Slaves at Work in Roman Antiquity," *Ancient Society* 38 (2008): 235–83. Although slave children were often sold as infants, it was assumed that a child could render service to her or his master by the age of five, and occasionally younger. Laes, "Child Slaves," 241, 259; Beryl Rawson, *Children and Childhood in Roman Italy* (Oxford: Oxford University Press, 2003), 160.

this? What kind of people would take children from their mothers? No matter how grand the story of the Romans, it was hard to believe that they were a people of justice, of peace, of salvation, when they tore children from their mothers, when the climax of their story was continual heartache. I was glad that the violence of the men who used me had resulted in my lovely babies, but when my son and daughter were stripped from me, I was convinced of the brutality of these people . . . and their gods!

Even though I knew that I should be careful not to betray my deep sorrow, I could no longer bring myself to tell the stories of Rome or sing the anthems of praise. I continued to care for my master's sons, but I could no longer pretend that I believed the stories of Rome. Our visits to the Forum and the temples became infrequent, just enough to keep up appearances.

Then, a few months ago, I noticed that one of the other slaves, Quintus, had given up his role in the household sacrifices. In a niche in the kitchen wall live the household gods, the *lares* and *genius*, whose blessing ensures the well-being of our household and our master and, through him, the well-being of us, his slaves.[13] Quintus had been accustomed to offering the cakes and oil on behalf of the slaves, but I noticed that he had begun to instruct another slave to take his place. One day, as we walked to the marketplace together, I asked him why.

Quintus looked around carefully and then lowered his voice. Bending his head toward me, he quietly began to tell me about someone named Jesus, whom the one true God had appointed to be our Savior. This Jesus was the true Lord who would bring peace and forgiveness to the world. He told me that Jesus had been crucified by the Romans; he had died the death of a slave. And then, unbelievably, he had been raised from the dead by the power of the Holy Spirit! Many had seen him alive before he ascended to the heavens.

This was an astounding story. I had never heard of someone who came back to life from the dead, and I told Quintus that I was surprised he had fallen for such a superstitious old wives' tale. He did not seem offended at my comments. Ever since Narcissus bought me, Quintus had cared for me like my own mother had, and he patiently explained more about this man, Jesus.

He told me how Jesus had been born in Galilee of the Gentiles and had healed the sick, made the blind to see and the lame to walk. He told me how Jesus had fed those who were hungry, how he had welcomed the shameful and sick to his

13. What actually happened at household sacrifices isn't exactly known; see Beard, North, and Price, *Religions of Rome*, 2:102; Beard, *Fires of Vesuvius*, 297–98.

table to eat with him, and how he had forgiven and healed gentiles, even though he was a Judean.[14]

At this point I interrupted him. "This Jesus is a *Judean*? You are following someone from that cursed and shameful people?"

Quintus told me that, yes, Jesus was the Jewish Messiah, whom God had sent to save the entire world.

"But that's impossible," I replied. "The Jews hate all other people. They won't even eat with us, and they refuse to worship the gods that bless us!"

Quintus was still very patient. "That is not the whole story," he said. "Those who follow Jesus know that their God has come to bless the whole world. And Jesus welcomed both Jew and gentile, and so do his followers." Quintus invited me to come see for myself, if I liked. There was to be a meeting of Jesus followers the next afternoon at the workshop of Prisca and Aquila, the awning makers. I could bring the children if I wanted. I confess that I was intrigued. And so the next day, when my mistress thought I was taking the children to the temples, I went to the awning makers' workshop.[15]

It was an astounding experience. When Quintus spoke to me, I assumed that this meeting would only be attended by slaves. But the whole household of Aquila and Prisca was present: their children and slaves and a couple of family members. There were also one or two other artisans and their slaves, a stoneworker, and a few more slaves from my household that Quintus had brought with the excuse of picking up some tile. There were also a few people who had just arrived in Rome, who had lost their land and were looking for a place to stay and work.[16] They were too old to sell themselves as slaves and had been sleeping in the tombs along the Via Appia.[17]

14. We use the term *Judean* rather than *Jew* to better reflect the Greek (*Ioudaios*) and to reflect the geographical connection that would have been made in the ancient world between *Ioudaios* and Judea, the land of their ancestors

15. On the relationship between slaves and the children they cared for, including the accompaniment of such children to meetings with their slave caretakers, see Rawson, *Children and Childhood*, 216.

16. This reconstruction of a house church in a craftworker's workshop is based on Oakes, *Reading Romans in Pompeii*, 89–96.

17. According to Lampe, the Via Appia was also a high-density slum area of the city (*From Paul to Valentinus*, 46, 56–58). Andrew Wallace-Hadrill points out that the nature of Roman housing (shops fronting the streets with larger homes behind; more spacious apartments on the second floor and smaller rooms for rent on the upper floors) meant that people of different socioeconomic levels lived in close proximity throughout the city ("*Domus* and *Insulae* in Rome: Families and Housefuls," in Balch and Osiek, *Early Christian Families*, 3–18). That said, some parts of the city, such as Transtiberium and the Via Appia, did have higher population density, a higher proportion of noxious trades (fullers, tanners), and a smaller proportion per capita of amenities such as bakeries. The statistics can be found in Lampe, *From Paul to Valentinus*, 51–54.

It was the oddest meeting I had ever attended. First of all, there was food that was shared with all equally. It didn't matter if you were a master or a slave, a man or a woman. We were all welcome to eat the same food, provided for all. When those of us who were slaves held back, we were encouraged to share from the same dish as the leader! I had never seen anything like it.

Second, the meeting was led not by Aquila but by his wife, Prisca! I had never seen a woman speak with authority when her husband was present. We opened with a hymn and a prayer, and then Prisca talked about the Judean Scriptures and Jesus. She then asked everyone to give their opinion on how the group could provide food and shelter—and even work—for those who were new to Rome. That's when I noticed another strange thing: everyone was allowed to speak—slaves, men, women, even one of the children piped up with an idea, one that turned out to be quite good. What was it about this community that honor was offered to all?[18]

Later I confessed to Quintus that the meeting had amazed me, and I was puzzled that Prisca knew so many of the Judean stories. He told me that Prisca and Aquila, their family, and the stonemason were all Judeans, even though they sounded Roman. Some of them were children of Judean slaves and had been in Rome for a couple of generations.[19]

"A couple of generations? But I thought that Judeans had been barred from Rome?" I said.

Quintus told me that many Judeans had not left the city, especially since there were many places to hide in Rome, and some of them sounded Roman. Also, some of the Judeans who did leave had returned under Nero. It turned out that Prisca and Aquila were two Judeans who had left and returned to Rome a year or two ago.[20]

Well, that meeting was three months ago. Very occasionally I was able to attend other meetings at Prisca and Aquila's. But more often Quintus and I met with a few other slaves from our household, when our master and his family were asleep. Gradually, I stopped going to the Forum of Augustus altogether. Rather than taking the master's sons to the Forum and telling the story of Venus, Aeneas's mother,

18. Bruce W. Longenecker, *The Lost Letters of Pergamum: A Story from the New Testament World*, 2nd ed. (Grand Rapids: Baker Academic, 2016), also engages in an evocative and imaginative reconstruction of what early Christian communities might have looked like to those who enter them for the first time.

19. On slaves brought to Rome as a result of conquest, see Keith R. Bradley, "On Captives under the Principate," *Phoenix* 58, nos. 3/4 (2004): 298–318 (plates for this article are on pp. 374–90). On Judean slaves' descendants in Rome, see Bradley, "On Captives," 309n17; Beard, North, and Prince, *Religions of Rome*, 1:272. Robert Jewett suggests that Aquila is of slave origin. *Romans: A Commentary*, Hermeneia (Minneapolis: Fortress, 2007), 955–56.

20. Acts 18:1–3.

or the story of Mars and his great blessings, which enabled Rome to conquer the barbarians and bring peace to the entire world, I began to tell them the stories of Jesus, who brought peace not by killing his enemies but by forgiving them as they killed him. Here was a strange story of a lord and savior who took violence on himself rather than inflict it on others. Here was a story of one who is a son of God not because his father had become a god after death, but because he rose from the dead. Maybe it was in the quiet telling of these stories, or maybe it was the welcoming community of those who followed the Way of this Jesus, but after some time I found that I believed this story. I found myself on the Way with Jesus. And for the first time in my life, I felt like I had come home, even though I couldn't really understand what that meant. When my mother and I were separated some years ago, I was left without a family, until I had my own children. But when they were taken away, I knew the bitter truth: home and family could never be claimed by a slave. But there was something about Jesus and the people of the Way that gave me a sense of home, even in my slavery, even in Rome.

There was still a problem, however. You see, even though I was no longer telling the story of the Roman people, I couldn't quite bring myself to tell the children those other stories, the stories of the Judean people. That Jesus had come with healing and forgiveness and justice for the shamed I was willing and eager to accept. I even believed that he had risen from the dead because of those who followed him. I just couldn't see how the stories of the Judean people could *matter* to those who followed Jesus, especially for non-Judeans like me.

And now Paul had sent a letter to the assemblies in Rome. It turned out that only Quintus was able to go that night and hear Paul's letter. He is our master's manager and was not required at the banquet. When I asked him the next day what was in the letter, he looked unusually smug. "Tonight we will meet in the kitchen," he said, "and there will be a surprise! Phoebe is coming to read the letter to us here, to those of us who follow Jesus in the family of Narcissus!"

Here! In our kitchen! I could hardly believe it. An important person coming to the *kitchen* to speak to us, to share Paul's letter! I wished that we had another place to meet, but even though only six of us could fit in the kitchen, it was still the safest place to do something in secret, and the presence in the wall of the household shrine with the *lares* and *genius* was our insurance in some way. Although it was odd praising Jesus in front of those statues that are not gods, if we *were* discovered it would be assumed that we were praying for household prosperity.[21]

21. On the presence and possible implications of *lararia* (household shrines) in the kitchen and other service areas, see David L. Balch, "Rich Pompeiian Houses, Shops for Rent, and the

When the time came, I was surprised to see that not only were the slaves present (the slaves who slept in the kitchen were followers of Jesus and they were used to having cramped meetings in their space) but one of the master's sisters, who lived in the house, was present as well. I had never seen her at Prisca and Aquila's before. But she had heard about Paul's letter from a friend who was part of the household of Aristobulus and who had seen Quintus at Prisca and Aquila's the night before.[22] She had no idea that there were followers of Jesus among the slaves of her household and was overjoyed to be able to meet with us that night.[23] While we were happy to see her, one of us had to sit in the hallway just outside the door to make space inside.

After we had quietly sung a hymn and had passed around some barley cakes that the cook had made and saved for us, Phoebe began to read Paul's letter. From the very first sentence it was not what I had expected. Paul began by calling himself a slave of Jesus the Messiah—he identified himself not with the honorable, not with the freeborn, but as the slave of another Master, Jesus, whom his followers called the Messiah, a Judean name for a King. I found this startling. Why would a free person call himself a slave, even of someone who was such a good Master as Jesus? To be a slave meant you were shameful. To be a slave meant that no one ever showed you honor. To be a slave meant that you could be beaten, even tortured at will, and no one would defend you. To be a slave meant you had no place, no father to belong to, no son to care for you, no homeland, no home.[24] Why would Paul say that he was a slave? How could he even understand what the life of a slave was like? How could he even *imagine* knowing what it was like to be a slave? How dare this free man, this Roman citizen who was also a Judean, describe himself as if his life were even remotely like mine?[25]

Huge Apartment Buildings in Herculaneum as Typical Spaces for Pauline House Churches," *Journal for the Study of the New Testament* 27, no. 1 (2004): 38–40. On the role of slaves in looking after the cult of the *lares* (household gods) or the master's *genius* (guardian spirit), see Lampe, *From Paul to Valentinus*, 379. Beryl Rawson indicates that slaves had a larger role in the cult of the *lares* and *genius*, as evidenced by their more frequent presence in service areas. "'The Roman Family' in Recent Research: State of the Question," *Biblical Interpretation* 11, no. 2 (2003): 119–38, esp. 123.

22. Paul sends greetings to those who belong to the family of Aristobulus in Rom. 16:10.

23. The involvement of women as leaders in the early Christian movement is described by Margaret Y. MacDonald, "The Role of Women in the Expansion of Early Christianity," in Balch and Osiek, *Early Christian Families*, 157–84. While the daily business of women would have facilitated opportunities for sharing the gospel, this did not mean that no risk was involved. MacDonald says, "This combination of boldness, affront and concealment is for me one of the most interesting and little understood features of the rise of early Christianity" (184).

24. On natal alienation and slavery, see Glancy, *Slavery in Early Christianity*, 25–26.

25. Our thanks to Grace vanOudenaren for this line of thought.

I was almost unable to listen any further, but immediately another phrase caught my attention: "the triumphant good news of God, concerning his Son."[26] Usually the triumphant good news is what Caesar offers after a fresh victory—and we know what that good news means.[27] More captured people will be brought as slaves to Rome, just as my mother and I were brought from Mauretania twelve years ago.[28] Caesar's good news is always bad news for most of us.

But Paul said that the good news of Jesus and his God is the power of salvation—oddly enough to the Judean first and then to the Greek! Why to the Judean first? I didn't really get this emphasis on the Judeans throughout the letter. It is true that the pagan people Paul goes on to describe who worship idols lead lives of sexual violence, and it is true that greed and envy manage to keep us all in our places. But Paul admitted that the Judeans are just as bad. He even said there would be anguish and distress for the Judean first and then the Greek. He said that God is not partial and that the external marks of Judaism do not matter![29]

So why did he spend so much time talking about a famous Judean ancestor, Abraham? The story of Aeneas was never my story, and now it had lost all appeal to me. Why would I abandon the story of one alien ancestor for another one? I was neither Roman nor Judean. And why should the descendants of this Judean Abraham receive a promise to inherit the world when it was clear that Jesus was not the Savior of any one people? Couldn't Jesus be the Savior of all without Abraham's story?

Other parts of the letter were much easier to understand. As I have already said, when Paul condemned all the sexual violence of the imperial house—and the violence of our own master too!—I knew what he was talking about.[30] Paul also seemed to understand at least something of what it meant to be a slave when he said that with his mind he is a slave to the law of God, but with his flesh he is a slave to the law of sin.[31] That's exactly what it is like—wanting to live a life of virtue and piety but being forced to do things my master demands even when they are shameful.[32] That's why Paul talked about our groaning as we wait for

26. Rom. 1:3 our translation.

27. The Greek *euangelion* can be translated as "gospel" or "good news." In the Roman Empire, the term was used for a the good news of a military victory. See sources in chap. 1, note 24.

28. Bradley, "On Captives under the Principate," 301–4. Rome was fighting to subdue Mauretania from 40 to 44 CE (p. 302). Ancient Mauretania was located in what is today western Algeria and northern Morocco.

29. Rom. 2:9–10, 28–29.

30. Rom. 1:26–27.

31. Rom. 7:14–20.

32. So also Oakes, *Reading Romans in Pompeii*, 147.

our bodies to be redeemed.[33] We cry out until we are fully free—the freedom of the children of God, he said. When that freedom comes, we will no longer be in bondage, forced to be a slave to sin. I have always known that groaning deep within me, and it seems to have only become more intense since I've started following Jesus.

It was a long letter, with parts that were hard to understand, and I was tired after a long day. But I remember a few other bits. Paul seemed to be describing some things that our community tries to do already. We try to be welcoming to strangers. We try to show honor to everyone, slave and free. I confess that I missed the rest of the letter until the very end where Paul sent greetings to us, those in the family of Narcissus!

There was silence as Phoebe finished. Then Quintus said, with a grin, "So, who would like the first holy kiss?" And we all began to laugh, so that we had to shush each other. Someday Quintus, with his weird sense of humor, will be the reason that we are caught!

Finally, Phoebe suggested that we pray together and meet again in six days. She would stay in the city for a bit and would come back to talk with us about this letter. In the meantime, some other slaves from the house of Prisca and Aquila would come and talk about it with us as well.

I left to sneak back into my mistress's room, very tired.[34] Paul's letter had comforted me in places—I thought he said that nothing could separate us from God's love—but it had been difficult and confusing in others. It was many months before I understood more of what Paul had written. And the person who helped me understand most of it turned out to be a Judean named Nereus whose grandmother had come as a slave to Rome almost one hundred years ago.[35] He is a free man, a worker with clay, who usually lives over the Tiber. Prisca and Aquila recently hired him to make some lamps, dishes, and jars for them. Then Quintus hired him to replenish some of the clay items in our kitchen. If my master had known he was a Judean potter from the tenement slums of Transtiberium, he

33. Rom. 8:23.

34. It appears that in most households slaves would sleep in the kitchen, the store rooms, the hallway, or even the master's or mistress's bedroom. Michele George, "Domestic Architecture and Household Relations: Pompeii and Roman Ephesos," *Journal for the Study of the New Testament* 27, no. 1 (2004): 7–25, esp. 13–14. However, Oakes provides evidence of very basic sleeping space for at least some slaves. Oakes, *Reading Romans in Pompeii*, 40.

35. Bradley, "On Captives under the Principate," 309n17, indicates that "Philo could report in his day (*Leg.* 155) that the Transtiberine community of Jews at Rome was descended from captives fortunate enough to have been manumitted." The majority of occurrences of the name Nereus in ancient Rome were people of slave ancestry. Lampe, *From Paul to Valentinus*, 174.

would never have permitted him to be hired. Nereus was overjoyed with Paul's letter to our communities here in Rome because he and some of his fellow Christians who met in his tenement house were greeted directly by Paul at the end of the letter.[36] Paul had heard of them! Probably from Andronicus and Junia, who were in prison with Paul and who also lived in the Judean ghetto over the Tiber.[37] That tells you a lot about Nereus, actually. He has pride in his people and maybe just a little more pride than he should have about being well known among the saints.[38] But maybe I should let him speak for himself.

Nereus's Story

When they told me about Paul's letter, I had no idea how deeply it would change my life. Almost all I had known for most of my thirty-four years was the crowded, noisy, smelly streets of Transtiberium, the lowlands by the Tiber, where the dockworkers, warehousemen, sailors, ivory carvers, cabinetmakers, millworkers, and brickmakers lived.[39] The smell came mostly from the leather makers, although the dyers also used urine for their work. Of course, growing up there, I had never noticed how crowded and smelly it was. I didn't notice that until I crossed the river to another part of Rome. And it was Paul's letter that gave me that chance.

See, it was this way. One day Alexandra, a slave from Prisca and Aquila's house by the Aventine hill over the river, came to find one of my kin, Julia.[40] She asked

36. Rom. 16:15.

37. Rom. 16:7 refers to Andronicus and Junia as Paul's kin, a reference to their shared Judean ancestry.

38. For the purposes of this book, we are suggesting that those greeted in Rom. 16:15—Philologus, Julia, Nereus and his sister, and Olympas—are a group of Judean followers of Jesus who live in the Transtiberium quarter of Rome. We make this suggestion on the following basis: (1) all four of these names have a high probability of slave ancestry (Lampe, *From Paul to Valentinus*, 174–79); (2) the majority of Judeans in Rome would have come as slaves at the time of Pompeii in 63 BCE (see note 35 above); (3) the majority of Judeans in Rome lived in the Transtiberium (Lampe, *From Paul to Valentinus*, 38–34; Beard, North, and Price, *Religions of Rome*, 1:269); and (4) the detailed work done by Lampe indicates that a high concentration of Christians also lived in the Transtiberium (Lampe, *From Paul to Valentinus*, 42–47). It is therefore plausible that if any of the groups in this letter were Judean followers of Jesus, they would have lived in the Transtiberium quarter of the city and would have had slave ancestry. We also assume that their status would have been far too low to have been among the more high-profile Judeans evicted from Rome by Claudius in 49 CE. While not wanting to assert definitively that this was the character of this group, the slave origins of their names make this a possible scenario.

39. Lampe, *From Paul to Valentinus*, 50–51.

40. On the basis of various data, Jewett, *Romans*, 956, situates the house of Prisca and Aquila in the Aventine, although he attributes a higher status to Prisca than we do. In accordance with

Julia to let the other followers of the Messiah know that Phoebe had arrived with a letter from Paul, a letter that would be shared with the believers that evening. Now some of the others had been to Prisca and Aquila's workshop at one time or another for a gathering of those on the Way, but I had never managed to make it. You need to understand how it is, just my sister and I, trying to keep our heads above water here, and if I don't stay at my patron's pottery workshop making lamps as long as there is light in the sky, I don't make enough money to buy food. And I didn't want to go across the city after dark. Not alone. A Judean walking around Rome after dark without security is asking to be beaten up; sometimes Judeans are even attacked in the daylight. My sister had gone to a meeting or two with Philologus. They would leave late afternoon while it was still light and return early the next morning. (Blessed be he who shelters us under the shadow of his wings for moving the hearts of Prisca and Aquila to allow my sister to sleep in their workshop all night!) They would bring me the news from the meetings and tell me about any new teachings. We would also let Julia know and try to meet with the other saints in the garden behind Julia's workshop. My sister and I rent a tiny room on the top floor of our building where there is only room to sleep, so we never host the meetings. To be frank, the floor couldn't hold that many people![41]

Anyway, what with the need to work, you can understand why I told Alexandra that I could not join them. They could bring me the news like they always did. I was fine with that.

But this time Alexandra was stubborn about it. I should be there, she said. My sister and I, and Olympas, Philologus, and Julia, should all come. She wouldn't say why it was important for the five of us to be there. And when I told her that if I left work for that long, we wouldn't eat the next day, or I might even lose my place, she was curiously unworried. She promised us that all things would work together for our good. So I gave in and we prepared to leave. It only made sense

---

Wallace-Hadrill's "*Domus* and *Insulae* in Rome," it is likely that a craftworker household like Prisca and Aquila's coexisted with wealthier dwellings.

41. Some of the tenement houses had rooms as small as ten square meters (approximately one hundred square feet) on the upper floors, with a shared latrine and water available from a cistern on the ground floor. See Janet DeLaine, "Housing Roman Ostia," in *Contested Spaces: Houses and Temples in Roman Antiquity and the New Testament*, ed. David L. Balch and Annette Weissenrieder (Tübingen: Mohr Siebeck, 2012), 341–43. Since most of the flats have no traces of cooking facilities or indoor sanitation, it is likely that "public baths and nearby cook shops and bars formed a key focus of communal life." Wallace-Hadrill, "*Domus* and *Insulae*," 13. On meeting in gardens, see David L. Balch, "The Church Sitting in a Garden (1 Cor. 14:30; Rom. 16:23; Mark 6:39–40; 8:6; John 6:3, 10; Acts 1:15; 2:1–2)," in Balch and Weissenrieder, *Contested Spaces*, 201–35.

to travel with Alexandra, even though as a slave she could be bullied in the streets just as easily as any Judean.[42] So we kept our heads down, stayed together, and tried not to draw attention to ourselves.

It was a slow walk through the crowded streets, over the river to the foot of the Aventine Hill. After a while I noticed that the air had changed. It still smelled like donkeys and rotting food; that was normal, and dust and smoke were everywhere, but the pungent stink of the tanners was gone. The shopfronts also had more carvings and bigger figures of the gods with more colorful murals. And although apartments still rose on the third and fourth stories, they looked more solid, slightly better built. It wasn't a long journey, but I felt as though I had entered a different city.[43]

The meeting that night was unusual. First of all, it was incredibly crowded. My sister explained that normally only thirty or so people came to these meetings. But that night there were fifty of us trying to cram into the workshop. Not only was every stool and bench taken but people were also sitting on the folded awnings stacked against the wall, standing in the doorway, sitting on the floor, and even standing outside the doorways on benches from the kitchen so they could see over the crowd. We contemplated meeting in the garden instead, but there was hardly more room there, and no awnings to sit on. There were so many different kinds of people! Tradesmen, merchants, slaves, men and women, children, some people who looked well fed, and others even thinner than I am, if you can believe it—all of us crowded in to hear what Paul the apostle had to tell us about Jesus the Messiah, the holy one of God, and the fulfillment of our Scriptures.

It was an amazing letter. Paul clearly knows the suffering we have gone through in Rome. In fact, right at the outset he named the idolatry that shapes so much of life in the capital. I know about that. Even though I make lamps, every now and then my patron tries to convince me to make the clay figures that gentiles use for their charms and even for worship sometimes. When I won't make items for pagan worship, he threatens to throw me out, but he never does. Although most of our lamps are made using a mold, I have a light touch with the clay, and I can make specialty items that are perfectly shaped and beautiful to the eye. He commands a high price for my work and can't afford to lose me. But he is a hard man,

42. For the most part, freeborn people had the right to speak harshly to slaves they encountered and even to subject them to physical abuse. Glancy, *Slavery in Early Christianity*, 12.

43. On the intermingling of commercial and domestic space, as well as the close proximity of various classes of housing throughout the city, see DeLaine, "Housing Roman Ostia," 327–51; Wallace-Hadrill, "*Domus* and *Insulae*," 10–15; and in Pompeii, Beard, *Fires of Vesuvius*, 62–63.

and Paul described him perfectly at the start of his letter. He is sexually violent, using his boy slaves to satisfy his lust. He is greedy and arrogant, telling tales about fellow merchants and the quality of their work to harm their businesses, and he is devious in his dealings. He really is heartless and ruthless. It was as if Paul had my patron in mind when he wrote those words.[44]

The letter was also full of comfort. When Paul described how famine and nakedness and persecution couldn't separate us from the love of the Messiah, I felt that he was talking directly to me about the way my sister and I have struggled. I've known famine and persecution, and in the winter my clothing is never quite enough.[45] If I would consent to use my skill for carving pagan statues, I could probably have enough to eat and new clothes on my back. But none of these things matter as much as faithfulness to Messiah Jesus, whose love enables us to wait for that new creation where justice will be at home.

Oddly enough, Paul's letter felt like a lament to me. Right from the start where he lamented how idolatry has led to violence, through the psalms of lament that he returned to again and again (these psalms are my prayers day and night), to his lament over our people who do not know the way of the Messiah, Paul seemed to be in anguish.[46] I was not surprised that he wrote about the groans of creation, the cries of believers, and the groaning of the Holy Spirit.[47] How could he not? Our God lamented our faithlessness through the prophets, and now Paul, a prophet for our time, lamented that same faithlessness, joining with the lament of the Spirit of God.

But the letter was also puzzling. This was the first time I had met with gentiles who were Christians. Though Paul told them not to be boastful, he did seem to make our story, the story of Israel, a little more welcoming to gentiles than I had remembered it. And while I was glad that he told the community not to condemn those of us who ate no meat, I expected him to talk a little more positively about the law. Surely the Torah is still at the heart of the covenant, just as Jesus is its fulfillment.

But the biggest surprise was at the end, when Phoebe read out the greetings. All five of us—Philologus, Julia, Olympas, me, and my sister—were mentioned (although Paul didn't know my sister's name!). He must have heard about us from Mary, who told us about Jesus so long ago. Or maybe from Andronicus and

44. Rom. 1:24–32.
45. Rom. 8:35.
46. Rom. 9:2.
47. Rom. 8:18–26.

Junia, two of the apostles who also know us well. At any rate, now we understood why Alexandra had insisted we all be there.

It was a long letter, and it was late before we finished. All five of us were offered space on the floor to sleep, although I chose a pile of awnings for myself. The next morning Aquila himself came to see me and asked if I would walk with him to the marketplace. I knew what this meant. In the crowded busyness of the awning workshop, it is hard for anyone to speak privately. Clearly he wanted to talk to me alone. So I went.

Aquila is an abrupt man of few words; last night in the meeting he had not spoken at all. Even though we had never met, it seemed that he knew of my work and my difficulties and had given them some thought. He offered me a chance to stay for a while to make some lamps, dishes, and jars for his household. He also wanted some tile made for one of his clients. I was surprised; usually it is easier and cheaper to buy lamps, dishes, and tile from one of the potters. But Aquila wanted plain lamps. No images of the empire and none of the gods.[48] He also asked me to train someone else as a potter—not one of his slaves but one of the refugees at last night's meeting who was new to Rome. He offered me the use of a kiln belonging to another follower of the Way on the next street over, a place to sleep in the workshop, and food with his slaves if I decided to stay. Of course, I did not intend to accept this offer because it would leave my sister without any support, but when I mentioned that to Aquila, he said that Prisca had offered my sister a chance to stay and help with sewing the awnings.

I still had some hesitation. I knew the offer was generous, but the problem was food. You see, although Prisca and Aquila are Judean, their household has both gentile and Judean members, and it is clear that we interpret our laws differently regarding what a Judean may eat. Even though I usually bought prepared food from one of the tavernas or cook shops, I did not eat meat.[49] Our laws forbid the eating of pork, which is the most common meat in Rome, and even if my closest cook shop has stews with other meat available, I am never sure if the meat was slaughtered properly or offered to idols.[50] Not that I usually have to worry about

48. Zanker, *Power of Images*, 274, describes lamps with the goddess Victoria on them. The story of Aeneas was also popular on lamps. See Galinsky, introduction to *Age of Augustus*, 3.

49. Most of the poorest people in the city did not have cooking facilities and hence purchased their meals. John M. Wilkins and Shaun Hill, *Food in the Ancient World* (Oxford: Blackwell, 2006), 40, 67.

50. Lampe, *From Paul to Valentinus*, 73. It appears that at this time there were no standard expectations around meat eating among Diaspora Jews. Meat that was forbidden in Leviticus was avoided, but the rabbinic laws around crockery and cutlery and the prohibition against mixing meat and dairy were later legal developments. There was no standardized Judean practice, as

these things, because eating meat costs more money than I generally have. I don't even eat meat when the other residents of my tenement house have it, during the festivals where meat is provided for all the inhabitants of Rome. Such festivals are in honor of pagan idols, so I quietly stay at home on those days and hope that no one notices my absence.[51]

But even if I could afford meat, I wouldn't eat it. In Rome, meat and wine are central parts of the festivals to the gods and goddesses that give favor and blessing to Rome. At those sumptuous banquets the gods and goddesses are toasted with libations and honored with sacrifices. In fact, my patron celebrates such banquets with his friends in his home.[52] I know not only is meat part of the sacrifice and wine offered as a libation to the gods,[53] but those banquets are also a way of celebrating the so-called favor of the gods on those who have plenty. From where I stand, these parties look like a way to give thanks for the injustices between rich and poor that shape everyday life on the streets of Rome and in Roman households. The status of patrons and their clients is strengthened in such feasts.[54] I want nothing to do with such eating and drinking because the meat and wine are the result of lives rooted in inequality, injustice, and excessive pagan worship. Rome's story is not mine, and I refuse to participate in the practices that such a story supports.[55] And I have rejected this story not just because I am a follower of Jesus but because I am a Torah-observant Judean. If there is one thing clear about our traditions, one thing that sets us apart as children of the covenant, it is that we reject all idolatry and all food connected to idolatry. So how could I move into a household, even a Judean Christian household, where

far as we can tell, that forbade the eating of all meat or the consumption of wine. See John D. Rosenblum, "Jewish Meals in Antiquity," in *A Companion to Food in the Ancient World*, ed. John Wilkins and Robin Nadeau (Chichester, UK: Wiley and Sons, 2015), 348–56. Some have suggested that because of the edict of Claudius in 49 CE, it was likely that kosher meat was no longer readily available in Rome. See Jewett, *Romans*, 838, and references there.

51. On eating meat in ancient Rome, see Wilkins and Hill, *Food in the Ancient World*, 54–46.

52. Wilkins and Hill, *Food in the Ancient World*, 81, 143.

53. Wilkins and Hill, *Food in the Ancient World*, 166. See also Mark Reasoner, *The Strong and the Weak: Romans 14.1–15.13 in Context* (Cambridge: Cambridge University Press, 1999), 73; Jewett, *Romans*, 869.

54. This was how food was transformed into "social capital." See Martin Pitts, "The Archeology of Food Consumption," in Wilkins and Nadeau, *Companion to Food*, 96; Katherine M. Dunbabin, *The Roman Banquet: Images of Conviviality* (Cambridge: Cambridge University Press, 2003), 8–11.

55. Interestingly, in 1 Cor. 11:17–34 Paul counters the practices of a clearly imperial meal (some get drunk while others go hungry) by telling a different story, the story of Jesus, whose death is remembered every time the community practices a different kind of meal—a meal where the hungry are fed.

such loose eating habits were practiced? Paul had called our little group of Jesus followers "saints." I wanted to live up to that name and not compromise our holiness.

When I shared these concerns with Aquila, he admitted that this has been a point of tension in the community. Some of the gentile followers of Jesus did look down on those who ate no meat, just as they looked down on those who could not afford to eat meat. It had been a point of discussion for some time. In fact, Aquila said that this issue alone had caused more ill will in the gathering than any other question. And then he suggested that perhaps this was why I needed to stay. He said that he knew of my deep faithfulness not only to Jesus but also to the Scriptures of Israel. He said that Philologus and Julia often shared insights of deep wisdom that I had taught them. And while he and Prisca were able to interpret the Scriptures and tell the stories, they needed help. They needed the wisdom of other Judeans who had struggled with being followers of the living God in a city like Rome.

While I could appreciate that, I told Aquila that I didn't want to be at the center of conflict. It would be much easier to go home and continue meeting with my fellow Judeans who were in agreement about these matters. Then, rather than focusing on the issue of meat eating, we would be free to focus on the other parts of what it meant to be faithful followers of the Messiah.

Aquila thought for a while after that. He was never quick to speak, and he took his time. Finally he asked me if I remembered how Paul had discussed the issue of food in his letter. Well, I didn't pretend that I remembered it all, but what I could remember was that Paul said that those who ate meat should not condemn those who didn't. And I was pleasantly surprised by that.

Aquila then told me that this community would likely spend a fair bit of time talking about Paul's writings on this issue. They would do so because how the community deals with such different eating habits isn't a side issue. It is at the heart of the gospel. That is why Paul spent so much time talking about this matter in his letter. Aquila said that it would be too easy for me to go back to Transtiberium and continue to meet only with those other Judeans who agreed with me. The community needed both Judeans and gentiles, those who followed Torah and those who didn't, because if we couldn't learn how to live peaceably with those we thought dishonorable, if we couldn't live with those who differed from us in practice, then we wouldn't be the community of welcome that Jesus was shaping us to be. If we were a new family in Jesus, then we would need to find ways to be at home with one another.

Aquila has a rare gift for persuasion. When he had finished his argument, he held his tongue and waited. The problem was that I could see his point. I knew that how we eat is not a side issue. I knew that food and feasting and the call to justice were all connected in my Scriptures. Maybe I would be able to convey something of that to those in this community. So I told him that if my sister agreed, we would stay.

And that is how we came to join the household of Prisca and Aquila. And we heard Paul's letter read again, section by section, after Phoebe had returned from sharing it with other assemblies in Rome. By the time I finished my work for Prisca and Aquila, and for a few of their patrons and one or two of their clients, I almost knew the letter by heart.

So when I began to do work for Quintus, the slave who managed the household and business of Narcissus, Prisca and Aquila encouraged me to attend the meetings of believers in that household, to help them understand what Paul's letter was about. Narcissus needed lamps, some dishes, and mosaic tile for his atrium. It would be a while before that work was done, so there would be time to talk through Paul's letter in some detail. In the meantime, I was welcome to make my home with Prisca and Aquila and continue to train other members of their household in exchange for food.

The discussions in the household of Narcissus were often intense as we talked and sometimes argued about what Paul meant in his long letter to the assemblies of the Way in Rome. And sometimes it wasn't just that the apostle was confusing and complicated in what he was writing to us but that we ourselves seemed to be speaking different languages as we tried to come to some understanding about what all of this meant for us as followers of Messiah Jesus. It made for some rather tense and frustrating conversations, especially between Iris and me. And it was in my conversations with Iris that I really began to see how much of the letter was difficult for a gentile to understand. For instance, she did not know our Scriptures. She didn't know that Paul was referring to psalms of lament. She didn't know who Abraham was or even who Adam was. She did not know the prophet Isaiah, nor did she understand why a Judean Messiah could save the world. But maybe I should let her tell this part of the story.

Iris Again

Let me confess right at the start that I didn't really like Nereus. I know, I know, as followers of Jesus we are called to a life of love. But Paul also said that we needed to let our "love be genuine," and there would be nothing genuine or honest about saying that I loved Nereus when I first met him, because I didn't. And, I'm embarrassed to admit, I certainly did not outdo anyone else in showing him honor.[56]

You know that Nereus has certain misgivings around food. Well, when I first saw him at Prisca and Aquila's house, it was his behavior around food that got my back up. I've already told you that one of the things that was so attractive about these meetings of Jesus followers was that the food was shared equally by all. There was no difference between slave and free or male and female. We were all welcome to eat together. Even though it was no banquet, it felt like an abundance because it was shared equally with all at these gatherings. And the first time that someone brought meat to share, something that was usually reserved for those with the most honor in the household, I could hardly believe it, and I was so excited. I don't know, but I think that the generosity of the community eating together was one of the things that helped me to understand and believe in the generosity of the love of Jesus. Being welcome at the table was such an act of respect that it turned on its head everything I had known and been taught about my place as a slave. At least here, in this community, I was an equal.

So when I saw Nereus at these meetings, and then in our own household meetings, refusing to eat the same food that was generously provided to the rest of us, I could hardly contain my anger. How dare he refuse the generosity of the community! I mean, Nereus was as poor and as low in the eyes of the world as the rest of us, so when he was offered respect and honor in our midst that he didn't receive anywhere else, why wouldn't he receive it? I thought that his disrespect for our generosity was an insult to the community. It was ingratitude. And if he refused to receive the respect offered by the community, then he didn't deserve that respect anyway.

I know that sounds awful. And it is hard to tell you of my attitude toward Nereus in this way, especially considering all that I have learned from him and how, since those early days, I have come to respect him. But you need to understand how difficult all of this was for me, and for him. It was almost as if the apostle Paul knew how divisive food practices would be in our assemblies when he wrote that we should not pass judgment on matters of food and drink but rather that we should pursue peace with one another for the sake of mutual upbuilding.[57] It took both of us some time before we could follow the apostle's advice when we were eating together.

56. Rom. 12:9.
57. Rom. 14:13, 19.

But as I've already told you, this wasn't my biggest problem with the letter. I was taken aback right at the beginning when Paul described himself as a slave. I was, quite frankly, insulted by this. What right did a freeborn man, with all the rights that went with being freeborn, have to identify himself with slavery? How could he have even the remotest idea of what it was like to have no honor, no place, no family? How could he even imagine the violence and risk that shaped the life of a slave? Maybe I was overreacting, but I was insulted that he would try to identify himself with those who had lost everything.

So that is where my conversations with Nereus began. And it was clear that I didn't know much about Paul. Nereus told me that Paul was an awning maker like Prisca and Aquila; that he worked day and night and suffered from hunger, thirst, and cold like many of us.[58] He told me about how Paul had been captured and beaten, how he had been whipped and imprisoned for telling people about Jesus. Well, I knew that this kind of thing happened to slaves all the time. Maybe the shame that others meted out on Paul for following Jesus *was* like the shame of slavery. Maybe Paul *did* know something about the insecurity and violence that we lived with as slaves. Maybe he *did* know what it was like to be a slave. But how could he say this about himself as if it were a *good* thing? Nereus agreed with me that this opening was puzzling. It is clear from the letter that Paul realizes the powerlessness that comes with slavery. Later he talks about being enslaved by sin. In fact, this is precisely what we are freed from when we become part of the story of Jesus—if we are crucified with the Messiah, we will be resurrected to new life, just as he was.[59] And the spirit that has been given to us is not a spirit of slavery that creates fear in us, but a spirit of sonship.[60]

Slavery and fear. Paul certainly got that right. As a slave, fear permeated every part of my life. I was always afraid: afraid of being raped by my master or one of his friends, afraid of being whipped if I was too slow, afraid of being hit in the marketplace or sold to another household. For a long while I had also been afraid that I would lose my children, but now that they were gone, I was afraid of what was happening to them. Every day, every moment, I lived in fear for my children. And now that I was following Jesus, I was also afraid of being found out by my master.

58. 2 Cor. 11:27. Elsa Tamez points out that this is the experience common to most artisans in the first century. *The Amnesty of Grace: Justification by Faith from a Latin-American Perspective*, trans. Sharon H. Ringe (Nashville: Abingdon, 1993), 53.

59. Rom. 6:5–8.

60. Rom. 8:15. The Greek word for adoption, *huiothesia*, is translated literally as "sonship." We use that word instead of "adoption" because in Roman society it was, literally, being a *son* that mattered.

But I knew that other spirit too, the spirit of sonship, that sense of privilege and place. I could see it in the household of Narcissus. The son of my master knows who his father is. He knows who his siblings are. He knows what his place is in society and the honor that is due to him in that place. And while that honor of being someone's child, that honor of a place of respect in a household, was not something that I had known since my mother and I were brought to Rome as slaves, I had now found precisely such a place in the family of those on the Way. Slavery and fear had stripped me of any sense of home. Freedom in Jesus had given me a sense of being adopted and welcomed into a new home, with sisters and brothers where the honor of sonship was shared by all, male or female, free or slave. And in some ways, people like Prisca and Aquila became a mother and a father to me.

So when Nereus and I talked about Paul's language of slavery in these ways, I began to appreciate that opening greeting a little more. And then Nereus explained to me that the language of slavery and sonship is found throughout the Scriptures of Israel. He told me the story of Israel's slavery to the pharaoh of Egypt, and how God heard their groaning and then came and set them free from their bondage.[61] He explained how it was during this exodus from slavery that God first referred to Israel as God's son.[62] I loved it that in this story God *knows* the suffering of God's people; God knows their misery, the violence that shaped their lives.[63] If this was the God of Jesus, no wonder I was so drawn to him. As Nereus was telling me the story, I came to see that this God even knows what it is like to have your children taken away, for that is what the Egyptians were doing to the Israelites: all their sons were to be taken and thrown into the Nile. This is what God came to deliver them from. I often dreamed of escaping the bonds of slavery, and Nereus told me that such a dream is always alive in the hearts and memories of Judeans. The God of Israel, the God of Jesus, is the slave-freeing God. He is the God who leads his people out of slavery, and this is what the exodus story is all about: the exodus from slavery to freedom.

While all this helped me understand why slavery was such an important thing in Israel's story, and therefore for Paul's understanding of the triumphant good news of Jesus, it still didn't make sense to me why Paul would introduce himself

61. Exod. 1–3. On this whole theme as a background for Rom. 8, see Sylvia C. Keesmaat, *Paul and His Story: (Re)Interpreting the Exodus Tradition* (Sheffield: Sheffield Academic Press, 1994), 54–154.

62. E.g., Exod. 4:22–23; Hosea 11:1.

63. Exod. 3:7.

as a slave. Why was being a slave something to brag about? And then Nereus said something that changed everything for me. He said something that gave me a sense of what was going on throughout this letter.

"Maybe that's exactly what Paul is getting at," he said. "A slave has nothing to brag about, and neither does a follower of Jesus." So rather than introducing himself with terms of honor and status, Paul says that he comes with no authority or honor of his own but only with the great honor of being a slave of Messiah Jesus. And when we started to think of everything else that Paul had written in this letter, Nereus's suggestion made a lot of sense. We are all slaves to sin, Paul wrote, and we have all fallen short of the glory of God.[64] None of us has anything to brag about. Nothing whatsoever. Our redemption, our being set free from slavery, is a total gift, an act of utter grace. There is nothing here that anyone can boast in.[65] And so Paul makes it clear from the beginning that he too has nothing to brag about, except his redemption in Messiah Jesus.

Even when Paul reflects on what it means to be set free from slavery to sin, to be transferred from being slaves to being children of God, he still uses the language of slavery. We are freed from sin and enslaved to God, and that means that we are to be slaves of justice![66] Both Nereus and I sat in silence for a few minutes when we got to this insight. While some of what Paul wrote made more sense to Nereus than it did to me, and other parts made more sense to me than they did to Nereus, this was something that stunned us both into silence. Both of us knew that slavery was a result of injustice. Whether you were gentile or Judean didn't matter on this one. And here Paul had the nerve to call us to be set free from slavery to injustice in order to embrace the slavery of justice. Whatever we would make of this, one thing was clear: this would be a slavery totally different from what I experienced in my life, because if I was to be a slave, and if Nereus was to join me in that slavery, then we would be slaves of Messiah Jesus. We would be slaves in his kingdom, not in Nero's empire. We would be slaves of a justice that could only set the captives free. We would both be slaves in the household of Jesus.

Something about this conversation had already begun to change my view of Nereus. We hadn't even got to talking about what Paul said about food, but the fact that Nereus took seriously my negative reaction to Paul's identification as a slave meant a lot to me. And the way he helped me to understand what this might

64. Rom. 3:23.
65. Rom. 3:24, 27.
66. Rom. 6:17–22.

mean, and then how we came to an understanding together of what it meant to be slaves to justice—well, I've never had a conversation like that with a man—or with anyone else—before. And maybe that is why I became more willing to learn from him. Maybe it was because he was willing to learn from me as well. If we were to be a community of slaves to justice, then there needed to be more justice in the way men and women related as well. I don't know, but maybe what we had already seen modeled for us in Prisca, Phoebe, Junia, and so many other strong women leaders in our midst began to shape how Nereus and I struggled together to understand Paul's letter to our communities.

As we continued to talk over the weeks that followed, we found that many other things in this letter made total sense to both of us. Just as Nereus could see his own patron in Paul's descriptions of idolatry, I could recognize the sexual violence of my own household and the ruthless character of my own master in Paul's words.[67] We could both also see our own suffering in Paul's words later on.[68] And, as I've said, when Paul talked about the imperial rule of death, as opposed to the imperial rule of justice that comes through Messiah Jesus, well, that made so much sense.[69] We could both see how the imperial rule of Caesar brought death for so many—death to those who were conquered, death for those who worked in the fields and built the roads, death for those who worked in the mines, death to slaves who were beaten by their masters, death to the children starving on the streets while one more temple was built to honor Rome, and, yes, death to so many Judeans. And we could both see how Jesus was a different sort of Messiah, a different Lord, a different King. In his communities there was not death but life, not shame but honor, not hunger but justice, not violence but forgiveness. We both knew that Paul was describing a community in which a slave and a Judean would have no shame anymore, indeed where both would be welcome. And we both understood the heart of the matter—that although we were both weak, both sinners, both undeserving of honor, the Messiah had died for us, to show God's love to us, so that we could be reconciled not only to God but also to each other—gentile slave woman and free Judean man.

These were wonderful and life-changing conversations, and I am so grateful to Nereus for all the time he took with me to help me understand. While it is true that I was increasingly enjoying his company, the fact is that we spent so much

67. Rom. 1:24–32.
68. Rom. 8:35–39; 12:14–15.
69. Rom. 5:14–17.

time together because there was so much to talk about, so much to explain, so many questions to struggle with. And I can tell you that we were both hungry to learn more, to understand more deeply what Paul was teaching us about Jesus and what it means to be followers of Jesus. It felt as if our lives depended on the things we were talking about. It was really that important.

But there was another major stumbling block for me in hearing Paul's word to the assemblies in Rome. As a slave I had to struggle with the language of slavery, but as a gentile I had an even bigger problem. When Paul says, right at the beginning of the letter, that he is not ashamed of the gospel of Jesus because it is the power of God for salvation to everyone who has faith, "to the Judean first and also to the Greek," I admit that my earlier irritation about the slavery language only got worse.[70] Why would the Judeans have any priority over anyone else? I mean, I was neither Judean nor Greek, so whether it was the Romans privileging the so-called wise over against anyone else dismissed as "barbarians," or Paul simply flipping it around and putting Judeans at the top of the heap, didn't matter much to me.[71] I was still left out. But if there was one thing I knew early in my walk with Jesus, it was that he included me and refused to give anyone a place of privilege over me. I heard something in a meeting once about a single lost sheep, and I was pretty sure that meant me. So the language about the Judeans was upsetting to me. And I really wanted to believe that this wasn't just me picking up on the Roman dislike of the Judeans as a "shameful" people but rather this was me not being able to see how any of this could be put together with what I had come to know about Jesus.

I was afraid to raise this question with Nereus. I was worried that he would be defensive. And at first, I think that he was. When I told him what was bothering me, he sat and thought for a long time. Then he said, "If this bothers you so early in the letter, then how do you react to all the discussion of Judeans and gentiles throughout the rest of the letter?" I told him that I didn't really see the point of it all. I then confessed that for large bits of the letter I was either bored or irritated. All this rehashing of the stories of Israel, all the quotations from ancient Scriptures that I knew nothing about—it almost felt as if Paul wasn't really addressing me and other gentile believers at all for an awful lot of the letter. When it came to these sections, my hunger turned into distaste. Nereus had his work cut out for him if he was going to explain all this stuff to me in a way that would feed my hunger. So maybe he should take over the story now.

70. Rom. 1:16.
71. Rom. 1:14.

Nereus Again

It is interesting that Iris says that she wasn't exactly trying to outdo others in showing me honor when we first met. We can laugh about it now, but the truth is that I didn't honor Iris much either in those early days. I must confess that my attitude toward those who ate anything and everything was contemptuous. I react to this kind of eating with disgust. Iris picked up on that disgust and wasn't going to put up with it. As long as I believed that my actions were morally superior, I could only be a stumbling block to Iris and other gentile believers. But if I was to be of the kind of service that Aquila had hoped that I would be, if I was to share my knowledge of the Scriptures of Israel with this sister who had embraced Messiah Jesus, then I would need to stop thinking of myself "more highly than I ought." I needed to discern my place in the body "with sober judgment."[72] And during those weeks, first in the assembly at Prisca and Aquila's household, then in the household of Narcissus, but especially in my conversations with Iris, I began to sense that I had the gift of a teacher.[73]

The truth is that while I was never bored with Paul telling Israel's story and quoting our Scriptures, I was often as irritated as Iris, but for different reasons. So explaining how Paul, a follower of Jesus with the highest Judean pedigree, was telling the story of Israel and constantly quoting from our ancient Scriptures was not going to be easy. You see, I had my own struggles with what Paul was teaching. His telling of the story was more generous, more welcoming to gentiles, than I was used to. And while I shared his anguish about our kin who have not embraced the way of the Messiah, who do not see the promises fulfilled in Jesus, I still struggle with how Paul addresses the question of God's faithfulness to his covenant people.

But before I could begin to struggle with my own questions about how Paul was retelling the stories of Israel and interpreting our Scriptures in light of Jesus, Iris had some more basic things that needed explanation. As I said earlier, she didn't know the stories of Abraham and Adam. The psalms of Israel had not been her language of prayer. The law and the prophets were alien to her. The covenant and its promises were unknown. But she wanted to understand Paul's letter, and even more importantly, she wanted to understand more about the Jesus she had put her faith in. Our conversation about Israel and slavery, along with the story of the exodus, had interested her enough to want to know more, even if she was

72. Rom. 12:3 NRSV alt.
73. Rom. 12:7.

still irritated at the pro-Judean stance that it seemed Paul was taking. When I told her that many, if not most, Judeans would see Paul as a traitor to Israel as much as the agents of the empire saw him as seditious to Roman rule, she seemed to be more accepting of his message.

Our relationship had moved from contempt to mutual respect. Iris appreciated that I took her concerns and bewilderment seriously, and I think she liked the fact that I was also bewildered by much of what Paul said. Her questions were piercing. For instance, why did Abraham, the father of the Judeans, matter to the story of Jesus? When Iris rejected the story of Rome, she did so because Jesus was the Savior of all peoples. None were to be put to shame. Why would she then accept the story of another people who considered themselves chosen by a god, a story of another ancestor who left his home to found a nation elsewhere?[74] Why embrace the story of Abraham after rejecting Aeneas? Didn't such nationalistic stories just end in violence toward other peoples, just like the story of Rome had been used to defeat Iris and her people?

I could see her point. So I began to tell her about Abraham, of his calling by God to be a blessing to *all* the nations, and how in Jesus we could now see that Abraham was the father not just of Judeans who were circumcised and followed the law, but of all of those who have faith in the justice of God.[75] Paul argued that it is our sharing in Abraham's faithfulness, not our obedience to the Judean law, that makes all of us Abraham's children and heirs to the promise that he would inherit the world.[76]

This was all so alien to Iris. I could see that she was struggling with what Abraham had to do with her faith in Jesus. Finally, I asked her these questions: "Who are the heirs of Aeneas? Whose story was this?"

"The Romans', of course," she replied.

"Not yours?" I asked.

"No, not mine and not yours. This is the story of our oppression, not our family history."

"And who does Paul say are the heirs of Abraham?" I continued. A look of astonishment came over Iris's face. "Come on," I pushed, "who are the heirs of Abraham?"

74. See N. T. Wright, *Paul and the Faithfulness of God*, book 1 (Minneapolis: Fortress, 2013), 307–11; and Neil Elliott, *The Arrogance of Nations: Reading Romans in the Shadow of Empire* (Minneapolis: Fortress, 2008), 125–38.

75. Gen. 12:1–3; Rom. 4:16–22.

76. Rom. 4:13–16.

"Paul says that I am . . . you are . . . we all are!" she said. "So if I am a follower of Jesus and Jesus is a descendent of Abraham, then *this* is my family story. That is why Paul says that Jesus is the firstborn of a large family, because we are now part of that family."

"That is certainly what Paul is saying, isn't it? *All* who have the faith of Abraham, *all* who believe the promises, *all* who confess that Jesus is Lord, that Jesus is the Messiah, are children of Abraham."

Now here is the problem. Iris was actually getting more excited about Paul's telling of the Abraham story than I was. You see, I wasn't quite convinced by what Paul was saying. He seemed to be taking some liberties with the story, as far as I could tell. I still thought that *both* obedience to the law *and* faithfulness to God's promise of justice and salvation in Jesus mattered. That's why I remained committed to Judean food laws. But I should say that Iris also had some ongoing problems with what Paul was saying. Her initial excitement aside, Iris still seemed worried that an emphasis on Abraham would result in some sort of nationalism. At a certain point in the conversation, we laughed when we realized that we both had problems with what Paul was saying but from exactly opposite sides. Iris was concerned about the Abraham story still giving too much priority to Judeans, while I was worried that his interpretation of the story gave too little. When I pushed back and reminded Iris that Paul did say, whether she liked it or not, that salvation came *first* to the Judeanss and *then* to Greeks, she pointed out that he said the same thing about the anguish and distress that would come to all who do evil, to "the Judean first and also the Greek."[77] Paul's point seems to be that, while Jesus comes as the Messiah of the Judeans, he is the Savior of all people and the Lord of all creation. And in Jesus, "God shows no partiality."[78]

That provided an opening to talk about Adam. Paul is clear that the problem isn't Abraham or nationalism. Abraham was part of the solution, part of the way that justice would come back into the world. The problem began long before Abraham in another part of the story; the problem was the sin that came into the world through Adam.[79] At first Iris thought that Adam was another Judean, but I assured her that, no, Adam was the father of all nations and that the rule of sin and death entered the world through him. It is because of Adam that Paul says

77. Rom. 2:10.
78. Rom. 2:11.
79. Rom. 5:12.

in this letter, "All have sinned and fall short of the glory of God."[80] Because of Adam, idolatry and injustice have shaped our story—the story of Rome, the story of the Judeans, and the story of all the peoples of the world. Paul's condemnation of the sexual and economic violence of Rome at the outset of the letter was the kind of thing that you could find in the prophets of Israel over and over again. Those who reject the living God, those who exchange their glory for idols, always end up in the deathly destruction of idolatry. And it is this death, this sin, this idolatry that the Messiah came to save us from. Because of God's love, the Messiah came to save the ungodly; while we were still enemies, we were reconciled to God through the death of his son.[81]

The story of Adam matters because it is the story of us all. And not only of us; it is also the story of creation. That is why Paul talks about creation waiting with eager longing and creation waiting for freedom. When we are set free to be the glorious image bearers of God once again, creation will be free as well![82]

Oddly enough, that made sense to Iris. She had heard the poets proclaimed at her master's banquets. She heard the stories of all of nature bursting forth in renewal when Augustus became emperor. And now that Nero was caesar, she had heard it said that the crops would harvest themselves and the cattle herd themselves.[83] If that wasn't creational renewal, what was? But Paul seemed to be saying something slightly different. We had to talk a lot longer to explain what it meant to be created in the image of God, especially in the context of a city that was full of images. And in a world where all "glory" points to the emperor and the gods, we had to spend a long time talking about how ordinary people are glorious when they obey their Creator.

So our conversations went, both of us trying to understand Paul. While I would try to explain and interpret Paul in terms of the story and Scriptures of Israel, Iris would always bring the conversation back to what all this means to a gentile follower of Jesus. She would also never let the conversation drift too far from the real world of life as a slave or, indeed, life as a Judean living in the capital of the Roman Empire. And behind all our questions and discussion was this question: How were we to live in light of this letter and in light of the forgiveness freely offered to us by Jesus? How could Iris be set free from slavery to sin when

80. Rom. 3:23.

81. Rom. 5:6–10.

82. Rom. 8:18–30.

83. See Robert Jewett's citation of Calpurnius Siculus's tribute to Nero in "The Corruption and Redemption of Creation," in *Paul and the Roman Imperial Order*, ed. Richard A. Horsley (Harrisburg, PA: Trinity Press International, 2004), 30–31.

her master required her sexual services?[84] How could she present her body as an instrument of justice when she was required to tell the stories of Aeneas to the children and when it was her duty to attend the theater and participate in the feasts of Venus and Cybele?[85] To not do these things would mean beatings and possibly even death. If she kept her head down, though, she could continue to teach the children the stories of Jesus—including her master's son, who would one day be head of the household.[86]

Iris wasn't the only one who struggled. Paul had made it clear, and Iris never missed an opportunity to remind me, that Judeans along with gentiles were sinners in need of God's forgiveness and grace. I know this, of course. But Paul seemed to have a loose relationship with the law. What does he mean when he says a person is a Judean who is one inwardly? And that circumcision is of the heart?[87] Of course, both Moses and Jeremiah said the same, but they meant that it should be *both*. Physical circumcision should be reflected in a circumcised heart.[88] Paul seems to be saying that physical circumcision is not necessary.

Thankfully we weren't the only people grappling with the implications of Paul's letter. As we met with the other members of the assembly, we realized that a whole body of believers was trying to faithfully follow Paul's command to "welcome one another." And we realized that Paul was right: no matter how hard it was to follow Jesus the Messiah, nothing could separate us from the love of God in the Messiah, Jesus our Lord.

84. Rom. 6:1. On this tension see Margaret Y. MacDonald, "Slavery, Sexuality, and House Churches: A Reassessment of Colossians 3.18–4.1 in Light of New Research on the Roman Family," *New Testament Studies* 53 (2007): 94–113; and MacDonald, *Power of Children*, 48–51.

85. See Rom. 6:13. Attendance at the theater "was one of the great collective experiences in Rome—festivals liberated everyone—even slaves—from everyday work." John R. Clarke, *Art in the Lives of Ordinary Romans: Visual Representation and Non-elite Viewers in Italy, 100 BC–AD 315* (Berkeley: University of California Press, 2003), 130.

86. Peter Lampe suggests that the early Christians would have lived in two social contexts: Hellenistic Roman society, where they behaved according to societal standards, and the context of the Christian congregation, where such social differences were invalid. When they were in the Hellenistic Roman world, the Christian context was internalized but not acted on. "The Language of Equality in Early Christian House Churches: A Constructivist Approach," in Balch and Osiek, *Early Christian Families in Context*, 79–80.

87. Rom. 2:28–29.

88. Deut. 10:16; 30:6; Jer. 4:4.

3

Empire and Broken Worldviews

Iris of the Broken Home

It was the children that broke her heart. It was the children that caused that rupture, that fundamental loss of faith, that profound alienation. It was the children that birthed her anger at the gods, her rejection of the master's story, her disdain for the stories of the empire.

Maybe Iris could have continued to accept her place as a slave in the household of Narcissus if it hadn't been for the children. Maybe she could have lived her life, kept her head down, and been obedient enough to court favor with her master and mistress. Maybe she could be useful enough to the household that she wouldn't be sold into a worse situation. She had already given up on any hope of ever seeing her mother or her homeland again. So maybe she had come to a place where she would simply make the best of what fate had dealt her. Maybe she could even suffer the indignity and violence of the sexual services she was required to provide. At least that sexual violence had resulted in her own two children. Her own two children. That was the crux of the issue. She could somehow make peace with her slavery as long as she had her own two children. She could somehow have a sense of home in this alienated place, at the heart of this empire, as long as she had her own two children. But that was always an illusion, and she knew it. These were not her own two children. These were bodies born of her body.[1] And her body, together with their bodies, were the property of the master, to do with as he pleased. One day it pleased him to sell those two little bodies to another.

1. Slaves were described as "bodies" in the ancient world. See Jennifer A. Glancy, *Slavery in Early Christianity* (Oxford: Oxford University Press, 2002), 10–11.

This was everyday life in the empire. An everyday transaction in the marketplace. This is what normal economic, sexual, and familial life looked like for a slave like Iris. But the normality of it all, the cultural legitimacy of it all, didn't erase the grief and anguish of a mother. And it is this grief and anguish, this brokenheartedness in our story, that breaks any spell that the empire might have had on this young slave woman from northern Africa. That tenuous sense of home that she held on to while she had her children was stripped away from her, and "home" was fundamentally broken.[2]

After her children were sold, Iris began to avoid trips to the Forum unless absolutely necessary. The symbolism of the empire, the statues of the gods, the rituals of the temples—all things that held a certain fascination to her young charges—became increasingly repugnant to her. The brutality of the sale of her children stood as an indictment of the Roman ideology of peace, virtue, and justice. In her anguish and grief she found that she could no longer teach the master's children the great story of Rome and its gods. The worldview of the empire, which had begun to seduce her into a numbed acquiescence, was shattered by the sale of her children. You see, even though she knew that her offspring were the property of her master, she just couldn't get over the deep, deep feeling that they were her own two children.

//////////////////

We have already begun to unpack something of the shape of worldviews in our discussion of Iris in these opening paragraphs, and it will be helpful to deepen this analysis a little further. Worldviews are storied visions of and for life.[3] Akin to what Charles Taylor describes as a social imaginary, we use the term *worldview* to get at the deep orientation that directs life, usually without much explicit consideration.[4] These communal orientations, these habitual ways of experiencing the world, are constitutive of all human life and shape our understanding of what the world is and how we should comport ourselves in that world.[5] As such, worldviews

2. The enormous public outcry over the separation of children from their parents at the border between Mexico and the United States in 2018 demonstrates that the taking of children is seen as reprehensible in our cultural narrative as well. On how the powers of empire target children, see Sylvia C. Keesmaat, "Separating Children and Parents at the Border Is Not about Safety. It's about Hate," June 25, 2018, Sojourners, https://sojo.net/articles/separating-children-and-parents-not-about-safety-its-about-hate.

3. See James H. Olthuis, "On Worldviews," *Christian Scholar's Review* 14, no. 2 (1985): 153–64; and Brian J. Walsh and J. Richard Middleton, *The Transforming Vision: Shaping a Christian World View* (Downers Grove, IL: InterVarsity, 1984), part 1.

4. Charles Taylor, *A Secular Age* (Cambridge, MA: Belknap, 2007), 172–73.

5. The habitual character of worldviews—that is, how they are shaped and sustained by certain repeated habits and provide a world in which we inhabit—is at the heart of Pierre

are not so much "systems of thought" as they are imaginative construals of the world. They tell us what is of ultimate significance, how we got here, and where we are going. "Worldviews answer ultimate questions at the heart of human life in terms of a grounding and directing narrative or myth that is encoded in symbols and embodied in a way of life."[6] We can diagram this model as follows:[7]

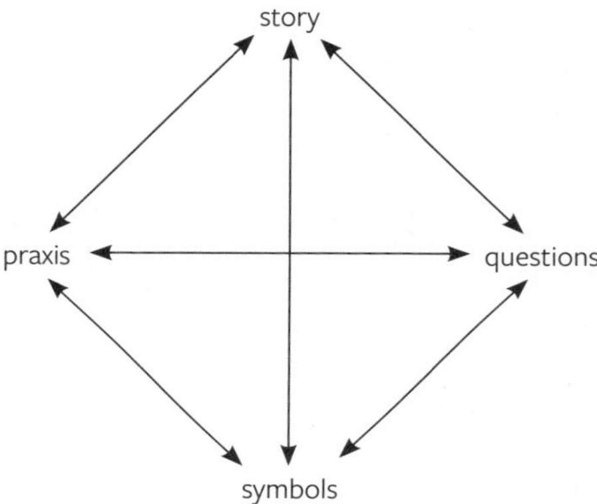

Iris knew that grand story of Rome. She had taught the children the great tale of Aeneas. The story of the rise of Augustus and the inauguration of the "golden age" was there to be seen in all of its symbolic power at the *Ara Pacis* and through any outing to the Forum. The household gods in the kitchen, together with the images on lamps, in a fresco in the atrium, on the coins in daily usage, all bore witness to this story. And if this narrative wasn't enough to shape the imaginations of all who lived in Rome, then the praxis, the very rhythms and structures of daily life in Rome, would have further reinforced the imperial worldview. From the daily sacrifices to the household gods to the many festivals in the annual calendar that celebrated the glory of the empire and the blessings of the gods to

---

Bourdieu's suggestive notion of *habitus*. Pierre Bourdieu and Loïc J. D. Wacquant, *An Invitation to Reflexive Sociology* (Chicago: University of Chicago Press, 1992), 5–24, 120–36. For helpful exposition of the idea of habitus, see James K. A. Smith, *Imagining the Kingdom: How Worship Works* (Grand Rapids: Baker Academic, 2013), chap. 2.

6. Steven Bouma-Prediger and Brian J. Walsh, *Beyond Homelessness: Christian Faith in a Culture of Displacement* (Grand Rapids: Eerdmans, 2008), 135.

7. This model was developed by N. T. Wright in collaboration with Brian Walsh and was first articulated in Wright's *New Testament and the People of God* (Minneapolis: Fortress, 1992), 122–24. Bouma-Prediger and Walsh put this model to work in discerning how a house becomes a home in *Beyond Homelessness*, 126–36. On the foundational nature of story in shaping the experience of home, see also J. Edward Chamberlin, *If This Is Your Land, Where Are Your Stories? Reimagining Home and Sacred Space* (Cleveland: Pilgrim, 2003).

the memory and recent stories of Roman military domination in the empire to the hierarchical system of honor and shame that dominated Roman life to her own condition as a slave, as property of a master who held her fate in his hands, Iris's daily life demonstrated the hegemony of the imperial imagination. It was hard to imagine her life outside of this social imaginary.

This imperial story, encoded and communicated through the ubiquitous symbols of the empire and embodied in the daily praxis or way of life in the city, and in the household of Narcissus, would have assumed ready answers to the worldview questions that any vision of life implicitly and sometimes explicitly must answer. In Rome those answers looked something like this:

Where are we? We are at the center of the universe, the heart of the empire, the apex of civilization. All roads lead to Rome, because Rome is the destination, the goal, of all things. The world is a cornucopia of natural blessings wherever the empire's rule reaches.

Who are we? We are Romans, blessed by the gods with virtue and abundance. We bear the historical weight and responsibility of empire to spread civilization, law, and justice. We are subjects of the divine Caesar, son of god, savior of the world. We are grateful children of the *Pater Patriae*, the Father of the Fatherland.

What's wrong? There are recalcitrant forces of resistance to the good news of the empire. There is barbaric and impious resistance to the lordship of Caesar. And there are resources that need to be liberated to the service of the empire.

What's the remedy? The triumphant good news of the empire must be spread throughout the world, bringing more and more peoples and lands to bow the knee and confess that Caesar is Lord. Barbaric resistance needs to be defeated, military control needs to be established, and the seaports and roads to Rome must be filled with goods, resources, and bounty coming to the heart of the empire.

What time is it?[8] We are at the climax of the world's story, living in the golden age of Augustus and his successors. It is the time of the *Pax Romana*. It is time for the peace of Rome to spread its net and encompass more and more people. And now, with Nero on the throne, we have entered a new golden age, a time when it is no longer necessary for Rome to rule by the sword.

These answers to the worldview questions would have made sense, we suggest, to most of the people in Iris's world. Given the daily rhythms (the praxis)

8. N. T. Wright in *Jesus and the Victory of God* (Minneapolis: Fortress, 1996), 138, added the fifth question, "What time is it?," to the original four articulated by Brian J. Walsh and J. Richard Middleton in *The Transforming Vision: Shaping a Christian Worldview* (Downers Grove, IL: InterVarsity Press, 1986).

of her life, the ubiquity of the imperial symbols, the power of that story, and her social status as a slave, it might have been tempting for Iris to believe it all. What alternative really was there for her? Whatever narrative she had been taught as a child had been ruptured by the conquest of her homeland, her separation from her mother, and her enslavement. If she had any alternative cultural practices or symbols to remind her of a previous worldview, they had been repressed. And so survival meant accepting her fate, perhaps enjoying the relative security of being a slave in the household of Narcissus, taking seriously her role in caring for the children, staying out of trouble, and enjoying her own children.

And then those children were stripped from her without a word. It was this event, this moment in the praxis of this worldview, that blew it all apart for Iris. This act of violence, this act of rupture, this act of unbearable cruelty put the grand story of Rome, the symbols of the empire, the daily praxis of the household, the marketplace, the temples, and the sacrifices to these gods all on trial. This could never again be her story. These symbols could never again be the lens through which she would look at the world. Indeed, the way of life to which she had been condemned through slavery had discredited this story of any claim to virtue and stripped these symbols of any allure that they might have once had. The answers of the empire to the worldview questions were revealed as lies by this one act of cruelty. Any temptation to make her peace with and be at home in this empire was wiped away by the empire's act of depriving her of the only semblance of home that she had left—her own two children.

So how might Iris have answered these worldview questions in those days, before Quintus began to tell her the story of Jesus? Her answers might have looked something like this:[9]

Where am I? I'm exiled in a foreign land, living at the heart of an empire of cruelty and oppression. I live with people who talk about virtue and civilization but who are brutal and heartless.

Who am I? I am the property of Narcissus. I am a slave, with no identity beyond that given me by my master. I am a sexual toy for my master and a victim of his violence. I am supposed to accept my lot, but I am burdened by the shame of my slavery.

What's wrong? I am brokenhearted. They have taken my babies, but I must not let them see my grief. I have no honor, no family, no place beyond my slavery. I am homeless.

9. While worldviews are always communal and never the idiosyncratic perspectives of individuals, we employ the first person in these worldview questions because we are imagining how Iris might have answered them, not how all slaves, for example, would have answered such questions.

What's the remedy? I don't know. I long for my children. I long to be someone's child. I desperately want a home, a real home in which I have honor. I guess that I want freedom, but that is almost impossible for me to imagine.

What time is it? It is a time they call "glorious," but I see it as shameful. It is a time they call "virtuous," but I see only debauchery. It is a time they call "peaceful," but I see only violence. They say it is a time when the great story has come to its climax, but I see it as a time in which there is no story of salvation, no story of real hope. It is time for lament.

Nereus of the Broken Covenant

Nereus never had any illusions about Rome. There was never a time in his life when he was tempted into any sort of accommodation with the empire. He knew the stories of what the Romans had done in his homeland of Judea. He knew of their continued occupation of what, to him, was land promised to his people by the Almighty, the Creator of all things, the covenant God of Abraham, Isaac, and Jacob. And the trouble a few years earlier that occasioned the edict from Emperor Claudius expelling Judeans from the city of Rome only underscored the tenuous place that Judeans had in the city. Viewed as a shameful people, they were constantly subject to suspicion and persecution.

While Nereus had heard that some Judeans praised Rome and even found ways to see the empire as part of the covenant God's plan—as an empire blessed by the God of Israel—to him this smacked of covenantal infidelity and treason.[10] No, it was clear to Nereus that you couldn't believe in both the story of Aeneas and the story of Abraham. You couldn't worship the one God in holiness and participate in the sacrifices to idols. Any Judean who could even countenance the idea of Caesar as "lord" or "savior" or "son of god" was guilty of blasphemy and should be cut off from the covenant people.

Like most Judeans in the Diaspora, Nereus was sure not only that Rome's story was not his story but also that this was a pagan, unholy story. This story, he believed, wasn't just different from the story of the covenant God; it was an idolatrous lie. Rome's story placed Nereus and his contemporaries in a "golden age" of fulfillment. For Judeans like Nereus, this was no golden age; rather, this was a time of deeply disappointing and painful exile. Prior to his embracing Jesus as

10. This was, of course, the position of Josephus after the Jewish revolt of 70 CE. See N. T. Wright, *Paul and the Faithfulness of God*, book 1 (Minneapolis: Fortress, 2013), 128–31. See Josephus, *Jewish War* 5.412, 6.312–15; cf. 3.399–408.

the Messiah, Nereus experienced his story as one of broken covenant and delayed promise. He knew enough from the law and the prophets to see that the present condition of his people and their homeland was not a mere accident of history, not a sad outcome of the rise of the imperial might of Rome. No, the problem was deeper than even the machinations of imperial history. For Nereus and many of his Judean compatriots, their continued exile in their own land, together with their occupation and dispersion throughout the empire, was a result of broken covenant.[11] And until the people of God returned to the covenant, the promises of restoration and return from exile would remain delayed.

So it was no wonder that Nereus did not want to make pottery and other objects that had any depictions of the gods or the glory of the empire. To depict such symbols would have contravened the Torah stipulations against graven images and made him complicit in idolatry. He knew all about the great Roman virtue of *fides*, the call to faithfulness. But for Nereus the question was faithfulness to what, or more specifically to whom? If God is the Lord of all, if the Almighty is king, then faithfulness to this covenantal God precluded faithfulness to any and all impostors, Caesar included. Participating in the dissemination of the symbols and images of the empire would have amounted to nothing less than continued complicity in the covenant breaking of his people that had rendered them homeless and extended their exile.

Of course, these were dangerous things to believe, and Roman authorities knew full well that Judeans both in their homeland and dispersed throughout the empire harbored such seditious views. So Nereus had to be careful in how he actually lived his daily life. The tension for him, as for Iris, came to its most profound and dangerous moment of conflict at the level of praxis, the everyday way of life at the heart of the empire. For Iris it was the children. For Nereus it was food. Like the apostle Paul, from whom they had received this letter, Nereus lived a life of deep agitation and distress as he walked through the streets of a city that was full of idols.[12] And that distress became intolerable when there was food involved. As we have imagined, Nereus would hide away in his room during festivals when meat was offered to all in the community in honor of a particular god or in celebration of the empire or the imperial household. As hungry as a

11. We follow here the key claim of N. T. Wright that exile remains a dominant motif in Second Temple Israel. We see this unfinished story and this longing for an ending of exile to be at the heart of Paul's letter to the Romans. N. T. Wright, "The Law in Romans 2," in *Pauline Perspectives: Essays on Paul, 1978–2013* (London: SPCK, 2013), 134.

12. When Paul visited Athens, "he was deeply distressed to see that the city was full of idols" (Acts 17:16).

poor subsistence laborer like Nereus might have been, that meat would turn his stomach. Nereus's emotional and spiritual distress in the face of idolatry became a physical repulsion when meat sacrificed to idols was on offer.

Nereus's withdrawal from the praxis of the empire was an expression of his rejection of the imperial story and, very importantly, a dangerous rejection of the symbols of the empire. You see, food is seldom just food. It has been convincingly argued in anthropological literature that food carries deeply symbolic meaning.[13] This was undoubtedly the case for a first-century Judean like Nereus. The allure that the symbols of the empire had on Iris was broken when she saw that these symbols represented a way of life that legitimated and even mandated her own oppression and grief. For Nereus, however, those symbols were always repulsive because he lived his life out of an alternative symbolic horizon. Torah itself carried powerful symbolic weight for a first-century Judean. The Torah was the covenant document, the promise, the seal of God's faithfulness. And within the Torah the stipulations of Sabbath, circumcision, and food purity were identified as the profound symbolic markers of the covenant people. Indeed, the land of Judea itself, now under occupation and profaned by Roman boots and Roman customs and rituals, carried the same symbolic weight for faithful Judeans as the images of a cornucopia of fruit and vegetables or a conquering emperor with vanquished enemies did for Romans.[14] Torah, land, circumcision, and food—these were the symbols of Israel that evoked and carried the story of the covenant God. And they stood in stark, and fatal, contrast to the symbols of Rome.

For Nereus, Jerusalem remained at the heart of his covenantal world, even as he lived in Rome, the heart of the empire. He was, in effect, doubly homeless. Homeless because, like all Judeans, he lived in an exile cruelly represented by the occupation of Jerusalem. And yet, as a Diaspora Judean, he was exiled even from the painfully exilic life of his fellow Judeans in their homeland. Both his own Judean identity and the history of Judeans in the capital city had demonstrated that Rome could never be home for a Judean exiled from his homeland.

Nonetheless, Nereus had to find a way to support himself and his sister by working for those who had oppressed his people and been instrumental in his

13. See Mary Douglas, *Purity and Danger* (London: Routledge, 1966), and Margaret Visser, *Much Depends on Dinner* (Toronto: McLelland and Steward, 1986). On the symbolism of food and especially the banquet in ancient Rome, see Katherine M. Dunbabin, *The Roman Banquet: Images of Conviviality* (Cambridge: Cambridge University Press, 2003).

14. On the weight of these symbols in the Roman Empire, see Paul Zanker, *The Power of Images in the Age of Augustus*, trans. Alan Shapiro (Ann Arbor: University of Michigan Press, 1988), 167–92.

own homelessness. There were compromises that he had to make. There were people he had to interact with whom he found morally repulsive. So he struggled to remain faithful to the covenant even as it seemed that the covenant remained broken and its promises delayed.

Prior to his embrace of Jesus as the Messiah, what would the contours of Nereus's worldview have been? Given his faithfulness to the story of Israel, his honoring of the symbols of that story, and his struggles to maintain a way of life that bore witness to that story and those symbols, how might Nereus have answered the worldview questions that this vision of life would have evoked?

Where am I? I am a stranger in a strange land, a land of exile, at the heart of the beast. I live on the margins of a great and wealthy city, in a slum of filth, poverty, and violence, among an unclean people.

Who am I? I am a son of Abraham, a child of the covenant, an heir of promise. I am a worshiper of the one true God.

What's wrong? I am a stranger in this strange land. I am despised as a shameful Judean. I am surrounded by idolatry, vile practices, and unclean people. My people remain in exile in their own land while I am exiled even from them, living here at the heart of the pagan empire that has oppressed us.

What's the remedy? Messiah must come. The restoration of Israel, the fulfillment of the promises, the return from exile must be accomplished. And in the meantime, I must remain faithful and thereby hold on to my identity and not betray the story of my people. I must keep Torah and strive for holiness, while also avoiding the negative attention of those who would do violence to me as a Judean.

What time is it? It is a time of disappointment and longing. It is a time when it is all the more important that we remain vigilant in our zeal for Torah and our longing for Jerusalem. It is time for Messiah to come. It is time for the end of our exile and liberation from our oppressor. It is time for Rome, in all its idolatrous debauchery, to fall.

The People of the Broken Treaty

We began this book with the story of our friend Iggy. But it wasn't only his story—it was also our story. It was the story of our grief, the sadness of a community, and the first performance of "Iggy's Song" that arose in response to our friend's death. We thought that we would call this section "Iggy of the Broken Treaty," but, as our interlocutor pointed out in chapter 1, Iggy's story, indeed the story of his people, is not ours to tell. Iris and Nereus are fictional characters who represent how we imagine a slave woman and a Judean man might respond to Paul's letter and to life at the heart of the Roman Empire, given their social location and history. We made up Iris and Nereus. Their stories, while rooted in historical research on first-century Rome, are constructs of our own imaginations. Iggy is no such construct. Iggy was our friend. So rather than presume to tell Iggy's story, let's take a look at the larger story of which Iggy's life was a part. This is a story of colonialism, the history of conquest and the relation of settler and Indigenous peoples in Canada. As we will see, Iggy's life was not only determined by this story; it was also a sacrifice required by the history of colonialism.

If you want to see how a people's story, together with their symbols and their way of life, can be the object of violent repression and attack, look no further than the First Peoples of the Americas and, indeed, Indigenous peoples throughout the world since the age of expansion. Here we find a profoundly tragic contemporary analogy to the homelessness of Iris and Nereus that we have seen in the context of first-century Rome.

The way in which Indigenous peoples would have traditionally answered the worldview questions dissolves when they can no longer practice a way of life in communion with their land, when their symbols and rituals are made into museum pieces at best and outlawed at worst, and when their grounding stories are eclipsed by the conquering and hegemonic narrative of Western civilizational progress.

In some countries all of this was done at the end of guns. In the United States, the war machine that had been constructed during the Civil War was then turned on the "Indians" after the hostilities between the Confederacy and the Union had ceased in 1865. The "Indian Wars" were not only a military program to dispossess the Indigenous peoples of their land, thereby creating room for settlers to spread west across the continent; they were also nothing less than an agenda of genocide. Dispossession and death always go hand in hand. Extermination invariably is a tool of expropriation.[15]

There is no story of colonial conquest that does not have an ugly dimension of such violence. But empires throughout the ages have known that it takes more than sheer military force to keep a vanquished people in their place. Unless complete genocide is enacted (and we know from history that genocide is seldom complete), imperial regimes need to assimilate conquered peoples or they will live with constant rebellion and "terrorism" on the margins, and sometimes at the heart, of the empire. Consider, for example, the assimilationist agenda of Babylon.

15. See the meditation on the story of Naboth's vineyard (1 Kings 21) in Bouma-Prediger and Walsh, *Beyond Homelessness*, 68–75.

Remove a people from their homeland, destroy their political and religious institutions and symbols, give them a Babylonian education, change their names, make them eat the food of the empire, and require them to pray only to the gods of the empire. This is, of course, the story of Daniel and his three Hebrew compatriots in the Babylonian court of Nebuchadnezzar, and then under the Persian reign of Darius.[16] The book of Daniel stands in Scripture both as a witness to the assimilating strategies of empire and as a testimony to the power of resistance.

The colonizing governments of the modern age might have come armed with the Bible, but it seems they hadn't read Daniel or, if they had, they didn't learn the lesson of the book. Indeed, in Canada and throughout the world the same assimilating measures have been employed as we see in Daniel. The final report of the Truth and Reconciliation Commission of Canada describes the Canadian government's former agenda in relation to the Indigenous peoples as nothing less than cultural genocide. The methods are familiar. Destroy the institutions, seize the land, impose forced migration, ban Indigenous languages, persecute spiritual leaders, destroy or confiscate objects of religious value, and disrupt family life. "Canada did all of these things."[17]

All colonizing and imperial forces throughout history justify such assimilation as a moral good, bringing "savages" (or "barbarians") into civilization and furthering the inevitable unfolding of history. It doesn't matter whether you have the mythology of Babylonian cultural supremacy, Aeneas's story of the ascendancy of Rome, or a modernist narrative of civilizational progress; all empires legitimate assimilation (regardless of the methods) by appeal to a grounding narrative of cultural supremacy rooted in the inevitable unfolding of history.[18] In 1883, Lord Rosebery (later to become the British prime minister) memorably and without controversy said, "It is on the British race . . . that rest the highest hopes of those who try to penetrate the dark future, or who seek to raise and better the impatient masses of mankind."[19] Call it "the white man's burden" or simply the arrogance of empire; such a view gives the moral high ground to forced assimilation. The Truth and Reconciliation Commission's report summarizes well the moral

16. Dan. 1:1–21; 3:8–30; 6:1–28.

17. Truth and Reconciliation Commission of Canada, *Final Report of the Truth and Reconciliation Commission of Canada*, vol. 1, *Summary: Honouring the Truth, Reconciling for the Future* (Toronto: Lorimer, 2015), 1. Hereafter cited as *Final Report.*

18. On the necessity of such narrative foundations to human life and to all cultural expression, see Christian Smith, *Moral Believing Animals: Human Personhood and Culture* (Oxford: Oxford University Press, 2003).

19. *Final Report*, 47.

legitimacy of such assimilation: "Taken as a whole, the colonial process relied for its justification on the sheer presumption of taking a specific set of European beliefs and values and proclaiming them to be universal values that could be imposed on the peoples of the world. The universalizing of European values . . . served as the primary justification and rationale for the imposition of a residential schools system on the Indigenous peoples of Canada."[20]

When the values of one culture, which are rooted in a particular narrative and worldview and armed with their own symbols and practices, are taken to be unequivocally universal, then they are assumed to be good news for everyone, whether the colonized recipients of this good news recognize it or not. And since it is unlikely that the first or even second generation of a colonized people will be willing to embrace the universal good news of the colonizing powers, it becomes imperative to assimilate the children. And so education becomes key to the process of cultural genocide and assimilation.

"Kill the Indian" through forced education became the mantra of the colonizing powers. Canada's first prime minister, Sir John A. MacDonald, argued that "Indian" schools on the reserves were inadequate because the proximity of children to their parents meant that the Indigenous child may well be educated but the child's mode of thought would remain "Indian." "He is simply a savage who can read and write," MacDonald observed. Mirroring the strategy of Roman masters who sold slave children away from their parents, MacDonald argued that "Indian children should be withdrawn as much as possible from the parental influence, and the only way to do that would be to put them in central training industrial schools where they will acquire the habits and modes of thought of white men."[21] Thus was born the residential school system in Canada. Echoing MacDonald, Public Works minister Hector Langevin argued in 1883 that "if you wish to educate these children you must separate them from their parents during the time that they are being educated. If you leave them in the family they may know how to read and write but they will remain savages, whereas by separating them in the way proposed, they acquire the habits and tastes . . . of civilized people."[22]

Habits, modes of thought, and tastes. Change these, it is assumed, and you will transform, convert, civilize, and thereby assimilate Indigenous peoples. The architects of the residential school system knew that you don't change a people's

20. *Final Report*, 49.
21. *Final Report*, 2.
22. *Final Report*, 45.

worldview simply by teaching them how to read and write. While replacing the stories embedded in traditional Indigenous myths with the powerful colonialist narrative of civilizational progress was at the heart of the assimilationist agenda, the architects also recognized that much more than book learning was necessary. If there was to be such assimilation, such a total reimagining of the world in the hearts of colonialist's young charges, then these children must acquire the habits of the colonizing culture. Yes, the narrative of empire must be embraced. Yes, the way in which that narrative answers the foundational worldview questions must be accepted as universally true. And yes, the traditional symbols of Indigenous culture must be supplanted by the symbols of the crown, of an industrial capitalist society, and of "civilized" culture (together with its religion). But none of this could happen without a transformation of day-to-day cultural practices. That is to say, old habits must die and new ones must be born in the lives of the children.[23]

And so children must be separated from their parents. Just as Iris was deprived of the chance to continue to teach her own two children, so Indigenous parents had to be stripped of the opportunity to pass on their cultural practices, language, symbols, and stories to their own children. In this way, Indigenous children were similarly reduced to mere bodies in the agenda of civilization.

The schools changed how the children ate, how they spoke, and how they dressed. As one of these children, everything from your table manners to games you played to how you submitted to authority to how you were treated when you were ill to how you prayed must be transformed. Especially how you prayed. This is where the churches became willing accomplices in the program of assimilation. Willing accomplices in cultural genocide. Willing accomplices in the rehabituation of the lives of Indigenous children so they would embrace the habits of a Christendom in league with colonialism. While Paul writes a letter subversive of empire, the modern church came to the Americas as an agent of empire. This is no surprise. Two papal bulls had legitimated conquest in the first place. "The 1455 [*sic*] Papal Bull, Romanus Pontifex . . . sanctified the seizure of the newly 'discovered' lands and encouraged the enslavement of the native peoples. Then in 1493 Pope Alexander VI issued Inter Caetera, which gave the Americas to

23. One does not embrace a worldview simply by thinking. Rather, one must be immersed in the habits of that worldview, the day-to-day practices wherein that grounding narrative is embodied. Here Pierre Bourdieu's notion of *habitus* proves helpful. A habitus, Bourdieu writes, is "a *way of being*, a *habitual state* . . . and . . . *a disposition, tendency, propensity*, or *inclination*" to behave in particular ways. Pierre Bourdieu, *Outline of a Theory of Practice* (Cambridge: Cambridge University Press, 1977), 214, cited in Bourdieu and Wacquant, *Invitation to Reflexive Sociology*, 18 (emphasis original).

Spain and Portugal."[24] Since the Catholic Church was not only a religious entity but also the most influential political power of the day, these papal bulls became part of international law. They are the basis for the "doctrine of discovery," which asserts that Indigenous lands belonged to those European Christians who "discover" them. This remains the legal basis for colonial policies today.[25] And because the church had provided sacred legitimation for the entire history of removal, extermination, and enslavement of Indigenous peoples, it was a logical step for the churches to take an active role in the "civilizing" and "Christianizing" of Indigenous children.[26]

The monumental task of the residential schools was to replace and render empty the active presence of a people's whole past, their whole history, together with the identity that such a history provided, and replace it with another. It was to somehow make an alien past—the story of European civilization stretching all the way back to its Greek (and Roman) roots—the "active present" and "second nature" to their young charges. And so, to change the inclinations, propensities, and dispositions of Indigenous children, the residential schools began a radical regimen of habituation to a new embodied history.

The problem was that this was an embodied history of terror. These "universal" values seemed somehow to legitimate severe corporal punishment, shockingly high death rates at the schools, the emotional trauma of children being separated from their families, and rampant sexual abuse. The daily habits of these schools invariably engendered a culture of victimization that "left many students feeling intensely betrayed, fearful, isolated, and bereft of home teachings and protection."[27] Rather than creating a sense of a new home in the colonizing culture, the schools rendered generations of Indigenous people deeply homeless.

24. This papal bull was actually written in 1454. Sylvia McAdam, "Dismantling the Doctrine of Discovery: A Call to Action," in *Wrongs to Rights: How the Churches Can Engage the United Nations Declaration of the Rights of Indigenous Peoples*, ed. Steve Heinrichs, 2nd ed. (Winnipeg: Mennonite Church Canada, 2016), 143.

25. The legal decisions rooted in the "doctrine of discovery" that continue to support colonization in Canada and the United States are described in Robert J. Miller, "The International Law of Colonialism," in *Yours, Mine, Ours: Unravelling the Doctrine of Discovery*, ed. Cheryl Woelk and Steve Heinrichs (Winnipeg: Mennonite Church Canada, 2016), 21–25. See also McAdam, "Dismantling the Doctrine of Discovery," 144; and Jennifer Reid, "Church and Land Theft," in Woelk and Heinrichs, *Yours, Mine, Ours*, 14–17.

26. In Canada, the residential schools were run by the following denominations: the Roman Catholic Church, the Anglican Church of Canada, the Presbyterian Church of Canada, and the United Church of Canada. In the United States, residential schools for Indigenous children were run by a variety of Catholic and Protestant missionary societies.

27. *Final Report*, 110.

This is why the legacy of the residential schools "is reflected in the significant educational, income, health, and social disparities between Aboriginal people and other Canadians."[28] Forcibly removed from their homes, these children were denied positive parenting and, in turn, had no opportunity to develop parenting skills themselves. Disconnected from their own culture, but not assimilated into the dominant culture, these children experienced profound cultural, religious, and linguistic alienation. Abused children became abusing adults. Addiction became a coping mechanism. And we see that "the path from residential schools to prison was a short one."[29]

Given this history, it is not at all surprising that Indigenous men and women are dramatically overrepresented in the Canadian prison system;[30] that suicide rates among First Nations are twice that of the total Canadian population;[31] that Indigenous children are one hundred times more likely to end up in foster care than non-Indigenous children;[32] or that alcoholism, together with shocking rates of fetal alcohol syndrome, is a pandemic in Indigenous communities.[33]

There is a thin line between cultural and physical genocide. Destroy a people's culture and you render them homeless. Cultural genocide is always a matter of

28. *Final Report*, 135.

29. *Final Report*, 136.

30. In 2011–12, 28 percent of the prison population in Canada was Indigenous, even though Indigenous people represented only 4 percent of the nation's population. Indigenous women represented 43 percent of the female prison population. *Final Report*, 170.

31. "Aboriginal youth between the ages of ten to twenty-nine who are living on reserves are five to six times more likely to die by suicide than non-Aboriginal youth." *Final Report*, 161.

32. In 2011, 3.6 percent of all Aboriginal children were in foster care, compared with 0.3 percent of non-Aboriginal children. When the residential schools began to close in the 1960s, there was a widespread forced removal of Indigenous children from their parents in what has become known as the "60s Scoop." It is not at all surprising to meet on urban center streets homeless First Nations men and women who have European or Asian surnames. Their assimilation into non-Aboriginal culture through adoption clearly failed. (*Final Report*, 138.) The situation has not improved, for "there are more indigenous children in foster care today than there were at the height of the residential school system" (Shari Russell, "Still Questioning: The Theft of Indigenous Children," in Woelk and Heinrichs, *Yours, Mine, Ours*, 30). The Moccasin Project works to raise awareness of Indigenous child-apprehension rates in Canada. For up-to-date information, see "Resources and Facts on Child Apprehension in Canada," http://www.sotheycangohome.com/resources.html.

33. The Truth and Reconciliation Commission did not mince its words: "The policy of colonization suppressed Aboriginal culture and languages, disrupted Aboriginal government, destroyed Aboriginal economies, and confined Aboriginal people to marginal and often unproductive land. When that policy resulted in hunger, disease, and poverty, the federal government failed to meet its obligations to Aboriginal people. That policy was dedicated to eliminating Aboriginal peoples as distinct political and cultural entities and must be described for what it was: a policy of cultural genocide." *Final Report*, 133.

cultural (and physical!) domicide—the murder of home. And where there is homelessness, there is death. Cultural genocide is a system of death, sacrificing whole peoples before the altar of an imperial colonialism.

All of this is devastating enough, but it gets deeply personal when you aren't talking about peoples but real individuals like Greg "Iggy" Spoon. Iggy wasn't just collateral damage in this cultural genocide. His life, like the lives of countless others, was taken as a necessary sacrifice on that imperial altar. As "Iggy's Song" put it, he was just "another f***ing drunk Indian better off dead."[34] But he was our friend. He was a deeply loved and respected member of our community. The death of a friend is always painful. But when that death was born of a colonialism of which we are the beneficiaries, and when the church was directly complicit in that history of genocidal colonialism, then the pain is deepened and mingles with guilt.

So how might we imagine those in the Indigenous community answering the five worldview questions? Or might we be asking the wrong questions of the Indigenous peoples here? Worldview questions are not worldview neutral. While the questions themselves assume a certain level of universality, it is undoubtedly the case that people living out of different grounding stories, shaped by different symbols, and embodying different ways of life would formulate these questions (if they were to do so at all) differently. For example, the worldview of the colonizers of North America was decidedly temporal in nature. Rooted in the myth of progress, the colonizers viewed the world primarily in terms of where it was going, how it was to be developed and changed. The Indigenous peoples, however, would frame these questions more spatially and relationally. Terry LeBlanc is a Mi'Kmaq-Acadian leader and the director of NAIITS: An Indigenous Learning Community. He reframed the worldview questions for us in a way that was more spatial and relational.[35] In gratitude for Terry's wisdom, we follow his lead and amend each of the worldview questions accordingly.

In light of these amended questions and recognizing the diversity of Indigenous peoples and traditions in Canada (and throughout the Americas and beyond), can we construe some general outline of how these questions might be answered by folks like Iggy in a post-residential schools era?[36] After the program of cultural

34. The publisher does not allow the rendering of certain expletives in print. The authors are not responsible for the alteration to the artist's original language.

35. In private correspondence. The website for NAIITS is www.naiits.com.

36. There is considerable diversity in Indigenous worldviews across Canada. As settlers we realize the danger of trying to speak on behalf of Indigenous peoples in Canada. Accordingly, we asked for advice from Mi'Kmaq-Acadian Terry LeBlanc. Our construal of answers to the worldview questions also depends on what we have gleaned about the Dene Nation of northern

genocide has disrupted Indigenous ways of life, attempted to destroy Aboriginal symbols and rituals, and sought to eradicate First Nation narratives and myths, how might the worldview questions now be answered? Perhaps it would look something like this:

Where are we? Where do we come from? Who are our people, our relations? And what is my relationship to the land? The land is our mother, all of creation our kin, and all creatures our relations. The Creator has brought forth a world of harmony, symbolized by the circle and the four directions.[37] But we have been torn from our mother's grasp. Forced to relocate to reserves that are in places alien to much of our traditional ways, and of little use to the colonial powers, we are in a place of alienation, poverty, and deprivation.

Who are we? What is our vision as a people? What are our responsibilities to each other and to the land? Once vibrant, independent, and free peoples of different nations and clans, who enjoyed "structured leadership, centuries-honed legal systems, and intimate relationships with all the diverse landscapes and waterscapes that make up Turtle Island," we are now children of broken treaties.[38] Betrayed by government and church alike, despised by the "mainstream" society, we are a people deemed unworthy to equal treatment in this, our truly native land.

What's wrong? How was the harmony destroyed? We have lost our life in the land. We have lost much of our language, our stories, our sacred rituals and places. The sacred circle has been broken, the harmony of creation has been ruptured, our mother has been defiled. The colonial powers have left us with broken spirits, broken families, and broken bodies. Our land has been stolen, our schools are substandard, we don't have clean drinking water, our housing is inadequate, our children continue to be taken from us, we populate the prisons and the downtown streets of the cities, and so many of us numb the pain through

---

Saskatchewan and Alberta. Foundational to our understanding was the Royal Commission of the MacKenzie Valley Pipeline Inquiry conducted by Justice Thomas R. Berger, *Northern Frontier, Northern Homeland: The Report of the Mackenzie Valley Pipeline Inquiry, Volume One* (Ottawa: Supply and Services Canada, 1977).

Other helpful resources include the collection of essays, poems, and reflections in Steve Heinrichs, ed., *Buffalo Shout, Salmon Cry: Conversations on Creation, Land Justice, and Life Together* (Harrisonburg, VA: Herald Press, 2013); John Mihevc, ed., *Sacred Earth, Sacred Community: Jubilee, Ecology and Aboriginal Peoples* (Toronto: Canadian Ecumenical Jubilee Initiative, 2000). Randy S. Woodley, *Shalom and the Community of Creation: An Indigenous Vision* (Grand Rapids: Eerdmans, 2012), and Richard Twiss, *Rescuing the Gospel from the Cowboys: A Native American Expression of the Jesus Way* (Downers Grove, IL: IVP, 2015), are indispensable reading for a Christian Indigenous worldview among the tribal traditions of the United States.

37. On the importance of the circle and harmony, see Woodley, *Shalom*, 71–73, 88.

38. McAdam, "Dismantling the Doctrine of Discovery," 142–43.

alcohol and drugs. Reduced to the image of another drunk and lazy "Indian," we are dismissed and shamed.

What's the remedy? How do we restore harmony and right relations? We must regain our voices, our languages, our stories, our spirituality, and our place in the land. The sacred rituals must be restored; our ancient ceremonies will bring healing. We must come home to our Mother, home to our land, home to our place as a vibrant, independent, and free people. We need to rebuild our families, our communities, our political structures. The sacred circle must be mended. And the colonizers need to keep their promises to us and honor our treaty rights. We signed treaties with the government in good faith and as nations in covenant with another nation. That nation-to-nation relationship must be restored, and our sovereignty as distinct nations must be respected.

What time is it? How do we live with integrity at this season of our life together and in the land? It is time to return to our ancient ways. It is time for us to remember who we are. It is time to live in gratitude again, and in harmony with all our relations. It is time for truth and reconciliation. And it is time for justice. The ideology of colonialism needs to be unmasked for the murderous lie that it is. The foundational doctrines of imperialism that legitimated cultural genocide must be repudiated. And it is time for a new "Covenant of Reconciliation" between the First Nations and the governments and people of Canada. This covenant would be "based on principles of mutual recognition, mutual respect, and shared responsibility for maintaining those relationships into the future."[39] And it is time for the churches to repent of their accommodation to genocide.[40] It is time for the long and painful path of healing to begin.

Broken Hearts, Covenants, and Treaties

Can we talk?

Of course.

I'm having a little difficulty figuring out why you've walked us through all this worldview stuff. I mean, we've already got an idea of the world of Iris and Nereus, which

39. *Final Report*, 200. The "Covenant of Reconciliation" is the Call to Action #46 in the report.

40. Many denominations in Canada have both paid reparations for the injustice of the residential schools that they ran in partnership with the government and offered apologies to the First Nations for their role in the attempt at cultural genocide. Many of these statements are collected in *Final Report*, 378–93. Call to Action #58 calls on the pope to issue an apology to the survivors of the residential schools, as well as their families and communities, akin to the 2010 apology issued to Irish victims of abuse.

is important for understanding Romans. But I'm not sure why knowing all this stuff about colonialism and Indigenous peoples matters. And even if the imperial contexts are parallel, the stories of people like Iris and Nereus were more central in Roman society than the stories of Indigenous people in our time. Isn't this kind of a marginal issue?

It is precisely because people like Iggy are marginal in our society that the parallel works. Nereus and Iris were considered irrelevant in ancient Rome. If one or the other died, it wouldn't matter; they would just be "another f***ing slave better off dead" or "another f***ing Judean better off dead" (to borrow language from "Iggy's Song"). If we ask ourselves who in our culture most closely parallels Iris and Nereus, who has been most devastated by colonialism and empire, and who has most deeply suffered the brokenness of our violent imperial narrative, it is the Indigenous peoples of North America. Unless we understand their brokenness, we will never understand why the gospel was good news for the community in Rome, or how it could be good news today. You'll notice that we described each of these scenarios using the word *broken*: a broken heart, a broken covenant, and a history of broken treaties. Both in the first century and today, that brokenness has everything to do with a disruption of life and an attempt to destroy a worldview.

So you are saying that creating brokenness is the intent of both the Roman Empire and the colonialism that shaped North America?

Deliberately so. For instance, one of the terrible betrayals of the treaty relationship between the governments of Canada and First Nations is precisely that Indigenous peoples entered into the treaties as if they were covenantal relationships of trust and mutuality, while there was no reciprocal covenantal commitment on the other side. The colonial invaders intended to break these covenants. Documents that were written in the language of covenant were in fact little more than legal mechanisms of social, economic, and religious control, expropriation, and, as we have seen, cultural genocide.

So why does the Truth and Reconciliation Commission still call for a "Covenant of Reconciliation"? Aren't Indigenous peoples a little suspicious of the language of covenant by now?

It is remarkable, isn't it? It seems that Indigenous peoples often have a deeper understanding of covenant than those who are rooted in the Judeo-Christian traditions.

While I see what you are saying, I still don't quite see how this helps us read Romans.

Perhaps one way to clarify this is to see whether there is something going on in all three stories that holds them together. Did you notice any similarities between Iris's, Nereus's, and the Indigenous peoples' answers to the "where are we" question?

Well, they all seemed to feel like they weren't at home. Iris and Nereus were not in their own countries, and Indigenous peoples have had their land taken from them.

Precisely. Whether we are talking about a North African slave in Rome, a Diaspora Judean in Rome, or the crises of Indigenous peoples in the wake of an attempted cultural genocide, all three are dislocated, alienated, and in a place of devastating homelessness. Moreover, these are not stories of people who for some reason of their own have up and left home to seek their fortunes elsewhere. Rather, they are all stories of forced relocation. They are all stories of people who have been stripped of their homes, both geographically and spiritually. Remember that in all three stories it isn't just a matter of moving people to a place that is not home but an imperial attempt to strip people of their very identity by replacing the stories and symbols that were foundational to their cultural distinctiveness with the stories and symbols of the conquering and colonizing forces.

But Nereus had managed to hang on to his stories and symbols.

Only because he came from a people who had special privileges in the empire to practice the Judean religion. Iris was not so lucky, nor were Indigenous peoples. It is very difficult to maintain your identity once those grounding stories and symbols are stripped away from you. This is why changing the habits of everyday life—from parent-child relationships to food to how you make a living to religious observance—has always been central to strategies of assimilation. And that is why Paul spends so much time in the later sections of his letter addressing precisely these habits of daily life in the Christian assemblies in Rome. Strengthening Christian unity and identity in these struggling and disparate communities will require engendering habits of the kingdom of God at the heart of the empire.

But the early Christians learned new habits—Nereus and Iris learned to live out of this different story, the story of Jesus. Couldn't that be called assimilation? And isn't that what we wanted for Indigenous peoples? To learn to function and thrive in a new story? To assimilate like new immigrants do?

That is a popular description of colonization, but it paints a picture that is far too rosy. You see, the corollary of an empire's sense of its own moral exceptionality and civilizational superiority is always the denigration and shaming of the people it has come to control. Those who are the "losers" of history are clearly people of less value. Slave, Judean, and "Indian"—all are seen to be a shameful people in their respective contexts. So there was no way for Nereus or Iris to ever be a part of Roman society as an equal to a male Roman citizen with wealth.

And there was no way for Indigenous peoples to thrive in Canada. The parallel with new immigrants is instructive, for native peoples were treated as inferior to new immigrants. Their land was often taken and given to new immigrants, and when they were permitted to keep the land, they were not allowed to farm with modern tools or to own machinery in common like immigrant farmers did.[41] The shaming of Iris, Nereus, and Iggy is central to how our three stories answer the "what's wrong?" question, and it is therefore also foundational for any answer to the question, "What is the remedy?" A renewed sense of identity and worth must overcome the shame that has been imposed by the empire.

Is this why Paul talks about shame in Romans 1?

Yes. Paul overturns the categories of honor and shame in Romans 1, and we'll see the same thing happening when he offers a charter for an alternative community in chapter 12. Precisely those who are deemed shameful in the empire are those whom the Christian communities are called to honor the most.

Honor *and* dishonor *seem like archaic terms. I mean, who really talks that way anymore?*

Well, Indigenous peoples do. Maybe it is only those who have lived under the weight of being dishonored, disrespected, and despised who understand how important something like honor really is. And if shame is the problem, then something like honor must be integral to the solution.

But what would that honor look like?

If shame is one of the devastating implications of being an alienated, despised "outsider," then honor must have something to do with being welcomed in, welcomed home. All three of our stories are about people who have been rendered homeless by the imperial realities in which they live. Whether a captive slave torn from her family and community and land, a Diaspora Judean alienated from his homeland and exiled in Rome with the longing for Jerusalem, or our friend Iggy, walking the streets of Toronto and alienated from his land and his people and his heritage, the result is the same. The empire has rendered each of these people profoundly and devastatingly homeless.

And if this kind of homelessness is common to all three of these stories, then it isn't surprising that we would find certain parallels between how each story answers the first four worldview questions: Where are we? Who are we? What's

41. The argument was that Indigenous peoples were "peasants" who had to learn farming in the proper order, beginning with the use of hand tools. See Rebecca B. Bateman, "Talking with the Plow: Agricultural Policy and Indian Farming in the Canadian and US Prairies," *Canadian Journal of Native Studies* 16, no. 2 (1996): 201–28.

wrong? and What's the remedy? But when you get to that fifth worldview question (What time is it?), there is still some similarity but an even more important difference. In all three scenarios the future requires a radical dismantling of the imperial forces that have left people homeless—whether slaves, Diaspora Judeans, or the Indigenous peoples. And, given the narrative we have created for Iris and Nereus, that dismantling of the imperial forces happens in Jesus. We'll need to reflect further on how Paul is reconstructing life around Jesus in such a way that the empire is dethroned in the lives of the Christian communities in Rome. We will also need to explore how this story of Jesus, together with the core symbols of that story and the way of life the story calls forth, will provide both Iris and Nereus with a new family and a profound home at the heart of the empire. In other words, the household of Jesus is the church, wherein homelessness is replaced by a deep homecoming.

All of that is very interesting, and it may even help me to understand Paul's letter to the Romans, but I still don't think that this works when you talk about First Nations.

Why not?

Well, if what you are saying about shame is true, doesn't it fail with the church? You are saying that the church became a place of homecoming for Iris and Nereus. But in North America, the church helped to take away the symbols and stories of First Nation peoples.

Sadly, this is true. That is why the churches are called to repudiate the doctrines that legitimated their role in colonization and repent of how they have participated in cultural genocide. The irony of all this in relation to Paul's letter to the Romans is tragic. On our reading, Romans is an anti-assimilationist letter. By reweaving story, symbol, worldview, and praxis around Jesus, Paul strives to foster a vision of life for the Christian assemblies in Rome that would give them the resources, resilience, and unity to resist assimilation into the empire. You are right. The church, which was part of the solution for the homelessness of Iris and Nereus, is at the heart of the problem for the First Nations. The counter-imperial and anti-assimilationist gospel that we meet in the letter to the Romans became captive to, and an instrument of, empire and assimilation.

So what do we do?

We do exactly what our Indigenous brothers and sisters call us to do. We repent. We repent of our complicity in cultural genocide. We repent of being agents of assimilation. We repent of the imperial captivity of the church. And to do that with our eyes wide open, we need to take stock of the empire that has so beguiled the church.

People of the Broken Worldview

In *Colossians Remixed* we offer this definition of empire: "Empires are built on systemic centralizations of power and secured by structures of socioeconomic and military control. They are religiously legitimated by powerful myths that are rooted in foundational assumptions, and they are sustained by a proliferation of imperial images that captivate the imagination of the population."[42]

It is no surprise that colonialism is the natural impulse of empire. Driven by a consuming appetite for ever-wider realms of influence and power, all empires develop programs of colonization that require socioeconomic and military control over lands and peoples. But, as we have seen, no empire can maintain its rule through economic and military force alone. Hence all empires legitimate themselves through overarching myths or metanarratives that tell a story in which the empire is the natural and necessary culmination of history. From the perspective of empire, colonized people like Iris, Nereus, and Iggy should be grateful to have been taken up into such a wondrous story. Moreover, this metanarrative is reflected and powerfully conveyed through the ubiquitous images and symbols of the empire that sustain an imperial imagination. Whether the symbol is of the household gods in the kitchen of Iris's master or the cross at the front of a residential school classroom, the purpose is the same—to shape the imagination of the people in such a way that the empire's colonization receives sacred legitimacy.

Just as we cannot understand the lives of people like Iris and Nereus apart from their context at the heart of the Roman Empire or the cultural genocide of the First Nations of the Americas apart from the terms of the colonial empire of the modern age, so also we cannot understand our own lives at the beginning of the twenty-first century without taking stock of our own imperial context. Any reading of Paul's letter to the Romans that ignores the dynamics of empire in both its ancient context and contemporary interpretation is a theological abstraction at best and a denial of its radical message at worst. So how shall we name our imperial reality? If we also live in an empire, then what empire is that?

If the collapse of the Soviet Union at the end of the twentieth century, with the resulting emergence of the United States as the only remaining "superpower," made it tempting to speak of the "American Empire," then the events of September 11, 2001, created a context in which such a depiction of our imperial reality became a historical necessity. A month after 9/11, former *Wall Street Journal* editor

42. Brian J. Walsh and Sylvia C. Keesmaat, *Colossians Remixed: Subverting the Empire* (Downers Grove, IL: IVP Academic, 2004), 31.

Max Boot wrote an article titled "The Case for American Empire," in which he argued that the "most realistic response to terrorism is for the United States to unambiguously embrace its imperial role."[43] Other analysts argued that the United States needed to recognize the imperial burden that history had thrust on this nation and that it was time for the United States to get over its "imperial denial" and embrace the responsibilities of empire.[44] Joseph Nye went so far as to say, "Not since Rome has one nation loomed so large above the others. Indeed, the word 'empire' has come out of the closet."[45] The front cover of the *New York Times Magazine* on January 5, 2003, said it all: "American Empire: Get Used to It." If the analogy between the Roman and the American Empire is at all apt, then we will need to ask how Paul's letter in the context of that ancient empire resonates in our own.

If empires are characterized by a centralization of power, then where else might that world-historical power be centralized but in the only superpower left standing at the end of the twentieth century? Of course, like all empires before it, the American Empire presents itself as a benevolent force in history, protecting order from chaos, civilization from barbarity, culture from savagery, and freedom from oppression. In this ideology the United States is at the vanguard of history precisely because of the providence of God. President George W. Bush gave voice to this imperial piety when he proclaimed, "The Author of Liberty has anointed the United States as the Agent of Liberty. Unique among great powers, this nation pursues interests larger than itself. When it acts, it does so on behalf and at the behest of higher authority."[46] The United States as God's agent of freedom in history is a conviction so deeply rooted in the American experience that it is shared by every president, regardless of party.

"Freedom," writes Andrew Bacevich, "is the altar at which Americans worship, whatever their nominal religious persuasion." He continues, "In our public

43. Max Boot, "The Case for American Empire," *Weekly Standard*, August 25, 2003, 27.

44. See Deepak Lal, *In Praise of Empires: Globalization and Order* (New York: Macmillan, 2004); and Niall Ferguson, *Colossus: The Price of America's Empire* (New York: Penguin, 2004).

45. Cited by Jim Wallis, "Dangerous Religion: George W. Bush's Theology of Empire," in *Evangelicals and Empire: Christian Alternatives to the Political Status Quo*, ed. Bruce Ellis Benson and Peter Goodwin Heltzel (Grand Rapids: Brazos, 2008), 25.

46. Cited by Andrew J. Bacevich, *The Limits of Power: The End of American Exceptionalism* (New York: Holt, 2008), 75. A less pious, more secular articulation of the same view of history can be discerned in Francis Fukuyama's infamous essay "The End of History?," *National Interest*, Summer 1989, 3–18, and the subsequent book *The End of History and the Last Man* (New York: Free Press, 1992). For a critique of Fukuyama's ideological view of history, see Brian J. Walsh, *Subversive Christianity: Imaging God in a Dangerous Time*, 2nd ed. (Eugene, OR: Wipf & Stock, 2014), chap. 3.

discourse, freedom is not so much a word or even a value as an incantation, its very mention enough to stifle doubt and terminate debate."[47] But what exactly is this freedom? Freedom, within this ideology, is little more than satisfying consumptive appetites and desires with as little interference or responsibility as possible. Within this economic worldview, the freedom of the individual is mirrored in the systems of free enterprise, free markets, and free trade. And the American Empire is called to protect such freedom domestically while exporting such liberty around the world. In the face of a terrorist attack, consumerism at home is as patriotic a duty as is fighting the "forces of tyranny" in foreign lands.

Developments on the US political landscape over the past number of decades have demonstrated that the strongest support for this American notion of freedom can be found in the ranks of the Christian church, especially conservative churches. Wendell Berry does not mince his words when he addresses the church in the context of empire:

> [The church] has, for the most part, stood silently by while a predatory economy has ravaged the world, destroyed its natural beauty and health, divided and plundered its human communities and households. It has flown the flag and chanted the slogans of empire. It has assumed with the economists that "economic forces" automatically work for good and has assumed with the industrialists and militarists that technology determines history. It has assumed with almost everybody that "progress" is good, that it is good to be modern and up with the times. It has admired Caesar and comforted him in his depredations and defaults. But in its de facto alliance with Caesar, Christianity connives directly in the murder of Creation.[48]

What has been devastatingly true of the church in relation to the plundering and division of First Nations' families and lands has been just as true in the church's overall complicity in empire throughout the modern age. And Berry begins to name the specific character of this particular empire. It is an empire rooted in a narrative of "progress" in which history is determined by economic and technological forces. This is an economy that preys on both the most vulnerable in the human community and the very creation that is the foundation of any economy. Through all of this, Berry laments, the church has entered into a de facto alliance with Caesar. How far from Paul's letter to the Romans we have come!

47. Bacevich, *Limits of Power*, 5, 6.

48. Wendell Berry, "Christianity and the Survival of Creation," in *Sex, Economy, Freedom and Community* (New York: Pantheon, 1993), 115.

But it is important to note that even though there is a profound continuity between the colonialism of the so-called age of discovery and settlement and the colonialism of our present context, there has also been a radical shift in the imperial reality in which we live. While the colonialism of the eighteenth to the early twentieth century was driven by the imperial aspirations of European nation-states, we have now entered into a new form of corporate colonialism. Instead of the planet being carved up geographically into competing colonies, the world is now opened up for corporate control and exploitation, unfettered by national interests or borders. Again, Wendell Berry proves insightful: "The global 'free market' is free to the corporations precisely because it dissolves the boundaries of the old national colonialisms, and replaces them with a new colonialism without restraint or boundaries."[49]

The supplanting of the nation-state with transnational corporations was always inherent in the dynamics of colonialism. Insofar as the expansion of empire was economically driven from the outset, it was inevitable that the logic of free enterprise capitalism, of a world driven by market forces, would at some point shake off its nationalistic shackles. This is the political coming of age of corporate power, and with it politicians become servants of corporate interests, subject to billions of dollars of lobbying and manipulation. When the "democratic" state (as ambiguous as that has always been) morphs into the "corporate" state, the citizens are disenfranchised, reduced to engaging in farce elections that have no real bearing on the shape of their lives or the power dynamics of the world in which they live. As Berry wisely observes, "A merely political freedom means little in a totalitarian economy."[50] It means even less when that economy dominates the political realm.

In the new imperialism of global capitalism, the state serves as the guardian, promoter, and safety net of the processes of globalization. The state privatizes public resources for corporate exploitation, deregulates the corporate sector to allow for unrestrained taking of profits, breaks down all trade barriers so that nation-states have limited control over their own economies, and reduces corporate taxes. And when it all begins to fall apart as it did in 2008, the state intervenes to bail out failing financial institutions and giant industrial firms.[51] The strategy

49. Wendell Berry, "The Total Economy," in *Citizenship Papers* (Washington, DC: Shoemaker & Hoard, 2003), 66.

50. Wendell Berry, "Sex, Economy, Freedom and Community," in *Sex, Economy, Freedom and Community*, 129.

51. "The characteristic of Globalization is that it will do for the private sector what it will not do for the public." John Ralston Saul, *The Collapse of Globalism: And the Reinvention of the World* (Toronto: Penguin, 2009), 105.

of the terrorist attacks of 9/11 understood well the symbolism and dynamics of empire. Targeting the World Trade Center and then the Pentagon not only identified the economic/military heart of the American Empire but the attacks also happened in the right order. First the World Trade Center, then the Pentagon. First go to the heart of the empire, the heart of the world economic order wherein the real power lies, and then attack the heart of the military system that serves to protect and expand that economic order.

Richard Bauckham brings all of this together well when he writes that "the reality of our world is not the end of grand narratives, but the increasing dominance of the narrative of economic globalization." This "is the new imperialism," where we see "the domination of politics by capitalist economics."[52]

The narrative of economic globalization is the latest and most virulent chapter in the myth of progress that has dominated the modern (and postmodern) age. This is a story that sees economic growth as the force that drives history. Unlimited economic growth and prosperity is the telos of history, which moves toward its realization as the economy is unleashed from all forms of social and political control. If allowed to follow its natural course, the "Market," together with its "invisible hand," will lead us into an era of unprecedented prosperity through an ever-expanding economy that will eradicate poverty, usher in an era of peace, and do it all in a way that is environmentally sustainable.

At the heart of this narrative is the self-interested autonomous individual. One of the most famous architects of this ideology, Milton Friedman, wrote that "one of the strongest and most creative forces known to man [is] the attempt by millions of individuals to promote their own interests, to live their lives by their own values."[53] Once all of life is reduced to a commodity, once the Market is the arbiter of all value, and once individual self-interest, avarice, and greed are elevated to supreme virtues, all sense of the common good, social responsibility, restraint, and moral responsibility dissolves. No wonder Friedman also argued that "few trends could so thoroughly undermine the very foundations of our free society as the acceptance by corporate officials of a social responsibility other than to make as much money for their stockholders as possible."[54] Notions of communal care, responsibility, cooperation, and love are supplanted by a view

52. Richard Bauckham, *Bible and Mission: Christian Witness in a Postmodern World* (Grand Rapids: Baker Academic, 2003), 94.

53. Milton Friedman, *Capitalism and Freedom* (Chicago: University of Chicago Press, 1962), 200. This is a world, of course, dominated by "man."

54. Friedman, *Capitalism and Freedom*, 133.

of history in which human beings live in constant tension and competition with each other. This is, most fundamentally, a narrative of war. "Capitalism orders human relations as struggle and conflict. In the absence of a shared end or common good, individuals are left to struggle to secure private goods and interests against other individuals, who must now be viewed as a threat."[55] We are all looking for the competitive advantage.

Such a war, such economic violence, is integral to the story that capitalism has always told. In war there are winners and losers, and it is clear who is who in the empire of global capitalism. While this imperial order has no single state as its sponsor nor a demagogue who rules over the empire, a remarkably small number of people are in fact controlling the majority of the world's wealth.[56] We have entered into a new Gilded Age of massive inequality in the midst of the richest nations on earth.[57]

If the story of the late colonial empire of economic globalization is a utopian tale of history driven by the liberated forces of the Market fueled by an unquestioned belief that "all economic growth benefits humankind and that the greater the growth, the more widespread the benefits,"[58] then the praxis of this worldview is clear. If the telos of human history is found in unlimited economic growth, then life will be shaped around the insatiable consumption of goods produced at the cheapest rate. An economic lifestyle of insatiability finds it incredibly difficult to imagine that one ever has enough, let alone too much. When human life is reduced to consumption and "competition becomes the defining characteristic of human relations,"[59] daily life becomes a struggle to stay ahead, to climb the

55. Daniel M. Bell Jr., *The Economy of Desire: Christianity and Capitalism in a Postmodern World* (Grand Rapids: Baker Academic, 2012), 104.

56. Jeff Sparrow, "By Every Meaningful Measure, Today's Elites Are Gods. This Should Make Us Angry," *The Guardian*, January 21, 2016.

57. This has been carefully documented by Thomas Piketty, *Capital in the Twenty-First Century*, trans. Arthur Goldhammer (Cambridge, MA: Belknap, 2014). Writing specifically about the American economic experience, Obery M. Hendricks Jr. argues that wealth trickles up, not down. As evidence he points out that from 1981 to 1990, corresponding with the Reagan administration in the United States, the poorest 20 percent of the population saw their incomes drop by 12 percent while the wealthiest 1 percent saw their incomes increase by 136 percent. Obery M. Hendricks Jr., *The Universe Bends toward Justice: Radical Reflections on the Bible, the Church, and the Body Politic* (Maryknoll, NY: Orbis, 2011), 157. Empires always have their elite, their aristocracy, regardless of the official rhetoric of equality and liberty. And so Hendricks argues that "when the richest 1 percent of the American people owns more than the entire bottom 95 percent combined, that is an aristocracy" (177).

58. John Perkins, *Confessions of an Economic Hit Man* (New York: Penguin Putnam, 2006), xiv.

59. George Monbiot, "Neoliberalism: The Ideology at the Root of All Our Problems," *The Guardian*, April 15, 2016.

corporate ladder, to purchase the newest technology, and to be a winner in the war that is our economy.

And, as we have already noted, in war there are winners and losers. The praxis of empire is always a praxis of inequality. Moreover, an economic lifestyle of *more* will always require an extractive economy, dependent on an infinite supply of cheap resources. In this worldview we are also at war with the rest of creation. Commenting on the warlike character of the Market, Wendell Berry argues that international capitalism is a force of total dominance and control in which "no place and no community in the world may consider itself safe from some form of plunder."[60] Toxic pollution, land destruction, soil erosion, loss of biodiversity, and an attack on the very biosphere are all expressions of an economics of violence. As Naomi Klein succinctly puts it, "Our economic system and our planetary system are now at war."[61] And in war there are sacrifices. If the environment must suffer in this bargain, then that is a sacrifice that must be made. So it is not at all surprising that we are a wasteful society, filling landfill sites, the oceans, and the atmosphere with the refuse of our industrial and consumptive lifestyles. The planet is a loser in this story. Indeed, the degree to which the planet yields its riches for human consumption is precisely the degree to which the story is fulfilled. A never-satisfied praxis of consumption is always a praxis of waste and despoliation.

In such ecological destruction, we are also throwing our children and our grandchildren into the hands of this idolatrous economy. As we sacrifice the planet, we also sacrifice future generations. But what else could be expected from humans whose are reduced to competitive consumers? The future generations end up being little more than additional competitors, people who would strip us of our entitlement to prosperity now. Let's not mince our words here. This is a praxis of child sacrifice.

But perhaps something else is going on here. The story of ever-accelerating economic growth produces a lifestyle of speed and mobility. As the economy speeds up, so must the society and so must we. If this dynamic of acceleration is the very life pulse of history, then those who are too slow, those who decide to remain where they are and become committed to a particular place, indeed those who conclude that they have "enough" or perhaps even "too much" and decide to opt out of the race to "more," will be left behind and become the castoffs of

60. Wendell Berry, "The Failure of War," in *Citizenship Papers*, 27.

61. Naomi Klein, *This Changes Everything: Capitalism versus the Climate* (Toronto: Knopf Canada, 2014), 21.

history. An accelerated life of mobility and speed, whether we are talking about the demands of an automobile culture or the imperative to always be prepared to move on, is a necessary requirement of global capitalism. Just as "production needs a mobile and temporary labor force that will keep the wages low, set worker against worker, and severely undermine labor solidarity," so also "capital needs to be free to invest, disinvest, and reinvest wherever it can reproduce itself at the greatest speed, regardless of place."[62] By the terms of this worldview, neither labor nor capital can have any loyalty to place or to community. And so we see that a praxis of mobility is also a praxis of homelessness. In his social-psychological study *The Poverty of Affluence*, Paul Wachtel writes, "Our present stress on growth and productivity is intimately related to the decline in rootedness. Faced with the loneliness and vulnerability that come with deprivation of a securely encompassing community, we have sought to quell the vulnerability through our possessions."[63] Consumerism and rootlessness go hand in hand. David Orr concurs: "Compulsive consumption, perhaps a form of grieving or perhaps evidence of mere boredom, is a response to the fact that we find ourselves exiles and strangers in a diminished world that we once called home."[64]

If the story of our imperial worldview is one in which economic growth drives history, and if the praxis and way of life that such a narrative engenders is indeed a praxis of compulsive consumption, waste and despoliation, child sacrifice, mobility, and homelessness, then we don't have to look too far to identify the symbols that encode this narrative in our daily life. The automobile itself functions as more than just a mode of transportation; it is a symbol in a culture of mass production, consumption, and mobility. What better technological symbol of an autonomous individual than the automobile?[65] So also the credit card, the cell phone (and the ever-present and narcissistic selfie), and the shopping mall (online even more so than the physical assembly of retail outlets) take on

62. Bouma-Prediger and Walsh, *Beyond Homelessness*, 258. See also James Howard Kunstler, *The Geography of Nowhere: The Rise and Decline of America's Man-Made Landscape* (New York: Simon & Schuster, 1993); and William Leach, *Country of Exiles: The Destruction of Place in American Life* (New York: Vintage, 1999).

63. Paul Wachtel, *The Poverty of Affluence: A Psychological Portrait of the American Way of Life* (New York: Free Press, 1983), 65.

64. David Orr, *The Nature of Design: Ecology, Culture, and Human Intention* (Oxford: Oxford University Press, 2002), 175.

65. And once we have achieved the autonomy of individual mobility through the automobile, the logical next step would be to grant the automobile itself increased autonomy even from the individual who would master it. Hence, the advent of driverless cars—the autonomy of the automobile.

symbolic meaning in our imperial context. In a warlike economy of anonymous transaction and efficiency, might the drone be not just a tool of assassination but also a symbol of this worldview?[66] And just as the cornucopia overflowing with fruit and vegetables from the far reaches of the empire had a profoundly symbolic power in ancient Rome, one wonders whether the produce section of the local grocery chain, itself overflowing with fruit and vegetables from around the world, regardless of the season, isn't also deeply symbolic of the worldview of global consumerism.

So in light of this story, these symbols, and the kind of praxis that we have discerned in our imperial context, how might we answer the five worldview questions from the perspective of global consumerism? How do we discern within our imperial context the worldview answers of the empire?

Where are we? We live in a world where everything has a price—life forms, DNA, human bodies, resources, the environment, commodities, abstract financial products, cultures, images. All value in this world is determined by the omniscient and benevolent will of the Market. While this is a finite world, it can sustain infinite economic growth. The world presents itself as a resource to human production, a domain for domination, and a recipient of human waste. The world is the object to the human subject, fit to be molded, constructed, engineered, and exploited for human prosperity.

Who are we? We are *Homo autonomous*, heroic individuals, creatures of freedom and liberty. We are *Homo economicus*, realizing our freedom most fully in the expansion of our economic prosperity and power. Following our own self-interest, we are creatures of insatiable desire. Covetousness and greed, once seen as vices, are now recognized as constitutive dimensions of the human condition. We are a people who live in hope of the coming utopian age of freedom, prosperity, and peace. Refusing to be tied to any place and embracing the accelerating speed of the economy, we are a people on the move with little commitment to place. We are pilgrims on a path of prosperity, with no home that is not up for sale at the best economic opportunity.

What's wrong? Whatever inhibits the full realization of human freedom, economic growth, and the free mechanisms of the Market. Agents of terror who reject our worldview and our cultural narrative, government regulations that would restrict the free and unfettered growth of the economy, taxation that takes from

66. Of course, no transactions are truly anonymous given the power of the internet to collect our personal data and sell it to corporations. Ironically, our "anonymous" online activity has created the lowest levels of privacy in history.

the rich to unnaturally redistribute income to the poor, environmental activists who think that the needs of nature are more important than the economy, economic contraction—all of these pose a mortal threat to the unfolding of history and the utopian vision of a consumer society.

What's the remedy? We must eradicate all that inhibits economic growth, all that would restrain the free unfolding of history, all that restricts the freedom of the Market, strips us of our right to prosperity, and threatens our consumptive way of life. We must privatize the public sphere, deregulate both international trade relations and financial institutions, reduce corporate taxes, and subject environmental standards to the dictates of economic growth.[67] And all of this makes it necessary that we enter into a period of permanent war against all those who would pose a threat to our economic liberty.

If this is at all a fair summation of how the empire of global capitalism would answer the first four worldview questions, then how might we discern an answer to the fifth question, the question of discerning the time?

What time is it? As we have seen, some would argue that now is the time for the American Empire to take up the mantle that history has placed on this nation. Now is the time for the United States of America to answer the call of liberty by providing the military and economic leadership that will remedy the problems that beset us. Even recognizing that the shift in colonialism that we have traced has left the nation-state supplanted by the corporate state, there is still lots of work for that nation-state to do in service of the universal mission of global capitalism. So what time is it? It is time for American Empire.

Others, however, aren't so sure. Millions of US citizens (and this is paralleled throughout the nations of the affluent West) have a profound sense of disappointment that emerges as anger at both the state with its interference in their lives and at the corporate elite who seem to have left them behind. Unemployment, underemployment, high debt rates, and the overall contraction of the economy has understandably left many Americans feeling that the core American value of liberty has been sacrificed. If liberty is the right to the American way of life, to fulfilling the American dream, then when that dream is a nightmare and that way of life seems to be experiencing foreclosure, anger is an inevitable response. So what time is it for this large portion of the population? It is time for America to be great again, for America to take care of its own rather than getting caught up in the affairs other nations. It is time to put America back to work. It is time, in

67. Cf. Klein, *This Changes Everything*, 19.

short, for a strong leader who is outside the corrupt political system of Washington to come and reignite the vision of American liberty.[68]

Proponents of both of these options believe, in their own way, that it is time to get the story of freedom and prosperity back on track. The vision of economic prosperity may have faced some challenges, but the empire itself remains viable. Others, however, think that this story has run its course, that the empire is in decline, and that it is time to abandon a bankrupt worldview.

Chris Hedges is such a prophet of decline. Within weeks of Barak Obama's first inaugural address, Hedges broke through the optimism of the moment by writing, "At no period in American history has our democracy been in such peril or has the possibility of totalitarianism been as real. Our way of life is over. Our profligate consumption is finished. Our children will never have the standard of living we had. And poverty and despair will sweep across the landscape like a plague. . . . Our empire is dying. Our economy has collapsed."[69] Two years later, Hedges almost seemed to predict the cultural eruption that we witnessed during the Republican presidential nomination race of 2016: "The mounting anger and hatred, coursing through the bloodstream of the body politic, make violence and counterviolence inevitable. Brace yourself. The American empire is over. And the descent is going to be horrifying."[70] So if the empire, together with its self-indulgence and gluttonous consumption, is coming to an end, then what are we to do? How does an empire respond to its political, economic, and military decline? Hedges says that "we can continue to dance to the tunes of self-delusion, circling the fire as we chant ridiculous mantras about our greatness, virtue and power, or we can face the painful reality that has engulfed us." While there is nothing that we can do to reverse this decline, "if we can break free from our self-delusion," we can "dismantle our crumbling empire and the national security state with a minimum of damage to ourselves and others."[71] From the perspective of the history of empires, this seems highly unlikely. Things are going to get much

68. The attentive reader will recognize that we wrote this during the ascendancy of Donald Trump to the Republican nomination for the presidential election in 2016 and his subsequent victory in that election. The irony that so many struggling Americans would embrace a member of the economic elite as their source of hope is not lost on us. Nor is the frightening prospect that the election of Donald Trump would give us the demagoguery of classic totalitarianism within the structures of the inverted totalitarianism of the corporate state. Revisiting this analysis during the first year of the Trump presidency, we see that this prediction was, sadly, accurate.

69. Chris Hedges, *The World as It Is: Dispatches on the Myth of Human Progress* (New York: Nation Books, 2013), 2.

70. Hedges, *World as It Is*, 81.

71. Hedges, *World as It Is*, 267.

worse before any significant cultural, economic, or political change will happen. So what time is it? It is a time of cultural decline, with all the threat, vulnerability, and precariousness that such decline entails.

Naomi Klein shares Hedges's prophecy of decline and even his call to dismantle the empire. In the face of the crisis of climate change, Klein has persuasively argued that when the ecological rules of our planetary system conflict with the economic narrative and praxis of unfettered economic expansion, it is time for nothing short of a new worldview. As the reality of climate change shatters the imperial worldview in which we live, move, and have our being, this will set off a battle of worldviews that will be much more radical than the ideological struggles we saw during the Cold War.[72] The myth of human domination of a passive world in the service of an expanding economy must be overthrown, and we will need new stories "to replace the ones that have failed us."[73] "Fundamentally," Klein argues, "the task is to articulate not just an alternative set of policy proposals but an alternative worldview to rival the one at the heart of the ecological crisis—embedded in interdependence rather than hyper-individualism, reciprocity rather than dominance, and cooperation rather than hierarchy."[74] So what time is it? It is time for a new worldview, a new story, together with new symbols and a praxis that is both sustainable and regenerative in a terribly wounded world suffering under a broken worldview.

Empire, Broken Worldviews, and the Letter to the Romans

A broken home, a broken covenant, broken treaties, and a broken worldview. And in the midst of it all, Iris's brokenness is paralleled in the experience of Diaspora Judeans, Indigenous peoples, and the late modern culture of global consumerism. Like Iris, we are all homeless. Whether we are talking about a slave woman who had her children taken from her, a Judean ripped from the land that was promised as home to his people, First Nations children removed from their families and their home on the land, or a whole rootless culture committed to mobility

72. Soviet communism and liberal democratic democracy shared the same view of the world as a domain for domination in which value was determined by economic transaction. This is why both systems were based on an extractivist economics with equally dismal environmental records. Their conflict was on how to manage economic growth and who owned the means of production. The worldview shift that Klein is imagining is much more radical, going to the very heart of the relationship between humanity and nature.

73. Klein, *This Changes Everything*, 461.

74. Klein, *This Changes Everything*, 462.

and consumption that has no commitment to place, no deep sense of home, the result is the same.

Empires are always cloaked in the language of home. The emperor is the *Pater Patriae*, the Father of the Fatherland. All are to find their place, their home, within the imperial household of which Caesar is the father. In modern colonialism, Indigenous peoples were treated as children, subject to a sovereign father in a faraway land, and reduced to wards of the state. By means of an educational program of enculturation, they were to learn the stories, adopt the practices, be shaped by the symbols, and embrace the worldview of their new family, their new home. And when the forces of terror threaten the American Empire by launching an attack on the symbolic heart of global capitalism, the result is, of course, a "Homeland Security Act" and a "War on Terror." Empires are all about home, even as they render so many of their subjects completely homeless.

So we must now return to Paul's letter to the Romans. Addressed to disparate Christian assemblies at the heart of the empire, might this letter have anything to say to the homelessness that we have discerned in the lives of Iris and Nereus? And if Paul addresses their homelessness, might this epistle be overheard in a way that speaks to the piercing homelessness of our own time? If this is a letter that offers a radical alternative to the imperial realities of its first recipients, does it have a counter-imperial word to say to us? If homelessness in one way or another is at the core of the broken worldview of empire, if the story, praxis, and symbols of empire, together with the homeland rhetoric that is part and parcel of all imperial discourse, are all a front for dispossession, then does Paul's letter to the Romans offer an alternative story, as well as subversive symbols and a liberating praxis, in the face of empire and its decline? To these questions we must now turn.

4

Homeless in Rome

Homecoming, Empire, and Romans

Iris and Nereus are homeless in Rome. The emperor cannot be their father, and the empire is not their homeland. Indeed, it is the empire itself that has rendered them so homeless in the empire's capital. Much of their conversation, as we have imagined it, has addressed the question of what it means to be at home (in slavery and in exile) together (as slave and Judean) in Jesus. Our friend Iggy was also homeless. Though a loved member of our community and sometimes housed, though usually living on the street, Iggy was also rendered homeless by empire. That is why we had to tell the story of the residential schools, cultural genocide, and the way that colonialism stripped Indigenous peoples of their home. And, we have argued, there is something domicidal at the center of the corporate colonialism that characterizes the narrative, worldview, symbols, and praxis of global capitalism. The home-stealing colonialists of the modern age have become homeless themselves on so many levels—homeless in empire.

So we began to wonder. If empire is a force of homelessness, its self-understanding as the only true "homeland" notwithstanding, and if Paul's letter to the Romans is written, with clear intent, to folks at the center of that empire, then might themes of home, homelessness, and homecoming be woven throughout this ancient letter? And if so, could that provide a lens for interpreting this letter in relation to the various forms of homelessness that we face in the twenty-first century?

Our thesis is simple. Almost too simple. But perhaps it can help us make sense of a text that has been alien to many of us for so many years. For this is a text that has been used to justify the tearing of the church asunder. How one interprets this text has been seen as a litmus test of biblical "orthodoxy," demarcating who is in and who is out. Romans has been wielded as a weapon, often in service of theological violence. We know this can't be right. We know that somehow we need to disarm Romans. Somehow we need to hear this text anew in a way that brings together and heals rather than tears apart and hurts. Somehow we need to find an angle on this text that places its large claims and sometimes complex argumentation into a clear and simple story. So our thesis began to develop.

Set in the context of the expulsion and return of Judeans to Rome, Paul's letter to the Christian communities amid the empire is fundamentally about home. If Judeans are consistently considered a shameful people who do not deserve the security of home in the empire, then how does a mixed community of Christian Judeans and gentiles make home together? And how does a mixed community of tradespeople and dependents, educated and illiterate, free and slave, men and women find home together in Messiah Jesus? What does homecoming look like for a community shaped fundamentally by the story of Jesus? How does that community embrace the story of Israel in light of the story of Jesus? And how does that story shape this community into a place of home? These questions are central to the epistle. Other more traditional theological topics such as righteousness and justification, the "faith of Jesus Christ," and the status of Israel in Paul's theology can be helpfully set in the broader context of home and homemaking for a young Christian community of diverse ethnic, religious, social, and economic backgrounds.

This is our thesis. Or perhaps it is better to say that this is our "hunch" based on these historical observations. If we read Paul's letter contextually (and how else can we read?), then there is a good historical argument to be made for the kind of reading that we are proposing.

We need to be clear, however, that contextualization is never a matter of only attending to the geopolitical, symbolic, and cultural context of the ancient text. We also read Scripture from our own geopolitical, symbolic, and cultural context, whether we acknowledge and account for that context or not.

Forced expulsion, economic migration, oppression of minority communities, and denial of place and citizenship are as common in our day as they were in the first century. "Never before," writes Elie Wiesel, "have so many human beings fled so many homes."[1] Or go to the other side of the Israeli/Palestinian divide

1. Elie Wiesel, "Longing for Home," in *The Longing for Home*, ed. Leroy S. Rouner (Notre Dame, IN: University of Notre Dame Press, 1996), 19.

and you hear a similar perception from Edward Said: "Our age, with its modern warfare, imperialism and quasi theological ambitions of totalitarian rulers . . . is indeed the age of the refugee, the displaced person, mass migration."[2] And just as empire had something to do with the precariousness of homemaking in the first century, so also can we discern similar dynamics in our own world of global capitalism.

We live in a culture of displacement. Not only have we seen an alarming rise of socioeconomic homelessness (or houselessness) in most industrialized nations, so also has a wider sense of displacement or homelessness been manifest even among those who are well housed. In *Beyond Homelessness*, Bouma-Prediger and Walsh put it this way: "Whether we are talking about the upwardly mobile who view each place as a rung in the ladder that goes to who knows where, or the postmodern nomad with no roots in any place or any tradition of place, or the average consumer who doesn't know anything about the place where she lives or the places her food comes from, the reality is the same—we are a culture of displacement."[3] But it is not merely a sense of displacement that permeates our world. As we write this, our world is witnessing the largest migration due to war since the Second World War. Refugees are pouring into Europe from Syria and Africa. Images of children lying dead on the beach, of refugee camps struggling with overflow, and of overturned boats in the Mediterranean are shaping political discourse not only of European nations but also of Canada and the United States.

All this displacement, all this homelessness, is a product of empire. A global capitalist empire with no sense of or commitment to the "common good" cannot begin to reflect on the "right of housing" for the poorest of our neighbors. This vision of life cannot really take seriously the importance of place because this "rootless and placeless monoculture of commercial expectations and products"[4] must "be ready at any moment, by the terms of power and wealth in the modern world, to destroy any place."[5] No one's home is safe; everything is up for grabs by the terms of power and wealth. All communities, all peoples, all habitats can be offered as sacrifices to the gods of our age. And so "a creeping dread of

2. Edward Said, "Reflections on Exile," in *Out There: Marginalization and Contemporary Cultures*, ed. R. Ferguson, M. Gever, Trinh T. Minh-ha, and Cornel West (Cambridge, MA: MIT Press, 1990), 357.

3. Steven Bouma-Prediger and Brian J. Walsh, *Beyond Homelessness: Christian Faith in a Culture of Displacement* (Grand Rapids: Eerdmans, 2008), xii.

4. Wendell Berry, *Sex, Economy, Freedom and Community* (New York: Pantheon Books, 1993), 151.

5. Berry, *Sex, Economy, Freedom and Community*, 22.

homelessness" permeates our culture as we are rendered geopolitically, socio-economically, culturally, ecologically, and spiritually homeless.[6] For the recent wave of refugees, things have moved from dread to the literal nightmare of running for their lives. And for the countless homeless on the streets of our most affluent cities, the reality of homelessness has moved from dread to numbness.

Reading a biblical text requires a double discernment—of both the historical context of the text at hand and the context of the reading community. If our reading of Romans in light of the themes of home and homelessness suggested by both the geohistorical and the symbolic context of the text is justified, and if our discernment of the inherent homelessness of our own culture of displacement is at all on target, then might this give birth to a biblically faithful and fruitful alternative reading of this ancient text? We are not proposing this reading as one that should eclipse all others. Nor are we arguing that the categories of home and homelessness function as *the* hermeneutical key that will unlock Paul's epistle to the Romans. More modestly, we are suggesting that this particular angle on the text could provide fruitful interpretation of the epistle in both its ancient context and its contemporary reading. As with all biblical interpretation, the proof lies in whether a particular reading faithfully opens up the text and helps to shape a community of radical discipleship.[7] Before we turn to that reading, however, we need to briefly review the wider biblical context.

Biblical Homemaking in the Face of Empire

The longing for home has always been central to biblical faith. This has always been the dream; this has always been the hope. If you put together the biblical themes of covenant, shalom, land, and inheritance, they all add up to home. We were created for home; our sin is an act of home-breaking, and the longing and hope of all biblical faith remains that of homecoming. The traditional triad of creation, fall, and redemption is helpfully deepened and elucidated by the triad of home, homelessness, and homecoming.

6. John Della Costa, "Outsourcing, Downsizing, Mergers and Cutbacks: Folks Are Living with a Creeping Sense of Homelessness," *Catholic New Times*, May 3, 1998, 10.

7. Or as Richard B. Hays puts it, "No reading of Scripture can be legitimate . . . if it fails to shape the readers into a community that embodies the love of God as shown forth in Christ." And further: "True interpretation of Scripture leads us into unqualified giving of our lives in service within the community whose vocation is to reenact the obedience of the Son of God who loved us and gave himself for us." Richard B. Hays, *Echoes of Scripture in the Letters of Paul* (New Haven: Yale University Press, 1989), 191.

The promise to Abraham and the patriarchs was of a homeland. This was the promise to the slaves in Egypt and to those exiled in Babylon. And this was a promise always made in the shadow of empire.[8] It was in the demise of the imperial project of Babel and the culture that followed it that Abraham was given a vision of home beyond empire. It was in the face of the homelessness of imperial slavery that the promise of home beyond Egyptian bondage was renewed. It was in the wilderness, a place that was uninhabitable, a place that could not be home, that Yahweh made home with his people and gave them the Torah as a charter for homemaking. And when the people proved themselves to be incurable home breakers and found themselves in the homelessness of exile, the promise was renewed once again. "Lift up your eyes and look around," proclaimed Isaiah. Open your eyes and see; "they all gather together, they come to you; your sons shall come from far away, and your daughters shall be carried on their nurses' arms" (Isa. 60:4). Sisters and brothers are coming home.

The longing for home cannot be extinguished. As Bruce Cockburn sings, "To keep a million homeless down takes more / than a strong arm up your sleeve."[9] And there have been many strong arms, many home-destroying arms. From Pharaoh's brick quotas for the slaves in Egypt to Solomon's forced labor in which we see home recast once again as empire, the story is the same. Home is defiled. And it continues in Israel's story. From Assyrian and Babylonian exile to oppression by the Romans, the covenant people found themselves homeless in the empire. Whether we are talking about Caesar Augustus or General Augusto Pinochet, imperial regimes are always murderers of home, invariably in the name of home. Tragically, the defense of home, together with the expansion of the boundaries of home (often in the name of the "Fatherland"), seems to legitimate and require the destruction of the home of others and the displacement of that home's inhabitants.[10]

8. Cf. Walter Brueggemann, "Always in the Shadow of Empire," in *Texts That Linger, Words That Explode: Listening to Prophetic Voices*, ed. Patrick Miller (Minneapolis: Fortress, 2000), 73–87.

9. Bruce Cockburn, "Santiago Dawn," track 7 on *World of Wonders*, High Romance Music Inc., 1985. Cockburn is reflecting on the imposed homelessness perpetrated by the regime of Augusto Pinochet ten years after the US-backed coup that overthrew the democratically elected government of Salvador Allende on September 11, 1973.

10. It needs to be asked whether the establishment of home for some *always* and *necessarily* entails the homelessness and displacement of others. It is clear enough that this was a dynamic in the history of Israel, rooted in the promise to Abraham. For the children of Abraham to have a home required the genocide of the inhabitants of the land. Paul, we will see, reinterprets the promise to Abraham in a way that insists on inclusion, not exclusion. For a liberating reading of the story of the conquest of the Canaanites from the perspective of Jesus's engagement with the

This was Israel's story. By the time of Jesus, exile had become a permanent state of being. The people of Israel were exiled in their own land, subject to military thugs, enslaved to their own fear, with crucifixion for those who dared to have a voice.[11] We meet in this story one home-destroying empire after another. The people of Israel were exiled in their own land and in the lands of others. Dispersed throughout the empire, a Judean Diaspora was cut off from home, subject to the imperial whim, and dismissed as a shameful and foolish people who resisted the imperial constructs of home. So Paul stands in the best of biblical traditions by deconstructing the imperial construction of home.

We now turn to a reading of Paul's letter to the Romans from the perspective of homemaking in exile, homemaking in the face of a home-destroying empire.[12]

Deconstructing the Imperial Home (Rom. 1:1–17)

As we have seen in the opening salutation, "Paul, a slave of Jesus Christ," the apostle has already begun to dismantle a home divided between free people and slaves. He has already begun to deconstruct a household that is built on the institution of slavery by identifying himself not as an insider of that household, not as an educated citizen of Rome with all the privileges that such status entails, but as a slave, the lowest status within the house that Rome built. And to make it clear that this is a deliberately subversive move, the apostle identifies his slavery as subject not to the emperor, the supreme "father" of the Roman household, but to Jesus Christ.

The imperial construction of home is rooted in an imperial gospel, the good news proclaimed by the empire. Imperial announcements of military victories, triumph over more people and lands, and the extension of the boundaries of the empire were called *gospels* or "good news" from Rome. The gospel of the empire told a story of the expansion of a homeland, rooted in the victories of the goddess Roma and bestowed with the blessings of Zeus. When Paul counters all of this by

"Canaanite" woman, see Grant LeMarquand, "The Canaanite Conquest of Jesus (Matt. 15:21–28)," *ARC: The Journal of the Faculty of Religious Studies, McGill University* 33 (2005): 237–47.

11. This understanding of first-century Israel as a context of exile is indebted, of course, to N. T. Wright, *The New Testament and the People of God* (Minneapolis: Fortress, 1992) and *Jesus and the Victory of God* (Minneapolis: Fortress, 2002). The broader analysis of home as central to the story of Israel is indebted to Walter Brueggemann, *The Land: Place as Gift and Challenge in Biblical Faith* (Philadelphia: Fortress, 1977); *The Prophetic Imagination* (Philadelphia: Fortress, 1978); and *Cadences of Home: Preaching among Exiles* (Louisville: Westminster John Knox, 1997).

12. Many of the texts from Romans that we deal with as part of the narrative of home in this chapter will receive more in-depth discussion in subsequent chapters.

repeating the word *gospel* five times in the first sixteen verses of the epistle, you know that this is not a coincidence:

> "called to be an apostle, set apart for the *gospel* of God" (v. 1)
> "the *gospel* concerning his Son" (v. 3)
> "announcing the *gospel* of his Son" (v. 9)
> "my eagerness to proclaim the *gospel* to you . . . in Rome" (v. 15)
> "for I am not ashamed of the *gospel*" (v. 16)

Home is always a storied place. Home is rooted in deep memories, in shared narratives. And Paul identifies the story that he is about to tell, the good news that he will proclaim in the face of all imperial gospels, as a decidedly Judean gospel that is rooted in Judean stories and "promised . . . through [God's] prophets in the holy scriptures" (1:2), concerning God's son "who was descended from David" (1:3). This is the good news of God's Son, not a son of Augustus, not a descendent of another Roman emperor. *Home is always rooted in story. The question is, Whose story? Whose patrilineage?*

Home is also a site of order, of rule. The Roman construction of home is rooted in the lordship of Caesar, who more often than not is a self-deifying lord. The emperor is literally the son of a god because his father has joined the pantheon of the gods upon death. Paul, however, speaks of a gospel concerning a son, descended from David, and "declared to be Son of God . . . by the resurrection from the dead." This is "Jesus Christ our Lord" (1:4). This is a home subject to a Lord, but not the lordship of Caesar. This is a home subject to a Son of God, but one who is declared Son not by some imperial pronouncement or because of the death and deification of his father. No, this Lord is Son of God because he defeated death and rose from the dead. Home is a matter of establishing a domicile, but domiciles are ordered places. *Home requires order. The question is, What kind of order? Whose order?*

Home is always a site of inclusion and exclusion. Homes have legitimate boundaries, legitimate distinctions between who is in and who is out. Imperial homes tend to specialize in exclusion over inclusion. In Rome, Greeks were favored because so much of Roman culture and mythology was dependent on the wisdom of the Greeks and because the Greeks were willing and enthusiastic members of the empire. Barbarians were those who refused membership in the household of Rome and resisted the hegemony of the empire. Similarly, the wise were those educated elite who ruled by natural right, while the foolish were hoi polloi, the common folk who had a lower status in the household. And while Judeans might well have been educated and were certainly not barbarians, they were nonetheless viewed as a shameful people because they refused to acknowledge the pantheon of the gods, tended to avoid the rituals of the imperial cult, and were a constant source of resistance to the empire back in their home territory of Judea. All of these were shameful behaviors that functioned to destabilize the imperial home.

So when Paul says, "I am a debtor both to Greeks and to barbarians, both to the wise and to the foolish. . . . For I am not ashamed of the gospel; it is the power of God for salvation to everyone who has faith, to the Judean first and also to the Greek" (1:14, 16 NRSV alt.), he turns imperial categories of status and shame, inclusion and exclusion, on their heads. Indebted to barbarians and the foolish? His gospel is to Judeans first and then to Greeks? The whole cosmic order is overturned in such language. *Home is a matter of inclusion and exclusion. The question is, Who is in and who is out?*

Finally, in the rhetoric of the empire, the Roman home is a home of justice. A flourishing of *iusticia* was seen as one of the divine blessings on the empire after Augustus. And the close companion of *iusticia* would have been *fides* (in the Greek *dikaiosynē* and *pistis* respectively). Justice and fidelity: on these two the empire was built and the imperial home established. Paul goes to the heart of the empire's self-understanding when he wrote, "For in [the gospel] the justice of God is revealed, through faithfulness for faithfulness; as it is written, 'The one who is just will live through faithfulness'" (1:17 our translation). *Home requires fidelity. Home must be rooted in the practice of justice. But whose justic*e? *Whose faithfulness? And faithfulness to whom?*

We are only seventeen verses into the epistle—perhaps three paragraphs—and it is clear that the apostle is at it again. Once again he is writing an anti-imperial tract, but this time he writes to the center of the empire. All the clues are there to indicate that this is a subversive letter that will undermine the imperial imagination, disarm the imperial ideology, deflate the imperial arrogance, dethrone the imperial lord, overturn the imperial hierarchies, and deconstruct the imperial architecture of home.

Homemaking Glory or Home-Destroying Shame? (Rom. 1:18–32)

Paul, the Judean, then takes us back to the beginning of Israel's narrative and to two of the most radically distinctive Judean beliefs. He reminds us of who humanity is in the foundational story of Genesis and in the crucial Torah prohibition of idolatry. Image of God or graven images? That is the question.

Created in the image of God, we are called to homemaking in God's good creation as faithful and grateful servants of creation, caretakers in the creational house of God. This is our glory, this is the mantle that we wear, and this is our wisdom.[13] But we exchange our glory for idolatry; we give up our homemaking service to our homemaking God and serve and worship the creature rather than the Creator. And that is how we become home wreckers. By rejecting our call to homemaking subject to the true and only Lord of creation, we become home breakers, not homemakers. All creation knows that the world is for attentive and loving care, that the world is for homemaking. Because all creation is founded in Wisdom[14] and "there is a wisdom worked into the very fabric of things,"[15] when we turn away from the Creator and the creation to embrace idolatry, we are cut off from that wisdom and become "fools" (1:22).

Home is built into the very fabric of creation and all creation knows what humans willfully miss. There's all this glory shining around: the glory of God, the glory of creation, and the glory that we bear as servants of creation.[16] But we exchange our glory, we exchange our homemaking call, for graven images. The creature called to be the image of God in creation gives up its proper calling and glory in order to bow the knee to false images, to idols. And once we bow the knee to graven images, our imaginations are taken captive. We can hardly dream of what life outside the grip of idolatry could look like. We can scarcely imagine what a life that isn't enslaved to the dominant mythology and ideology could look like. We don't have the imaginative resources to even consider what home might be without the hierarchies, divisions, and lifestyle of the empire. Justice and fidelity get distorted, and we find ourselves living the lie of exclusion that has been planted and nurtured in us by the empire.

As a result, home collapses all around us. Sexual fidelity devolves into sex as power and sex as consumption. This is the home-destroying sexuality of the empire. Things move from bad to worse. Home is a site for the care and protection of children, but idols always require sacrifice. And they have an insatiable

13. The definitive study of the biblical understanding of the image of God is J. Richard Middleton, *The Liberating Image: The* Imago Dei *in Genesis 1* (Grand Rapids: Brazos, 2005).

14. See Prov. 3:19; 8:22–36; Ps. 104:24. See also Sir. 24:1–22.

15. Ellen Davis, *Scripture, Culture, and Agriculture: An Agrarian Reading of the Bible* (Cambridge: Cambridge University Press, 2009), 34. See her further discussion of wisdom on pp. 33–36, 142–47.

16. Cf. Ps. 8.

appetite for children. So not only does the intimacy and fidelity of sexuality get reduced to promiscuous entertainment in the empire, but children are offered up in service of such entertainment. Imperial sexuality mirrors the rest of the empire's practices by being predatory. Always wanting more. Always looking to control and to consume. And children are the most vulnerable victims of such sexual predation. This is the bitter fruit of idolatry. This is the sexuality of empire.[17]

What is true of our sexual lives is manifest in every dimension of imperial life, in every aspect of the home. Home rooted in covenant is undermined by faithlessness. Home as a place of truth is destroyed by deceit. Home as a refuge of respect is undermined by gossip and rebelliousness.

Idolatrous copulation bears the bad fruit of a deeply distorted life, full of evil longing, greed, hatred, envy, the breaking of community and destroying of families, arrogance, insolence, disrespect, foolishness, infidelity, and a ruthlessness that is born of a heart that has turned its back on love.

It has always been about home, but we are incurable home wreckers. It has always been about home, but we engage in domicide. No wonder we can't find our home in the empire.

We Are All Home Wreckers (Rom. 2:1–3:20)

The problem with any diatribe against a particular way of life is that it can so easily be construed as being about someone else. We criticize the lives of others as being distorted, as having no potential for homemaking, while we are blind to our own home-breaking practices. And in a community as diverse as the house churches in Rome, there would be great potential for such self-righteous critique of one another, especially between the Judean and gentile members of the community. For the gentile members of the church there would invariably have been a bias against their Judean brethren as a divisive group of people who had consistently been a threat to the *Pax Romana* and therefore a threat to the very foundations of the Roman household. But the Judean members of the community could well have heard Paul's diatribe against idolatry as addressing the domicidal way of life of gentiles in the empire. If home is a matter of inclusion and welcome, then Paul is going to have to address this division within the Christian community from the outset. If home "is a place of belonging, of recognition and acceptance rather

17. We will return to the theme of sexuality in the empire in chap. 9, and we will explore what Paul might have to say to us as we struggle with questions of sexuality in our own context.

than disdain and rejection,"[18] then the apostle will need to find a way to break through that disdain and rejection so that the disparate Christian communities in Rome will be forged into a home of covenantal belonging in Messiah Jesus.[19]

So the apostle immediately asks his listeners, Who among us can judge another? Who among us can enact home-excluding judgment? Do any of us have some special virtue, some higher understanding, some preferred place in the home that God builds? No, he insists, we are all home breakers, whether we are gentile or Judean. "Whoever you are," the apostle repeats, you are subject to the wrath of a God who seeks to make home but is constantly thwarted by the home-breaking of his image-bearing creatures (2:1, 3).

It is true that the Torah of Israel is a word for homemaking. And while some gentiles obey this Torah without knowing it (2:14–16), many Judeans disobey it in their home-breaking ways, and that is why they remain in exile to this day, says Paul, the onetime Pharisee (2:17–24). And not only are the children of the promise homeless in their exile, but their home-breaking also perpetuates the homelessness of the rest of the world! Isn't that why the prophet wrote that God's name is blasphemed among the gentiles (2:24)?[20]

Moreover, while home is always rooted in rules and traditions, no real home can be sustained simply by the dutiful observation of those rules and traditions. Yes, circumcision was the foundational symbol of (male) membership in the covenantal household, but the old adage has some truth in it—home is where the heart is. And if your heart is not rooted in the depths of covenant, then all the rule-keeping and tradition-honoring of the world still won't build home. Home is a spiritual reality, and if you get the rules but miss the spirit of the covenant, then you will find yourself to be profoundly homeless.

So pagan idolatry meets Judean Torah-breaking and we are all rendered homeless. Home requires faithfulness, yet we are all faithless. Home requires justice, yet we all practice injustice. So if Judeans are, like everyone else, incurable home breakers, do they have any advantage over gentiles? Of course they do, for they were given God's homemaking words. Even though they broke home, God continued to faithfully build home for and with them. Their story shows us how God won't let lies, injustice, or faithlessness get in the way of making truth, justice, and faithfulness our promised home. But we aren't there yet. Quoting, respectively, Psalms 14, 5, 10, and 36, all written against pagan oppressors of Israel,

18. Bouma-Prediger and Walsh, *Beyond Homelessness*, 65.
19. Paul addresses this disdain and rejection further in Rom. 14 and 15.
20. Isa. 52:5. See also Ezek. 36:20.

Paul levels out the home-breaking guilt, describing both Judean and Greek as under the power of sin.[21] "All have turned aside . . . ; there is no one who shows kindness, there is not even one" (3:12). "Their throats are opened graves; they use their tongues to deceive" (3:13). "Their mouths are full of cursing and bitterness" (3:14). Without kindness, and with a discourse of constant deception and violence, how can home ever be achieved? And in the middle of a careful compilation of quotations from the Psalms against pagans, Paul inserts one prophetic voice that is clearly directed not at gentiles, not at those "outside" the covenantal community, but at the people of Israel in exile, at those "inside" the bounds of the covenantal home.

> Their feet are swift to shed blood;
> ruin and misery are in their paths,
> and the way of peace they have not known. (Rom. 3:15–17, quoting Isa. 59:7–8)

Home is a place of safety, yet in Israel—like in Rome—it has become a place of violence. Home, in its deepest covenantal meaning, is about shalom. It is a place of well-being, of wholeness, reconciliation, and restoration of all our relationships. But in Israel—like in Rome—the path of shalom has not been known.

Paul sums it all up by proclaiming that "all have sinned and fall short of the glory of God" (3:23). All have distorted the image of God. All have failed in their homemaking stewardship.

All . . . save one.

Homecoming Is at Hand (Rom. 3:21–31)

There has been one righteous one, writes Paul. There has been one faithful one who can atone for the violence of our home-breaking by bearing that violence and shedding his blood. All of us have sinned—Judean and Greek alike—and fallen short of the glory of God (3:23). All of us have given up the glory of bearing God's image in homemaking faithfulness. All of us have defiled the creational home. All of us are destroyers of home. And there is nothing that we can do to restore this home on our own. There is nothing that we can do to set ourselves free from

21. See Sylvia C. Keesmaat, "The Psalms in Romans and Galatians," in *The Psalms in the New Testament*, ed. Steve Moyise and Maarten J. Menken (London: T&T Clark, 2004), 139–61 (esp. 145–48).

our idolatrous captivity and become homemakers anew. No, if there is to be a restored glory, a restored stewardship, a restored image of God in our lives, then it will come as radical gift. Rooted in grace, restored homemaking is never finally a human accomplishment but a gift of the divine homemaker. Because we have sold out our home to idolatry, another needs to accomplish this redemption of home. If it is our injustice that has rendered us homeless, then the justice that is required for homemaking must be found in another. If we are to be justified in coming home, then that justification will not be of our own making. If it is our infidelity that so fundamentally broke home, then we will need the faithfulness of another to restore home anew. This, says Paul, is the faithfulness of Jesus Christ.[22]

The faithful one, the one who maintains the fidelity that is the very foundation of all covenantal homemaking, is the place of mercy, so that home is restored in him and our home-wrecking ways are passed over by God. And all those who trust in the faithfulness of Jesus Christ are made right at home (3:24–26).[23]

Homecoming is at hand, not as something that we have attained through our own hard work, but as a gift. Homecoming is at hand, not by a steely resolve to obey the Torah (as good as the Torah is), but through grace. There is no home without grace, there is no homecoming without gift, and it doesn't matter whether you are a Judean or a Greek. Through Jesus the righteous one, through Jesus the just one, through the faithfulness of Jesus Christ, homecoming is at hand for those who embrace, and are embraced by, his faithfulness.

Renarrating the Story of Home (Rom. 4:1–5:11)

Home is a gift that is received in humble faithfulness. Isn't that what the story has always been about? Isn't that the story that is the very foundation of our homemaking?[24] All constructions of home are storied, we have suggested. Another way to say this is that all homes have family roots. And Rome's memory goes back to the story of the pious and godly Trojan hero, Aeneas, who escaped the Trojan

22. On translating *pistis Christou* as "faithfulness of Christ," the ground-breaking book remains Richard B. Hays, *The Faith of Jesus Christ: An Investigation into the Narrative Substructure of Galatians 3:1–4:11*, SBL Dissertation Series (Chico, CA: Scholars Press, 1983).

23. N. T. Wright's summary is helpful: "*The Messiah, the faithful Israelite, has been faithful to death, and through him the faithful justice of the covenant God is now displayed for all, Jew and gentile alike.*" N. T. Wright, *Paul and the Faithfulness of God*, book 2 (Minneapolis: Fortress, 2013), 841 (italics original).

24. For a richly holistic telling of the biblical story, see J. Richard Middleton, *A New Heaven and a New Earth: Reclaiming Biblical Eschatology* (Grand Rapids: Baker Academic, 2014), esp. chap. 3.

War with his son, his father, and his household gods and became the founder of Rome.[25] For the people of Rome, the piety and faithfulness of Aeneas shapes the character of their fatherland and their homes.

Paul, however, looks elsewhere to provide a narrative foundation for the home-making community that is the church in Rome. And, not surprisingly, his memory goes back to the beginning of the covenant with Israel, back to Abraham. While Aeneas achieves home through military conquest, Abraham has nothing to go on except a promise. He was promised a home, and he received that promise in faith. Like all great stories, all metanarratives, Paul tells a story of leaving home on the way to a home. But the protagonist is called to a home that he can only receive as a gift, never as an accomplishment of either his piety or his military prowess. And Paul brings us back to the foundational story of Abraham not just for Judeans in Rome but also for gentiles who have followed Messiah Jesus to the fulfillment of this promise.

So whose father is Abraham? Who are welcomed into the home that was promised to him? Who shares in the inheritance of Abraham? Those who share his faith, of course. Those who enter this home-constituting story through faith. The children of Abraham are those who claim him as father, not by family lineage, but by embracing the promise of covenantal homecoming. Iris is welcomed home in Abraham, and Nereus needs to understand the promise to Abraham in the world-embracing terms that were always at the heart of the covenant.

Remember, the promise was that he would inherit the world (4:13)! The whole world, not just the land of Israel, is to be a home of righteousness. The justice of the covenant God is not limited to one people or to one place. No, the promise is for the whole world. All creation will be restored to a habitation for homemaking, and many people will become Abraham's descendants. Many people will embrace Abraham and Sarah as their great-great-grandparents.

Do you want to come home? Do you want a home that the empire can never provide? Then abandon the empire's story of home and embrace the story of Abraham. Abandon all exclusionary home constructions. This has a double edge to it. By interpreting the promise to Abraham in cosmic and inclusive terms, Paul is undermining both Judean *and* Roman exceptionalism. All are invited home to father Abraham, and the only house rule that counts is faithfulness—a faithfulness that goes beyond the family boundary markers of circumcision and beyond the boundaries of the law, even Israel's law.

25. See Neil Elliott, *The Arrogance of Nations: Reading Romans in the Shadow of Empire* (Minneapolis: Fortress, 2008), 125–38.

So, hoping against hope, Paul counsels these diverse communities of the Way to follow Abraham and trust the promises, even against the evidence. Though the imperial forces of homelessness are forces of death, and the darkness of the grave is deep, there is a dawn to be embraced—the dawn of resurrection. The faithful one who incarnates justice, invites us home, and keeps the promise of Abraham, has died at the hands of the empire and has risen in the homemaking power of God (4:24–25).

Faith in this Jesus, Paul insists, will make us just. And in that justice we meet a peace that the *Pax Romana* can never understand (5:1). This is a peace with God through Jesus, the messianic Lord. This is a peace through the one executed by the empire, and therefore believers are bold to proclaim that Jesus is Lord, not Caesar. Jesus is our Savior, not Caesar. There is no home without grace, and through Jesus we can enter the house of grace. Through Jesus we can stand in grace, and without such standing there can be no home (5:2).

A home built on grace, however, is a home that will suffer at the hands of those who cannot comprehend such grace. This is a home that will reject the exclusionary categories of the empire and suffer for that rejection. But that suffering, mirroring as it does the very suffering of Jesus, will shape the community with the virtues of homemaking. This will be a community in which suffering produces endurance, a stubborn commitment to the vision of the homecoming kingdom, come what may. And that endurance gives birth to a depth of character in the community that produces hope. Home is a site of hope. Without hope the home dies. But the hope of the gospel, writes the apostle, will not disappoint. This is a hope that will be fulfilled because the Holy Spirit has filled our hearts with love, which, of course, is the only secure foundation for any home (5:3–5).

A home built on grace is not a home that will easily set up barriers of exclusion against those who are seen to be unworthy of home or unclean and therefore unwelcome. No, this is a home in which God has proven his love for us "in that while we still were sinners Christ died for us" (5:8). Sinners are welcome in this home. Indeed, Paul can't imagine any other kinds of members of the household.

If all of this flies in the face of the ideology of purity that had taken hold of some segments of first-century Judean theology, then what Paul says next radically undermines and disarms the ideology of the empire. Surely if home is to be a site of safety, then it needs to be a place of protection from and exclusion of those who are perceived to be enemies of the home. But Paul will have none of it.

You see, "while we were enemies, we were reconciled to God through the death of his Son" (5:10). If home was broken because we became enemies of God, our creational home, and each other, then renewed homecoming can only happen through reconciliation. While we were far off, God opened the arms of welcome and brought us home. And somehow, though Paul does not deem it necessary to spell out how this all works, the death of the faithful one, the homelessness of the Messiah's shed blood on a Roman cross, is how enemies are reconciled and welcomed home. In the mystery of the cross, the injustice of violent exclusion paradoxically makes us just. Home is to be a site of reconciliation, not enmity. Home is a place of forgiving welcome, not judgmental exclusion. Home is a place of love, not anger. Now that is something worth boasting about in the face of the empire (5:11)!

We could sum up the heart of Paul's theology here by saying that while Rome makes peace through the shedding of the blood of others, Jesus makes peace through the shedding of his own blood. Rome's peace, as well as Rome's sense of the security and identity of home, requires shedding the blood of its enemies. Only then can Rome rest secure. Paul describes an alternative vision of homecoming, together with an alternative vision of how we deal with our enemies. Jesus welcomes all home through his outstretched arms on a cross. All are welcomed home through his blood. Sinners, enemies, and all other kinds of home wreckers are welcomed and reconciled in this restored home.

Back to the Beginning (Rom. 5:12–21)

This is where the whole story has been going from the beginning. So Paul now reaches back before Abraham. He goes back to the very beginning, to Adam. Just as the foundational call to stewardly homemaking was given to Adam, so it is Adam's sin, Adam's broken stewardship, Adam's trespass, that gave death its rule in our lives. It is Adam's failed service, failed homemaking, and rebellion that reduced the house of life to a domicile of death.

If Adam's sin is the primordial moment of home-breaking, then it is the obedience of Jesus Christ, his faithfulness and free gift, that births the kingdom rule of life. It is the Messiah's righteousness, his justice and his grace, that opens the door to the household of life.

So where do you want to live? The domicile of death or the household of life? Under the imperial rule of death or the kingdom rule of life? Homeless in the empire or at home in Christ?

Baptism as Homecoming (Rom. 6:1–23)

Paul ends chapter 5 by contrasting two kingdoms, two realms of kingly rule, two conflicting sovereignties—the dominion of death identified with Adam and the dominion of righteousness or covenantal justice through Jesus, the messianic Lord. Now in chapter 6 Paul asks the question of identity, but he begins with the question of where we will dwell. Where is our home? What's the upshot of all of this? Paul asks. If the rule of grace abounds in the face of sin, should we remain in sin? In which realm should we find our identity?

It seems like a nonquestion, like a setup, but our hunch is that some folks actually thought that making peace with the empire and its way of life would be an implication of Paul's theology of grace. More importantly, however, Paul knows that we always need to be reminded about *where* we are, *who* we are, and *whose* we are.

Where are you? You are in the dominion of life, not death. You live in the kingdom of God, not the empire of death. How do you know? Because when you were baptized *into* Christ Jesus, you were baptized into his death. And that means that you have been buried *with* him in his death, and therefore you are raised *with him* in his resurrection.

The question is, Do you want to come home? Do you want to live in the kingdom of life? If so, you must die to the domicidal story of sin, die to the rule of death, and die to the culture of death. You must die with Christ in baptism and be raised with Christ to the life-giving rule of his kingdom. The door is wide open and all are invited to come home. But even the most hospitable home still has a doorway and a threshold. We must walk through the door and cross that threshold. And baptism is the doorway. Or, to put it differently, the waters of baptism are boundary waters. They are a watershed moment. Paul's retelling of Israel's story in light of Jesus has moved from Abraham to Moses, and now he speaks of baptism with clear echoes to the waters of the exodus narrative.[26]

Do you see what Paul is doing here? He is saying that in baptism, not only do we confess our belief in the Jesus story, but we are actually taken up into that story, so that what happened (and happens) to Jesus happened (and happens) to us. This is a profound move akin to the way in which Israel's story identifies each successive generation as being present when God liberated them from Egypt through the waters of the exodus.

26. See N. T. Wright, "The Letter to the Romans: Introduction, Commentary, and Reflections," in *The New Interpreter's Bible*, vol. 10 (Nashville: Abingdon, 2002), 534.

You are in the kingdom of life because in Christ you have died to the empire and its culture of death and have been raised to new life. His story is our story. If you are welcomed home in Christ and embraced by the kingdom of life, then you are no longer at home in or subject to the dominion of death. The dominion of home-wrecking sin must have no more power over you.

Who are you? You are *in* Christ, and therefore you are to consider yourself dead, buried, and raised with him to new life. You will not be a pawn to the prince of darkness any longer because you belong to Christ.

Well then, *whose are you?* If you are subjects of the kingdom of Christ, then you are no longer slaves of the empire of death. But notice that Paul won't actually allow us the comfort of that distinction between subjects and slaves. Rather, Paul insists on using the same language for our relationship to either the imperial kingdom of sin or the messianic kingdom of Jesus. In both instances we are slaves. And it seems that Paul is aware of the oddness of his language when he admits that he's using human images here because of the limitations of our understanding (6:19).

Echoing the imagery of the exodus, Paul says that we were once slaves to sin, but that in Christ, in sharing in his baptism, we have come through the waters in a new exodus of liberation. But then he says that we have not simply come out of slavery into freedom, but that in being set free from sin—set free from the empire of death and all its oppressions—we have become slaves of righteousness, slaves of justice. Here we come to a deeper meaning of Paul's self-identification as a slave in the very first words of this epistle.

Paul says that we shouldn't allow sin to reign over our embodied lives, because we present every dimension of our lives as weapons, not of injustice, but of justice. In an empire rooted in the injustice of an economic system of slavery, we are to become slaves of justice, presenting our bodies, our imaginations, our economic transactions, our political lives, our cultural comings and goings, our sexual expressions, our family structures, our intellectual theorizing, our daily work as slaves to justice. Because only in such an embodied life of justice will our lives bear witness to our baptism. Only in seeking covenantal justice will we demonstrate *where we really live* and where we find our most fundamental identity. Only in walking a life of justice in all that we do will we bear witness to *whose we are*. And, ironically, only in being slaves to justice will we be *who we really are*: sinners set free from our sin, sinners no longer subject to the kingdom of death because we have embraced the free gift of God—eternal life in Christ Jesus our Lord. This is homecoming. Leaving the false home of sin, we are called to cleave to Christ as our covenantal partner. Married to Christ, we are called anew to be fruitful and multiply.

Incurable Home Breakers (Rom. 7:1–25)

But there is a problem. Paul knows it, the community in Rome to whom he writes knows it, and we know it through painful experience. We may be married to Christ, but it seems that we are still incurable home breakers. Fidelity doesn't come naturally to any of us. We are still screwing around with idols, and we are still, it seems, slaves to adultery.

In fact, Paul mounts a failed analogy in chapter 7 that seems to be intentional. A married woman is bound to her husband until he dies. If he should die, then she is no longer bound to him and is free to be bound to another. We were bound to the law but have now "died to the law through the body of Christ, so that [we] may belong to another, to him who has been raised from the dead in order that we may bear fruit for God" (7:4). Now this is already a little odd: the analogy has shifted because here it is the wife who has died, not her husband (the Torah), yet Paul identifies her death *to* the Torah as setting her free, without fear of adultery, to be joined to Christ and to bear fruit with him. The argument is strained, but the point is clear. We are now discharged from the law and set free to the new life of the Spirit, without fear of adultery.

But here's where the analogy moves from being odd to being broken. Paul goes on to describe, with a painful and disarming honesty, that though we are liberated for a life free of adultery, we are, nonetheless, still all adulterers.[27] We have been both set free and "sold into slavery under sin" (7:14) at the very same time! We know that God's law calls us to homemaking, yet we sabotage home all the time. We are called to be at home in Christ, but sin dwells in us, has taken up residence in us, and it seems that homemaking is not at home in our lives. We are torn, taken captive by forces that are deeper than our will for home; we find ourselves slaves to homelessness, condemned to always live outside the home we so deeply long for. Our lives seem to persistently disqualify us from the very home that has been put on offer in Christ, the very home that we entered through the waters of baptism.

So now we find ourselves in a different place and with a different identity than the one we just heard about through our baptism. Who are we? People who have

27. We are indebted to Amy Fisher for this insight from a very fine sermon at Wine Before Breakfast, University of Toronto, November 10, 2009.

been "sold into slavery under sin" (7:14). Sin now "dwells within me" (7:17), and therefore "nothing good dwells within me" (7:18). The very sin to which we have been enslaved has been so internalized that it has literally taken up residence in our lives. It is not just that we dwell in sin; it is much worse. Sin dwells in us, and all of our dwellings are dwellings of death. We are back to radical homelessness all over again.

Redemptive Homecoming in the Spirit (Rom. 8:1–38)

Here's the good news. There is no condemnation for those who are in Christ Jesus! This is not a house of condemnation! Slavery is never the last word in this story. Liberation is always at hand. Homecoming remains available. And the promise is not nullified and cannot be nullified even by our home-breaking ways.

Yes, sin dwells in you. Yes, sin has become at home in you. But, more powerful than sin, the Spirit of God also dwells in you. That's what your baptism was all about! That's where your incorporation into the story of Jesus brings you. Christ is in you! The Spirit that raised Jesus from the dead is at home in you, and the home-renewal project is clearly under way. As Paul played off the language of dominion in chapters 5 and 6, in chapters 7 and 8 he plays with the metaphor of dwelling. Both involve the language of home. In contrast to the sin that "dwells" in us in chapter 7, Paul tells the community in Rome that, in Christ, the Spirit now dwells in them (8:9, 11).

Paul, the Judean, is talking about a salvation that entails being led by the Spirit (8:14) out of slavery and into full adoption as children of God (8:15). As God's children, we receive our inheritance as true heirs (8:17) when we are crowned with glory (8:17–18). This happens all because in the midst of our slavery we cried out, "Abba! Father!" (8:15). If what Paul says is true, what do you think he might be talking about? When did anything like that ever happen?

Of course, this language echoes the exodus from Egypt. When a Judean talks about being set free from slavery, the exodus is the memory being evoked. When a Judean says that we have not received a spirit of slavery to fall back into fear, the story of fearful Israel in the wilderness longing to return to Egypt resonates through these words. When a Judean talks about being led by the Spirit, a pillar of cloud by day and a pillar of fire by night is the unmistakable reference. When a Judean speaks of receiving a spirit of adoption, wherein their slave status is overturned through covenant promise, then the nation-constituting event of the exodus is undoubtedly ringing in the background. When a Judean refers to the Spirit bearing witness with our spirits that we are children of God, and if children, then heirs of God, their language of inheritance reaches back to Moses leading the children of God toward their inheritance. And when a Judean places all of this in the context of our crying out, "Abba! Father!," then it is impossible not to hear the Israelites "crying out" to God in the midst of Egyptian bondage, groaning under the weight of Egyptian brick quotas.[28]

If the problem is slavery, then the solution is exodus. And so Paul maps out, in evocative and liberating terms, a new exodus in Jesus Christ. The apostle takes the metaphor of exodus already echoed in the discussion of baptism in chapter 6 and deepens it considerably.

And just as Moses in the wilderness set before the people two paths—blessing and curse, life and death—so Paul insists that the same choice lies before us in Jesus Christ. To set the mind on the flesh, he writes, is death. To set the mind on the Spirit is life and peace (8:3–8; cf. Deut. 30:15–20). The homeless violence and self-serving of the flesh or the homecoming peace and hospitality of the Spirit—that is the choice.

How you imagine the world, Paul seems to be saying, depends on who has taken up deep residence in your life, who "dwells" in you. Whether you have a mind of flesh or of the Spirit, whether you want to remain in Egypt or take the risk of exodus, and whether you are comfortable in the empire or long to be set free depends on who or what is the most deeply animating force in your life. It depends on which story you want to be in. Paul again tells his listeners that their story is ultimately the story of the exodus.

What time is it? Is it the new golden age inaugurated through the reign of the benevolent Nero? Is it time to rejoice in the virtues of the empire? Is it time to make our peace with the hegemony of Rome? Is it the end of history?

No, says Paul. It is new exodus time. It is time to be set free and come home. It is time to put away the spirit of slavery that falls back into fear. It is time to get out of the empire of death and get the empire of death out of us. It is time to cry "Abba! Father!" and to hear the very Spirit of God pronounce us children of God, no longer slaves. We are the ones who will inherit the home of creation. We are not only welcomed home; this home was meant to be ours all along.

There is, however, a catch, says Paul. You see, if we are children, if we are heirs—heirs of God and joint heirs with Christ—then we will suffer before we

28. See Sylvia C. Keesmaat, *Paul and His Story: (Re)Interpreting the Exodus Tradition* (Sheffield: Sheffield Academic Press, 1999), 54–154.

enter into our glory (8:17). No one ever said that this was going to be easy. If we are heirs with Christ, if we are set free to follow Christ on this new exodus, if Christ has come to dwell in us, if with Christ homecoming in the kingdom of God is our inheritance, then we will walk the path of this Christ. We will leave the empire and embrace the kingdom. We will follow the one who set us free on a cross, and we will suffer with him at the hands of the very empire of death that put him on the cross and at the hands of every empire to follow. Only then will we share in the glory of a full and restored humanity.

This young Christian community in Rome will have to decide where they want to live. Will they live in an empire of slavery, hierarchy, violence, and oppression? Or will they live at the margins, subject to the ridicule and persecution of the empire? Will they be at home in the empire or will they embark on an exodus journey with Jesus, a path of suffering? You see, although there is suffering in this homecoming, that suffering is overshadowed by the restored glory, the restored fruitfulness, indeed nothing less than the restoration of all creation as the home it was always meant to be.

From the very beginning of the story, creation has been our home. So Paul evocatively tells us that all creation now waits, with bated breath, for our redemption, for our restored servanthood, for our homecoming. And not only the creation but the Spirit herself, Paul writes, is waiting, groaning, longing, interceding in hope of our homecoming. Waiting for when humans will be conformed anew to the image of God and take their place again as faithful homemakers. At that homecoming we will respond to our homemaking responsibility in obedience. Then will we be made just again, and our proper glory will be restored.

So who cares about the machinations of the empire? Who needs to worry about the persecutions of the empire? If we are welcomed home in Christ, then who can render us homeless? If Christ has died and risen and now sits at the right hand of God, then who can separate us from his love? No one and no thing! The home-murdering forces of the empire are impotent before the resurrection power of this hope. Nothing can separate us from the love of God; nothing can make us homeless again.

Nothing, that is, except ourselves. The empire has no power over us, but we can still render ourselves homeless. We can reject the promise. And this is Paul's deepest anguish. What the empire can do to his fellow Judeans is of little consequence. What his sisters and brothers are doing to themselves is another matter altogether.

The Tragedy of Self-Exclusion and the Faithfulness of God (Rom. 9:1–11:36)

The apostle now moves from powerfully confident anti-imperial pronouncements at the end of chapter 8 to a deep and unbearable sorrow at the beginning of chapter 9. His anguish is unceasing because Israel refuses to come home. This homecoming in Jesus that is received with joy throughout the world is the homecoming of the Messiah. This is the homecoming promised to Abraham that has been the covenantal hope from the beginning. And yet most of the apostle's Judean brothers and sisters reject this homecoming, and they remain in exile. This does not simply create a theological conundrum for the apostle but occasions "great sorrow and unceasing anguish" (9:2). He says, "They are Israelites, and to them belong the adoption, the glory, the covenants, the giving of the law, the worship, and the promise; to them belong the patriarchs, and from them, according to the flesh, comes the Messiah, who is over all, God blessed forever. Amen" (9:4–5).

This is their story, but now that it comes to a climax, they find themselves on the outside looking in. There is a double tragedy here. A people rendered homeless and exiled by the external forces of the empire now seem to render themselves homeless through a rejection of the very Messiah for whom they have been waiting for so long.

How do we make sense of this? How does it make sense when those who have not been looking for the salvation of Israel's God are stumbling into this homecoming, while those who have been eagerly longing and waiting for this salvation are stumbling over it? There is a cornerstone in Zion, the foundation stone for the kingdom of God, but some will trip over this stone (9:32–33). The very stone that is the foundation of this house has become a stumbling stone, barring the entrance of those to whom it was first promised.

When things don't turn out exactly as you thought they would, what do you do? You do what Paul has been doing throughout this letter. You retell the story in a way that attempts to make sense of things. Home is always storied. When home is broken, the story needs to be revisited. And the question that Paul brings to this retelling is how we put together Israel's unbelief with God's faithfulness. If this is a story about Israel and its faithful covenant God and yet Israel finds itself excluded at the climax of the story, then what is really going on here?

This isn't just an admittedly anguished theological problem for the apostle, however. He addresses this retelling of Israel's story to the church communities in Rome precisely to counteract the arrogance that gentile Roman Christians felt in comparison to Judeans that in fact mimics how the empire has always seen these troublesome people from Judea. So he continues to tell a narrative that undermines and disarms the dominant narrative of Rome itself. The apostle writes that this story all comes to a resolution in a Messiah "who is over all" (or better, who is "God over all, blessed forever"[29]). The rhetorical conflict with an ideology that enthroned Augustus as lord of the world could not be clearer.

So with an eye toward both Israel and Rome, Paul revisits the story, and again the issue is the justice of God. How will that justice be realized? And what does that justice look like? Paul says that because the chosen people are ignorant of the justice of God, unenlightened about the hospitable, healing, forgiving, generous, compassionate, and redeeming justice of God, they seek to establish a justice of their own (10:3). A "justice of their own." That has a familiar ring doesn't it? This is what empires always do. They seek justice of their own and on their own terms but not the justice of God. So perhaps Israel is starting to look like the empire once again.[30]

Paul then engages in a little rabbinic exegesis that will undoubtedly be alien to anyone who studies in a modern seminary. What was implicitly alluded to in the contrast between flesh and spirit in chapter 8 is now explicitly referenced in Paul's use of Deuteronomy 30 in Romans 10: this passage from Torah that anticipates exile and God's gracious provision of a return from exile is now interpreted, line by line, in terms of Christ.

Where is this righteousness? Where is this justice? Where is the hope of a return from exile, a fulfillment of our waiting and longing? Is it in heaven? Is it in the abyss (an interesting misquote from Deuteronomy, but we'll leave that for now)? No, we don't need to go to heaven (in order to bring Christ down, adds Paul) nor do we need to descend into the abyss (in order to bring Christ up from the dead, adds Paul), because this word—this testimony of fulfillment, this announcement of the advent of the kingdom and the end of our exile—"is near you, on your lips and in your heart" (10:8, quoting Deut. 30:14). It is so close that you can taste it, feel it, and know it so deeply that you can entrust your life to it. Why? Because, says Paul, the gospel has been proclaimed! The good news has been announced!

29. Wright, "Letter to the Romans," 624.

30. This has been a recurring temptation throughout Israel's history, perhaps most notably present with the establishment of the monarchy with "a king like the nations" who rules Israel and expands its boundaries just like its imperial neighbors. This is also the historical reality that underlies many of the passages from Isaiah that Paul quotes in Rom. 9–11. Israel has attempted to find security in alliances with other powers rather than trusting in the covenant God (Isa. 1:9; 8:14; 10:22; 11:10; 28:16; and 29:10—all referenced in Rom. 9–11). Paul also quotes from Isa. 45; 52–53; 59; and 65. On all of these see J. Ross Wagner, *Heralds of Good News: Isaiah and Paul in Concert in the Letter to the Romans* (Leiden: Brill, 2003).

All it takes to taste this kingdom, to be released from exile, is to confess with your lips and believe in your heart the word that is near you—that Jesus is Lord. Confess this, believe in your heart that Jesus has been raised from the dead, and salvation is yours.

But there's the kicker. To embrace this kingdom, to embrace this Messiah, is to reinterpret the story of Israel as pointing to Jesus. He is that word that is so near that Moses speaks of. To embrace this Messiah is to embrace his story of death and resurrection as the fulfillment of the story of Israel, as the hope that all Israel has been waiting to see revealed. And that isn't very easy to do. Sometimes you can miss the fulfillment of the promises by insisting that it must come on your terms. And then, of course, there is the difficulty of this public profession that Paul talks about. Believe in your heart and profess with your lips that Jesus is Lord. In Rome, whether you are a Judean or a gentile, such a confession could cost you your life. You see, everyone knows that Caesar is Lord. But for a Judean to confess Jesus not only as Messiah but also as the messianic Lord puts that person in a difficult position both with Judeans and with the imperial authorities. It is much easier to proclaim that Caesar is Lord, to meet the empire on its own terms.[31]

So while it is not surprising that very few Judeans had accepted Messiah Jesus, it still broke the apostle's heart, as it broke the heart of Isaiah before him. You see, in the midst of exile Isaiah says, "How beautiful are the feet of those who bring good news!" (Isa. 52:7; cf. Rom. 10:15)—that is, how redemptively beautiful are gospel pronouncements of homecoming in the face of the empire. Yet the same Isaiah laments, "Who has believed our message?" (Isa. 53:1; cf. Rom 10:16).

Paul shares that lament. Paul is still waiting for the fulfillment of the promises to Israel. Indeed, earlier he said that all creation was waiting, all creation was longing for the coming of the messianic kingdom. And now he elicits the voice of all creation in the proclaiming of the gospel. Citing Psalm 19, he says that a voice has gone out to all the earth, words have gone to the end of the world—and this is the voice, these are the words of all creation bearing witness to the one who comes, the one whom the stones on the side of the road would proclaim as the king of Israel, the redeemer of all creation (10:18–19). The very creation that was called to bear witness against the idolatry of the empire in 1:18–23 now

31. Neil Elliott suggests that the attempt of Judeans in Alexandria to put their trust in Roman citizenship lies behind this passage. These Judeans tried to make their peace and find their place in the empire—precisely the opposite of Paul's approach to the empire. Elliott, *Arrogance of Nations*, 93–96, 117–18.

bears witness against Israel's refusal to hear the good news of homecoming in Christ. And if the people of Israel won't listen to creation, then they likely won't listen to Moses either. It was Moses who said that God would respond to Israel's idolatry by making the people jealous and angry by showering his blessing on a nation that did not seek him (10:19, quoting Deut. 32:21). Well, that's exactly what's happening under Paul's gospel. Nations that did not seek him are recipients of exile-ending good news. Then, as if to rub the salt in the wound (his own wound!), Paul references Isaiah again. God will be found by people who did not seek him and will reveal himself to a people who did not ask for him (Rom. 10:20, quoting Isa. 65:1).

So what is God up to? Has God said, "Your waiting is over, and if you can't see that I have come in Jesus to fulfill the promises, then you can continue to wait as long as you want, but your waiting will be in vain"? Does he say that waiting is over because fulfillment has arrived? No, God says, with a lamenting voice of his own, "All day long I have held out my hands to a disobedient and contrary people" (Rom. 10:21, quoting Isa. 65:2). All day long, indeed for ages upon ages, God has held out God's hands—hands of healing, hands of forgiveness, hands that will lead the exiles home. And God's hands are still held out. God's hands are still reaching out—bloody hands, nail-pierced hands. Is the wait over? No. God is still waiting. This is God's justice. This is God's covenantal faithfulness.

The exile is over, the return has been announced, and all creation echoes with the good news. And grace remains even in the face of rejection of the Messiah. If we might reach back and expand a gospel parable to help us catch what Paul is saying here, the prodigal has returned, and he has brought his pagan friends with him. The homecoming party has begun, and the elder brother remains outside. Indeed, the homecoming party has begun, and all the prodigal's pagan friends have been adopted into the father's household, grafted into the covenant community (11:17–21). So what will happen to the elder brother? What will happen to the one who refuses to join the party? What will happen if he refuses to come home?

The generosity and love of the father is constant. This is a God of covenantal faithfulness, a God of covenantal justice. And that justice extends to the elder brother. That welcoming justice, those open hands, are still extended to him. He is still part of the household. While he may be an enemy of the gospel (11:28), an enemy of the homecoming good news, the promise-keeping father's house is still his home. This is still Israel's story, and they remain beloved. God's gift and promise of homecoming is irrevocable (11:29). This is a home of mercy to all (11:32), even enemies (5:10; 12:20), and the doors are never shut.

Can we ever get our heads around all of this? Of course not. The wisdom of God is too rich for us. The knowledge of God is beyond us. All that is left for us is to offer our worship and praise (11:33–36).

Worship, Community, and Hospitality (Rom. 12:1–21)

The apostle then moves from the doxology of 11:33–36 to the "therefore" of Romans 12:1: "I appeal to you therefore, brothers and sisters, by the mercies of God, to present your bodies as a living sacrifice, holy and acceptable to God, which is your spiritual worship."

Therefore. If it is true that we are all home wreckers and that our home-breaking idolatry and infidelity are met by the home-restoring faithfulness of Jesus Christ; if it is true that the dominion of death is overthrown by the dominion of life; if it is true that while home-wrecking sin still dwells in us, the Holy Spirit has also taken up residence in our lives; if it is true that the mercy of God extends to all people and to all creation; if all of this is true, says the apostle, then he is bold enough to call his Roman Christian listeners to offer up their bodies, their whole lives as a living sacrifice in the renewed house of God.

So then, Paul appeals, in response to the creation-restoring mercy of God and the homecoming power of Jesus Christ, offer up your embodied lives as a body of believers, alternative to the body politic of the empire. Only such radical sacrifice and devotion can be considered true worship. No longer held captive by the home-destroying imagination of empire, allow your imagination to be transformed by the renewing of your minds, by seeing the path of homecoming in the midst of homelessness. Only when you have minds renewed for homecoming will you be people of discernment. Then you will see the world through the tear-filled eyes of the Creator. Then you will share God's anguish and partake of God's hope.

In Romans 12 we have the charter of the homecoming community. Here is what home looks like if it is to be faithful to the story of Israel culminating in Jesus the Messiah. Story shapes character. So if this story of God's covenantal faithfulness and justice is the story that is now foundational to this community's life, then what is the character of that life? What does it look like inside the home that is the church in Rome?

Just as we have seen that home is not an accomplishment but a gift, so also does Paul root this homemaking community in gift. But note that these gifts, different from the empire, are received in grace: "By the grace given to me I say . . ." (12:3). In the imperial household, gifts were tied to socioeconomic status and biology. For example, if you were a man, you would have the gift of rationality, and if you were a male child, you would develop this gift. If you were a woman, you could have the gift of rationality, but without authority. A slave, however, would never have this gift.[32] And this would be the case with most gifts of leadership. Within the structure of the paterfamilias, it would only be natural that such gifts would be discerned in the ruling males of the household.

Paul, however, calls for sober judgment on these matters. Don't "think of yourself more highly than you ought to think," but "think with sober judgment, each according to the measure of faith that God has assigned" (12:3). The arrogance and superiority of the imperial household is inappropriate to a community rooted in the alternative narrative of Jesus. Your place, Paul says, is established not by the terms of the empire but by the gifts of God manifest in the faithfulness of the community.

And just as the empire is a body (*sōma*), indeed a body politic, so also is the church a body (12:4–5). Paul's description of the church in Romans and elsewhere as the body of Christ is deliberately provocative. Bodies have members, and it is the cooperative functioning of the diverse members that make the body whole. In the empire these members consist of a stratified system of slaves, migrants, homeless people, tradespeople, farmers, soldiers, priests who are part of the aristocratic ruling classes, the imperial household, and the emperor as the head of the body. The body Paul speaks of consists of people exercising a diversity of gifts that are profoundly different from the structure of the empire. This is a body of people who exercise the gifts of prophecy, ministry, teaching, exhortation (or encouragement), generous giving, leading, and compassion (12:6–8). Who would have ever thought of things like ministry, encouragement, generosity, and compassion being at the heart of any body politic? Moreover, given the narrative that is the foundation of all this, the very shape of the prophetic, teaching, and leading gifts would have been directed to forming a community of ministry, encouragement, generosity, and compassion. And if we look ahead to the greetings in chapter 16, it also becomes clear that this is a body in which these gifts are celebrated and exercised across gender and class boundaries.

Paul then describes the kind of community that the exercise of these gifts will produce. Understanding your rightful place and your unique gifts in the shaping of this redemptive home, you should shape your communal life by the kind of love that is the heart of any covenantal home (12:9). If this is a story of

32. Aristotle, *Politics* 1.1260a.

homecoming, then be a people of hospitable homemaking. Such a home cannot be built on the feigned love you see in the imperial world of patronage, where clients and lower members of the household offer service and devotion to the patron in hope of favors down the line. No, says Paul, let love be genuine; let it be a matter of deep mutual affection, not the fake love of the lower toward the higher (12:10). Indeed, the apostle makes his point very explicit, saying that in an empire that honors only the elite, Christians are called to outdo one another in showing honor to all. Don't court favor with the powerful, but "make your way with the oppressed" (12:16 our translation).[33] As a community of compassion, rejoice with those who rejoice and weep with those who weep (12:15). In an empire of rich and poor, Paul calls for a community whose way of life is shaped by economic generosity (12:13).

This is the charter for the church in both its internal relationships and to the broader community in which it finds itself. In a culture of fear and self-enclosed protection, extend hospitality to strangers (12:13). Bless those who would persecute you and render you homeless (12:14). If those who would destroy your homes are hungry, then feed them (12:20). This is the home of God, so don't be overcome by evil, but overcome evil with good (12:21). "So far as it depends on you, live peaceably with all" (12:18). You live in a city that proclaims the *Pax Romana* and yet is built on violence and persecution. Do not be taken up in the deathly way of repaying evil with evil (12:17). That is only a path of violent homelessness. Rather, be a household that demonstrates to Rome a peace that passes all understanding.

We can hear echoing through this household charter Jeremiah's counsel to the exiles in Babylon: "Seek the peace of the city" (Jer. 29:7 our translation), even as it threatens you and seeks to strip you and your neighbors of such peace.[34]

Be Careful with the Domicidal State (Rom. 13:1–14)

An astonishing thing about the traditional reading of Romans 13 is not only that it is divorced from the prophetic traditions of Israel and disconnected from everything that we know about Jesus in the Gospels but also that it fails to take seriously the context of Romans 13 in relation to Romans 12 or to the whole of the epistle.

Paul has been writing a letter to a community at the very heart of the empire, and from the beginning it has been clear that he is proclaiming a counter-imperial

33. "Making one's way with the oppressed" catches the meaning of 12:16 better than "associate with the lowly." See Elliott, *Arrogance of Nations*, 152.

34. We will discuss Rom. 12 at more length in chaps. 6 and 8.

gospel. He is striving to engender an alternative imagination that will shape a new and liberating household of faith at the center of the empire.

At this point in hearing the letter, members of the community might well be asking, "If we are not conformed to this age, to the rulers and authorities that are the cause of our persecution, then how do we relate to these authorities in the present, before the full dawning of the day of our Lord's coming?" How does the household of Jesus relate to the household that is subject to a "Lord Caesar" who is the embodied opposite of the Lord Christ?

Could Paul possibly be counseling the community to be part of the household of Caesar? Could he possibly be dividing the legitimate lordship in this community's life between Christ and the emperor? In light of all that has gone on in the previous twelve chapters, this seems highly unlikely.

In a city where Caesar was made head of the household by the gods, Paul is clear: the household belongs to God, and any authority that Caesar might have is from the God whose Son is the true Lord (13:1). It just so happens that even with that designated authority, Caesar managed only to create a household of judgment, terror, fear, wrath, and the sword (13:2–4). This is quite the contrast with the household of welcome, generosity, solidarity, and forgiveness that Paul has just described in chapter 12. The body that is the church is a radical alternative to the body politic that is the empire. So, Paul counsels, because this Roman body politic is rooted in violence and the sword, don't neglect to offer fear and honor where they are prudent and necessary, recognizing all along that you belong to the household of another Lord, Jesus Christ. Be careful around the state, remembering that in the end you are called to offer what God has offered you—to love one another—even to those who are in the violent Roman household. For this is how the story is fulfilled.

Then, as if to make his point painfully clear to anyone who hadn't caught the earlier irony, Paul cites the injunctions against murder, adultery, stealing, and coveting, in the face of an imperial household that is based on precisely such sins. Nero's household was, after all, established by the murder of Claudius. Nero's bedroom was a playground in which he would copulate with whomever he liked. Nero's economy was based on the pillaging of lands and their populations far and near. And Nero's empire was filled with insatiable greed.[35] If Paul is calling forth a new kind of household, rooted in Jesus, then the contrast with the household

35. Elliott remarks, "The instructions of Nero to a newly appointed governor around the time Romans was written: 'You know my needs. See to it that no one is left with anything.'" Elliott, *Arrogance of Nations*, 43.

of the emperor couldn't be clearer. Another law, the law of love, rooted in Israel and deepened in Jesus, trumps and passes judgment on Roman law.

And in case anyone hasn't quite caught on to the dismissal of the imperial order yet, the apostle pushes it all further with a comment about what time it is. "Besides this, you know what time it is." You know that "the night is far gone, the day is near" (13:11–12). Contrary to public opinion generated by the imperial household, you know that this is an age of darkness, not light, and that this is an empire that is stuck in the night. You know that time is up for this imperial house of cards. A "home" rooted in deceit and violence, in sexual predation and greed, is no home at all. So lay aside the practices of darkness. Abandon this imperial facade of a home, together with its debauchery and petty jealousies, and live in the day, clothed in Christ.

Be discerning in your homemaking life together, Paul is saying. We make home in the shadow of empire. We make home in the dark. But remember this: "The night is far gone, the day is near." So live in the light, live in the day of homecoming, even as the home-destroying darkness persists.[36]

Getting Personal in Community Life (Rom. 14:1–15:13)

Do you want to know what it means to live in light of homecoming and not in the darkness of the empire? "Welcome in faithfulness those who are weak" (14:1, our translation). "Welcome one another . . . as Christ has welcomed you" (15:7). This is a community of radical hospitality, radical welcome. Therefore, you "must not pass judgment," Paul says (14:3). "Who are you to pass judgment?" (14:4). "Why do you pass judgment?" (14:10). We are all "accountable to God" (14:12). "Let us therefore no longer pass judgment on one another" (14:13). Welcome precludes judgment in this household, and Paul has taken great pains to find a way to embrace a diversity of faithful expressions of gospel life. Because "the kingdom of God is not food and drink but justice and peace and joy in the Holy Spirit" (14:17 NRSV alt.), this community must "pursue what makes for peace and for mutual upbuilding" (14:19). This is a community that is committed to "the good purpose of building up the neighbor" (15:2) and seeks to "live in harmony with one another, in accordance with Christ Jesus, so that together you may with one voice glorify the God and Father of our Lord Jesus Christ" (15:5–6).

Peace, harmony, welcome. We do not live in a home that practices exclusionary judgment toward others; rather, we seek to shape a home in which all are

36. We discuss Rom. 13 in chaps. 6 and 8.

welcomed. So welcome in faithfulness those who are weak. And for heaven's sake, don't place a stumbling block before anyone who has already found a way to not stumble over Jesus.

However, Paul does not offer this counsel of inclusion in service of any naive pluralism or out of a simple desire that everyone will get along. No, this is fundamentally a matter of lordship. Paul says, "We do not live to ourselves, and we do not die to ourselves. If we live, we live to the Lord, and if we die, we die to the Lord; so then, whether we live or whether we die, we are the Lord's. For to this end Christ died and lived again, so that he might be Lord of both the dead and the living" (14:7–9). Our friend Rachel Tulloch has wisely argued that for Paul "unity is found not in *agreement* of all particulars, but in the *direction* of our actions and convictions. To whom do we eat or not eat? To whom do we celebrate or not celebrate? More crucially, to whom do we live or die? To whom do we belong?"[37] The question is, Who is your Lord and what does it mean to live in community, to make home together, under that lordship?

In this home there is a profound and deep commitment to including those with whom we have serious disagreements. Tulloch expands:

> There is a dying involved here. It is fascinating how Paul moves so quickly from a discussion of church disagreements to talking about living and dying for the Lord. Because a community of welcome is also a community of the cross. That's why it matters so much who our master is. We have to give of ourselves in order to welcome others. Embracing even those I am fully convinced are wrong on some things is just an extension of the embrace of the One who gave himself for those who rejected him. He is the one whom we live and die for and the one to whom we all have to answer.

The house of Lord Jesus is a stark contrast to the house of Lord Nero. The Roman Christians—Judean and gentile alike—need to decide in whose house they will make their home.[38]

Home: Rome to Jerusalem and on to Spain (Rom. 15:14–16:27)

That is why Paul has written to these sisters and brothers in Rome. He has written so that in the midst of the tensions in their city, and in the midst of a culture of

37. Quotations here and below are from a sermon preached at Wine Before Breakfast, University of Toronto, February 27, 2007.

38. We will explore Rom. 14 and 15 in more detail in chap. 7.

exclusion—with its systems of status and honor, shame and persecution—they will be a home of welcome. If the good news is that the faithfulness of Jesus Christ has opened the door to the home we have always longed for, then Christians are called to be a community of hospitality and homemaking. In this community, Paul proclaims throughout this letter, siblings are coming home, in the resurrection dawn of the new creation.

This homecoming is happening everywhere. Believers in Achaia and Macedonia have sent the apostle with gifts for the poor among the saints in Jerusalem. Paul longs to go to Spain to proclaim the good news because even those "barbarians" are welcomed home. In fact, Paul looks for assistance in welcoming the barbarians from people who are at the center of the empire.

The epistle ends with an extensive list of greetings to many people in the community. The breadth of Paul's homecoming vision is matched by the expansive generosity of his greetings. Male and female, powerful and powerless, slave and free, elite and the lowest of the low are all greeted and welcomed home in Jesus. In a community in which there is tension between Judean and gentile, he conveys greetings to all. And he also appears to be calling Jesus followers from the various communities listed to likewise greet one another. Those close to the imperial household and those far from the corridors of power, those who have high status in the empire and those who are dismissed as shameful—all are called to mutual acknowledgment and greeting that breaks down these imposed divisions. Embrace those who the empire has excluded, Paul says, and honor those whom the social hierarchy despises. And it goes both ways. In the household of Jesus all are welcome; even those who have been oppressors are now welcomed as sisters and brothers.

Moreover, mutuality within this new body politic, this body of Christ, is a decidedly bodily welcome. "Greet one another with a holy kiss" (16:16). Not the lewd and aggressive kiss of a master raping his slave. No, this is a holy kiss that the apostle enjoins the community to share with one another. This is a kiss of embrace in one family. This is a kiss between sisters and brothers, breaking down the racial, political, gender, and economic boundaries of the empire. This is the loving and respectful kiss that characterizes the family of Jesus, in contrast to the imperial family of father Caesar.

If Paul's goal has indeed been to foster a new sense of home rooted in Jesus, then it isn't surprising that he moves to some of his strongest language in the whole letter right at the end. After calling his addressees to be an embracing, welcoming community, he then tells all who are listening to keep an eye on those who will cause dissent and offense, opposing the gospel that Paul has expounded in this letter (16:17). If we are the family of God, if we are in the household of God, if in Jesus Christ we have come home to God, to ourselves, to all of creation, and to each other, then beware of those who would create divisions in that household. Be careful around those who would re-inscribe oppressive boundaries, rebuild walls of division, and reconstitute the excluding categories of the empire.

And, counter-imperial to the end, the apostle delivers a final disarming blow against the empire. Knowing full well that what Rome calls peace is in fact oppression, and having undoubtedly seen the *Pax Romana* symbolized on imperial coins by a Roman boot on a captive's head, Paul offers his most abrasive and explicit denunciation of the empire. "The God of peace will shortly crush Satan under your feet" (16:20). The God of peace—the one who breaks down these walls of division, these categories of honor and shame, these structures of power and hierarchy—overthrows the *Pax Romana*. Instead of Roman boots on the heads of those whom the empire has conquered, Paul dares to imagine the tables totally turned. The Satan, that real force of violent power that is at the heart of the empire, is now crushed, proclaims the apostle, under the feet of those who have believed in and pledged their allegiance to another Lord. Just as Paul will bring grave warnings at the end of his letter about those who would tear asunder the household of God, so also will he pronounce apocalyptic judgment on that force of home-breaking that has plagued the biblical story from the beginning.

Now to the homemaking and home-redeeming God, the only wise God, through Jesus Christ, be the glory forever. Amen.

5

Creation and the Defilement of Home

A Lament for the Land[1]

When did you first notice?
When did you realize that delight
had turned to grief?
When did it become painful
to merely open your eyes and see
    the land,
    the rivers,
    the marshes?
Do you remember the moment
that joy turned to mourning?

Was it when you led your grandchildren
to the traditional sites and there were
    no blueberries,
    no herons,
    no hawks
    to be seen?

1. This section of the chapter was first presented by Sylvia Keesmaat as a keynote address on October 2, 2015, at the Rooted and Grounded Conference hosted by Anabaptist Mennonite Biblical Seminary in Elkhart, Indiana.

Was it when you went to catch frogs with your niece,
and they were deformed?
Was it when your grandson went out on the ice
to hunt on the ancient trails
and the ice, too thin, let him fall?
Was it when you drove past
the field and woods
where you saw your first rabbit,
but now there were streets named
after the birds that used to live there:
  bobolink,
  meadowlark,
  oriole?

Was it the spring your apple trees blossomed
but there were no bees to pollinate the fruit?
Was it the day you realized that the river
was a valley of dry rocks, dry plants, dry bones?

Was it the morning you watched the oil
seep up through the ground,
  into the muskeg,
  into the water,
  into the fish,
  your food,
  your children's blood?

Was it the day you looked up
and saw the sands piled on the horizon,
while the trucks drove deeper and deeper
into the tar-soaked earth?

Was it the day your mother,
your child,
your neighbor,
your sister,
your nephew
was diagnosed?

Was it the summer you realized that the sandhill cranes
no longer nested in the marsh,
or that the Karner blue butterfly no longer visited your garden?

Or the year you found only one monarch caterpillar in your
  milkweed?
Only one.

When you first noticed,
did you weep?
Did you open your mouth in lament?

Lament was the response of the prophets
to the devastation of their land.
Lament was the response of Jesus
to the suffering of his land.
Lament was the response of Paul
to the mourning of the earth.

Paul. Yes, Paul.
Paul the apostle.

Just think about Paul and his travels,
his journeys on the straight stone roads of the empire,
walking, walking.

Each road itself a carefully constructed environmental disaster,
forty feet wide, twelve feet of foundation,
  eating up land,
  cutting off streams,
  felling forests,
  creating erosion.[2]

Roads constructed for the movement of soldiers,
to enable the rape of the land.
Roads for the intensive agriculture and mining that
turned Italy and Greece into dry, arid landscapes.

Paul walked through the bare landscapes,
trees gone, earth blowing in the wind.
The trees taken to shore up the mine shafts,
trees taken for the fires to heat Roman baths,
Roman cooking fires,
Roman kilns for bricks for pottery and smelting.
Paul walked through Rome's first provinces,

2. J. Donald Hughes, *Environmental Problems of the Greeks and Romans: Ecology in the Ancient Mediterranean*, 2nd ed. (Baltimore: Johns Hopkins University Press, 2014), 180.

the first to be denuded and then abandoned
as Rome marched northward, cutting, stripping, raping as it went.

Paul had seen it before his travels, of course.
In Judea, the land of his ancestors,
he had seen the Roman destruction of villages,
the Roman annexation of the fertile land,
the cash crops on what had been family farms,
the movement of troops through the countryside,
their animals grazing on the crops of the people.

Seeing the victims of empire then,
Paul would not be surprised by the same victimization now.
Occupation then, like now, means water diverted for the cities,
peasants prevented from farming.
The hopeless hunger of the Galilean peasant then
mirrors the Palestinian farmer now.
The forced migration of Judeans then
repeated in the dislocation of Indigenous peoples now.
The dry-mouthed despair of the Judean desert then
and the West Bank now.
All casualties of empire.

No doubt Paul had also heard the hollow promises,
as we have heard them:
the promises of imperial abundance.
He had heard the poetry celebrating imperial fertility and fruitfulness,
and he saw the images of Augustus with Gaia and her cornucopia,
and Roma with her fertile breasts.

It was nothing he hadn't heard before.
Deep in his tradition,
in the Scriptures,
in the prophets,
he had heard the promises of idolatry to provide fertility.
Baal, the god of Canaan,
Nebo and Marduk, the gods of the Babylonians,
and now the gods of Rome.
The gods of empire always promise abundance
while they suck the earth dry,
grind down the heads of the poor,
and destroy the inheritance of the meek.

Paul had heard it all before.
And that is why he writes a lament
to those who live at the heart of empire:
to the followers of Jesus who live in Rome,
those who were slaves,
and ex-slaves.
Those who had migrated to Rome when they lost their land,
and those who had been captured and bought and sold and bought again.
Those who had no place to lay their heads,
and those who slept in a corner in their master's kitchen.
Those who could call themselves citizens,
and those who were not considered human.
Those who suffered oppression, famine, and sword,
who hungered and thirsted for bread and water,
who had no coat on a winter's night,
who suffered violence at the hands of the state,
and at the hands of the powerful;
those who couldn't breathe,
who had not yet been shot with their hands up,
or died in police custody.

All these, to whom Paul wrote,
knew about land loss,
either their own or their forebears.

They knew that the promises of abundance
didn't apply to the poor,
the hungry,
the sexually desirable boy slaves,
the sexually useful female slaves,
the bath stokers,
and stoneworkers,
weavers,
dyers,
shipyard workers,
grain handlers,
leather tanners,
garbage movers,
laborers in the mines,
fieldworkers,

migrants,
homeless.

No abundance for them.
No meat in their bellies.
No water for their thirst.
No safety for their bodies.
No justice for their cries.
No wonder that Paul
wrote to them with a profound
sense of lament.

Yes, lament.
Lament is where Paul goes,
as soon as he has proclaimed the good news of the gospel,
the saving power of the gospel by which God rights injustice.

Paul declares God's astounding good news
for justice in Romans 1:16–17,
and then moves into lament.
Prophetic lament,
a lament for the earth,
for the violence of idolatry,
and for the economic abuse
of the empire.

It is no surprise, really.
After quoting Habakkuk's
astounding confession of faith,
"the just shall live by faith,"[3]
Paul really had nowhere else to go.
After all, lament was the context for Habakkuk's confession too.

It is always in the midst of lament that the prophets confess their audacious hope.
Against all the evidence
they proclaim that God will save,
that God will make all things right,
that the creator God *will* restore the earth and those in it.

Maybe all of that was in Paul's mind as he quoted Habakkuk.
Maybe he remembered the stories of his people.

3. Hab. 2:4 our translation.

Maybe he remembered how the prophet condemned the arrogant
with their treacherous wealth,
those who, in their greed, never have enough,
so that they even collected people as their slaves.[4]
Maybe he remembered how Habakkuk graphically described
the greedy hoarding of the debt holders,
who keep the poor on the hook with insupportable debt,
who murder people and commit violence to the earth.[5]
Those who build habitations of injustice,
homes of exclusion.
Creation bears witness against them,
they are without excuse.
The stones cry out in judgment
and wooden beams join the chorus.[6]
Why do they cry?
  "Because of human bloodshed,
  and violence to the earth,
  to cities and all who live in them."
And the prophet says it twice.[7]

Paul knew these prophetic words.
He had seen such cities.
He knew such violence.
Greed, shame, profanity against the earth,
it's all there in the oracle of the prophet,
and it is all echoed in the apostle's letter.[8]

And Paul knew that Habakkuk's confession
"the just shall live by faith"
was embedded in a contrast with the proud and the greedy,
was offered as the alternative to the spirituality of empire.

4. Hab. 2:5.
5. Hab. 2:6–8, 17.
6. Hab. 2:9–11.
7. Hab. 2:8, repeated in 2:17.
8. "Between these two identical verses in Hab. 2:8 and 2:17 there is a movement between greed (Hab. 2:9; cf. Rom. 1:29), shame (Hab. 2:10; cf. Rom. 1:16), and the profanation (Hab. 2:8, 17; cf. Rom. 1:18) of not only the earth in general but also of a specific piece of land (Lebanon), and the destruction of the animals (Hab. 2:8, 17). The verbal echoes with shame, greed, and profanity (usually translated *ungodliness* in Rom. 1:18) in Rom. 1 are striking." Sylvia Keesmaat, "Land, Idolatry, and Justice in Romans," in *Conception, Reception, and the Spirit: Essays in Honor of Andrew T. Lincoln*, ed. J. Gordon McConville and Lloyd J. Pietersen (Eugene, OR: Cascade Books, 2015), 93.

Habakkuk's astounding affirmation, against all the evidence,
that there is life for the just,
occurred in a context of bloody, idolatrous economic exploitation
with deadly consequences for the land and those who lived in it.

This is, of course, the language of idolatry.
Idolatry is what makes the stones cry out
and the wooden beams answer.
Idolatry is what makes the earth
lose its reverence.
Idolatry is where Paul moves next
in Romans.

Ever since the creation of the world,
says Paul,
ever since that first creative word,
    the "let there be,"
ever since God planted the forest garden for the earth-creatures,
    the trees for beauty,
    for food,
    and for seed,
and entrusted us with serving
and observing the growing things
that bind us to life,
ever since the spirit of God was breathed into our lungs
    as God knelt there in the earth,
ever since then, we have known about God
by the things God has made.
The creation itself is not mute, but eloquent.
The creation tells us about God.

Did Paul know, when he wrote this,
that so many things God had made
could no longer speak?
Did Paul know that idolatry renders creation mute
by destroying the creatures?
Did Paul know about the extinction of whole species?
Probably not.

But we do.
And so we need to ask ourselves:
    What profound knowledge have we lost
    because we no longer see the five-lined skink or the king rail?

What does the delicate dance of the woodcock tell us about God?
    Or the candy-striped leafhopper?
    Or the loggerhead shrike?
What did you learn about God when you saw your first barn owl,
    your first massasauga rattler,
    your first lady's slipper orchid
    under the cedars, surrounded by deer flies?
Even though Rome caused extinctions
in North Africa, Europe, Greece, and Iran,[9]
it is hard to imagine that Paul knew that voices in the choir
of creation's praise of God
had been silenced forever.[10]

But *we* know.
We know that there are things we can never know about God,
because we have silenced creation.
We know that the psalmist's words about creation's praise
no longer describe our reality.
We know that the songs of praise are now groans of longing.
And, as we shall see, Paul knew about those groans too.

Paul may not have known of extinction,
but he did know that idolatry leads to futility,
    unfruitfulness,
    impotence.
Paul knew that exchanging our glory for idols,
refusing to be faithful image bearers,
and giving that power to other images
    leads to violence,
    to land loss,
    to mourning.
So it had been again and again in Israel's story that Paul echoes.

9. Hughes describes at some length these extinctions, attributing them to the games, hunting, war, trade in exotics, and habitat destruction. He sums up in this way: "The Romans were persistent, efficient, could pay well, and came to dominate the commerce in animals and animal products throughout the Mediterranean basin, so the major responsibility for extinctions was theirs." Hughes, *Environmental Problems*, 104.

10. Hughes indicates, however, that there were concerns about declining animal populations at this time. Cicero, when he governed Cilicia, refused to make his provincials collect leopards, because of their scarcity, and various African rulers enacted conservation laws in order to preserve animals from the Roman games. Hughes, *Environmental Problems*, 98–99.

Didn't Psalm 106 tell the story of how
the people in the wilderness exchanged their glory
for the image of an ox?[11]
Didn't the psalmist recount how in their idolatry
they forgot their God
and despised the arable land
into which God led them?[12]
And didn't that story find the people
sacrificing their children to the fertility idols
so that the land was polluted with blood?[13]
We know this story too, don't we?
Settlers conquering a land in the name of the gods of empire,
  placing their trust in gods of profit and affluence.
Didn't the colonizers despise the land,
  plowing up the fertile prairie,
  destroying the buffalo,
  cutting down the forests
  that were food, medicine, shelter, and clothing
  for the Wendat, Anishnaabeg, Mississauga, Haudenosaunee.
What else can we call the stripping of children from their families,
  the agenda of genocide,
  except child sacrifice before bloodthirsty gods?
They polluted the land with blood, says the psalmist.
Polluted with blood, indeed.

Don't we also hear Jeremiah's lament echoing through Paul's
  language?
Israel had exchanged their glory
  for that which did not profit,
  for futility,
  for impotence,
so that the fruit of the good land was defiled.[14]

And surely Paul knew Hosea's cry of the heartbreak of the land,
  its mourning,
  keening over the violence
  to which it had been subjected.

11. Ps. 106:19–20, echoed in Rom. 1:23.
12. Ps. 106:24.
13. Ps. 106:37–39.
14. Jer. 2:7–11, echoed in Rom. 1:23.

With the prophet, the apostle knew
that murder, adultery, and stealing
will always lead to death for the creatures of the land:
    the wild animals,
    the birds of the air,
    even the fish of the sea are perishing.[15]
When the people exchange their glory, continues Hosea,
they exchange it for shame.[16]

We know those parts of the story too,
don't we?
The fertile land sacrificed for so-called profits,
for oil, for gas, that bring profitless death, not life.
We know the mourning of the land,
    the oil-covered birds in the Gulf of Mexico
    or the tailings ponds of Alberta;
    the fish stocks collapsed,
    the salmon attempting their futile journeys up dammed rivers;
    the shame that we wear in the Roundup Ready
    cornfields and soy fields of our lands.[17]

And we know, like Paul, where the stories of empire go.
Hosea knows, Paul knows, and we know
that idolatry always leads to sexual and economic violence.
Exchanging glory for shame, declares the prophet,
leaves us with a consumptive insatiability
that results in a sterility,
a loss of fruitfulness,
in every dimension of our lives,
not least, our economic and sexual lives.[18]

There is no separating these things.
We cannot speak of violence to the land,
    or violence to the earth,

15. Hosea 4:2–3.

16. Hosea 4:7 is clearly alluded to in Rom. 1:23.

17. Roundup Ready seeds have been genetically modified to resist the killing effects of the herbicide Roundup. An initial application of Roundup ensures that fields have no living vegetation before seeds are sown, and partway through the season a second application ensures that no vegetation besides the crop can live. These are fields of death for plants and for the birds, butterflies, bees, and insects that depend on diversity for food and habitat.

18. Hosea 4:7, 10, 14.

apart from violence toward
  the bodies of the poor,
  the bodies of women,
  the bodies of refugees.
If we have exchanged our glory,
if we don't realize that we are image bearers of the Creator,
  that our glory is in our care and love
  for one another and for all creation,
then violence becomes inevitable and legitimate.

In a context of imperial violence,
where the imperial house modeled an abusive sexuality
toward slaves, young boys, and women,
where such abuse was practiced all the way down the domination system,
Paul is condemning the abusive use of slave boys by their masters,
of women forced into prostitution for the goddess religions,
of the imperial sexual violence at the top.

The rape of the land and the rape of the vulnerable are always linked,
  from the socioeconomic structure of ancient Rome
  to the residential schools,
  from the practices of war
  to the life of the most vulnerable in our own time.
Imperial idolatry always, always, always
stokes the fires of abuse against land, women, children, and the poor.

And such sexual violence goes hand in hand
with economic violence, according to Paul.
Those who get in bed with idols are filled
with every kind of injustice.

So Paul names the economic sins that a violent heart permits:
  greed, malice, envy, bullying, whispering rumors, murder.
He calls out the attitudes that go with such economic violence:
  craftiness, insolence, haughtiness, boastfulness.
Deformed by their own idolatry, such people
  are inventors of evil, foolish, faithless, heartless, ruthless (1:29–31).

If you get in bed with idols, you're gonna get raped,
  and you will become a rapist of one sort or another.

In biblical faith, such economic sins are always linked to the land:
  who has access to land,
  who is able to foreclose on land,
  who can bribe the judge to strip someone of their land,
  who has access to food and resources from the land.
Idolatry permeates it all: land, sexuality, economics.

And us? Are we willing to confess our idolatry?
As we lament the rivers turned into valleys of dried bones,
and the pollution of our watersheds;
as we watch the topsoil running off our fields,
bees dying,
oil seeping, seeping, seeping
into the heart of life itself,
are we willing to name the idolatry,
are we willing to repent of the idolatry that brought us here?

A renewed sense of "creation care" simply isn't enough.
We can do our organic farming,
plant more pollinators,
attend the farmers market,
and join community-shared agriculture programs.
We can oppose pipelines
and march for climate and jobs
all we want.

But Paul is telling us that the problem is deeper than
a lack of concern for creation.
When the apostle laments
our covetousness, insolence, and ruthlessness
  —and mark well, these are ecologically disastrous vices—
he is talking to our hearts,
about the way that we bind ourselves to betray,
about our constant turn to our own desires,
  our own safety,
  our own security.

Safety and security.
Let's state this as clearly and baldly as possible:
in a world where "safety and security"
is a slogan for excluding the stranger,
building larger walls,

and justifying violence,
Jesus calls us to give up our safety and security
for the sake of the gospel.

In our world, as in Paul's,
safety and security is the language of idolatry.

It is the language of greed
and the language of selfishness.

It is the language of those who are faithless,
who have no covenant with God, with other people, or with creation.

It is the language of those who guard their own interests before others,
the language of those who are close fisted, not openhanded.

It is the language of the those who opposed the prophets,
and it is the language of those who opposed Jesus,
who had a maddening habit of throwing security and safety to the wind
if it meant welcoming the outcast and forgiving the unforgivable.

Safety and security is, in short, the language of those who trust themselves
rather than God.

Trusting our economic system for such safety and security
is the way that we bind ourselves to betray our creaturely kin.
Trusting our own violence and military might for such safety and security
is the way we bind ourselves to betray people who are not "us."

So, what might it look like
to renounce the idolatry of our culture?
The economic idolatry,
the technological idolatry,
the militaristic idolatry,
that shapes our imagination from day to day?

What might this look like for creation?
What would it look like if Christians
refused to work at jobs that would harm community or creation,
questioned the use of technology that would harm community or creation,
said no to goods produced in a way that did harm to community or creation?

Why don't our communities do this?

Because it is hard to opt out of the economic idolatry of our culture;
it is hard to embrace an economics of generosity, justice, and care;
it is hard to secede from the system of slavery that produces our food and toys;
it is hard to renounce the technology that would harm community and creation;
it is hard to find products that haven't harmed community or creation.

Indeed, such a renunciation of idolatry sometimes seems impossible.

So let us try one small step.
Have you got a cell phone?
Pull it out and put it in front of you.
You know how these phones are made, right?
You know that the toxic chemicals that are in the plastics pollute our groundwater
and give cancer to our neighbors.
You know that the metals are mined on the backs of slave labor
by companies that displace Indigenous communities
and engage in murder and theft.
We are afraid that there is no way to avoid this disturbing conclusion:
the making of cell phones harms community and creation.

You know how these devices function in our lives, right?
We interrupt conversations for them;
we depend on them for a frightening amount of information;
we use them for company ("Good morning, Siri");
we interrupt sermons and talks with them;
we refuse to commit to meetings and plans because of them;
we take inappropriate pictures and send inappropriate texts.
We indulge ourselves in viewing the same.
We have become addicted.
And this addiction, like so many others,
takes energy.
We use fossil fuels to do these death-dealing things,
and we reap the rewards of depression and isolation.[19]
The use of cell phones harms community and creation.

19. See Jean M. Twenge, *iGen: Why Today's Super-Connected Kids Are Growing Up Less Rebellious, More Tolerant, Less Happy—and Completely Unprepared for Adulthood* (New York: Atria Books, 2017).

And you know what happens when we are finished with these devices,
right?
You know how the toxic chemicals leach into the groundwater.
How they contaminate those who dismantle the phones.
How they become toxic waste.
When we are done with cell phones, they harm community and
creation.

So why are we carrying these things around?
Why?

Because we create what destroys and bind ourselves to betray.
Because they are part of the technological idolatry of our culture.
Because we think that we have no choice.
We cannot live without these devices.
There is a technological inevitability about it all.[20]

But here's the thing:
"no choice" is the language of empire,
the language of idolatry,
the language of slavery to sin,
the language of the dominion of death.

And it is because we are slaves to sin[21]
that Paul begins with lament.
It is because we are under the power of sin
that Paul is drawn to the psalms of lament in Romans 3.
And it is because such sin permeated not only the believing community
but all of Roman culture
that such lament comes to full expression
in the longing and groaning of creation in Romans 8.

Paul begins in lament and continues in lament
because he knows this is not how the story is meant to be.

Creation, called to reveal the loving
and joyful character of God (1:20),
has been subjected to futility (8:20).
Adam, failing to exercise a dominion of life-giving justice (5:12–14),

20. In his very fine MA thesis, Robert Miller engages in provocative analysis of this kind of technological inevitability in terms of idolatry and the disconnection from place. "Idolatry, Technology, and Place" (master's thesis, University of St. Michael's College, Toronto, 2017).
21. See Rom. 7:14–25.

was the one who subjected creation to bondage (8:21).
Abraham's offspring,
who were to inherit the earth (4:13),
now groan in bondage (8:23).

Again and again Paul gives us a vision of God's hope
for humanity and the earth,
a vision that was betrayed.
You may remember that when Peter realized his betrayal,
he got up, went out,
and wept.

This, then, is the first reason why we are a people of lament.
Because we recognize the truth of Romans 7:
we do not do what we are called to.
We are a people of betrayal.
And so we weep.

But there is another reason why we are a people of lament.
We are the people who live in the tragic gap
between what should have been and what is.
We live with heartbreak because the vision of God's good creation
has so captured our imagination,
has so permeated our bodies,
that we can't help but mourn the loss.
When you first noticed that delight had turned to grief,
did you weep?

Aldo Leopold once said that
"one of the penalties of an ecological education
is that one lives alone in a world of wounds."[22]
We live in that wounded world
And because we do so, we groan,
we cry out.
But unlike Leopold, we are not alone.
We are not alone because the cry of the earth,
and the cry of the creature
become the cry of the Spirit,
who groans along with us,
who cries at our side,
who enters the grief of our hearts.[23]

22. Aldo Leopold, *Sand County Almanac* (New York: Ballantine, 1996), 197.
23. Rom. 8:26.

Paul's letter to the Romans is threaded with grief
because the God of whom he writes
is a brokenhearted God of grief.
From grief over the violence humanity
brought to the earth before the flood,[24]
to grief over Israel's destruction of the land,[25]
to grief over the exile of the people,[26]
to the grief of Jesus over
Jerusalem's embrace of violence in the land,[27]
the story of God in the Scriptures is one of grief.

No wonder the Spirit groans along with us;
her lament has been the subtext the whole story through.[28]

And because we are people of the Spirit,
because, Paul tells us, we are children of God,
that lament is our lament as well.
For once the kingdom vision
has grabbed hold of us,
once we want nothing more
than the new creation,
we can't help but live with heartbreak
over the reality of how things are.
We can't help mourning the world
that hasn't come into being.
We can't help seeing the pain
of our world.
Indeed our hope exposes us to that pain;
it uncovers the pain;
it says, "This is not how the world should be,"
and all we can do is grieve.
And that grief,
that lament,
that mourning,
becomes the place that we must live,

24. Gen. 6:5–7.
25. Isa. 24:4–6, 11, 19; 9:10; Jer. 2:4–8.
26. Hosea 11:8–9.
27. Luke 19:41–44.
28. Profoundly helpful in seeing this as a theme throughout the biblical story is Terence Fretheim, *The Suffering of God: An Old Testament Perspective* (Philadelphia: Fortress, 1989).

the tragic gap
between the hope and the reality.

This is what it means to live in the Spirit of Jesus.
Not the place of a spiritual high or continuous joy.
No, at the center of empire,
in the midst of a culture of death,
in a world where powerful countries
refuse to take climate change seriously
and oil leaks by the million liters into the muskeg,
where Indigenous women continue to disappear
and Palestinian teenagers weep over their barren future—
in that world,
living in the Spirit
looks like the agony of childbirth.

Living in the Spirit
looks like the tear-stained face of someone
who can't quite believe how bad it is,
and who knows
that this isn't how it is meant to be.

This too is part of the suffering that demonstrates
that we are led by the Spirit.[29]
This too is at the heart of a suffering
that shapes Christian endurance, character, and hope.[30]
If the Spirit of Jesus is the same Spirit
that hovered over the face of the deep
at the dawn of creation,
then in the face of ecological despoliation
there can be no life in the Spirit
without such suffering,
without such lament.

And that lament can only be real
if we know what it is that we have lost.
Maybe you've never mourned the loss of the Karner blue butterfly.
Maybe you've never seen the lady's slipper
or the five-lined skink.

29. Rom. 8:14–17.
30. Rom. 5:3–5.

Maybe you don't know what part of the music is missing
now that the Eskimo curlews
are gone;
maybe you don't know
what part of the chorus has been silenced.

We can only lament what is lost if we know what is gone.
So we are called to learn the story of our place.
Not the story of progress.
Not that story of cultural amnesia that erases the names of old,
redraws the maps,
blocks the streams and rivers,
wants us to think that civilization brought this land into being,
and that it is here only for our consumption.
This is a story of placelessness.
No, if we want stories of our place,
then we need the stories of old,
the stories that the First Peoples told,
before the stories of conquest
and genocide shaped our world.

Learn the stories of the people indigenous to your place,
the stories of the Anishnaabeg and the Mississauga,
the Wendat and the Coast Salish.
Learn the stories of plants for medicine as well as food:
  the tansy and the yarrow;
the stories of trees for shelter and transport:
  the mother basswood and the birch;
the stories of wolf and song-dogs,
  of turtle and beaver;
the stories that were the sinews binding
the peoples of the past to the land.

We need to hear these stories
because we cannot mourn what we do not know we have lost.

You can go to look at the oil sands of Northern Alberta
and be overwhelmed by the devastation.
But it isn't until you speak to the people of Fort McKay
and the people of Fort Chipewyan,
or the Mikisew Cree First Nation,
and hear their stories of a land

and a way of life that has been lost
that you can begin to understand the depth of the loss,
that you can begin to mourn what is gone,
that you can begin the hard work of lament.

This place of lament would be unbearable
if it weren't for one thing.
If grief is the subtext,
then God's love is the text.
For I am convinced, says Paul,
that the love of God goes all the way down,
  past the death of the creatures,
  the angels that do the bidding of evil,
  the rulers who mandate destruction,
  the present reality of a culture of death,
  the future plans to destroy,
  the powers that seem to be in control,
  the height of our military aspirations,
  and the depths of our tar sands.
None of the wounds we have inflicted on creation
can tear us away from the love of God in Christ Jesus our Lord.[31]

And it is because of such love,
the same love that reconciles us to all creation,
that we can confidently see through the tears of lament
to the biblical promise of a new heaven and a new earth.
We are waiting, says Paul, for the redemption of our bodies.[32]
We are waiting for resurrected life in the new creation.
Not some rapture to heavenly bliss,
but a new heaven and new earth where justice is at home.

And in the end, it is by being surrounded by such deep love
that we have the power to abandon safety and security and say
  no to the idolatry of our culture,
  no to the death-dealing hopes of our world,
  no to the ways in which our technology would seduce us.

This is the challenge of Paul's letter to the Romans:
realize that you are a people of lament.

31. Rom. 8:38–39.
32. Rom. 8:23.

Don't move too quickly and cheaply to the stories of hope
that blind our eyes to the critical nature of our situation.
Allow the pain of creation to find its voice in your life,
dare to bring that pain to expression,
realize that this is what it means to live in the Spirit.

But don't stop there.
If the crisis is communal,
then to community we must return.
And so Paul says to the followers of Jesus in Rome:
let love be genuine, hate what is evil, hold fast to what is good.
Rejoice with those who rejoice and weep with those who weep.
Live in harmony with one another.
Do not be haughty, but walk with the oppressed,
and do not claim to be wiser than you are.[33]

Dare we imagine what this looks like for creation?

What would it look like not only to love our places
but also to hate the injustice that harms the beloved?
Could this actually call us to abandon our cell phones?
Are there other technological devices
that fail the test of love for creation?
Is it crazy to imagine life without a dryer or a microwave?
How about the automobile,
that symbol of modern autonomy?

And what would it look like to really hold on for dear life,
hang on against the odds and the evidence to what is good,
to the delight, joy, and faithfulness of creation?
Could rejoicing with creation go so deep that we rejoice
even when the exuberant, profligate,
wild fertility of insects, plants, and animals
infringes on our own interests?

And what would it look like not only to weep with creation
but also to give up our arrogant pretension that we actually know what we are doing?
What would it look like to have creational humility?

33. Rom. 12:9, 15–16. We reflect on the ecological shape of the virtues that Paul describes in Col. 3:12–17 in Brian J. Walsh and Sylvia C. Keesmaat, *Colossians Remixed: Subverting the Empire* (Downers Grove, IL: IVP Academic, 2004), 193–200.

What would it look like to walk with creation and experience its
oppression,
to walk with the people of the Athabasca and Mikisew Cree,
to try to breathe the contaminated air of the tar sands,
to eat the fish, see the cancer of oil grow in our bodies too?

What would it look like to walk with the people Flint, Michigan,
thirsty for water,
to accompany the black lives of the food deserts,
to walk with the Indigenous women before they disappear,
along with the animals and the earth itself under our violent care?

What would it look like to do this in such a way
that their lament becomes our deep sorrow,
their hope our deep hope?

And so we come to the end and find it the place of our beginning.

When did you first notice?
When did you realize
that delight had turned to grief?

Mark that moment.

For it was then
that you began to image
the suffering servant of creation
that you are called to be.

Paul's Context, Our Lament

That certainly was an impassioned call for us to engage in lament because of the destruction of the earth. I feel like I need a few moments to let it sink in. I can feel the sense of loss that you talk about here. I can think of the places that I love that have been lost as the suburbs have expanded. So I resonate with what you are saying and I agree with you. But I also have a feeling of discomfort. Not because I disagree with you. Rather, I'm a little skeptical that you can root this call to lament for creation in Romans. As you point out, we know that species are going extinct, but I don't think that Paul had that kind of environmental awareness. Isn't this just our concern projected back onto Paul?

This is the most common question we are asked about the Bible and creation care. And while it is true that the biblical writers weren't concerned about issues like climate change and species extinction—how could they be?—a close look at the biblical texts reveals that they *were* concerned about the fertile land where God had placed them and the health of their communities in that land.

In her book on an agrarian reading of the Old Testament, Ellen Davis points out that "the Hebrew Scriptures [have a] pervasive interest in land, not only as national territory, but also, and more fundamentally, [an] interest in land as fertile, and further, in the primary human vocation to maintain its fertility (Gen. 2:15)." This means that Torah is concerned with faithful life in a particular place, the land of Canaan, "shared with other creatures—trees (Deut. 20:19) and birds and animals (Deut. 22:4, 6–7; 25:4)—whose own lives are precious and valuable."[34] Another way to put this is that Israel's "faith revolved around the question of land, either a desperate yearning for it, or a problematic possession of it."[35]

This was true not only for the writers of the Torah and prophetic literature, as Davis has shown, but also for an urban writer like Paul. Jeremiah, Hosea, and Isaiah have specific realities in sight when they describe the mourning of the land and the reversal of creation brought about by Israel's lack of covenantal faithfulness.[36] We rob Paul's language of its prophetic power if we neglect to ask what he might have meant when he said that creation was "wait[ing] with eager longing," "subjected to futility," and "groaning in travail" (Rom. 8:19, 20, 22). Reading Paul on the level of theological abstraction and dogmatic discourse prevents us from asking what, precisely, he might have meant. It is clear that *human* suffering had a solid, rooted referent for Paul. Why is it that we do not assume the same for his creational references?

So are you suggesting that Paul was referring to specific things that were happening around him when he talked about creation groaning?

Yes. And we are suggesting that this was not something new to Paul. Throughout the Scriptures of Israel, and especially in texts that Paul alludes to, the writers link unfaithfulness and disobedience to the destruction of the land and the suffering of creation.

34. Ellen F. Davis, *Scripture, Culture, Agriculture: An Agrarian Reading of the Bible* (Cambridge: Cambridge University Press, 2009), 9, 82.

35. Walter Brueggemann, "Israel's Sense of Place in Jeremiah," in *The God of All Flesh: And Other Essays*, ed. K. C. Hanson (Eugene, OR: Cascade Books, 2015), 45.

36. Davis points out that "from the eighth century BCE on . . . the economics of food production was a matter contested between the crown and its agents, on the one hand, and the bulk of the population, on the other." Davis, *Scripture, Culture, Agriculture*, 3. See her discussion of Jer. 4:23–28 on pp. 10–11.

I wondered about that. I have never noticed those connections in the Hebrew texts that you referred to.

All of these texts show how idolatry has deadly effects for humanity, animals, and the earth. That is why Paul begins by talking about being blind to the face of creation, a blindness that is at the heart of such idolatry. Those who practice injustice do not recognize that creation reveals God's nature to them (Rom. 1:19–20). Their futility (1:21) and foolishness (1:22) mean that they misunderstand both creature and Creator (1:25). We referred above to the three passages that scholars widely acknowledge that Paul is alluding to here: Psalm 106:20 (105:20 LXX),[37] Jeremiah 2:11, and Hosea 4:7. What is striking is that all these passages link idolatry with abuse of the land. In Psalm 106, for instance, after describing Israel's judgment for their idolatry with the golden calf, the narrative describes Israel's turning aside from the land they had desired, because of lack of faith in God's word (Ps. 106:24).

Similarly, Jeremiah 2:11 comes as the climax to a section in which the Israelites are described as those who go after worthless things and become worthless (*emataiōthēsan*: Jer. 2:5 LXX), the same word that is usually translated as "became futile" in Romans 1:21. In Jeremiah, this futility meant that the Israelites defiled the plentiful and fruitful land that they were brought into by their God (Jer. 2:7). Idolatry destroys the land.

Even more striking is Paul's echo of Hosea 4:7. Hosea 4 begins with God's indictment against the people who have been abusing the land. The prophet proclaims that there is no faithfulness or loyalty, no knowledge of God in the land; there is swearing, lying, murder (*phonos*: Hosea 4:2 LXX; cf. Rom. 1:29), stealing, and adultery—and bloodshed follows bloodshed. *Therefore*, the prophet concludes, the land mourns, and all who live in it languish, together with the wild animals of the fields, the reptiles of the earth, and the birds of the heavens, and the fish of the sea are dying (Hosea 4:2–3 LXX; the Hebrew text omits the reptiles of the earth, which Paul includes in Rom. 1:23). Hosea then goes on to describe the greed, injustice (*adikiais*: Hosea 4:8; cf. Rom. 1:18), and worship of idols practiced by the people (Hosea 4:7–19).

The imagery is heartbreaking. The land is mourning, keening over the violence it has been subjected to. Every creature is languishing, has grown feeble,

37. The initials LXX refer to the Septuagint, the Greek translation of the Hebrew Bible. The Hebrew Bible is referred to by the initials MT, for Masoretic Text. Paul's quotations of texts from his Scriptures show that he was familiar with the Septuagint. On occasion the verses are numbered differently in the Septuagint than they are in the Hebrew Bible. For that reason, we have given references to the Greek versification where the two differ.

lost vitality. Mourning, the sapping away of life, and death: this is where idolatry leads.

I admit that the parallels between Romans 1 and these texts are striking. But isn't it an overstatement to argue that a misuse of the land is at the heart of idolatry? Isn't idolatry about worshiping false gods?

Yes, it is, and that is precisely why idolatry is so devastating for the land. You see, whom or what you worship shapes your whole life. It determines how you conduct your economic affairs, how you relate to the poor, and how you treat the land. Our worship is indicative of our deepest trust. If your trust is in an economic system—any economic system—that operates by destroying the land, then you are practicing idolatry. If we are living a lifestyle that demands the destruction of creation in order to continue, then we don't even have to ask who or what we worship. Our creation-abusing lives bear witness that we have put our trust in idols and not the Creator God, the God of the Scriptures. When it comes right down to it, our economic life and our lifestyles always become enfleshed in the land. That is the only place where we live.

I'm not sure I understand what you mean by "trust." This doesn't sound like any scriptural definition of idolatry that I've ever heard.

Let's look at what the biblical writers say about idolatry and see if that clarifies anything. Paul's description of idolatry in Romans 1 parallels prophetic literature and the Psalms at every point. Idolatry prevents knowledge of the true Creator,[38] it is rooted in falsehood,[39] and it always ends up in futility and foolishness.[40] Idolatry results in a loss of glory[41] and a misunderstanding of creation.[42] Finally, idolatry engenders greedy patterns of consumption both sexually and economically.[43] And such consumption and greed always manifests itself in the lives of ancient Israelites in abuse of the land. So Davis notes that "beginning here [Gen. 3] and continuing throughout the Old Testament, land degradation (e.g., Lev. 26:18–20; Deut. 28:15–18) is a sure sign that humans have turned away from God. Conversely, the flourishing of the land (e.g., Lev. 26:3–6, 10; Deut. 28:2–5, 11–12; Isa. 35; Pss. 65; 72) marks a return to God.

38. Rom. 1:20–21; Hosea 4:6.

39. Rom. 1:25; Jer. 10:14; 51:17; Hab. 2:18.

40. Rom. 1:21–22; 2 Kings 17:15; Pss. 97:7; 115:3–8; Isa. 44:9; Jer. 2:5; 10:2, 15; 51:17–18; Hosea 5:11.

41. Rom. 1:23; Pss. 106:20; 115:8; Isa. 42:8; Jer. 2:11; Hosea 4:7.

42. Rom. 1:25; Isa. 44:10–20; Jer. 10:3.

43. Rom. 1:24–31; 1 Kings 21; Isa. 2:6–8; Jer. 5:7–9; 22:9–17; Ezek. 18:1–19; 22:1–16, 22; Hosea 4:10–12, 17–19; Amos 2:6–8; Mic. 6:9–16; Hab. 2:9–10. Cf. G. K. Beale, *We Become What We Worship: A Biblical Theology of Idolatry* (Downers Grove, IL: IVP Academic, 2008), 203.

In short, the Old Testament represents the condition of the land as the single best index of human responsiveness to God."[44]

Psalmic and prophetic texts on idolatry consistently contrast those who know God as the Creator of heaven and earth who gives good gifts to God's people with those idolaters who do not know God, who practice deceit, who are greedy for dirty money, and whose unfaithfulness brings ruin to the land.[45] If we read carefully, we can see that these contrasts are central to Romans 1. In a letter that has God's gift of grace at its heart, seeing God's power, and indeed God's very nature through the revelation of creation, is crucial. Idolatry, however, is blind to the gift that the Creator has offered, and attempts to seize the abundance and fertility of the gift on its own terms—terms that result in economic exploitation, control, and death. Idolatry always renders creation mute, silencing its praise. And, Paul will argue, idolatry leads to a certain kind of violent consumption that results in an abusive sexuality and an economics of greed rooted in deceit and unfaithfulness. This is where an inability to see the earth as gift will lead.[46]

So you are saying that because idolaters can't see creation as the abundant gift that God has given them, they can't trust that God will provide for them? That instead they trust in their own violent and controlling economic practices?

That's exactly the point.

Okay, I get that. But I still have a couple of questions. First of all, I'm not sure how this shows that Paul is concerned with creation and its care in Romans. And, second, I don't see any discussion of violent economic practices in Romans.

We are coming to Paul's concern for creation soon. But first, you need to notice that in Romans 1 Paul's argument moves from idolatry to talk about exploitive and violent consumption in both sexual and economic terms. We'll spend much more time on this in later chapters of this book, but for now notice that Paul describes those who practice idolatry in terms that would have both resonated with those who knew the imperial household and evoked the goddess religions.[47] But even if

44. Ellen F. Davis, "Learning Our Place: The Agrarian Perspective of the Bible," *Word and World* 29, no. 22 (Spring 2009): 114.

45. E.g., Pss. 97; 115; 135:1–7; 146; Isa. 41:17–20; 45:1–8; 45:18–19; Jer. 8:10; 9:3–14; 10:14; Hosea 4:6; Hab. 2:4–19.

46. On idolatry and wealth, see Joel Marcus, "Idolatry in the New Testament," *Interpretation* 60, no. 2 (April 2006): 152–64; Brian S. Rosner, *Greed as Idolatry: The Origin and Meaning of a Pauline Metaphor* (Grand Rapids: Eerdmans, 2007), 103–29. Helpfully, Beale refers to Ezek. 22:1–16, where idolatry is described as the root of economic and sexual sin. Beale, *We Become What We Worship*, 203.

47. Neil Elliott has made much of the parallels between Paul's description of violent sexuality in Rom. 1 and the imperial household. Elliott, *The Arrogance of Nations: Reading Romans*

his hearers had no firsthand knowledge of the life of the imperial household, they still would have recognized the lifestyle of the elite in his description because the characteristics of the rulers of Rome shaped the whole of Roman society.[48] In addition, the exploitive practices of sexuality found in various religious contexts were reflected in the practices of the household. What kind of sexuality was practiced at all levels of Roman society? A violent and predatory sexuality of exploitation and consumption. The sexual exploitation of women, slaves (of either gender), and temple prostitutes is validated by the idolatrous narrative of the empire, where social division and exploitation is rooted in the divine cosmology. People can be used and treated as sexual commodities when they are merely slaves of the gods rather than images of God.[49]

So because idolatry denies the position of humanity as the image of God, it enables the abuse of other people, who are no longer seen as image bearers.

Precisely. Human beings are then viewed as commodities to be bought and sold and used as their owners see fit. This enabled the colonizers to deceive, enslave, and kill Indigenous people and steal their land: they were barbarians, not real people.[50] It was no different in the Roman Empire. This is how Iris would have experienced her life in the household of Narcissus, as a commodity for his pleasure and use. And this is all part of a larger economy of abuse and exploitation. We'll talk about this further in the next chapter, but for now it is important to see that Paul's description then moves from an exploitive and predatory *sexuality* to an exploitive and predatory *economics*.[51]

---

in the Shadow of Empire (Minneapolis: Fortress, 2008), 78–83. Jeramy Townsley has convincingly argued that these verses reflect the idolatrous sexual practices of the goddess religions. Townsley, "Paul, the Goddess Religions, and Queer Sects: Roman 1:23–28," *Journal of Biblical Literature* 130, no. 4 (2011): 707–28.

48. See Margaret Y. MacDonald, "Slavery, Sexuality, and House Churches: A Reassessment of Colossians 3.18–4.1 in Light of New Research on the Roman Family," *New Testament Studies* 53 (2007): 94–113.

49. On human beings as slaves of the gods found in Sumero-Akkadian and Babylonian creation accounts in contrast with human beings as the image of God in Gen. 1, see J. Richard Middleton, *The Liberating Image: The* Imago Dei *in Genesis 1* (Grand Rapids: Brazos, 2005), 149–219.

50. Similarly, the US Declaration of Independence declares that "all men are created equal" but also decries the "merciless Indian Savages, whose known rule of warfare, is an undistinguished destruction of all ages, sexes, and conditions." In other words, "those 'red' Indians . . . are not truly human. They are 'merciless' savages incapable of kindness." Iris De León-Hartshorn, "Dismantling Injustice through Balance and Harmony," in *Yours, Mine, Ours: Unravelling the Doctrine of Discovery*, ed. Cheryl Woelk and Steve Heinrichs (Winnipeg: Mennonite Church Canada, 2016), 121.

51. For the link between violent sexuality and violent economics, see Walter Brueggemann, "Land, Fertility and Justice," in *Interpretation and Obedience* (Minneapolis: Fortress, 1991), 235–60. On the link between the violent abuse of women and the violent abuse of the earth

I can see that Paul has been talking about sexuality, but the verses after that don't mention economics or money at all.

Maybe we don't see such economic allusions here because we have been so conditioned to read these kinds of texts in such a narrowly spiritualized way. Paul's lists of vices and virtues are invariably interpreted as referring to our "spiritual lives," as if our spirituality doesn't become evident in our daily economic and household practices. Paul's language here refers to very specific actions that everyone would have been familiar with in the ancient world. When Paul describes the debased mind and practices of the empire in Romans 1:29–31, he does so in a way that highlights a context of injustice, greed, and heartless, merciless economic conceit and violence. His was a world where some were the victims of the malicious and faithless actions of those who could afford to boast about their wealth and social standing, a world where envy fed backroom dealings (inventors of evil), and where the covenant ideals of economic justice had no place.[52] This was, in short, the predatory economy of the Roman Empire.[53] As Peter Oakes points out, it is quite likely that a slave would have recognized the behavior of her master in these verses, not just in terms of sexual abuse, but also in terms of economic and social practice.[54]

I've never heard those verses described as referring to economics. I thought that they were just about our attitudes.

Our attitudes are always embodied in specific practices in daily life. In the biblical story one's economic practices are where these attitudes most often find expression.

I still don't see what this has to do with the land.

It is important to note that throughout the Hebrew Scriptures, as well as in the Roman Empire (and indeed throughout history), economic oppression is always linked to the ownership and control of land.[55] Consequently, as Paul goes on to describe injustice in Romans 3:10–18 by means of a complex unit of quotations

throughout history, see Susan Griffin, *Women and Nature: The Roaring inside Her* (New York: Harper, 1980); and Derek Jensen, *Endgame*, vol. 1, *The Problem of Civilization*, and vol. 2, *Resistance* (New York: Seven Stories, 2006).

52. We describe the economic overtones of Paul's vocabulary in Rom. 1:29–31 at greater length in chap. 6.

53. Described by Neil Elliott, "Disciplining the Hope of the Poor," in *A People's History of Christianity*, vol. 1, *Christian Origins*, ed. Richard A. Horsley (Minneapolis: Fortress, 2005), 180.

54. Peter Oakes, *Reading Romans in Pompeii: Paul's Letter at Ground Level* (Minneapolis: Fortress, 2009), 133.

55. E.g., 1 Kings 21; Hosea 4:1–3; Mic. 7:1–3; Hab. 2:6–17. This, of course, is true in every economy, including our own.

from various psalms, land is never far from his sights. We can hear strong echoes of classic Hebrew texts against idolatry as Paul describes the unjust who have no understanding and do not seek God, those whose mouths are full of death-dealing and poisonous lies that create a curse and bitterness, those whose way of walking only leads to death and creates ruin and misery for the innocent who get in their way. Such people have no knowledge of what makes for peace because they do not know or seek God. And when we realize that in this passage Paul is mostly quoting from psalms of lament—where the faithful cry out to God for justice in the face of economic oppression that results in the loss of land—we can see that Paul links idolatry with economic abuse as readily as the prophets did.[56] Just as the prophets were engaged in naming the sexual, economic, and creational abuse of their times, so Paul's evocative echoes carried a whispered judgment of the powers of his own day. These judgments do not remain a whisper, however, as the letter progresses.

But the only place where it seems to me that Paul offers any explicit judgment of the idolatrous powers of his own day is at the end of chapter 8. And even there he has moved on from talking about the land.

Maybe it would help if we looked again at the movement of the whole letter. The narrative arc of Romans as a whole draws on the story of Israel, in all its complexities around land, land loss, and land promised. As we began to see in our discussion of Romans as a text of homemaking, the stories of Adam, Abraham, the exodus, the deuteronomic promises of blessing and curse with their effect on the land, and the prophetic promises of restoration are all explicitly referenced in the letter.[57] Even more striking, however, the narrative arc of Romans 8, in a richly allusive way, evokes the story of the calling of human beings in relation to creation, the subjection of creation to futility, creation's bondage to decay, the groaning of creation, believers and the Spirit, and the future expectation of the freedom of the glory of the children of God, which is somehow linked to the redemption of their bodies.

56. The psalms quoted by Paul with these themes are Pss. 10 (9 LXX); 14 (13 LXX); 71 (70 LXX); 140 (139 LXX). See also Isa. 7:6, 9; Hosea 4:1–13; Mic. 7:1–13; Hab. 2:6–17. W. Derek Suderman shows how Ps. 35 can be read as giving voice to the Indigenous peoples of the Six Nations as they cry for justice. This is, we suggest, precisely the kind of context in which these psalms were originally sung. Suderman, "Reflections of a Christian Settler in the Haldimand Tract," in *Buffalo Shout, Salmon Cry: Conversations on Creation, Land, Justice, and Life Together*, ed. Steve Heinrichs (Harrisonburg, VA: Herald Press, 2013), 263–77.

57. Adam: Rom. 5:12–21; Abraham: Rom. 4; exodus: Rom. 6–8; deuteronomic promises: Rom. 8:1–2; prophetic restoration: Hosea 2:23 in Rom. 9:25; Isa. 10:22 in Rom. 9:27; Isa. 59:20–21 in Rom. 11:26; Isa. 11:10 in Rom. 15:12.

That's a tightly packed narrative you've just outlined. So what you are saying is that Paul has used language that recalls the story of creation right from the beginning of the biblical narrative, and he does so not just in Romans 8 but throughout the letter.

Not only does he recall that biblical narrative, but he explicitly situates the current experience of creation within that story. Paul does this in three ways. First, in Romans 8:20 he uses the language of futility to describe the bondage that creation is suffering. Futility is the language of idolatry throughout the Scriptures,[58] and as we saw, such idolatry is overwhelmingly linked to abuse of the land. By returning to the theme of futility at this point in his argument, Paul is bringing to completion the circle that he began in Romans 1:21–22, where he explicitly linked an idolatrous blindness to creation with "futile" thinking and "senseless minds." The idolatry that manifests itself in Roman society is merely one act in that larger narrative of creation that stretches throughout Israel's Scriptures. Just as the prophets named the specific imperial realities of their day within God's larger story in the world, so also Paul sees the suffering of creation under Rome as rooted in the idolatrous and violent practices of the empire.

Second, Paul's description of the groaning of creation in Romans 8 echoes those places in the Scriptures that describe Israel's cry to God under a situation of violent economic oppression, beginning with the exodus event, where Israel's bondage enabled Egyptian economic exploitation of the land (the building of storehouses for food and slave labor in the fields).[59] The groaning of creation has often been viewed as generic metaphorical language, a poetic way to describe the fact that creation also suffers as a result of human sin. However, just as such language pointed to specific economic and social practices in the Scriptures of Israel, so also Paul is describing specific economic and social practices in relation to the land.

58. Contra David Horrell, Cherryl Hunt, and Christopher Southgate, *Greening Paul: Reading the Apostle in a Time of Ecological Crisis* (Waco: Baylor University Press, 2010), 77. They argue that the word for futility (*mataiotēs*) only occurs in the LXX in Psalms, Prov. 22:8, and Ecclesiastes, noting especially Eccles. 3:19. Words formed from the root of *mataio-*, however, occur throughout the historical books and the prophets in relation to idolatry, e.g., 2 Kings 17:15 // Isa. 2:5; Isa. 44:9; 10:3, 15; Hosea 5:11.

59. These linguistic parallels are drawn out at some length in Sylvia C. Keesmaat, *Paul and His Story: (Re)Interpreting the Exodus Tradition* (Sheffield: Sheffield Academic Press, 1999), 107–10. See also Terence Fretheim, "The Reclamation of Creation: Redemption and Law in Exodus," *Interpretation* 45 (1991): 354–56; and "The Plagues as Ecological Signs of Historical Disaster," *Journal of Biblical Literature* 110 (1991): 385–96.

Third, when Paul describes the suffering of the Roman believers in Romans 8:35, he includes both poverty (oppression, distress, famine, and nakedness are all economically rooted) and political repression (persecution, peril, and the sword). Paul's language of the groaning of believers in 8:23, therefore, is not just a theological formulation of the suffering that precedes the inauguration of the new age but also has a specific face on the ground in this place, in this community. It looks like poverty and abuse.[60] We suggest, therefore, that Paul's language of the groaning of creation means not just that creation is undergoing suffering because it is "unable to achieve its purpose or emerge from the constant cycle of toil, suffering and death"[61] but also that creation is groaning for the same reason that believers groan: because it is suffering under the exploitive economic practices and violent militarism of Roman imperial rule.

Environmental Destruction and the Roman Empire

But how likely is it that Paul was referring to environmental destruction in the first century? Do we even know anything about Roman environmental practices?

As a matter of fact, we know quite a bit. For instance, we know that this letter was written at the time of Nero. Like the mythology of a creational "golden age" that accompanied the rule of Augustus, it was claimed that under Nero nature had been restored "to its original state in the primeval Age of Saturn, when beasts of the field were so tame that they herded themselves and when the earth brought forth its harvest without the use of the plow."[62]

The reality, however, was considerably different. In the face of official economic affluence, the *practices* of Rome betrayed the land-destroying economic oppression that underpinned the empire. While Rome (like so many empires before it) *claimed* to be the source of creational renewal, descriptions of the creation-destroying character of empire were common. Not only did Roman victory often require destroying the infrastructure of the conquered, continued Roman control depended on an ongoing exploitation of both people and land. The army alone needed enormous resources: wine, olive oil, pork, garum, pepper for food,

60. See also Oakes, *Reading Romans*, 114–15.

61. Horrell, Hunt, and Southgate, *Greening Paul*, 77.

62. Robert Jewett, "The Corruption and Redemption of Creation: Reading Romans 8.18–23 with the Imperial Context," in *Paul and the Roman Imperial Order*, ed. Richard A. Horsley (New York: Trinity Press International, 2004), 31. On the importance of the imagery of fruitfulness in the empire and the challenge to such imperial assertions throughout Israel's history, see Walsh and Keesmaat, *Colossians Remixed*, chap. 4.

horses, pack animals, animals for sacrifice, and feed for this livestock. Leather was needed for everything, as was metal.[63] Mining metal consumed enormous amounts of wood to shore up the mine shafts, to burn for smelting, and to create the infrastructure for washing the ore.[64]

Roman roads, along with ships, enabled produce to stream more quickly from the exploited provinces to Roman garrisons and Rome itself.[65] In addition, the growing need for grain in Rome led to the systematic ruin of forests and pastureland, not only in Italy but also in Africa, contributing to its desertification.[66]

Further, many ancient authors mention air quality in Rome itself, which had very high levels of pollution due to fires for cooking, heating baths and houses, cremations, and industrial activities.[67] Cities were also the locus for epidemics such as tuberculosis and malaria.[68]

Underlying all environmental concerns was the loss of arable land by individual farmers. Low yields, erosion, conscription, and inability to work as a result of illness, affected a farmer's ability to subsist on the land, making it possible for those with more socioeconomic power to take it over. At the heart of all this consumption, therefore, is a carefully hidden reality of land loss, a reality that the official poets and artisans did not depict when extolling Roman virtue and might. While the empire claimed to be at the apex of world renewal and abundance, life on the ground was dramatically different.

Wait, are you saying that ancient authors not only described Rome's practices, which we can now see were destructive, but that they themselves also realized that these were destructive practices?

63. Neville Morley, "The Early Roman Empire: Distribution," in *The Cambridge Economic History of the Greco-Roman World*, ed. Walter Scheidel, Ian Morris, and Richard P. Saller (Cambridge: Cambridge University Press, 2007), 276. On the increased burden that the army placed on the land, see Elio Lo Cascio, "The Early Roman Empire: The State and the Economy," in Scheidel, Morris, and Saller, *Cambridge Economic History*, 632–38. On the sheer amount of marble quarried, metal mined, and wood burned in the empire, see Willem M. Jongman, "The Early Roman Empire: Consumption," in Scheidel, Morris, and Saller, *Cambridge Economic History*, 609–11.

64. Dennis Kehoe, "The Early Roman Empire: Production," in Scheidel, Morris, and Saller, *Cambridge Economic History*, 567.

65. Klaus Wengst, *The Pax Romana and the Peace of Jesus Christ*, trans. John Bowden (London: SCM, 1987), 30; and Herbert Girardet, "Rome and the Soil," in *Far from Paradise: The Story of Man's Impact on the Environment*, ed. John Seymour and Herbert Girardet (London: BBC, 1986), 60.

66. Girardet, "Rome and the Soil," 59; Wengst, *Pax Romana*, 35; and David J. Hawkin, "The Critique of Ideology in the Book of Revelation and Its Implications for Ecology," *Ecotheology* 8, no. 2 (2003): 169.

67. Robert P. Saller "Ecology," in Scheidel, Morris, and Saller, *Cambridge Economic History*, 22.

68. Saller, "Ecology," 35–37.

Yes, in a book called *Environmental Problems of the Greeks and Romans*, J. Donald Hughes carefully and convincingly argues not only that environmental destruction was widespread at Paul's time but also that ancient authors such as Vitruvius, Strabo, Aristotle, and Theophrastus described and decried the devastation.[69] Poets sang of the disappearance of wild animals, caught in Caesar's nets in such numbers that "the former lofty lairs of wild beasts are now pasturages."[70]

But that doesn't mean that Paul would have shared their concerns.

Actually, his context suggests that he *did* share these concerns. There are two reasons why we think so. First, Paul had spent a considerable amount of time in Judea, where imperial economic policies wrought destruction both for the people and for the land itself. Hughes graphically describes the environmental impact of Roman military practices, agricultural technology and economic practices, and population relocation, all of which were widespread in Galilee and Judea.[71] Paul would have seen the effect that decades of military occupation had on the land, the expansion of imperial estates with the loss of familial land, and the despair that accompanied such violence.[72]

Second, the cities in which Paul stayed and worked had varying relationships to the land surrounding them. In general, their inability to live sustainably within their immediate environment was evidenced by the eroded and desiccated landscapes that surrounded them.[73] Moreover, larger urban centers were filled with those who had been forced off their land for various reasons and who were now part of the urban poor.[74] Many of these urban residents not only had recent memories of their land but also had close ties to the agrarian contexts from which they came.

69. Hughes, *Environmental Problems*, 1–16, 56–68, 144–45; Norman Wirzba, *The Paradise of God: Renewing Religion in an Ecological Age* (Oxford: Oxford University Press, 2003), 11, cites both Homer (*Iliad* 16.389–92) and Plato (*Critias*, book 3) as concerned about deforestation and soil erosion. As mentioned above, Hughes indicates that there were also concerns about declining animal populations at this time, and Cicero refused to make his provincials collect leopards. See note 10 above.

70. Hughes, *Environmental Problems*, 88.

71. Hughes, *Environmental Problems*, 70–76, 110–20, 124–26.

72. Richard A. Horsley, *Galilee: History, Politics, People* (Harrisburg, VA: Trinity Press International, 1995), 207–21. See also Ekkehard W. Stegemann and Wolfgang Stegemann, *The Jesus Movement: A Social History of Its First Century*, trans. O. C. Dean Jr. (Minneapolis: Fortress, 1995), 47–52, 108–13.

73. Hughes, *Environmental Problems*, 2, 163–64, 183.

74. Oakes, *Reading Romans*, 95, refers to the large number of migrant workers and immigrants in Rome. Walter Scheidel indicates that rising population levels created competition for cultivable land at this time. He also notes that many of the slaves in Rome were transported from outlying rural areas in the empire. "Demography," in Scheidel, Morris, and Saller, *Cambridge Economic History*, 49.

The Roman Empire was still by and large an agrarian culture, and hence concerns regarding the land, its fertility, its abundance, and its economic exploitation were never far from the consciousness of those who lived there, including those with whom Paul lived and worked.

Given this context, Paul's description of idolatry at the outset of this letter, alongside his graphic description of the suffering of creation in Romans 8, could only have been heard as a prophetic critique of the dominant mythology of creational abundance and renewal that sugarcoated the violent, land-destroying practices of the empire.

Lament Revisited

If this is prophetic critique, why did you spend so much time talking about lament? Paul's judgmental language about idolatry seems more angry than grieving, and isn't anger more in line with the prophets he refers to?

This, it seems to us, is a fundamental misreading of the story. The first description of God's reaction to the violence that is inflicted on creation is one of grief. In Genesis 6:6, when the Creator looks at the violent imaginations of those created in the image of God, the Creator experiences heartsick grief and regret. This means that "God's grieving goes back to the morning of the world."[75] This language of grief occurs again in the Psalms (78:40–41) and in Isaiah 63:7–10.[76] In fact, throughout the prophets, the grief and suffering of God in reaction to the unfaithfulness of Israel is palpable. Take, for instance, Jeremiah 3:19–20:

> I thought
> how I would set you among my children,
> and give you a pleasant land,
> the most beautiful heritage of all the nations.
> And I thought you would call me, My Father,
> and would not turn from following me.
> Instead, as a faithless wife leaves her husband,
> so you have been faithless to me, O house of Israel,
> says the Lord.

75. Fretheim, *Suffering of God*, 112.

76. It is perhaps typical of humanity's easy attribution of anger to God that the LXX of Gen. 6:6; Ps. 78:40–41; and Isa. 63:7–10 substitutes "anger" for "grief."

The poignancy of God's grief over this betrayed hope is almost unbearable. Or consider Isaiah 65:1–2, where we meet the image of the Creator holding out imploring hands in supplication to a people who refuse to take the gifts those hands are offering. Although the prophets also speak of God's judgment and wrath, this wrath is always rooted in God's hopes for what the people could have been. God always wills salvation for God's people.[77] As a result, "grief is always what the Godward side of judgment looks like."[78] The pain and anguish of God over Israel's unfaithfulness is always present in the text.

The land shares in this pain and anguish throughout the story. We have already talked about Hosea 4:1–3, where all parts of creation—land, seas, animals, insects, birds—suffer for and lament humanity's violence. Such mourning is also found in Jeremiah 12:1–13, where the mourning of the land is referred to repeatedly (vv. 4, 11). We know that this passage is moving in Paul's thought because the lament of Jeremiah 12 is echoed in Romans 8:27 and 36.[79]

The prophetic texts that Paul evokes, therefore, are rooted in the grief that both the prophets themselves and God express in relation to Israel. But it should also be noted that of the many psalms that Paul quotes in Romans, the majority are psalms of lament. He is placing himself firmly within the lament tradition right from the outset of the letter.[80] That lament builds to a crescendo in Romans 8 and it continues into chapter 9 where he talks about the great sorrow and unceasing anguish in his heart when he considers his own people. The first eleven chapters of Romans, we suggest, have an undercurrent of lament.

And just as the prophets give voice to God's lament, so in Romans Paul doesn't stop with the lament of creation, or of believers. Romans 8:26 describes the Spirit groaning with sighs too deep for words. The very Spirit of God does not know what to say as she joins in with the lament of creation and believers. The grief of God is ongoing.

77. Hosea 11:5–9. On the dynamic of God's suffering over Israel's infidelity and God's constant desire for salvation in the midst of such suffering, see Scott A. Ellington, *Risking Truth: Reshaping the World through Prayers of Lament*, Princeton Theological Monograph Series (Eugene, OR: Pickwick, 2008), 44–52, 136–41; Fretheim, *Suffering of God*, 109–48; Abraham Heschel, *The Prophets*, vol. 2 (New York: Harper & Row, 1962), 263–65.

78. Fretheim, *Suffering of God*, 112.

79. Keesmaat, *Paul and His Story*, 130–31.

80. As early as his assertion "I am not ashamed of the gospel" in Rom. 1:16, the apostle is alluding to the laments of Israel in which they complain about being put to shame. Moreover, in these psalms, the themes of shame and justice are found together. Most notable is Ps. 71:1–2 (70:1–2 LXX): "O Lord in you I hope, / never let me be put to shame. / In your justice deliver me, / turn your ear to me, and save me" (our translation).

I guess part of my question has to do with the implications of this. Why does it matter that Paul is writing a letter rooted in lament?

Apart from the way in which it makes sense of the tone, narrative arc, and pathos of the letter? Isn't that enough?

Look, from the beginning you have been saying that things like lament and grief are necessary ways into this book, and it has been clear that this has all kinds of very personal implications for you two. That's what I'm getting at with my question.

Fair enough. We began this book by talking about the Sanctuary Community in Toronto and our Indigenous brothers and sisters in that community. We did so because we saw deep parallels between the grief and loss of that community and the grief and loss of those who made up the community of Jesus followers in ancient Rome. The stories of Iris and Nereus are representative of life for the majority of people in the Roman Empire. Their stories, as we saw, were stories of loss: loss of identity, loss of family, loss of safety, loss of home. And lament wells up in the deep springs of such loss.

As we have argued, for too long Romans has been read as an intellectual exercise in which Paul has tried to systematize a "theology." As a result, it has been read as disconnected from the real struggles and hopes of those people who actually heard the letter in the kitchens or workshops of Rome. And, as a further unfortunate side effect of a narrowly "theological" reading, we have been unable to see that Paul himself is writing an epistle deeply embedded in the lament of the prophets, in the lament of the psalms, in the lament of the earth, and in the lament of God's very self for God's wayward people.

So to understand this letter properly we need to see lament at its heart?

Understanding is only one part of it. You see, if this letter is written to the most oppressed and marginalized people in the Roman Empire, if it is a letter of gospel, good news for those people and hope for those who have no hope, then it can only be a life-giving word if we read it as written to the same kind of people today. To read Romans as addressed only to upper-middle-class, privileged churchgoers or to well-salaried academics is to strip it not only of its intent but also of its power. We need to ask ourselves: Who are the marginalized, the neglected, the despised people today for whom Romans is a word of good news, a word of hope? We need to read this letter for and with those sisters and brothers. That is why we began with our friend Iggy. But in this chapter we have followed Paul further and seen that we need to read his letter to the Christian assemblies in Rome, not just with our human kin but also for and with those creatures who have been abused, violated, and destroyed by our own imperial economic systems. We need to ask how this letter is good news for the earth, for the creatures on the earth and in the seas, for the whole extent of suffering creation.

From Lament to Ecological Repentance

But you haven't been talking about good news. You've been talking about lament. This doesn't seem like good news to me. Or maybe I should put my question this way: Why does it matter that we groan with creation? Isn't it enough to acknowledge that we've messed things up and get on with making things right?

Okay, what do you suggest?

What do you mean?

Well, you've admitted we've messed up, and you want to make things right. Where do we start? What would you suggest our first steps should be?

So, um, you want me to suggest some ways forward for dealing with environmental degradation? I mean, there's lots of stuff out there: use energy efficient appliances, buy organic and local food, only purchase from "green" companies, use cloth diapers, ride a bike instead of driving your car. Is that what you mean?

No, that definitely is *not* what we mean.

It isn't? But surely we need to do these things if we want to live sustainably.

That may well be true. But we need to take Paul more seriously when he says that those who have the first fruits of the Spirit groan along with creation. He doesn't say, "Those of us who know there is a problem should be the first to find the solutions." Face it, we have known what the solutions are for fifty years, but we haven't managed to actually change our lives in any meaningful ways. One of the reasons Paul calls us to lament, to grieve, to enter into the groaning of creation, is that genuine grief and lament is a sign of repentance. Grief is the doorway to repentance. Without grief we will not come anywhere near comprehending the depth of the problem nor will we have a profound enough grasp of our need to repent. Unless we enter into that place of grief, it is too easy just to jump into solutions without having realized the depth of our sin. And if we haven't recognized the depth of our sin, we will think that our lives are shaped by our choices rather than our habits and even our addictions. It will be too easy to think that if we just tweak our behavior here and there, things will change. And any solutions that assume our choices are the only problem will be shallow. You can change your lightbulbs and use energy-efficient appliances until the cows come home, but it won't make a difference. We need to probe more deeply the assumptions of a worldview that shapes a way of life that ruins the planet and condemns future generations. We need to acknowledge how that worldview feeds our addictions, and we need to grieve deeply a life that destroys our creational home. Only then can we begin to hear and embody Paul's rich vision for homemaking in the letter to the Romans.

Kind of reminds me of the old "Romans Road" approach to this letter. It is only after you realize that you are a sinner and feel remorse for your sin that you will recognize your need for a savior. You are saying that unless we have entered into the lament of creation, it is hard to genuinely repent.

Well, no reading of Romans gets it all wrong all of the time. That old approach to reading Romans was right about sin and repentance, even if it was hopelessly individualistic and had no grasp of the communal nature of redemption, let alone a sense of the creation-wide implications of Paul's gospel.

Nor did that reading of the text grasp the importance of lament. Lament and repentance go together and form a circle of shared relationship, a dance of lament between God's people and the groaning earth, one sharing the pain of the other, both knowing the sinfulness that has led to this deep pain. Lament is what happens when we name the deathly ways of our culture and our own complicity in this culture of death. Walter Brueggemann says that in lament we acknowledge "the complete collapse of the contrived world of royal construction, which had no contact with reality," and give anguished voice to "*the public practice of pain*, which touches both guilt and grief, guilt at being responsible for so much of value that is being denied, and grief that it is gone and irretrievable."[81]

So that is why you spent so much time in your reflection at the start of this chapter talking about what we have lost.

It is hard to feel grief for the rich diversity and complexity of God's creation if all we have fed ourselves and our children is a cartoon version of reality. We need to wake up to what we have really lost in order to grieve it, and "in this awakening there [will be] a good deal of pain."[82]

So where do we begin?

Maybe we begin by asking not "What are the solutions?" but rather "Where is the pain?" And that question leads us to repentance, especially if we ask how we have been caught up in creating that pain. Note that this is different from the heavy guilt of the "Romans Road." There is still guilt here, but it is deeper,

81. Walter Brueggemann, "Unity and Dynamic in the Isaiah Tradition," *Journal for the Study of the Old Testament* 20 (1984): 95.

82. Wendell Berry, "A Native Hill," in *The Art of the Commonplace: The Agrarian Essays of Wendell Berry*, ed. Norman Wirzba (Berkeley: Counterpoint, 2002), 8.

almost more devastating, more painful. It isn't just a matter of our personal guilty conscience but a matter of being caught up in something that is bigger than our own moral failings. And it should make us wonder about whether we've bought into the idolatry of our time without even thinking about it. That's where Paul begins in this letter. He isn't just naming the idolatries but calling the Roman Christians to repent of them. So what do you think? What are some of the idolatries of which we need to repent?

When you say idolatries, do you mean where we put our trust?

Yes.

Okay, would economic growth be the kind of thing you mean?

Definitely. Our election campaigns focus on economic growth, and we look to economic growth to provide jobs and security for our futures. Yet it seems clear that we ought to sacrifice our farmland, animals, people, and the well-being of our communities to it. Whenever economic growth is in tension with ecological health, the "economy" wins. And "winners and losers" is precisely the right metaphor. If the ideology of empire has us in a perpetual state of war, and if a competitive economic system is also an economics of war, then who is the enemy? Unfettered economic growth in a finite world invariably creates a competition between ecology and economy in which ecology invariably loses.[83] But ecology, or creation, isn't the only loser in the war that our economic system wages. Many of those seeking to protect the earth, the animals, and the well-being of our communities are considered a threat that needs to be destroyed. This is the real reason that colonizers seek to destroy the peoples who resist their rule. In ancient Rome the conquest of Africa and the steady movement northward to Britain were necessary primarily for resource extraction. The mines that provided the metal for weapons, clasps, harnesses, tools, and coins needed enormous amounts of wood, as noted earlier. As wood was used up around a mine, the Romans simply moved farther out. Of course, wood was also needed for ships to move goods to Rome, and in Rome itself wood was needed for cooking fires and heating the baths. The luxurious life of Rome was built

83. Indeed, this is a contradiction within the very structures of home. Steven Bouma-Prediger and Brian J. Walsh put it this way: "The Greek word *oikos* (eco-) means house or household, thus 'ecology' is the logos of the *oikos*, that is the study of the household, and 'economics' is the *nomos* of the *oikos*, the law or the rules of the household." When the practices of economics are at war with the very ecological structures of life, then we have the most profound and dangerous contradiction. If the human household is in conflict with the household of creation, then this is a house seriously divided and it will inevitably collapse. Bouma-Prediger and Walsh, *Beyond Homelessness: Christian Faith in a Culture of Displacement* (Grand Rapids: Eerdmans, 2008), 185.

on subduing other peoples in order to extract their resources. Wood was the fossil fuel of the ancient world.[84]

Closer to home, the attempted genocide of Indigenous peoples on Turtle Island was in the service of this same deathly economy. Why did the explorers want access to the land? Because of the vast wealth of its resources: gold, timber, and furs. Even now our own economy is based on breaking treaties and dispossessing peoples so that we can continue to extract resources from Indigenous lands. The examples are countless: Shoal Lake, Manitoba, where pumping clean drinking water from Shoal Lake for nearby Winnipeg has created a boil water advisory in Shoal Lake 40 First Nation for twelve years; Fort McKay, Alberta, whose people have been losing more and more land to the tar sands and who, along with Fort Chipewyan and Athabasca First Nation, have had their water, plants, and air contaminated. Grassy Narrows, where the local water has been contaminated with mercury from a paper mill for the past fifty years. More prominently, the Sioux of Standing Rock, North Dakota, have been fighting to protect their sacred waters from the Dakota Access Pipeline, and even more recently the Secwepemc land defenders, the Squamish Nation, the Coldwater Indian Band, and the Tsleil-Waututh Nation are defending their land and sacred waters from the building of the Trans Mountain Pipeline from the Alberta tar sands to the West Coast.[85]

We are addicted to the wealth generated by the exploitation and desecration of Indigenous resources.[86] And, like all addicts, we justify the violence that is necessary to maintain our wealth. We mean that literally. Worldwide, the death toll of Indigenous peoples seeking to protect their lands from mining, cash cropping, and resource extraction is steadily rising.[87]

Naomi Klein's recent book on climate change is a powerful testimony to this conflict within the structure of home. The rules of the planet and the rules of the economy are on a devastating collision course. "What the climate needs to

84. Kehoe, "Production," 567; Hughes, *Environmental Problems*, 68–70.

85. Grassy Narrows, www.freegrassy.net; Standing Rock, www.standwithstandingrock.net; Secwepemc Land Defenders, https://www.secwepemculecw.org; the Sacred Trust initiative of the Tsleil-Waututh, https://twnsacredtrust.ca; and Protect the Inlet, which is the umbrella organization for Indigenous and non-Indigenous resistance against the trans mountain pipeline, https://protecttheinlet.ca.

86. Grace Li Xiu Woo, "Is Exorcism Necessary: Casting Our Colonial Ghosts," in Woelk and Heinrichs, *Yours, Mine, Ours*, 41.

87. See the reporting from Global Witness: https://www.globalwitness.org/en/. *The Guardian* also documents deaths of Indigenous peoples who are protecting their land, along with profiles of Indigenous land defenders from around the world: www.theguardian.com/environment/series/the-defenders.

avoid collapse is a contraction in humanity's use of resources; what our economic model demands to avoid collapse is unfettered expansion. Only one of these sets of rules can be changed, and it is not the laws of nature."[88]

But an economy that is not growing is assumed to be an economy in crisis. The idea of voluntarily contracting or limiting our economy and resource extraction is pretty much unimaginable.

It is unimaginable because our imaginations have been taken captive by idolatry, as Paul says in Romans 1:22–23. And because we are captives, the idea of contracting the economy for the sake of a habitable planet, insisting that the rules of the human household are subject to the rules of the household of all creation, is literally unthinkable to so many people. To put this in terms of our earlier worldview analysis, a radically different way of living in the world, a deeply ecological vision of our economic lives, seems so unthinkable because the dominant worldview of global capitalism, rooted as it is in the story, symbols, and practices of empire, has blinded us to such alternatives. This is why Klein calls for a new worldview in the face of the climate crisis: "Fundamentally, the task is to articulate not just an alternative set of policy proposals but an alternative worldview to rival the one at the heart of the ecological crisis—embedded in interdependence rather than hyper-individualism, reciprocity rather than dominance, and cooperation rather than hierarchy."[89]

So are you saying that Paul's letter to the Romans can provide that worldview?

We want to be careful about our own colonizing past. We want to be careful about arrogantly offering an interpretation of Romans as the answer to all of our ecological questions. But when Klein says that this process of worldview transformation will require debating which "new stories can be told to replace the ones that have failed us,"[90] then, with grace and humility, we think that the counter-imperial narrative that Paul is telling in Romans is precisely such a story. Paul's vision of redemption breaks through both hyper-individualism and anthropomorphism because he has a redeemed community in a redeemed creation in view. His dismantling of imperial systems of shame, dominance, and hierarchy calls forth a vision of reciprocity and cooperation. Indeed, his theology is one in which God the Spirit is herself in a relationship of cooperation and reciprocity with all creation.

88. Naomi Klein, *This Changes Everything: Capitalism versus the Climate* (Toronto: Knopf Canada, 2014), 21.
89. Klein, *This Changes Everything*, 462.
90. Klein, *This Changes Everything*, 461.

Klein's strategy for worldview transformation is "think big, go deep, and move the ideological pole away from the stifling fundamentalism that has become the greatest enemy to planetary health."[91] In Paul's terms this could be stated as follows: allow your imaginations to be liberated by a vision of creational redemption, be drawn deeply into the story of this redemption, and repent of all idolatry.

Yes, but that isn't going to convert the environmental movement to Paul's worldview. The epistle to the Romans isn't going to be the charter document for a postcapitalist world order!

No, of course not. But it might mean that Christians will have a more constructive role to play in that world order and begin to be a more healing force in a world of ecological disaster. At the very least, we hope that our reading of Paul can help liberate Christians from our captivity to an ecologically destructive worldview and give birth to a praxis of ecological homemaking. Paul's ecological vision calls us to imagine and enact alternative economic models and join forces with others who are passionate about sustaining life on this planet, protecting habitats, and seeking eco-justice for the most vulnerable.[92]

This is exciting stuff, but I've got to confess, it is all more than overwhelming. I can name the idolatry easily enough. But I don't know what to do about it.

Remember when we talked about Bourdieu's notion of habitus? Any cultural pattern of life is rooted in, sustained by, and inculcated into people's lives through the habits that make up everyday life. The ideology of economic growth is based on the buying habits, educational habits, and vocational habits of all of us who support the system by living as though money is more important than creation or community or our families. The small daily habits of consumption and abuse make it possible for the larger abuses to happen in our culture. Wendell Berry points out that "soil is not usually lost in slabs or heaps of magnificent tonnage. It is lost a little at a time over millions of acres by the careless acts of millions of people. It cannot be saved by heroic feats of gigantic technology but only by millions of small acts of restraint, conditioned by small fidelities, skills and desires. Soil loss is ultimately a cultural problem; it will be corrected only by cultural solutions."[93]

91. Klein, *This Changes Everything*, 26.

92. There are many fine organizations that bring together people of various worldviews into a unified movement for a sustainable planet. One of the finest Christian conservationist NGOs is A Rocha. This international organization provides hands-on opportunities for creation care at their various sites around the world: www.arocha.org. A broader-based movement that is at the heart of advocating for real and deep economic, political, and environmental transformation with specific reference to climate change is 350.org.

93. Wendell Berry, "Conservation and Local Economy," in *Art of the Commonplace*, 202.

This is not just true of soil loss. It is our small daily acts of carelessness, or of care and restraint, that will bring either hurt or healing to our economy. While we need to be involved in the big movements of radical structural change, that activism needs to be grounded (literally) in "small fidelities, skills and desires," small but significant shifts in our daily habits that will help us to embrace and nourish a healing habitus for habitation, an ecology and economics for homemaking.[94]

So one way to repent of this idolatry would be to ask how the way I spend my money is destroying the people or communities that I love.

Yes. But not only the communities that you love. We should not be willing to sacrifice *any* community anywhere, or anyone else's welfare, for our own idolatry.[95] Otherwise we remain seduced by the "colonialist principle" of the industrial revolution: "the assumption that it is permissible to ruin one place or culture for the sake of another."[96] This was the colonialist principle of ancient Rome as well. So the question then becomes, What ways of living, what habitual daily practices do I engage in that destroy people, communities, or the creation?

Hmm. That would require some thought.

We can think of one thing that is an unconscious habit for most people that we know. How often do you use your cell phone?

My cell phone? I don't really pay attention to how often I check it. Quite a bit, I would say.

This seems to be an incredibly sensitive issue these days. When we mention that we don't have cell phones, people tell us that they wish they weren't so dependent on their phones. But they can't imagine living without them.[97] The cell phone has become such a ubiquitous part of daily life that it is ludicrous to even question whether this device is a particular habit of communication that needs

94. Bouma-Prediger and Walsh develop an "economics for homemaking" at some length in *Beyond Homelessness*, 141–52. See also Bob Goudzwaard and Harry de Lange, *Beyond Poverty and Affluence: Toward an Economy of Care* (Grand Rapids: Eerdmans, 1995); Herman Daly and John Cobb Jr., *For the Common Good: Redirecting the Economy toward Community, the Environment, and a Sustainable Future* (Boston: Beacon, 1989); and Bill McKibben, *Deep Economy: The Wealth of Communities and the Durable Future* (New York: Holt, 2007).

95. In his essay "The Failure of War," Wendell Berry asks, "How many deaths of other people's children by bombing or starvation are we willing to accept in order that we may be free, affluent, and (supposedly) at peace?" He continues, "To that question I answer pretty quickly: *None*. . . . Please. No children. Don't kill any children for *my* benefit." Wendell Berry, *Citizenship Papers* (Washington, DC: Shoemaker & Hoard, 2003), 29.

96. Wendell Berry, "Sex, Economy, Freedom, and Community," in *Sex, Economy, Freedom and Community* (New York: Pantheon Books, 1993), 166.

97. Ironically enough, a young friend of ours was asked in a job interview recently if he had a cell phone. When he responded that he didn't, the interviewer said, "You're hired!" His boss is tired of telling her employees to get off their phones and get back to work.

serious reconsideration. But as more and more studies come out showing that we are actually addicted to our cell phones, we need to ask whether cell phones are the culmination of our slavery to an oppressive economic system.

You don't literally mean addicted *do you?*

Studies are now out showing that the use of a cell phone produces the same chemical as gambling or drug use.[98] They are literally addictive. Literally enslaving. And, like all slavery does, cell phones make us homeless, disconnecting us from community and creating depression.[99]

That's a pretty strong statement.

How else would you describe something that cuts us off from the earth, legitimates bullying and violence, and increasingly controls the information we receive and the people we interact with?

That almost sounds like the definition of an abusive relationship.

With the exception of violence and bullying, which is just a gratuitous by-product, these are not only the results but also the *goals* of the social media industry.[100] Our willing participation in such a relationship points to idolatry. And if we're talking about idolatry, then we also need to question the technological imperative of needing the newest, most powerful, and most efficient electronic device. This sure looks like the idolatrous ideology of technicism.

Technicism?

Yes, a close cousin to economism.[101] Technicism is the absolutization of human tool-making ability. Once you make technique into a god, then, like all idols, it begins to distort your life and remake you in its own image. Just as we cannot imagine life that is not driven by economic growth and the increase of affluence, so also do we find it almost impossible to imagine life without the tools that an ever-accelerating technological culture has on offer. This is the root of our addiction to electronic devices that we think lead to a quicker and more efficient life.

Living for the last number of years in a solar-powered, off-grid house, we have become painfully aware of the amount of power that is thoughtlessly used in our society. Being dependent on solar power for our electricity needs makes us

98. See Adam Alter, *Irresistible: The Rise of Addictive Technology and the Business of Keeping Us Hooked* (New York: Penguin, 2017).

99. See Twenge, *iGen.*

100. See James Williams, *Stand out of Our Light: Freedom and Resistance in the Information Economy* (Cambridge: Cambridge University Press, 2018).

101. J. Richard Middleton and Brian J. Walsh write of the false trinity of scientism, technicism, and economism in *The Transforming Vision: Shaping a Christian World View* (Downers Grove, IL: IVP, 1984), chap. 9, and *Truth Is Stranger Than It Used to Be: Biblical Faith in a Postmodern Age* (Downers Grove, IL: IVP, 1995), 16–17.

aware that there is no way of supplying energy to our devices that doesn't harm communities or creation. And we are not exempt from these habits of ecological harm. There is no one who is righteous, says Paul, not one. While we may protest coal mining that removes mountaintops and fracking for gas while polluting the local water supplies and creating geological instability, the fact is that our solar panels feed into a bank of batteries in our basement that is itself an ecological hazard. So we try to reduce our use of electricity as much as possible, preparing for a future when this might not be choice but necessity. Some days we begin to wonder whether it might be the case that as long as we use electricity, we are part of the problem.

But you aren't asking me to live without electronic devices?

We aren't asking you to do anything until you engage in a process of discernment, lament, and repentance. And we encourage you to do that in the context of community, not just as an individual. The habits of life are communally formed, and so they need to be communally transformed as well. Maybe that process of discernment will lead you and your community to decide that there are some devices and appliances that you don't need in your life. For instance, perhaps you will decide that many of the things that you do using electricity can be done another way. Perhaps you will decide that owning or using a clothes dryer is a luxury that is too ecologically costly and therefore unfaithful, when clothes dry naturally over time on their own. We have raised three children to adulthood without ever owning a clothes dryer. Maybe you will decide the same thing about a hair dryer. Or machines that knead bread, chop things, open cans, steam milk, or make coffee out of little disposable cups. At some point you will perhaps look at these appliances and conveniences and be deeply troubled, even appalled, that you own them at all.

Or if you have to use an appliance, maybe you will decide not to own one yourself. We go to the laundromat to do our laundry. All the water at this laundromat is solar heated. While there, we use a washing machine used by many others, keeping at least one out of the landfill. We also talk to the laundromat owner, find out what is going on in town, visit the library, the post office, and the secondhand bookshop, and we talk with other neighbors. Doing our laundry becomes a chance to build community. And then we take our laundry home to dry on the line outside or on drying racks in the house. Again, this is where community is at the heart of a faithful response. What happens if you decide that a number of people will share one washing machine together? Then doing the laundry requires communal coordination and creates more communal interaction.

The way you've described it, you don't just give something up by not owning a washing machine; you've also gained other things.

That isn't just true for the washing machine. If we chop our pickles by hand rather than using the food processor, we can talk to the children or to the friends that we have roped into helping us. We've gained community while we work (although, to be fair, our children might be a little annoyed with us).

But lest we paint too rosy a picture, we do need to be clear here. Doing the laundry at the laundromat and hanging it to dry takes more time than throwing a load in the washer at home before supper and tossing it in the dryer after supper. Changing our habits will not be an easy process because we have become comfortable in our idolatries and our addictions. We have become what Berry calls "environmental parasites." And he has some uncompromising words for what change will look like:

> If you are fearful of the destruction of the environment, then learn to quit being an environmental parasite. We all are, in one way or another, and the remedies are not always obvious, though they certainly will always be difficult. They require a new kind of life—harder, more laborious, poorer in luxuries and gadgets but also, I am certain, richer in meaning and more abundant in real pleasure. To have a healthy environment we will all have to give up things we like; we may even have to give up things we have come to think of as necessities. But to be fearful of the disease and yet unwilling to pay for the cure is not just to be hypocritical; it is to be doomed.[102]

I guess I wonder how this could possibly work without the support of a community of other people doing the same things. If I want to get off the technological treadmill, am I going to need a whole new set of friends?

We can't answer that question for you. But we all need to approach this with our eyes wide open. We cannot discern paths of healing without being rooted in an alternative story, and such a story is necessarily shared in community. In the context of empire today, as in the first century, redemptive healing requires us to develop communities of discernment. Such deep communities can also help us struggle through these issues of repentance and faithfulness. In community we need to ask questions of discernment when making our decisions, questions that encompass the whole life span of the things we purchase and the way we use them.

Questions of discernment?

102. Wendell Berry, "Think Little," in *Art of the Commonplace*, 87.

Yes, when thinking about products that we may or may not incorporate into our lives, we ask a series of questions about production, use, and disposal. These three questions help us discern whether to purchase something or engage in a specific practice.[103]

1. Does the *making* of this item harm community or creation? Was a habitat or species destroyed in its manufacture? Were people exploited or made ill? Does the making of this item undermine the shalom of God's creation?
2. Does the *use* of this item harm community or creation? Is habitat destroyed, or are species harmed in its use? (This question pertains to electricity use as well.) Are people exploited or harmed when it is used? Does the use of this item undermine the shalom of God's creation?
3. When this item is discarded, does it harm community or creation? Is habitat or species destroyed when it is discarded? Are people exploited or made ill? Does the *discarding* of this item undermine the shalom of God's creation? Or does this item, at the end of its life span, decompose to feed new life?

It seems to us that when Paul says that we are no longer to let sin rule over our mortal bodies and that we should no longer be tools of injustice but rather of justice (Rom. 6:12–13), he is talking about these kinds of things. Do our daily practices serve injustice or justice? Paul is clear about what the answer should be.

Those are pretty far-reaching questions. And pretty limiting. Would I be able to buy anything made of plastic if I used these criteria?

Both the manufacture and disposal of plastic poisons our ground water and elevates cancer rates—and that isn't even considering the extraction of the oil from which plastic is manufactured.[104] So questioning your use of plastic is important. The good news is that there are people all over the world manufacturing things that are alternatives to plastics.[105] You can also refuse to buy plastic.

103. Pushing beyond the standards of profitability and utility that are preeminent in an industrial worldview, Wendell Berry gets at a similar process of discernment with the following questions about work and its product: "Is the worker diminished or in any other way abused by this work? What is the effect of the work on the place, its ecosystem, its watershed, its atmosphere, its community? What is the effect of the product on its user, and on the place where it is used?" Berry, "Going to Work," in *Citizenship Papers*, 38.

104. For a clear summary of plastics in our environment, see Sasha Adkins, "Plastics as Spiritual Crisis," in *Watershed Discipleship: Inhabiting Bioregional Faith and Practice*, ed. Ched Myers (Eugene, OR: Cascade Books, 2016), 154–67.

105. For help on transitioning to a plastic-free life, go to the website of the Zero Waste Institute (www.zerowasteinstitute.org; www.zerowasteeurope.eu/2015/3/zero-waste-a-key

Or ask how things were done before we had plastics. Admittedly, this is all very difficult because some things are only available in plastic. But even though it is hard to come up with satisfactory answers sometimes, these are deeply faithful questions. And we haven't even talked about food yet.

What do you mean?

One of the first areas of our lives that needs repentance is our food production and consumption. How we produce our food has far-reaching ramifications for the health of creation. But how food is *controlled* demonstrates our attitudes toward land and how it is cared for. Throughout the biblical story there is a contrast between imperial powers who view land as a commodity to be exploited and the people of the land who see their lives and health as interwoven with the health and care of the land. For instance, when Joseph controls all the food in Egypt, during the first year of the famine he provides food in exchange for all the money that the people have. In the second year he provides food in exchange for all their animals. In the third year the people offer themselves *and* their land to be slaves to Pharaoh. It is clear that not only do they see no hope for themselves apart from the land; they also see only desolation for the land if they are separated from it (Gen. 47:1–19). Similarly, in the story of Naboth's vineyard, King Ahab and Queen Jezebel embody the royal dynamic of the powerful, stripping Naboth of his *nahala*, the land to which his family belongs (1 Kings 21).

Similarly, the history of colonization in our country, Canada, has shown that forcing Indigenous peoples off their lands was intended to have a double effect. First, the land was separated from the care of the people whose lives were bound up in it, so that it could be mismanaged, abused, and exploited by settlers seeking wealth and maximum short-term profit. And second, deprived of their land and food sources, Indigenous peoples faced starvation and disease.[106] Denying access to food and food sources became a tool of genocide.

When you said that we needed to talk about food, I thought you were going to talk about organics and that kind of thing.

-solution-for-a-low-carbon-economy/). For ideas on alternatives from highlighters to contraceptives, see www.rubbishfree.co.nz. The founders of this site, Waveney Warth and Matthew Luxon, produce one large bag of rubbish per *year*. See also Bea Johnson, *Zero Waste Home: The Ultimate Guide to Simplifying Your Life and Reducing Your Waste* (New York: Scribner, 2013); and Amy Korst, *The Zero-Waste Lifestyle: Live Well by Throwing Away Less* (Berkeley: Ten Speed Press, 2012).

106. For an evocative essay linking Naboth's vineyard with contemporary abuse of Indigenous lands, see Matthew Humphrey, "A Pipeline Runs through Naboth's Vineyard: From Abstraction to Action in Cascadia," in Myers, *Watershed Discipleship*, 121–37.

That is certainly important as well. If we ask the questions above about where we get most of our food, we will see that industrial agriculture makes it impossible to love our neighbor and impossible to serve the earth. In practice, industrial agriculture is rapidly making it impossible for the whole world to be fed; you can only let the topsoil blow away for so long until it is completely gone, and you can only pour petroleum-based fertilizers into the soil for so long before the land is left barren and infertile.[107]

This is one place where the public imagination is already way ahead of the church. The worldwide movement toward local food, farmers markets, sustainably raised meat, and urban agriculture isn't just a trendy food fad; it is a biblical imperative. This is because the problem is not a lack of knowledge about what's wrong; the problem is our *moral ignorance* and *weakness of character*.[108] That is to say, we know the costs of our imported industrial food, but our idolatrous appetites mean that we won't say no. We know we should eat seasonally, but darn it, carrots and beets get so boring by spring. The insatiable consumption that is at the heart of all idolatry is manifest in our gluttonous eating habits.

Ironically, this is how sin is described right at the beginning of the story, when Adam and Eve engaged in that first culinary indiscretion in Genesis 3. God told them to contain their appetites; only one tree was off limits for them. And it is precisely that tree that they insist on eating from. The original sin was to eat something out of season, to eat something that they were not permitted to eat at that time.

A "culinary indiscretion"? That sounds like having an affair over dinner.

Eating out of season is like having an affair. It is eating in a way that is unfaithful to your place.

So why was the forbidden fruit "out of season"?

Because the prohibition was that while other trees were fine for harvesting, something about this tree made it wrong for human consumption at that time. Whether it might have come into season at another time, we don't know, but the fruit of this tree set a limit to human consumption. Responsible care for their garden home required Adam and Eve to respect the nature of this tree and therefore to constrain their own appetites. "As creatures that eat,

107. According to the UN Food and Agriculture Organization, there are only sixty more harvests' worth of topsoil left. See Chris Arsenault, "Only 60 Years of Farming Left If Soil Degradation Continues," *Scientific American*, https://www.scientificamerican.com/article/only-60-years-of-farming-left-if-soil-degradation-continues/.

108. Wendell Berry, "The Unsettling of America," in *Art of the Commonplace*, 44.

we have to live in terms of what a nourishing garden requires of us," writes Norman Wirzba.[109] The sin of the garden was one of misdirected desire, an overstepping of proper creational boundaries, and a declaration of independence from both the Creator and the rest of creation.[110] They took and they ate because it was a delight to the eyes and they desired it (Gen. 3:6). Kind of like strawberries in January in Canada. Or melons in March. Why do we eat them? Because they are beautiful to see, we want them, and we want them now. That's it.

Food outside of covenant, outside of seeking the shalom of creation, outside of justice for the food producers and for those who have no access to this food, is always "food out of season." Wirzba describes this as "eating in exile."[111] When we are exiled and alienated from our creational home, food becomes a commodity, and we become consumers. We lose touch with the production of food (or even the loving preparation of our food) and demand that our food be plentiful, inexpensive, and convenient. Eating in exile is invariably a matter of consuming "food out of season." Or to return to Paul's diatribe at the end of Romans 1, food consumed in greed and covetousness (and its culinary cousin, gluttony), and food produced by a foolish agriculture that is ruthless and faithless in relation to the land, is always "food out of season."

Really, it is astounding that we continue to behave this way. Do we want our children and grandchildren to live in even more extreme weather because we wanted grapes in February and tomatoes in April? What kind selfish indulgence is this? The oldest kind imaginable, according to the biblical story. It is these daily acts of indulgence that make it possible for a culture of indulgence to thrive; it is our complicity in these small-scale abuses that make it possible for large-scale abuses to be tolerated.[112]

Reflecting deeply on what we eat in terms of the three questions of discernment listed above doesn't seem that much of a stretch from Paul's vision of creation's groaning and longing for redemption. Is the shalom of God's creation frustrated or furthered in the production, consumption, and disposal of this food within its broader agricultural context?

109. Norman Wirzba, *Food and Faith: A Theology of Eating* (Cambridge: Cambridge University Press, 2011), 75.

110. Randy Woodley describes the fall as abuse of the land that "throws creation and our relationship with the Creator out of balance." Woodley, "Early Dialogue in the Community of Creation," in Heinrichs, *Buffalo Shout, Salmon Cry*, 100.

111. Wirzba, *Food and Faith*, chap. 3.

112. Davis, *Scripture, Culture, Agriculture*, 13.

From Lament to Resurrection Hope

Why do I have a sinking feeling that if I start asking these kinds of questions, I'm going to get depressed?

We wish depression on no one. Depression is debilitating and paralyzing. It leaves us with no resources with which to respond to the admittedly depressing state of affairs in which we find ourselves. But you are right in seeing that honestly asking these kinds of questions about our eating habits, and about pretty much everything else in the system of global capitalism, is a very sobering thing. That is why any serious engagement with a world of ecological wounds must begin in lament.

Another reason to engage in lament?

Yes. You see, lament is necessary because when we engage in lament, we are crying out for things to be different. We are holding up before God the hope and expectation of another world, and we are asking God to bring such a world into being. Lament calls God back repeatedly to the need for justice for creation and humanity.[113]

Are you saying that lament is an act of hope?

Yes, lament is an act of hope. In fact, it is an act of "passionate expectation."[114] While depression leaves us stuck in the brokenness of the present, lament entails a vision of life that calls us forward. Remember how Paul depicts creation in Romans 8. Creation is not only groaning in birth pangs but also waiting with eager longing for the revealing of the children of God (Rom. 8:19). And Paul describes us as groaning inwardly while we wait for adoption, the redemption of our bodies (Rom. 8:23). You see, lament is always asking "How long?" because lament is voiced in defiant hope of a restored world. The creation knows that when the children of God begin to live out their calling as the image bearers who will care for creation, then creation itself will be set free. And as believers we long for that day when we will be those true children and our very bodies will be redeemed.

Is this what you called "living in the tragic gap" earlier on?

Yes. The phrase is from Parker Palmer.[115] The tragic gap is that space between what creation can and will be and the place that we find ourselves in now. We

113. Walter Brueggemann, "The Formfulness of Grief," in *The Psalms and the Life of Faith*, ed. Patrick D. Miller (Minneapolis: Fortress, 1995), 91.

114. Brueggemann, "Formfulness of Grief," 91.

115. Parker Palmer, "The Broken-Open Heart: Living with Faith and Hope in the Tragic Gap," *Weavings* 24, no. 2 (March/April 2009): 1–12.

deeply long for that place of healing, of forgiveness, of restoration. But we aren't there yet. And so we live with the grief of knowing how it could be but having to deal with the deathly reality of how things actually are.

That's what depresses me. That gap is unbearable, and I find myself paralyzed. "Stuck in a moment that I can't get out of" is the way that Bono put it.[116] *And I just don't know what to do.*

Here's the thing. Living in the tragic gap doesn't actually get better if you are offered a list of rules to follow, as if to say, "If you care for creation, then do this and this and this and you'll be fine." We are stuck in a moment that we can't get out of because the story of our lives, that story of civilizational progress and affluence embodied in the produce section of our grocery stores, has reached a dead end. This is a story that provides no way forward. What we need is a transformed imagination, not a list of rules.

The grand story that Paul is telling and reinterpreting at the heart of the empire invites us to be taken up in a vision that calls us forward, calls us in, so that we can't help but want to live into the healing and redemption that God offers. This storied vision so captures our imagination that we can't bear to live any other way. While recognizing that the tragic gap runs right through the lives of all of us (see Rom. 7), we offer our whole embodied lives to God, seeking to be liberated from dead-end conformity to the idolatrous systems of the world. Rooted in this story, experiencing this liberation, our imaginations are set free from captivity to the globalist ideology of empire, and we begin to discern what is the good and acceptable will of God in our lives (Rom. 12:1–2).

Maybe this is crazy, but it seems to us that if our imaginations are set free by this vision, then simple things like buying strawberries in January, or owning a dryer, or even owning a cell phone, become things that we can't imagine doing because they are so far from fulfilling our desires for what the world can be.

Part of the problem is that my upbringing didn't involve a vision of hope for the earth. I mean, if your deepest longing is to live with Jesus in heaven, then you don't really have any powerful "desires for what the world can be." Heaven kind of eclipses earth. But you've made it sound as though God's vision of shalom includes the earth, not just now but in the future.

Where does Paul ever say in the epistle to the Romans that the Christian's eternal destiny is to live with Jesus in heaven? Nowhere. And how could he even imagine such a thing? It is not found anywhere in the Bible, nor would such a

116. U2, "Stuck in a Moment," on *All That You Can't Leave Behind*, Universal International Music, 2000.

vision have ever occurred to the apostle.[117] We need to remember that Paul's most foundational understanding of human identity and calling is rooted in the story told so vividly in Genesis 2. There we meet a God with dirty fingernails. The Creator kneels down into the earth and forms an earth creature. God takes *ʾadamah*, the earth, and makes *ʾadam*, the earth creature. The earth creature, formed from the earth, is who we are. Humans are from the humus. Randy Woodley describes us as "walking earth."[118] But it isn't enough to be an earth creature, for then the Spirit of God breathes out and fills our lungs—and the earth creature begins to live. We are creatures made of earth and the living breath of God.

Genesis 2 goes on to paint a captivating picture of where we are and what God has called us to do. This God of the dirty fingernails plants a garden for us—the image is less a carefully tended ornamental garden than a forest garden. The Divine Gardener causes trees to grow that are pleasant to the sight—trees for delight—and trees that are good for food: hazelnut and butternut, almond and acorn, walnut and chestnut, peach, apple, mango, pawpaw, pomegranate, fig, olive, grape, date, cherry, elderberry, and seaberry—all the trees that give life and shelter and medicine for the earth creature.

Of course, a forest is never just trees. It is a habitat, a home for animals, insects, birds, snakes, frogs, bushes, flowers, bacteria, fungi. The forest garden is a home for all creatures.

And then God places the earth creature in this forest garden to till it and to keep it. The earth creature bears the image of the Divine Gardener through gardening. The human bears the image of the Divine Homemaker by being at home and making home, protecting and enhancing the world as habitat to all creatures. "Till and keep" is the translation most of us are familiar with. Ellen Davis points out that a better translation would be "serve and observe."[119] We are to serve in

117. J. Richard Middleton calls us to repent of a dualistic doctrine of heaven that strips us of the profoundly new-earth hope of the biblical witness. Middleton not only demonstrates that biblical eschatology (throughout the whole canon!) is decidedly directed to the restoration of the earth, not eternal dwelling in heaven, but he also addresses every possible text that might suggest a heavenly destination. Rather than engaging each of these texts, thereby taking us away from our focus on Romans, we leave that detailed argument to Middleton. J. Richard Middleton, *A New Heaven and a New Earth: Reclaiming Biblical Eschatology* (Grand Rapids: Baker Academic, 2014), esp. 221–27, 300–305. Also extremely helpful is Barbara R. Rossing, *The Rapture Exposed: The Message of Hope in the Book of Revelation* (New York: Basic Books, 2004). The epilogue addresses the texts outside the book of Revelation ("Debunking the Rapture Verse by Verse," 173–86).

118. Randy S. Woodley, *Shalom and the Community of Creation: An Indigenous Vision* (Grand Rapids: Eerdmans, 2012), 86.

119. Davis, *Scripture, Culture, Agriculture*, 30.

the sense of being a servant of creation, as we are to be servants of one another. And we are to observe creation, as we observe the law by obeying its limits. We make home in creation through loving attentiveness. Attending to the limits and rules of the natural world, we attempt to live according to them.[120] We are placed in a forest of delight and beauty, a forest of food and sustenance, and we are called, quite simply, to pay attention to what it needs, and look after it. That is all.

The point of many of the prophetic texts that Paul alludes to in Romans is that we have forgotten who we are. The earth creatures have failed to live up to the calling we were given, this calling to make the earth fully our home.[121] This is what the language about exchanging the image of the living God is about. We were created as the image bearers, to engage in faithful rule over the creation. And we have abdicated our calling. We have failed to be the ones who imaged God, and we have forgotten our roots in the earth. We are no longer the earth creatures but the death bringers. We have replaced "till and keep" with "take and destroy." We have supplanted "serve and observe" with "dominate and discard."

This is the imagery that Paul refers to in Romans 8:19 when he says that all creation groans as it waits with eager expectation for the revealing of the children of God. Creation is waiting for the earth creatures to be revealed, waiting for us to fulfill our calling, waiting with longing for us to claim our identity. We are the earth creatures, come to serve and observe, to tend and keep the earth and those who live in it. Creation is waiting for us to remember who we are.

But, as we have seen, creation isn't the only one waiting. Paul says that those of us who have the first fruits of the Spirit, who have been enlivened anew by the life-giving breath of God, know our calling. We know who we are, and so we too groan as we wait for the redemption of our bodies (Rom. 8:23). We are longing and groaning with creation. We are waiting, waiting for resurrection.

And in talking about the redemption of our bodies, Paul says something not just about who we are but about who we are called to be. You see, we are the earth creatures, and our destiny in the Bible is never to live for eternity apart from our bodies and the earth.[122] That is why the book of Revelation describes our hope in terms of a new heaven and a new earth where God comes to dwell on the new earth with humanity, with the earth creatures. Then God will wipe every tear

120. In the beginning, there was no ecology-economy division.

121. Woodley, *Shalom*, 76.

122. Again, Middleton, *New Heaven*, 227–37, is very helpful on the matter of life after death. Through close exegesis of all the relevant texts, he demonstrates that the doctrine of a bodiless intermediate state of the dead in heaven has no biblical warrant.

from our eyes, death will be no more, and mourning and crying and pain will be no more (Rev. 21:1–5).[123]

I guess that does fit in better with Romans 8. After all, what would be the point of creation waiting for the children of God if we were just going to abandon the earth for heaven?

And it fits in with the biblical vision of who we are called to be. You see, if we accept the popular vision that we are all headed to heaven someday, then it becomes easy to turn our back on the earth, because it doesn't really matter. We will never foster an ecologically healing vision and practice in our lives as long as we hold on to an unbiblical heaven-focused theology.

Biblical hope, in Paul and throughout the canon, is decidedly this-worldly. Resurrection hope is always a bodily hope that encompasses all of creation. The Bible calls us to remember who we are: we are from the earth, we are for the earth, and we are destined for the new earth, where God will dwell with us.[124] Or, in the language of Romans 8, we are the children of God who will one day be agents of creation's liberation when our bodies are redeemed. This is language of resurrection, the language of hope (Rom. 8:19–24). Throughout the book of Romans, the longing for resurrection found throughout the Scriptures is answered in Jesus.

What do you mean by "the longing for resurrection found throughout the Scriptures"? I thought the resurrection of Jesus was a complete surprise for the disciples.

Oh, it was a complete surprise. But that is only because the resurrection of Jesus didn't quite match their expectations. If we look at those places in Paul's Scriptures that talk about resurrection, however, we can see how in Romans Jesus fulfills the expectations of those texts. But in order to talk about that resurrection hope, we need to say one more thing about idolatry. The problem with idols is their impotence. They have neither knowledge nor understanding, they cannot hear or speak, they cannot move, and, most importantly, they cannot save.[125] Idolatry can never deliver on its promises, can never live up to its ideological rhetoric, always disappoints, and therefore always breeds hopelessness. In

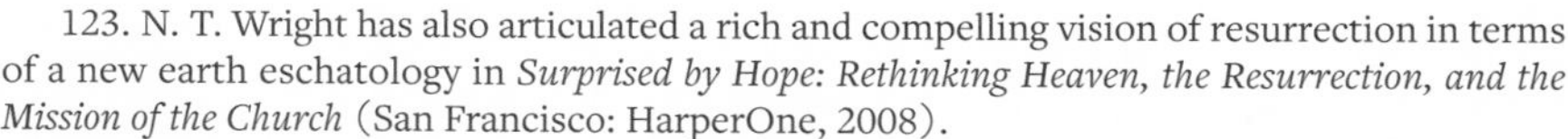

123. N. T. Wright has also articulated a rich and compelling vision of resurrection in terms of a new earth eschatology in *Surprised by Hope: Rethinking Heaven, the Resurrection, and the Mission of the Church* (San Francisco: HarperOne, 2008).

124. Wendell Berry puts it this way: "The Bible's aim, as I read it, is not the freeing of the spirit from the world. It is the handbook of their [i.e., the spirit and the world's] interaction. It says that they cannot be divided; that their mutuality, their unity, is inescapable; that they are not reconciled in division, but in harmony. What else can be meant by the resurrection of the body?" Berry, "The Body and the Earth," in *Art of the Commonplace*, 104.

125. See Walter Brueggemann, *Israel's Praise: Doxology against Idolatry and Ideology* (Philadelphia: Fortress, 1988), 94–95, 106–18.

contrast, the God of Israel is not only the Creator of all, but also the one who saves the weak and the orphan and maintains the right of the oppressed and the poor.[126]

In those psalms where God is called on to act in the face of the oppression and idolatry of gentile nations, the language of resurrection is central. "Rise up [*anasta*], O God, and judge the earth!" says the psalmist (Ps. 82:8).[127] Why should God rise up? Because of God's steadfast love toward Israel (44:26). Throughout his letter to the Romans, Paul is arguing that that call has been answered. How do we know that God is faithful? Because in Jesus, God has acted against injustice (Rom. 1:18); in Jesus, God has ended the dominion of death (5:17); in Jesus, God has ended the power of wickedness (6:17–19); in Jesus, God has proved his love for us (5:8); in Jesus, we have a sure hope to share in the glory of God (5:2); in Jesus, we are not only made just but also glorified (8:30); and in Jesus, we hope for the redemption of our bodies (8:23). All of this happens because Jesus rose from the dead (1:4; 4:24–25; 6:4–8; 7:4; 8:11, 34; 10:9; 14:9).

This hope of resurrection is intimately tied to the restoration of creation that Paul describes in Romans 8:19–21. As we have seen, creation not only waits for the children of God to take up their task as image bearers (8:19, 29) but also waits for "the freedom of the glory of the children of God" (8:21). The loss of glory that results from idolatry in Romans 1:23 is restored to those who are conformed to the image of the Son in Romans 8:30. In light of texts such as Psalm 8:4–9 and Daniel 7:14, as well as various texts from Qumran and the intertestamental literature that link the glory of Adam with care of the land, Paul appears to be working in a symbolic world where the loss of "glory" and its restoration has very tangible effects on the land.[128]

It seems to me that "glory" talk usually has a negative impact on the land.

What do you mean?

126. The classic articulation of this latter point is Ps. 82 (81 LXX), which uses the vocabulary of the oppressed (*tapeinō*), also found in Rom. 12:16. Cf. Walter Brueggemann, "Reflections on a Biblical Understanding of Property," in *A Social Reading of the Old Testament: Prophetic Approaches to Israel's Prophetic Life*, ed. Patrick J. Miller (Minneapolis: Fortress, 1994), 278. On the contrast between the impotence of the gods and the creating and saving action of God, see Deut. 4:25–31; 10:12–22; 32:36–43; 33:23–29; 1 Kings 18:20–38; Pss. 115; 135; Isa. 10:1–13; Hab. 2:18–19; and consistently in every chapter of Isa. 40–48.

127. See also Pss. 3:7 (3:8 LXX); 7:6 (7:7 LXX); 9:19 (9:20 LXX); 10:12 (9:33 LXX); 17:13 (16:13 LXX); 44:26 (43:27 LXX); 68:1 (67:2 LXX); 102:13 (101:14 LXX); 132:8 (131:8 LXX).

128. For documentation and further discussion of these motifs, see Keesmaat, *Paul and His Story*, 84–101.

Well, first there is the "going to glory" language that is identified with going to heaven, and you've already shown how that is a theology of little ecological benefit. But then there is the way in which "glory" is so often the language of empire. You know what I mean? As you've described it, the "glory of the fatherland," the "glory of empire," is always bad news for the land. Once something is glorified, it seems totally legitimate to sacrifice things before that glory.

Paul's emphasis on glory, however, comes as a radical challenge to the imperial story.

How so?

In the first place, according to Rome, the emperor is the one who images the gods and engages in a glorious rule over the world.[129] Paul tells a different story: rather than Caesar bringing restoration, abundance, and peace to creation, it is the restored people of God who bring such restoration as part of their creaturely calling. Paul applies the "image of God" language, usually reserved for the king, to those who are the children of God, those conformed to the image of Jesus (Rom. 8:29; cf. Col. 3:10). In this way the special status of the emperor as image of God is challenged by this motley assortment of people who claim to be followers of a different Lord with a radically different calling.[130]

In the second place, the so-called abundance and fertility of the empire are rooted in the power and strength of Roman military might. Violence is the basis for *all* that the empire offers. As Romans 8 progresses, Paul makes it abundantly clear that the children of God who will exercise right rule over creation are those who bear the first fruits of the Spirit and hence groan in travail with creation itself (8:23).[131] That is to say, not violent rule over creation but entering into the suffering of creation fits the children of God for the redemption of their bodies. If the "glorification" of the children of God (8:30) is a matter of being restored to our foundational identity and calling to till and keep, to serve and observe, then sharing in the anguish of creation is integral to realizing that true human glory. Paul thereby replaces the "glory" of Rome that results in abuse of the land with the redemptive glory of healing service.

129. In fact, throughout the ancient Near East the king as the image of god or the gods was ubiquitous, along with the corollary: the rest of humankind exists to serve the gods by serving the king. Already in Gen. 1, the description of humanity and not the king as the image of God was a challenge to these other stories. See Middleton, *Liberating Image*, 185–219.

130. On the contrast between Jesus as Lord and Caesar as Lord, see Sylvia Keesmaat, "Crucified Lord or Conquering Saviour? Whose Story of Salvation?," *Horizons in Biblical Theology* 26, no. 2 (2004): 69–93.

131. Of course, as the chapter continues, the Spirit also enters into this groaning (8:26).

That's a pretty attractive picture.

That's the whole point. Paul is offering this vision of the healing of the earth as an alternative imagination to that of the empire. If we truly are earth creatures, called to the care of creation, then the destruction of creation will leave us in lament and sorrow, even as we long so deeply for a life of ecological healing, love, and care. This is not a world that we can clearly see through the haze of our pollution and the tears of our despair. But hope, says Paul, is precisely for what is not seen. "But if we hope for what we do not see, we wait for it with patience" (8:25).

Hope on the Ground and in the Watershed

I guess the question then becomes, What does that hope look like? I mean, we've talked about repentance, and there are things we need to give up if we repent. But if we are to live into this hope, are there things we should be doing? Not that I'm looking for a list of rules, but can you help me to get a hopeful imagination off the ground?

Off the ground?

Okay, bad metaphor. I guess that what I'm looking for is in fact a hopeful imagination on the ground.

One place that hopeful imagination can be found is in Indigenous visions of the land. In the lament that began this chapter, we talked about remembering and learning what we have lost. In the process of that learning, in hearing the stories of our place, in learning what the indigenous species of plants and animals were, in learning about our watersheds and how they have changed, we will learn not only what to mourn but also what needs to happen for health to return.

That's a pretty tall order.

Begin, then, with your watershed.

What do you mean, my watershed?

There was a time, not that long ago, when the primary question for communities was where their water came from. Water is foundational for human life and for the life of the plants and animals on which human beings depend for food, shelter, tools, and clothing. So people not only knew where their water came from; they also knew what was necessary for that watershed to remain healthy.

Our farm is located in the Martin Creek watershed, which runs into the Balsam Lake watershed, part of the broader Kawartha Lakes watershed. This area is not prime agricultural land, but it has begun to be profitable for cash cropping. Cash crops like soybean and corn are beginning to be planted in large quantities. These crops are highly dependent on petroleum-based fertilizers and are laced with pesticides and herbicides. This kind of agriculture makes money while depleting the soil, wiping out beneficial insects and polluting the watershed.[132] In order to facilitate large equipment and to cultivate in every possible area of a farm, it is common to cut down tree lines between fields. The trees, of course, prevent erosion, increase fertility, provide habitat for numerous animals, insects, and plants, and help to keep water from running off the land.

We know that this kind of agriculture is killing our watershed. And so we actively support legislation to limit the pesticides that are being sprayed on those fields. We have recommitted ourselves to not purchasing any products that were produced using the pesticides that were killing our watershed, for surely they are killing the creatures in other watersheds as well. And then we have begun to think more intentionally about water on our farm. How could we contribute to the health of our watershed in our farming practices? Was there a way that we could keep water from draining straight into what is now an increasingly contaminated marsh? Could we somehow hold water on our own land so that it could seep down to the water table more slowly? We had been exploring these questions already, but our alarm at the increase of these cash-cropping methods in our area, together with worry about the health of creatures in our watershed, provided a context for our actions that fed the urgency of our work.

So what did you do?

We began to redesign our garden so that we planted along the contours of the land, rather than imposing straight lines of garden beds. Designing the garden on contour has meant that we have built swales and berms that will capture water during rain events in a way that slows down the movement of water across the land. In one of our pastures we have dug similar swales and planted hundreds of trees and bushes along the berms. Some of these plantings will result in food and berry crops in the future, both for human and animal consumption.

While the cash croppers are tearing out tree lines, you are creating new ones?

Precisely. On one level this is a very large project for us, but in the broader scheme of things this is a small fidelity, an attention to one place in order to live out that vision of creational restoration. But there is another aspect to this.

132. For a comprehensive picture of how industrial agriculture is one of the top contributors to climate breakdown, and of the alternatives for renewal, see Eric Toensmeier, *The Carbon Farming Solution: A Global Toolkit of Perennial Crops and Regenerative Agriculture Practices for Climate Change Mitigation and Food Security* (White River Junction, VT: Chelsea Green, 2016); and Paul Hawken, ed., *Drawdown: The Most Comprehensive Plan Ever Proposed to Reverse Global Warming* (New York: Penguin, 2017).

Before the colonizers came to this land, the Mississaugas of the Anishnaabeg people lived on this land, and it provided all they needed from season to season: maple syrup in the late winter; pan fish and pickerel in the spring; the berries in their seasons: strawberries, raspberries, blueberries, elderberries; the three sisters: corn, beans, and squash; wild rice and nuts in the fall along with ducks, geese, and deer; and ice fishing in the winter again. The land provided all the food they needed, as well as their medicines, clothing, and shelter. On our farm we are not just planting any trees and shrubs; we are trying to learn about the plants indigenous to our watershed. Those plants that can provide food, medicine, and shelter are the ones that we are planting. We are seeking, in a very small way, to bring restoration to our watershed.

But how can I find out about my watershed? I live in the middle of a city. My water comes from a tap.

You can access watershed maps that will show the larger watershed for your area, as well as smaller areas. And we are part of an exciting movement of Christians throughout the world who have coined the phrase "watershed discipleship" to describe the direction that their ecological vision and practice is taking.[133] You could start by banding together with these folks. And once you've started to learn about your watershed, you can then begin to discern what it means to be a creature of that watershed.

A creature of my watershed? I'm not sure I understand what you mean by that.

According to Norman Wirzba, "We need to recover the art of being creatures. By this I mean (a) an appreciation of how our lives are maintained by grace and (b) the practical skills necessary to act on that appreciation."[134] It won't be enough to know what we have lost; it won't be enough to grieve that loss. We must begin the difficult journey of relearning how to live so as to recover that loss. We must recover what some call an "agrarian vision,"[135] "educating our young in the ways

133. More information can be found on watershed discipleship at https://watersheddiscipleship.org. To find your watershed in Canada, and for a description of the major watersheds, go to Canadian Geographic: http://www.canadiangeographic.ca/watersheds/map/?path=english/watersheds-list. Kairos Canada has helpful information on their Reconciliation in the Watershed program as well as resources for learning about your watershed and learning about watershed discipleship. Go to http://www.kairoscanada.org/what-we-do/ecological-justice/reconciliation-in-the-watershed. In the United States you can find your watershed at https://water.usgs.gov/wsc/map_index.html.

134. Wirzba, *Paradise of God*, 15.

135. For a succinct articulation of an agrarian vision, you couldn't do better than Wendell Berry's fine essay "The Agrarian Standard," in *Citizenship Papers*, 143–52, as well as all the essays in the Wirzba-edited collection of Berry's essays, *The Art of the Commonplace*.

of home-coming or home-building, ways that promote dedication to places or community over the long term."[136]

I guess the problem with that is I wouldn't know how to educate anyone in the ways of homemaking or home building. I live so far from where I was born that I only go back for visits now. And with school and work, I haven't lived anywhere long enough to feel that it is a place in which I am rooted, a place that is my home.

You have articulated the central problem for many of us—we have forgotten the practical skills of homemaking in our place. So maybe one way to begin would be to disconnect from the technology that shields us from creation and begin with a garden.[137]

A garden.

Yes. Grow some of your own food, even if it is just a window box or a container on your porch. Through your garden, even if it is only two plants, you can learn "the patience of attention and the humility of service."[138] And if you garden on a larger scale, you will learn, in the words of Romans 12:16, what it is to "walk with the oppressed" (our translation), especially the oppressed and abused earth that we find in both the cities and our rural areas. And if you begin to realize what has already been lost in your place, you will realize that it isn't enough to just do something "sustainable." We would just be sustaining something that is already damaged. We need to go beyond that to restoration. There is a movement that we are quite involved with called *permaculture*.[139] At its most basic, permaculture is the marriage of two words: *permanent* and *agriculture*. In that context it refers to an agriculture that is rooted in the resilient and regenerative interaction between plants, animals, and humans for the long term. That means we should plant fruit and nut trees and shrubs, perennial grains and vegetables. We should create an ecosystem that will be resilient and endure from generation to generation (hence permanent). But permaculture is more than that. If you read the foundational

136. Wirzba, *Paradise of God*, 99. For further practical reflection on such homemaking, see Shannon Hayes, *Radical Homemakers: Reclaiming Domesticity from Consumer Culture* (Richmondville, NY: Left to Write Press, 2010).

137. Norman Wirzba helpfully describes the garden as "the world in miniature," in which we have "the most practical lens through which to feel and understand our engagement with the earth." He notes that the garden is also the context of both creation (Eden) and salvation (Gethsemane). Wirzba, *Paradise of God*, 113.

138. Wirzba, *Paradise of God*, 115.

139. An accessible introduction to permaculture in an urban context is Toby Hemenway, *Gaia's Garden: A Guide to Home-Scale Permaculture*, 2nd ed. (White River Junction, VT: Chelsea Green, 2009). A recent and excellent example of rural permaculture is Ben Falk, *The Resilient Farm and Homestead: An Innovative Permaculture and Whole Systems Design Approach* (White River Junction, VT: Chelsea Green, 2013).

theory of permaculture practitioners, you will notice an emphasis on the mess that we have created for ourselves. Permaculture acknowledges that we human beings have an unprecedented ability to affect our environment and an incredible lack of insight as to what the impact of our actions will be. And those effects have been, for the most part, disastrous.

This sounds a bit like Romans 1–3.

The biblical understanding of sin might be the only doctrine that is empirically verifiable. So it isn't at all surprising that folks who may not have any allegiance to biblical faith see the same thing that the Scriptures bear witness to. But there is more. People involved with permaculture also seek to explore ways of living that care for both creation and the human community. But they are concerned not merely with care but also with healing, regeneration, farming and gardening, building, and creating communities in ways that create fruitfulness and fertility for all concerned. They are concerned with relationships that are healthy, with food that is good for the community of all creatures, with buildings that bring healing to those who inhabit them.[140] And all of this is done with an eye to the fact that we are likely to mess things up. So there is a built-in system of feedback, of constant thoughtful and prolonged observation to ensure that what is undertaken really is for the healing of those involved.

Thoughtful and prolonged observation reminds me of what you were saying earlier about our calling to serve and observe the creation.

It is very close. Serving and observing become a constant feedback loop: observe continually so that you can make sure that you really are serving! Since we have a persistent tendency to serve ourselves rather than creation, this feedback is essential. We need to be vigilant in keeping our eyes open to what is really going on. We need a heightened attentiveness to creation.

This point is crucial, because the prophets make clear that at some point we will not have a choice. The land will vomit us out, and we will be forced

140. David Pritchett, "Watershed Discipleship in Babylon: Resisting the Urban Grid," in Myers, *Watershed Discipleship*, 42–59, describes ways that "re-villaging," "de-paving," and "food-mapping" subvert the infrastructure that distances us from the soil in urban contexts. For an example of how permaculture principles can shape resilient communities in a global context, see Trina Moyles, *Women Who Dig: Farming, Feminism and the Fight to Feed the World* (Regina, SK: Regina University Press, 2018); see also Rob Hopkins, *The Transition Handbook: From Oil Dependency to Local Resilience* (White River Junction, VT: Chelsea Green, 2008), and *The Transition Companion: Making Your Community More Resilient in Uncertain Times* (White River Junction, VT: Chelsea Green, 2011). Hopkins is the founder of the Transition Movement. A theological underpinning is provided by Timothy Gorringe and Rosie Beckham, *Transition Movement for Churches: A Prophetic Imperative for Today* (Norwich: Canterbury Press, 2013).

into a frightening place of exile.[141] That might be the exile of environmental devastation, or the exile of a new place because our city was flooded out or our farmland is a desert. But one thing is clear—the status quo, the energy use, and the stable economy and comforts of our middle-class North American lifestyle will no longer be possible. The question is, Will we have already been living into the vision of healing and redemption so that we know what that vision looks like when the time of exile comes? Will we know how to plant gardens and build houses? Will we have the skills of homemaking? Or we will have been so caught up with the idolatries and addictions that led to destruction that we won't know how to be the healing hands of God in the world? That, we submit, is the question.

I guess I am still struggling with another question. You talked earlier about how our economic system is built on taking resources from Indigenous peoples both in Canada and around the world. You've also talked about the need to be attentive to the effects of our actions and to what is really happening in creation. It seems to me that if we are talking of repentance, then we need to take seriously what is happening in our country to Indigenous land. And, I confess, when I start to think about those issues, they seem so huge and complex that I don't know where to begin.

Perhaps the place to start is where you are. Do you know the history of Indigenous people on the land where you live? For instance, one of us (Sylvia) was born in Caledonia, Ontario. Caledonia is located next to the Six Nations reserve. Her dad lived across the road (literally) from the reserve in his teenage years, and so she grew up hearing the history of the Six Nations—the Mohawk, Cayuga, Seneca, Tuscarora, Oneida, and Onondaga peoples, who form the Haudenosaunee (or Iroquois) Confederacy. When she was a child, her father would find arrowheads and tools in the fields near their house and tell stories of what life had been like for the people there, even before the Six Nations had moved into this area. (This land had belonged to the Mississauga people before the Six Nations moved up from what is now the United States, and before that it belonged to the Wendat.) In addition, her uncle married Ann Johnson, a woman from Six Nations.

But even with all of these connections, there were things she didn't know. She didn't know that her aunt had lost her Indian Status when she married her uncle. She didn't realize that Aunt Ann *couldn't* live on the reserve and that her children were not considered native. She didn't realize that originally the peoples of the Six Nations were given 950,000 acres, six miles on either side of the Grand

141. Lev. 18:25–28; 20:22.

River from mouth to source. She didn't know that now they lived on only 45,000 acres of that land.[142]

Now we live in the Kawartha Lakes, and we are slowly learning the history of the Mississauga people who lived here before they were confined to a reserve at Curve Lake. In both of these cases, where Sylvia grew up and where we live now, there are ongoing struggles concerning the land that we can learn about and support. The people of the Six Nations are currently asking the government for an accounting of the money that the government promised to hold in trust when treaties were made on the Haldimand Tract, the original lands that they were given. We can join their voices in demanding an accounting and restitution of these monies.[143]

In addition, members of Mennonite, Lutheran, and Anglican churches located on this treaty land are exploring something called a "Spiritual Covenant." Adrian Jacobs describes it this way: "Churches in the Haldimand Proclamation would acknowledge Six Nations jurisdiction over the lands, pay a token lease to Six Nations, and Six Nations in turn would permit the church to function as a church. If a church was ever decommissioned, the land would then revert to Six Nations with Six Nations' assurance that the land would be used for spiritual and community purposes, and not business purposes (like a smoke shop!)."[144]

In Curve Lake there are different issues. The traditional staple food of the Anishnaabeg people, who are located in an area called Kawartha Lakes, is wild rice, or *manoomin*. For many years wild rice no longer grew in the lakes, but because the lakes are becoming healthier, the wild rice is returning. James Whetung, a member of Curve Lake First Nation, has harvesting rights for the wild rice in the lakes, but local cottage owners have done their best to destroy his harvests. They consider wild rice a weed that makes it hard to use their motorboats and jet skis. When they were unable to get permission to cut and destroy the wild rice early in the season, the cottagers resorted to sabotage; now they suspend a

142. For a detailed history, see http://www.sixnations.ca/SixMilesDeepBooklet2015Final.pdf. Click on the "Six Miles Deep Booklet." On the same site you can access Chief Hill's speech at the United Nations Permanent Forum on Indigenous Issues, which contains recommendations for action (http://www.sixnations.ca/UnitedNationsApril2015PresentationChiefHill.pdf). See also Susan M. Hill, *The Clay We Are Made Of: Haudenosaunee Land Tenure on the Grand River* (Winnipeg: University of Manitoba Press, 2017).

143. Adrian Jacobs and Karen Kuhnert, "Seeking a Spiritual Covenant: Possibilities in the Haldimand Tract," in Woelk and Heinrichs, *Yours, Mine, Ours*, 157; Six Nations Council, *Six Miles Deep: Land Rights of the Six Nations of the Grand River*, http://www.sixnations.ca/SixMilesDeepBooklet2015Final.pdf.

144. Jacobs and Kuhnert, "Seeking a Spiritual Covenant," in *Yours, Mine, Ours*, 154.

chain between two motorboats and drag it through the rice beds, dumping the destroyed rice on the healthy beds that remain.[145]

Is that legal? Isn't that comparable to sabotaging a farmer's crop?

That's exactly what it is like. But because they have lived on a lakefront property for three generations (a grand total of forty-seven years), the cottagers feel entitled to destroy the food supply of the people who have lived there for thousands of years.

But how can anyone get away with destroying someone's food crop?

This is the basis on which settler peoples have always interacted with Indigenous peoples on the land—our private property (and the pleasure we derive from it) is always more important than morality or justice.[146]

But it doesn't have to be that way. We can stand with James Whetung and insist that his harvests be protected. We can tell people his story. We can educate cottage owners and farmers and try to return the lakes to common ownership in actual fact, not just on paper.

That sounds more manageable than trying to fix the whole system.

Well, maybe we need to realize that we aren't here to "fix" anything. That's part of the problem. One of the things we need to repent of is our desire to be the people who fix everything and solve every problem. Our Indigenous brothers and sisters are telling us to *listen*. Listen to what they have to say. Just shut up already and allow those who have been oppressed for so long tell us what liberation, healing, reconciliation, and reparations can look like.[147]

Did you just say "reparations"? What do you mean by that?

Well, the Bible makes clear that repentance and reconciliation are not easy. Leaving the reign of death and entering the reign of life (Rom. 5:17; 6:12–14) involves being crucified with Jesus (6:3–11). This isn't just something we say. Crucifying our old self means giving up all those things that have made for death, for us and for other people. It means giving up our addictions, our comforts, our pleasures that can only happen because someone else has been oppressed, because injustice has been done. This means that we will be called to *sacrifice*. We can't say we want reconciliation with the land and with the people we have dispossessed

145. The story has a few other complicating twists and turns. See Lisa Jackson, "Canada's Wild Rice Wars," *Al Jazeera*, February 20, 2016, https://www.aljazeera.com/indepth/features/2016/02/canada-wild-rice-wars-160217083126970.html.

146. Jennifer Harvey, "Dangerous 'Goods': Seven Reasons Creation Care Movements Must Advocate Reparations," in Heinrichs, *Buffalo Shout, Salmon Cry*, 324.

147. In *Shalom and the Community of Creation*, Randy Woodley discusses the importance of listening in an Indigenous worldview (144–47).

if we are not willing to engage in the hard work of making reparation, listening to what justice would look like, and then in humility standing with those seeking such justice. This is, we suggest, what presenting our members as instruments of justice (6:13) and walking with the oppressed (12:16) look like on the ground.

Kind of like those who went to Standing Rock to help protect the sacred waters of the Sioux from the Dakota Access Pipeline and those who have stood with the people of Grassy Narrows as they fight to have the mercury in their water cleaned up. Is that the kind of thing you mean?

That is part of it. But remember, you are a person with a place, wherever that place is right now. Explore your own history with that place. Where did you (or your ancestors) come from to end up here? What were the economic and political forces that brought you here? Learn the history of those who have been dispossessed in this place. Find those people. Hear their stories. Let them be your guide as they discern justice for their community and justice for the land on which you live.[148] The first peoples knew the watershed first; their wisdom will be necessary for your health and life.

On another level, and from your place, write your politicians. At the very least, urge them to enforce the treaties, where they exist.[149] And urge them to seek water justice. Protecting the watershed on which Indigenous peoples—and all of us—depend is crucial.

What if I can't find Indigenous peoples working on these issues?

We think that it is highly unlikely that that will be the case. However, there are examples of churches who have taken the lead on watershed regeneration. In Indiana, Benton Mennonite Church was preparing to do baptisms in the Elkhart River when they discovered that it was polluted with *E. coli* from sewage and agricultural runoff. So they began to explore where the pollution was coming from and worked to clean the river up. Throughout this process the river became more and more important to the community. Pastor Doug Kaufmann goes to check on the health of the river regularly, considering the river to be part of his community, whose health and well-being he is concerned about. In a sense, the river is now part of the congregation. This church is part of a network of Mennonite churches

148. For a richer and more detailed description of this process, see the very important article by Elaine Enns and Ched Myers, "Healing from 'Lies That Make Us Crazy': Practices of Restorative Solidarity," in Woelk and Heinrichs, *Yours, Mine, Ours*, 138–42.

149. Sylvia McAdam, "A Need for Courage: Discussing Settler Stumbling Blocks to Solidarity," in Woelk and Heinrichs, *Yours, Mine, Ours*, 63.

working for the health of their watersheds and creation.[150] A worldwide network of Christians in conservation called A Rocha also works with local communities on these issues.[151]

I guess that if all you are saying is true, it only makes sense for our churches to be the places where care for creation begins.

Romans is precisely about becoming a community that joins the lament of creation and walks with the most vulnerable. Your church community would be a good place to start. Not only are there quite a few curricular resources like those provided by the Mennonite Creation Care Network and A Rocha, but there is also a Green Church Network as well as a movement of churches that meet outdoors called the Wild Church Network.[152] Ched Myers provides an evocative description of watershed ecclesiology:

> Local congregations are ideally situated to become centers for learning to know and love our places enough to defend and restore them. But we must first re-inhabit our watersheds *as church*, allowing the natural and social landscapes to shape our symbolic life, mission engagements, and material habits. In some traditions, the older model of parish-as-*placed*-community still survives—though atrophied by market-driven member transiency and commuter mobility—and can be nurtured back into vibrancy. . . . Developing a watershed ecclesiology simply involves consciously rethinking our collective habits, large and small, inwardly or outwardly oriented.[153]

"Symbolic life, mission engagements, and material habits." Oddly enough, we can think of examples of all of these, although none of the churches doing them would consider themselves to be doing watershed ecclesiology. For instance, we've noticed that a lot of rural Anglican churches in Canada have windows that interpret the gospel stories in terms of the local geography—like a crucifixion scene that is clearly located on the Canadian shield. We could draw attention to these and become more intentional about locating our local geography in the places we

150. The Mennonite Creation Care Network has many resources concerning watersheds and creation care in general: www.mennocreationcare.org. Click on the link "Watershed Way" for information on watershed discipleship in your community. An extremely helpful curriculum for adults with practical resources can be found on the same website: https://www.mennocreationcare.org/every-creature-singing/.

151. In Canada the A Rocha website has very helpful liturgical and curricular resources: www.arocha.ca. The site also has links to Mennonite and A Rocha curricular materials.

152. See www.wildchurchnetwork.com.

153. Ched Myers, "Toward Watershed Ecclesiology: Theological, Hermeneutic and Practical Reflections," in Myers, *Watershed Discipleship*, 210.

worship. Another church we know takes a hike as a congregation every fall. And since various people on the hike point out plants and birds from the area, this could become a more intentional way for other members to inhabit and grow to know their watershed. Community gardens at churches and kitchens for teaching food preparation and preserving are venues for missional engagement as well. And many churches even occasionally have an outdoor service, usually for Easter.[154]

Imagine reflecting on these actions theologically with your congregation. That would be a way to build on practices that currently happen, walking into faithfulness and presenting your members as tools of justice rather than injustice (Rom. 6:13).

What you are describing seems to be an example of living in a way that denies the dominion of death and embraces the life that comes through Jesus (Rom. 5:17).

And maybe this is something of what Paul means when he calls us to walk in newness of life (Rom. 6:4). A new life for our communities, for ourselves, and for all creatures on the earth.

154. Myers, "Toward Watershed Ecclesiology," 200–217, cites examples like these and many more besides, with links to initiatives from a wide variety of denominations.

6

Economic Justice and the Kingdom of Life

We have argued that Paul is concerned about the shape of the *oikos*, the household of creation and the household of faith. This makes him, in the broadest sense of the term, an eco-theologian, not only because a theology of the land, a theology of creation, is woven throughout his epistle to the Romans, but also because his letter as a whole is an attempt to engender an alternative home among the followers of Jesus at the heart of the empire. Moreover, Paul's concern for creation is not something separate from his goal of shaping the disparate Christian communities in Rome into a unified home; it is integral to that goal.

We have also seen, however, that creational vision and economics are equally inseparable. Indeed, the despoliation of the creational household is invariably rooted in the practices of the human household. Ecology and economics are often on a collision course. Humans tend to make their home in the world in ways that destroy habitats and render that very world uninhabitable. And this domicidal tendency of human culture making, and specifically human economic practices, is only intensified, and provided with mythical and symbolic legitimation, in the dynamics of empire.

And so we must ask, Is Paul's creation theology broad and deep enough to also engender a theological vision of economics? If we have established that Paul has a creational vision running throughout his letter to the Romans, then can we make as strong a case that economic life is just as clearly within the purview of this epistle? How grounded is Paul's letter to the Romans in both the desecration of the land that he experienced all around him and the poverty, oppression, and economic injustice that was the daily life of so many of those to whom he addressed his letter? Does Paul's vision encompass both ecology and economics? And if it does, then how might we hear Paul's letter to the Romans speak into our own economic lives, especially within the imperial context of a global capitalism that has elevated the economic dimension of life to the pantheon of the gods? This chapter and the next will address these questions.

Idolatry, Ecology, and Economics

The desolation of creation is a prominent theme within the story of Israel. And the prophets make it clear that the destruction of creation is always a consequence of the economic practices that arise out of idolatry, out of a desire to live within the story of the gods of the nations. In the previous chapter we explored the ways in which idolatry leads to the groaning of creation, and the ways in which our own idolatrous and addictive lifestyles frustrate our attempts to work for the redemption and healing of the earth. We also argued that such destruction is rooted in the economic structures that are taken for granted and simply assumed to be the way that economic life works. This is as true of the economic structures that perpetuate the injustices of our own world as it was of the imperial economy of first-century Rome.

We have shown how Paul begins his lament in the letter to the Romans with an exposé of the idolatrous assumptions of the empire. Such idolatry, he argues, gives rise not only to an abandonment of our calling in relation to creation but also to sexual and economic violence. In this chapter we will focus on the dynamics of economic violence. The theme of economic justice, especially in relation to those who are rendered impoverished by the structures of empire, runs as a thread throughout Romans. Sometimes this theme is assumed in the symbolic world that the text moves within, and sometimes it overtly surfaces to remind us that this was a letter written to people who lived at the heart of an economically and socially stratified empire, where the vast majority of the population lived a precarious economic existence.[1]

1. Elsa Tamez calls them "the excluded." Elsa Tamez, *The Amnesty of Grace: Justification by Faith from a Latin-American Perspective*, trans. Sharon H. Ringe (Nashville: Abingdon, 1993), 37, 115. See also Peter Garnsey and Richard P. Saller, *The Roman Empire: Economy, Society, and Culture* (Berkeley: University of California Press, 1987); Walter Scheidel, Ian Morris, and Richard P. Saller, eds., *The Cambridge Economic History of the Greco-Roman World* (Cambridge: Cambridge University Press, 2007); Margaret Atkins and Robin Osborne, eds., *Poverty in the Roman World* (Cambridge: Cambridge University Press, 2006).

But before we begin with the specific texts, let us briefly review some points from earlier chapters. As we argued in chapter 1, the epistle to the Romans is deeply concerned with the question of God's faithfulness to Israel, or, as Richard Hays puts it, the question of theodicy.[2] Like all empires, the cultural narrative of Rome was one where the gods were on the side of those with power, those who were victorious. The persecution and suffering of Judeans in Rome (some of whom had been expelled in 49 CE and were not allowed to return until 54 CE) would firmly place them on the losing side of history in the narrative of Roman culture. Judean Christians were on the same losing side as their non-Christian kin. The theme of suffering, therefore, that runs through the letter (Rom. 5:3–5; 8:17–39; 12:12–21) was not merely an abstract discussion for Paul but had a wider sociocultural referent. In fact, it is clear that some of the vocabulary of the letter points to imperial persecution. The appeal for gentile acceptance of the Judeans throughout the epistle also highlights this theme.[3] In such a context, Paul writes a letter that draws deeply on the Scriptures of Israel to assert God's faithfulness to God's people. As we have shown, all of this is framed in terms of the justice of God (*dikaiosynē theou*), the covenantal faithfulness of God to God's people and, through them, to the world.

We suggest that this theme of suffering in Romans, as well as the question of God's justice, is linked not only to gentile-Judean relations but also to those who suffer economically. Such economic suffering has a twofold basis. On the one hand, as Peter Oakes has argued, those who began to follow Jesus would have provoked reactions from colleagues, clients, and patrons that resulted in increasing poverty from loss of business, possible exclusion from a guild, or loss of access to shared resources (such as ovens or kilns).[4] On the other hand, the community of believers in Rome consisted primarily of those who suffered as a result of the economic priorities and policies of imperial culture. Our depiction of Nereus and Iris in chapter 2 was based on recent work that has sought to uncover the economic complexities of the Pauline communities

2. Richard B. Hays, *Echoes of Scripture in the Letters of Paul* (New Haven: Yale University Press, 1989), 38.

3. That this theme is central in Romans is argued by Neil Elliott, *Liberating Paul: The Justice of God and the Politics of the Apostle* (Sheffield: Sheffield Academic Press, 1995); Sylvia C. Keesmaat, *Paul and His Story: (Re)Interpreting the Exodus Tradition* (Sheffield: Sheffield Academic Press, 2004); and Jewett, *Romans*, 70.

4. Peter Oakes, *Reading Romans in Pompeii: Paul's Letter at Ground Level* (Minneapolis: Fortress, 2009), 114–15; Peter Oakes, *Philippians: From People to Letter* (Cambridge: Cambridge University Press, 2001), 89–96.

in the Roman Empire.[5] While there is some disagreement over the details, it is clear that if subsistence is measured in terms of the calories necessary to keep one alive, then the overwhelming majority (more than 85 percent) of people in the empire lived in circumstances around or below the subsistence level.[6] Insofar as Paul's communities reflected the social and economic realities of the empire, they would have included a large number of members who lived in poverty. Moreover, it is clear from Paul's allusions to the social situation of his listeners that he both assumes and expects that there would be poverty in these early Christian communities.[7]

As we described the lives of Iris and Nereus, we tried to create a sense of the diversity of those who made up the communities of believers in Rome through a fictional portrayal of two typical members. We suggest that Nereus and Iris were the rule rather than the exception among Roman believers. Our reconstruction relied to some extent on the work of Peter Oakes, who, through a meticulous exploration of the material culture of those who lived at and above subsistence

5. In light of work by Steven J. Friesen, the question of the social location of the communities that Paul wrote to has become front and center (Steven J. Friesen, "Poverty in Pauline Studies: Beyond the So-Called New Consensus," *Journal for the Study of the New Testament* 26, no. 3 [2004]: 323–61). Friesen has, with his poverty scale, provided data as to the poverty level of most people in the empire and has determined, on the basis of references in Paul's letters (though, oddly, not Rom. 16), that the majority of those in Paul's churches (roughly 70 percent) lived at or below subsistence level. The number was likely higher in Rome, where the amount of money necessary for subsistence living was approximately 300 denarii higher per year than in other cities. See also Bruce Longenecker, "Exposing the Economic Middle: A Revised Economy of Scale for the Study of Early Urban Christianity," *Journal for the Study of the New Testament* 31 (2009): 243–78; Bruce W. Longenecker, *Remember the Poor: Paul, Poverty, and the Greco-Roman World* (Grand Rapids: Eerdmans, 2010); and a number of the essays in *Engaging Economics: New Testament Scenarios and Early Christian Reflection*, ed. Bruce W. Longenecker and Kelly D. Liebengood (Grand Rapids: Eerdmans, 2009). A fictional depiction that brings such economic dynamics to life is Bruce W. Longenecker, *The Lost Letters of Pergamum: A Story from the New Testament World*, 2nd ed. (Grand Rapids: Baker Academic, 2016).

6. The criteria used by Friesen in "Poverty in Pauline Studies." As Peter Oakes points out, however, such criteria do not take into account the fact that poverty levels begin well above the line of caloric subsistence. He therefore suggests a definition of poverty that is focused on the ability of someone to participate in the normal expectations of their culture (ironically, of course, in the empire such "normal expectations" would have been inaccessible to the vast majority of the population). Peter Oakes, "Constructing Poverty Scales for Greco-Roman Society: A Response to Steven Friesen's 'Poverty in Pauline Studies,'" *Journal for the Study of the New Testament* 26, no. 3 (2004): 367–71.

7. For example, Paul's depiction of the community in Corinth makes a point of bringing attention to the socioeconomic standing of many in that community as "weak in the world," people who are "low and despised in the world" (1 Cor. 1:27, 28). And in his discussion of the practice of the Lord's Supper, it is clear that he is concerned that those "who have nothing" are being humiliated and left out (1 Cor. 11:22). See Longenecker, *Remember the Poor*, chaps. 6–13.

level in the empire, provides a creative and illuminating glimpse into the lives of some of Paul's hearers by focusing particularly on Rome and the letter to the Romans.[8] However, we also want to ask whether Paul had economic issues in his sights in this letter and, if so, to what extent? We will look at Paul's language throughout Romans, particularly in the context of the Scriptures of Israel. Could it be that Paul is actually talking about poverty in this letter even more overtly than we had previously considered? Could it be that the question of poverty is at the heart of God's covenantal faithfulness and at the heart of a community where grace reigns through *justice* to eternal life (Rom. 5:21)? Could it be that the home that Paul is envisioning in this letter (our proposal in chap. 4) must be a home of economic justice? And if such economic themes are indeed crucial to Paul's letter, then does that provide us with the resources to address the economic distortions, injustices, and crises of our own time (introduced in chap. 3)?

The Suffering of the Roman Believers

We begin our exploration with Paul's descriptions of suffering throughout Romans, which points to a context of not only political oppression and persecution but also the suffering that results from poverty. Peter Oakes has noted the importance of the theme of endurance in suffering in Romans.[9] Such a theme is central in Romans 5:3–5, 8:17–39, and 12:12–21. In 5:3 and 8:35 the Greek word for suffering is *thlipsis*, which occurs repeatedly in the psalms of lament that Paul so frequently quotes in the letter.[10] As we shall see, in these psalms such suffering is consistently linked to injustice. In Romans 8:35 the list of those things that cannot separate believers from the love of Christ includes not only political persecution and the sword (presumably wielded by the state) but also hardship, distress, famine, and nakedness. This list suggests that members of this community were under threat not only from the direct actions of the state (as the "sword" and "rulers" of 8:35 and 8:38 suggest) but also from economic hardship. Who suffers from the hardship of nakedness and famine? Only the poor who have no access to scarce resources. Those who wield the sword and impose persecution, those identified with the "rulers" and "powers" (8:38), do not go hungry or unclothed.

Paul, of course, not only experienced such hardship himself; his travels and trade also exposed him to a wide diversity of people of low social standing. As

8. Oakes, *Reading Romans*.
9. Oakes, *Reading Romans*, 138–39, 173–79.
10. E.g., Pss. 9 (LXX 10); 43 (LXX 44); 70 (LXX 71); 139 (LXX 140).

Elsa Tamez points out, Paul was “a traveler, rubbing shoulders constantly with other travelers of every sort: sailors, slaves on the way to be sold, fugitive slaves, traders, teachers, soldiers, among others.”[11] In addition, his work as a tentmaker (or awning maker) meant that he spent time in workshops with others of his trade and with slaves and freed slaves, whose stories he most certainly heard.[12] And, of course, as a prisoner Paul would have heard the stories of those who were imprisoned as a result of debt or robbery. Many of those imprisoned would have been slaves. The full weight of the injustice of the Roman economic system would have been vividly portrayed in the lives of those whom Paul encountered in these contexts. Those whom Paul spent his time with were well acquainted with the grief that is the offspring of poverty and injustice.

We shall explore below how such poverty would have been the natural result of Roman economic practices—after all, the majority of the population contended with the challenge of having enough food to stay alive—but we should also realize that poverty would have been exacerbated by the kinds of suffering that resulted from becoming a follower of Jesus. Oakes outlines the consequences of abandoning pagan worship, the suspicions that neighbors, clients, patrons, and business associates would have had of secretive associations and Judean activities (both ways to describe Christian meetings), and the violence that could have erupted as a result of evangelism.[13] For those whose businesses depended on good relationships—whether with other bakers who were willing to share oven space, or suppliers who didn’t overcharge, or even patrons who placed a daily large bread order—the possible rupture of these relationships or the loss of honor as a result of following Jesus could have severe economic consequences.[14] Similarly, a wife with an unbelieving spouse could be divorced, or a child with an unbelieving father could risk being cut off, and slaves who might be trying to save up for manumission by saving tips or other earnings might see this small income curtailed by unbelieving masters. Similarly, freedmen or freedwomen could suffer from the disruption of a relationship with a former owner.[15]

Even the “sword” in Romans 8:35 could have economic repercussions. If a follower of Jesus is called before the magistrates as a result of his or her suspicious

11. Tamez, *Amnesty of Grace*, 48.
12. Tamez, *Amnesty of Grace*, 54.
13. Oakes, *Philippians*, 89–96.
14. Oakes outlines these dynamics in Oakes, *Philippians*, 89–91.
15. These scenarios are explored in Oakes, *Philippians*, 91–95.

behavior and receives a beating and a night in jail, the ensuing dishonor could easily result in a loss of business and a severing of some relationships.[16]

It is no surprise, therefore, that Paul's exhortation to "bless those who persecute you" (12:14) follows on from his appeal to "contribute to [or share in] the needs of the saints; extend hospitality to strangers" (12:13). Such economic sharing could have been made necessary by the persecution that the community faced. The extending of economic grace to those in the community and strangers alike is paralleled by the extension of the grace of forgiveness to those who have caused this hardship. The two come together in 12:20, where such sharing of food and drink is extended to the enemies who have caused hardship to the community. (Why would there be language of vengeance or repayment unless a wrong had been done?)

Furthermore, when Paul employs the word used here for sharing (*koinōneō*) in other contexts, it is clear that he has in mind a financial sharing of resources (Gal. 6:6; Phil. 4:15; cf. Rom. 15:27).[17] It is notable, however, that Paul couples this injunction for economic generosity within the Christian community with extending hospitality to strangers. This would undoubtedly include the sharing of food and clothing to those outside the Christian community who suffer the hardship and distress of hunger and nakedness (8:35). Such hospitality would require the sacrificial generosity of a community already acquainted with poverty within its ranks. If the home that Paul is envisioning for these Christian communities is to be worthy of the Lord they follow, then there will need to be an "opening of the social circles of the household and the tenement-assembly to others, not only in the city, but internationally."[18]

When Paul enjoins the community a few verses later to "make one's way with the oppressed (*tapeinō*)," usually translated "associate with the lowly" (12:16), we do well to hear echoes of those places in the Septuagint where the *tapeinō* are the humble poor, or those who have been "brought low" or "ground down," hence "the oppressed."[19] In fact, the *tapeinō* are linked with the poor in a number of passages that Paul quotes or echoes in Romans.[20] For example, in the depiction

16. Oakes, *Philippians*, 90.

17. Jewett, *Romans*, 764.

18. Neil Elliott, *The Arrogance of Nations: Reading Romans in the Shadow of Empire* (Minneapolis: Fortress, 2008), 152.

19. We owe this translation to Elliott, *Arrogance of Nations*, 152.

20. Throughout this book we have engaged in an intertextual reading of Paul's letter to the Romans. That is to say we have been attentive both to how Paul quotes older Hebrew texts and to how he is often alluding to Hebrew textual traditions even if he is not engaging in actual quotation. In this chapter we will also attend to the allusions (intentional references) and

of human sinfulness in Romans 3:9–18, Paul cites Psalm 10:7: "Their mouths are full of cursing and bitterness" (3:14). Whose mouths? Those who "murder the innocent," those who "seize the poor and drag them off in their net" (10:8–9); those who are "greedy for gain" (10:3) and whose discourse is that of "deceit and oppression" (10:7). And so the psalmist prays that, in the face of such economic violence, God will "do justice for the orphan and the oppressed [*tapeinō*]" (10:18). The psalm is rich with economic allusion that is surely not lost on the apostle, nor far from his understanding of human sinfulness, not least in the context of the Roman Empire.

Or consider the citation of Psalm 18:49 in the context of Paul's call to be a community of radical welcome in Romans 15: "Welcome one another, therefore, just as Christ has welcomed you, for the glory of God. . . . As it is written, 'Therefore I will confess you among the Gentiles, and sing praises to your name'" (15:7, 9). This declaration comes at the end of a psalm of praise in which the psalmist extols God because "you deliver a humble people [or the oppressed, *tapeinō*], but the haughty eyes you bring down" (Ps. 18:27; 17:28 LXX). Praising God among the gentiles and engendering a community of welcome resonate deeply with the deliverance of the economically oppressed.

Three verses later (15:12), Paul brings his message of radical welcome to a prophetic climax by quoting Isaiah 11:10: "The root of Jesse shall come, the one who rises to rule the nations; in him the nations shall hope" (our translation). And what kind of rule will this be but one of justice?

> He shall not judge by what his eyes see,
>   or decide by what his ears hear;
> but with righteousness he shall judge the poor [*tapeinō*],
>   and decide with equity for the meek of the earth.
>   (Isa. 11:3–4)

We see, then, that in Paul's depiction of the situation of the Roman believers and in the allusions within key psalmic and prophetic texts that he employs, he is naming a suffering that is a result of both persecution and poverty.

---

echoes (unintentional references) that can be discerned in a number of texts explicitly cited by Paul. In this immediate context we look at how three texts that Paul references—Pss. 10:7; 18:49; and Isa. 11:10—carry allusions to biblical concerns for the poor oppressed (*tapeinō*). Of course, foundational to any intertextual reading of Paul is Richard B. Hays's groundbreaking book, *Echoes of Scripture*. Building on Hays, Sylvia Keesmaat unpacks the method that we employ in *Paul and His Story*, 48–52.

What Injustice? What Sin?

In addition to these texts that give some insight into the situation of the community, Paul describes the injustice (*adikia*, Rom. 1:18) of the empire in terms that have strong economic resonances. This happens in two ways: first, in Paul's overt descriptions of those who have ceased to image God and, second, in Paul's quotations of and allusions to the Scriptures of Israel.

In Romans 1:18 and following, Paul describes how the wrath of God has been revealed against all the godlessness and the injustice of those who "imprison the truth in injustice."[21] Paul's description of the injustice of those who do not acknowledge God ranges far beyond the descriptions of abusive sexuality in 1:26–27. Paul describes behaviors that are rooted in a culture of greed and abuse, one that distorts both sexual and economic life. The list of vices (or types of people) in 1:29–31 is as follows: injustice, wickedness, greed, evil, envy, murder, quarreling, treachery, malice, whisperers/gossips (or informers),[22] slanderers, God-haters, conceited bullies, arrogant, boastful, inventors of evil, disobedient to parents, void of understanding, faithless (or bound by no covenant; cf. Jer. 3:6–25), heartless, and without mercy. This lists contains twenty-one behaviors that are manifestations of what Paul calls a base mind and improper conduct. Of those twenty-one, the first nine are used to describe the economic injustice that results in violence toward the vulnerable in Paul's Scriptures (injustice, wickedness, greed, evil, envy, murder, quarreling, treachery, malice);[23] three describe the deceit that the Psalms link to economic oppression (informers, slanderers, inventors of evil);[24] three characterize those who inhabit superior socioeconomic status (conceited, arrogant, boastful);[25] and three describe attitudes that shape an ethos of injustice: faithless (that is, bound by no covenant), heartless, and without mercy.

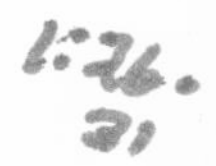

We have described eighteen of the twenty-one vices. The remaining three—God-haters, disobedient toward parents, and devoid of understanding, or foolishness—may not be directly economic, but they have clear economic implications. Indeed, to engage in the kind of economics that is implied in this list of vices, one would have to be a "God-hater." How else could one justify an

21. We owe this translation to Tamez, *Amnesty of Grace*, 58.

22. Jewett, *Romans*, 183.

23. See Deut. 2:13–15; Jer. 6:6, 9; Hosea 4:1–3; Mic. 6:9–16; 7:1–13; Hab. 2:6–17.

24. E.g., Pss. 5:9; 10:7; 36:3; 140:3. All of these are quoted in Rom. 3:10–18.

25. We reference here only those texts that use the same vocabulary as Rom. 1:29: Prov. 15:25; 16:19; Isa. 2:7–11; 13:11; Hab. 2:4–5. *Pleonexia* (greed; Rom. 1:29) occurs repeatedly in the LXX to denounce violent oppression and unjust gain: Ps. 10:3; Jer. 22:17; Ezek. 22:27–29; Hab. 2:9. A number of these texts also use *adikia* (injustice) and *phonos* (murder), both found in Rom. 1:29.

economics of covetous deceit and injustice unless one lived in profound disobedience and rebellion against the God who is known by the generosity of love, covenantal faithfulness, and justice, and who calls us to bear the image of God in every dimension of our lives, including our economics? "Disobedience to parents" can entail many different kinds of disrespect and insolence, but surely one form of such disobedience would be economic. Economic obligation toward parents was an assumed responsibility in the ancient world. Disobedience to parents could well entail a breaking of that responsibility.[26] And describing such people as "foolish" or "devoid of understanding" simply continues the line of argument that Paul has been using since he intoned that "claiming to be wise, they became fools" in their idolatry (1:22). The wisdom that is necessary to make good and responsible economic choices, the wisdom that is at the foundation of an economics of homemaking and justice, is totally lost on idolaters who are captivated by the vices that Paul has here evoked.

These verses describe the predatory economy of the Roman Empire,[27] an economy that bore a striking resemblance to the imperial economies against which the prophets, psalmists, and Torah had always invoked judgment. Iris and Nereus would have seen in this description not only a reflection of imperial society as a whole but also the economic dealings of, respectively, her master and his employer.[28] Moreover, they would have seen how those in the community of Jesus followers had suffered as a result of these behaviors. On the one hand, most members of this community knew that greed, envy, injustice, murder, treachery, arrogance, and faithlessness characterized the economic interactions that kept wealth circulating among the elite. On the other hand, their suffering had been intensified because of their new faithfulness to Jesus. Some would have lost customers because of informers or because of slander or because of those who responded with malice or invented evil about their new

26. It is a profound indication of the nature of late capitalist individualism that we see the erosion of such a responsibility to parents in our own time. Economics is a matter of caring for a household, but we delegate the care of the elderly to corporations that run nursing homes. Such abnegation of responsibility for our parents is simply the end result of living by corporate proxy. We give the whole of economic life—food, clothing, shelter, education, entertainment, care of the sick and the elderly—to corporate control. "Our major economic practice, in short, is to delegate that practice to others." Wendell Berry, "The Total Economy," in *Citizenship Papers* (Washington, DC: Shoemaker & Hoard, 2003), 64.

27. See the description in Neil Elliott, "Disciplining the Hope of the Poor in Ancient Rome," in *A People's History of Christianity*, vol. 1, *Christian Origins*, ed. Richard Horsley (Minneapolis: Fortress, 2005), 180.

28. Oakes, *Reading Romans*, 133.

allegiance. Such malice and slander would in turn have intensified economic hardship as clients, customers, and colleagues sought to distance themselves from those now considered dishonorable.[29]

The privatization of this list of vices as if they were a description of individual sinfulness devoid of socioeconomic and cultural reference has tamed this text, stripped it of its counter-imperial force, and rendered it economically benign. And to make matters worse, we have for so long been distracted by an unseemly preoccupation with the so-called attack on homosexuality in the previous verses that we have been happily blind to the radical economic critique that is contained in Paul's diatribe against the empire.[30]

From the outset, then, Paul has described injustice in unmistakably economic terms. What does the injustice of ungodliness look like? What does it look like when the truth is imprisoned in injustice? It looks like the oppressive rule of the rich over the poor, and the violence, envy, lies, and deceit that keep wealth concentrated in the hands of the rich. The apostle's language is unambiguous. When the knowledge of God is rejected and hidden, injustice is inevitable.

Paul, however, not only condemns economic injustice with his overt descriptions of sin and injustice; he also evokes this condemnation in his scriptural quotations and allusions throughout the letter. This is nowhere more powerful than in Paul's foundational citation of the prophet Habakkuk. We have already noted in chapter 1 that when Paul appeals to Habakkuk in Romans 1:17, his citation carries with it the broader context of Habakkuk's critique of empire. We do well to also note that this critique is focused on the economics of empire. Indeed, the very next line after the crucial insight that "the righteous live by their faith" (Hab. 2:4) reads, "Moreover, wealth is treacherous" (2:5). Habakkuk goes on to describe the insatiability of the arrogant. They are those who open their throats wide as Sheol and, like death, never have enough (2:5). They are loaded up with goods taken in pledge. They voraciously heap up what is not their own and get "evil gain" (2:6, *kakēn*) for their houses (2:9). This is precisely the term that Paul uses in Romans 1:29: *kakia*, usually translated as "greed." And for Habakkuk, as for Paul, all of this is rooted in the idolatry of empire (2:18–19).[31]

29. Oakes, *Philippians*, 89–91.

30. We will address the question of homosexuality in Rom. 1:26–27 in chap. 9.

31. For a contemporary cultural and liturgical engagement with Habakkuk, see Brian J. Walsh and the Wine Before Breakfast community, *Habakkuk before Breakfast: Lament, Liturgy, and Hope* (Toronto: Books Before Breakfast, 2016).

The conceptual overtones between Habakkuk 2 and Romans 1 are striking. The wider context of the Habakkuk quotation, of course, is judgment on the Chaldeans. Their sin is described in terms of both geopolitical and economic violence. The Roman believers would have recognized the parallels to their own imperial reality. In the midst of such violence, God promises that the just shall live by faithfulness. In the Septuagint, the version of the Scriptures on which Paul draws the most, this verse reads, "The just shall live by my faithfulness."[32] Faced with Chaldean pretensions of imperial fidelity, Habakkuk evokes God's faithfulness in the midst of economic and political oppression. Paul's quotation of Habakkuk evokes God's faithfulness for those in Rome as well.

Paul does something similar in the verse just before the programmatic statement "The just shall live by faithfulness." Indeed, he sets up that profound statement by insisting that he is "not ashamed of the gospel" (1:16), evoking thereby the psalms of lament in which "shame" and "justice" are concurrent themes.[33] Most notable of these is Psalm 71:1–2:[34]

> O Lord, in you I hope;
>   never let me be put to shame.
> In your justice [*dikaiosynē*] deliver me and have mercy on me;
>   turn your ear to me, and save me.[35] (Our translation)

The psalmist continues with a plea for God's rescue from the unjust (*adikountos*, 71:4 [70:4 LXX]; cf. Rom. 1:18, 29) and roots his hope in God's justice (*tēn dikaiosynēn*) and salvation (71:14–15 [70:14–15 LXX]). By asserting that he is not ashamed of the gospel in language that draws together themes from the psalms of lament, Paul has proclaimed that God is the one who acts for justice on behalf of those who would be shamed by the unjust. But Paul is *affirming* what

32. See Hays, *Echoes of Scripture*, 40–41, on how Paul's translation, by omitting the pronoun, makes possible the interpretation from either the Masoretic Text ("the just shall live by his faithfulness") or the Septuagint ("the just shall live by my faithfulness").

33. See Sylvia C. Keesmaat, "The Psalms in Romans and Galatians," in *The Psalms in the New Testament*, ed. Steve Moyise and Maarten J. Menken (New York: T&T Clark, 2004), 140. As Hays has indicated in relation to the language of shame, "*aischynein* and its near relatives *kataschynein* and *epaishynesthai* appear regularly in the very prophecies and lament psalms from which Paul's righteousness terminology is drawn" (Hays, *Echoes of Scripture*, 38). Hays also refers to Ps. 44:10; Ps. 24:2; Isa. 28:16 LXX (to which Paul appeals directly in Rom. 9:33); and Isa. 50:7–8.

34. Ps. 70:1–2 LXX; cf. Ps. 30:1–3 LXX.

35. We suggest that Rom. 1:17 is making an intentional allusion to Ps. 71. This psalm is also discussed in N. T. Wright, "The Letter to the Romans: Introduction, Commentary, and Reflections," in *The New Interpreter's Bible*, vol. 10 (Nashville: Abingdon, 2002), 424.

is held up as a *question* in the psalms of lament.[36] For these are the psalms that raise most deeply the question of theodicy—the problem of God's faithfulness to Israel.[37] However, the problem of theodicy isn't just a matter of whether God has abandoned Israel; it is also the question of why the poor continue to suffer and why those who practice injustice (*adikia*) appear to be triumphant.

Such a question is central to the psalms that Paul brings together in Romans 3:10–18, his largest collection of quotations from Israel's Scriptures. In this description of the power and pervasiveness of sin, the apostle refers primarily to various psalms of lament. Central to these psalms is the problem of the suffering of the just because of the lawlessness and oppression of the unjust. This oppression is accomplished through deceitful speech and the persecution of the poor and needy.

Perhaps the best way to see what Paul is doing here is to juxtapose Romans 3:10–18 with each of these psalms. (We have also indicated the allusions to and echoes of various other psalms and other texts after the appropriate verses in Romans 3.)

> There is no one who is just, not even one;
> there is no one who has understanding, [Ps. 14:2]
> there is no one who seeks God.
> All have turned aside, together they have become worthless;
> there is no one who shows kindness,
> there is not even one. [Ps. 14:1, 3]
>
> Their throats are opened graves;
> they use their tongues to deceive. [Ps. 5:10]
>
> The venom of the vipers is under their lips. [Ps. 140:3]
> Their mouths are full of cursing and bitterness. [Ps. 10:7]
>
> Their feet are swift to shed blood;
> ruin and misery are in their paths,
> and the way of peace they have not known. [Isa. 59:7–8]

36. Paul's intertextual allusion to these psalms both disrupts and regenerates this psalmic tradition in his own writing. "That is to say, the placing of a text in a different context can undermine the original meaning or context of the text. Alternatively, precisely by being placed in a new context, that text is preserved and renewed for a new situation." Keesmaat, *Paul and His Story*, 51. So Paul takes the question of shame in the lament psalms (specifically Ps. 71 here) and turns it into an affirmation of not being ashamed in Rom. 1:16.

37. Walter Brueggemann puts it this way: "In Israel's most knowing texts, the problem is not Israel's sin but God's doubtful fidelity." Walter Brueggemann, "Praise and the Psalms: A Politics of Glad Abandonment," in *The Psalms and the Life of Faith*, ed. Patrick D. Miller (Minneapolis: Fortress, 1995), 117.

There is no fear of God before their eyes. [Ps. 36:1]
(Rom. 3:10–18 NRSV alt.)[38]

Paul begins with Psalm 14. The psalmist complains that there is no one who shows kindness (Rom. 3:12; Ps. 14:1, 3) or does good. Believing that they are above the law (Ps. 12:4 describes them as the lawless ones, *anomia*), they are driven by an insatiability that consumes both bread and people, as they thwart and obstruct the plans of the poor (Ps. 14:4, 6). These are the greedy and treacherous bullies that Paul describes in Romans 1:29–31.

Psalm 5:10 (Rom. 3:13) refers to the discourse of death that characterizes all oppression. There is no life to be found in the deceit of the powerful, in the rhetoric of empire. Similar to Habakkuk 2:8, 17, the psalmist decries how the deceitful are "bloodthirsty" (Ps. 5:6), and it is clear that the thirst of the deceitful is only quenched by the blood of the poor.

Continuing on the theme of deceitfulness, in Romans 3:14 Paul alludes to both Psalm 10:7 and Psalm 140:3. Resonances between these psalms and Romans 3 are extensive.

As we have seen above, Psalm 10 is preoccupied with the oppressive relationship between the powerful rich and the vulnerable poor. The psalmist begins:

Why, O Lord, do you stand far off?
Why do you hide yourself in times of trouble?
In arrogance[39] the wicked persecute the poor—
let them be caught in the schemes they have devised.

For the wicked boast of the desires of their heart,
those greedy for gain curse and renounce the Lord.
In the pride of their countenance the wicked say, "God will not seek it out";
all their thoughts are, "There is no God." (Ps. 10:1–4)

Psalm 10 is in fact the second half of one longer acrostic poem that begins with Psalm 9.[40] References already in Psalm 9 to the oppressed (9:9), the poor and afflicted (9:12, 18), the one who suffers (9:13), and the needy (9:18) make

38. References given are to the Masoretic Text. Septuagint (LXX) references are in parentheses: Pss. 14:2 (13:2); 14:1, 3 (13:1, 3); 140:3 (139:4); 10:7 (9:8); 36:1 (35:1).

39. LXX *hyperēphaneuesthai*; cf. Rom. 1:30.

40. An acrostic poem begins each stanza with the subsequent letters of the Hebrew alphabet. Psalms 9–10 have such a structure.

it clear that "the speaker and those whom the speaker represents are the socially vulnerable and marginal."[41] The psalmist here represents and speaks for the vulnerable in direct and aggressive opposition to those who oppress them. With devastating clarity, the psalmist describes the powerful in terms of their penchant for violent injustice:

> Their mouths are filled with cursing and deceit and oppression [*dolou*;
> see Rom. 1:29];
> under their tongues are mischief and iniquity.
> They sit in ambush in the villages;
> in hiding places they murder the innocent.
>
> Their eyes stealthily watch for the helpless;
> they lurk in secret like a lion in its covert;
> they lurk that they might seize the poor;
> they seize the poor and drag them off in their net. (Ps. 10:7–9)

Of course, there is nothing new about any of this. The psalmist is simply giving voice to the dirty secret of most social reality by describing the normal course of affairs in the political and economic life of the poor.[42] However, this daring act of description, this giving voice to the voiceless, sets the scene for a radical reversal. Like Paul writing to the heart of the empire, the psalmist "speaks a countervoice *back against social reality* in a way that contradicts accepted social reality and . . . social power."[43] No wonder the psalmist goes on to appeal to God to remember the poor and the helpless (10:12–14), to punish the wicked (10:15–16), and to do justice for the orphan and the oppressed (*tapeinō*, 10:18; cf. Rom. 12:16). Walter Brueggemann describes this call for God to "rise up" and reverse social reality as "an act of political counterimagination rooted in theological passion."[44] If the broader socioeconomic themes of Psalm 9–10 are at all echoing through Paul's use of this psalm in Romans 3:12, then might we be justified in hearing a

41. Walter Brueggemann, "Psalms 9–10: A Counter to Conventional Social Reality," in Miller, *Psalms and the Life of Faith*, 220.

42. Naomi Klein, *The Shock Doctrine: The Rise of Disaster Capitalism* (New York: Picador, 2008), describes how the wealthy in contemporary contexts sit in ambush on the poor and stealthily watch for an opportunity to seize them and capture them in their net.

43. Brueggemann, "Psalms 9–10," 233. He also writes, "This psalm is an extraordinary act of counterspeech and counterpoint. It seizes the conventional, usually unquestioned, script of the strong, states it, mocks it, and overrides it, so that the psalm is itself a moment of social inversion and even social control for those who normally are left without speech and without power" (228).

44. Brueggemann, "Psalms 9–10," 230.

similar voice of political and economic counterimagination throughout Paul's letter to the Romans?

Not surprisingly, Psalm 140 is also a prayer for deliverance from the unjust:

> Deliver me, O Lord, from evildoers;
> protect me from those who are violent or unjust [*adikou*],
> who plan evil things in their minds,
> and stir up wars continually.
> They make their tongue sharp as a snake's,
> and under their lips is the venom of vipers. [see Rom. 3:13]
>
> Guard me, O Lord, from the hands of the wicked;
> protect me from the unjust [*adikōn*]
> who have planned my downfall.
> The arrogant have hidden a trap for me,
> and with cords they have spread a net,
> along the road they have set snares for me.
> (Ps. 140:1–5 NRSV alt.; 139:2–6 LXX)

And like Psalm 10, this psalm evokes a divinely sanctioned political and economic reversal.

> I know that the Lord maintains the cause of the needy,
> and executes justice [*dikē*] for the poor.
> Surely the righteous will give thanks to your name;
> the upright shall live in your presence.
> (Ps. 140:12–13; 139:13–14 LXX)

Paul's description in Romans 3:10–18 of the violence, ruin, and misery of sin is given depth by the echoes of the psalms that he quotes. The themes are consistent. The plotting and slander of the powerful oppressors grind down the poor and the needy. While the apostle is arguing that the *power of sin* has equal force over both Judean and gentile (3:9), it is clear from all of his allusions that the *sin of the powerful* has greater force to impose violence, oppression, and economic injustice on the powerless.

It is no accident that the progression of these verses in Romans 3 moves from the lack of understanding of the wicked (vv. 10–12), to their speech (vv. 13–14), to the paths that their feet walk (vv. 14–18). The injustice of their hearts is embodied in all that they say and do. Paul is, of course, mirroring the very same progression that we find in Psalms 10 and 140.

And it is no surprise that the apostle will also bring Isaiah into the conversation. When human sinfulness and its impact on socioeconomic life is depicted, it is hard to imagine someone like Paul not referring to Isaiah.[45] When Paul quotes Isaiah's critique of Israel, that "their feet are swift to shed blood, / ruin and misery are in their paths, / and the way of peace they have not known" (Rom. 3:15–17; cf. Isa. 59:7–8), he highlights the broader socioeconomic allusions found in this prophetic text. Again, the themes of bloodshed and violence (Isa. 59:3, 8) appear throughout the oracle. There is no justice in the land (vv. 4, 8, 9, 11, 14, 15), and the very juridical systems that should uphold justice for the poor are perverted and corrupted (v. 4). The prophet proclaims:

> Justice is turned back,
>   and righteousness stands at a distance;
> for truth stumbles in the public square,
>   and uprightness cannot enter.
> Truth is lacking,
>   and whoever turns from evil is despoiled. (Isa. 59:14–15)

Doesn't this sound incredibly similar to the argument in Romans 1:18? In their injustice they have suppressed the truth. Or, as Tamez puts it, "injustice was presenting itself as truth, that is to say as justice, preventing the truth from manifesting itself as such."[46] The deceitful structures that insist on the inevitability and "self-evident truth" of unjust economic and political systems can only lead to violence and death. Hence such deceit is called out and named, both by the psalmists and by Paul in Romans 1:18 and 1:29–30. Paul isn't just referring to the "personal" lies that reveal the deceptions in our personal relationships but to the systemic lies that are necessary to uphold a political and economic system that maintains the wealth and status of the rich and ensures the continued exclusion and enslavement of those without social, economic, or political power. Such lies ensure that "the poor and the weak are completely abandoned to the perverted logic of injustice."[47] No wonder Isaiah claims that the people do not know "the way of peace," for peace refers to the broad Hebrew notion of shalom

45. J. Ross Wagner has documented Paul's dependence on Isaiah. See J. Ross Wagner, *Heralds of the Good News: Isaiah and Paul "in Concert" in the Letter to the Romans* (Leiden: Brill, 2002).
46. Tamez, *Amnesty of Grace*, 98.
47. Tamez, *Amnesty of Grace*, 107.

as the flourishing of all of life in justice.[48] This is a peace that is fulfilled in Messiah Jesus and goes so much deeper than anything imagined by the *Pax Romana*.

The allusions back to Romans 1 continue with the final citation. Paul concludes his depiction of human injustice in Romans 3 by quoting Psalm 36:1: "There is no fear of God before their eyes" (Rom. 3:18). They are "God-haters" (1:30). Like all the other psalmic references in Romans 3, these are people whose words are deceitful (Ps. 36:3), they plot evil (36:4, 12), and in their arrogance they tread on the powerless (36:11). Again, the parallels to Romans 1:29–31 are unmistakable.

But perhaps even more is going on here. As we have seen, in Romans 1 the wrath of God is revealed against all injustice and wickedness because people have suppressed the truth (1:18; cf. Isa. 59:14–15). And they are without excuse, argues Paul, "for what can be known about God is plain to them, because God has shown it to them. Ever since the creation of the world his eternal power and divine nature, invisible though they are, have been understood and seen through the things he has made" (1:19–20). But what exactly is it that creation reveals about God, and how is that related to what Paul calls the injustice of the wicked? Psalm 36 gives us a hint. While the sinful have no fear of God as they plot evil, the psalmist goes on to proclaim precisely what the wicked cannot possibly see:

> Your steadfast love, O Lord, extends to the heavens,
> your faithfulness to the clouds.
> Your righteousness [LXX *dikaiosynē*] is like the mighty mountains,
> your judgments are like the great deep;
> you save humans and animals alike, O Lord. (Ps. 36:5–6)

What does creation proclaim about God? What of the divine nature has been known since the creation of the world? What is apparent about God from the things that God has made to all who have eyes to see? That all creation—the heavens, clouds, mountains, the deeps of the ocean, humans and animals alike—is held by and receives God's steadfast love, faithfulness, and justice. Economic injustice not only oppresses the poor and breaks the decrees of God; it is a pattern of life in

48. See Walter Brueggemann, *Peace* (St. Louis: Chalice, 2001). For a wide-ranging discussion of shalom in the New Testament, see Willard Swartley, *Covenant of Peace: The Missing Peace in New Testament Theology and Ethics* (Grand Rapids: Eerdmans, 2006). Steven Bouma-Prediger and Brian J. Walsh unpack the ecological meaning of shalom in *Beyond Homelessness: Christian Faith in a Culture of Displacement* (Grand Rapids: Eerdmans, 2008), chap. 6.

violent opposition to the very nature of God. Indeed, the one who lives without the fear of God not only is a fool and an oppressor but also is living against the grain of creation itself. Steadfast love, faithfulness, and justice extend to all creation, permeate all creation, and bring salvation to all creation.[49] Martin Luther King Jr. famously said that "the moral arc of the universe is long, but it bends toward justice."[50] It seems to us that Psalm 36, and by extension Paul in Romans 1:18–32, is making the same point.[51]

We conclude that Paul's description of sin, especially in Romans 3:10–18 and 1:18–32, would have evoked the psalms of lament that call on God to come to the aid of the poor, whose widespread and systemic oppression was evident throughout Roman society. Considering Paul's constant reference to these psalms of lament, together with his allusions to the critique of injustice throughout the prophetic literature, it is hard to miss the economic overtones of Paul's understanding of sin and injustice.[52]

Nor should anyone be surprised by this characterization of human sinfulness in terms of economic injustice. As Tamez points out, the first two chapters of Romans describe the sinfulness of human society using the word *adikia* (injustice), not *hamartia* (sin).[53] By the time Paul declares all people to be under the power of sin in Romans 3:9, it is clear that he is referring to the injustice he has previously described. But in case his hearers haven't quite gotten the point, he follows that statement with, "No one is just [*dikaios*], not one" (3:10 our translation) and launches into the psalm quotations we have just described.

Of course, it is hard to imagine how Paul, the converted Pharisee, could have thought any differently. Throughout Israel's story, idolatry *always* bears the bitter fruit of economic oppression and injustice. Idolatry is always a matter of covenantal amnesia (Deut. 6:10–15). Embracing idols, the people forget who their God is, and thereby forget who they are called to be. Forgetting that the covenantal God is a God who sets slaves free, and forgetting that Torah says, "Justice, and only justice, you shall pursue, so that you may live and occupy the land that the Lord your God is giving you" (Deut. 16:20), idolatrous Israel also

49. We will return to this exegesis in more depth, specifically in relation to the question of homosexuality, in chap. 9.

50. See Obery M. Hendricks Jr., *The Universe Bends toward Justice: Radical Reflections on the Bible, the Church, and the Body Politic* (Maryknoll, NY: Orbis, 2011).

51. This connection between knowledge and justice is also made by Tamez, *Amnesty of Grace*, 111.

52. Similar overtones can be discerned in Paul's echo of Ps. 94:14 in Rom. 11:2 and his reference to Ps. 69:22–23 in Rom. 11:9–10.

53. Tamez, *Amnesty of Grace*, 105.

forgets that they are called to be a people of mercy and justice who care for the vulnerable and are openhanded toward the poor.[54]

In light of this, it is telling that Paul writes explicitly of covetousness as an example of sin working in him (Rom. 7:7, 8). The final commandment of the Decalogue, "You shall not covet" (Exod. 20:17; Deut. 5:21), lies at the root of the economic sin that shapes all the false "taking" that Torah prohibits. One only "takes" in murder, adultery, and theft because one covets that which belongs to another. Moreover, it is such covetous "taking" that invariably occasions the bearing of false witness against a neighbor.[55] Paul's shorthand for the effect of sin is covetousness, the root of economic injustice.

The point is not that Paul is zeroing in on economic sin to the exclusion of other ways of being unfaithful. Rather, throughout the biblical story the economic life of the people—the way they treat the poor, the widow, and the vulnerable—reflects their character and displays their faithfulness (or lack of such faithfulness) to the covenantal God, who hears the cry of the oppressed (Exod. 3:22) and "who executes justice for the orphan and the widow, and who loves the strangers, providing them food and clothing" (Deut. 10:18). In Paul's Scriptures, economic faithfulness is fundamental to bearing the image of God. Insofar as the apostle is talking about covenantal faithfulness throughout Romans, themes of hearing the cry of the poor and caring for the oppressed are always resonating through his language.

That Paul combines direct description of economic injustice with these allusive echoes means that Iris and Nereus would have heard this theme at a different volume. Famine and nakedness would not have been an issue for Iris, who at least had the relative stability of slavery. But she would have been part of a household that worked together to ensure the economic well-being of her master's family, and this would have meant being in competition with other households.[56] The arrogance, greed, injustice, envy, haughtiness, insolence, and deceit that Paul describes in Romans 1:29–30 were evident all around her in the daily dealings of those with wealth in the empire, and they would have permeated her own household as well. After all, wasn't it precisely such injustice, deceit, heartlessness, and ruthlessness that had caused her to be taken as a slave in the first place,

54. E.g., Exod. 22:21–27; Lev. 19:1–17, 32–37; Deut. 15:1–11; Isa. 1:16, 17; 56:1; 58:6–10; Jer. 21:12; 22:3; Ezek. 34:1–4; Hosea 12:6; Amos 5:21–24; Mic. 6:8.

55. See Stephen Barton, "Money Matters," in Longenecker and Liebengood, *Engaging Economics*, 40. See also Patrick D. Miller, "Property and Possession in Light of the Ten Commandments," in *Having: Property and Possession in Religious and Social Life*, ed. William Schweiker and Charles Mathewes (Grand Rapids: Eerdmans, 2004), 17–50.

56. See Oakes, *Reading Romans*, 103–6.

and that had taken her children from her? So Iris also would have resonated with Paul's language of a suffering that produces endurance in Romans 5:3. She had been forced to endure deep suffering. She also would have resonated deeply with Paul when he wrote of Jesus interceding for those who suffer such hardship and distress (Rom. 8:34–35). Moreover, Paul's concern with her suffering, and with the violence that she experienced, would have been overwhelmingly evident in the community ethic of Romans 12. A community that showed honor to all, and would weep with those who weep while they walked with the oppressed (12:16, 15, 9), would have been a place where Iris's suffering was acknowledged. And while in the household of Narcissus she would have remained a slave, in Paul's transformed community she would have found a new identity. No longer was she reduced to a "body" owned by another. Now she could know herself as an indispensable "member" of a body of love. No longer was she a mere economic unit to be bought and sold on the market. She now had a new identity rooted in "gift." In the household of Narcissus she was a commodity, but in the home of Jesus she was a beloved and indispensable sister.

Unlike Iris, Nereus was familiar with hunger and nakedness. He had seen the oppressive economic practices of his employer, who abused his slaves, paid his workers the barest minimum he could get away with, and charged as much as he possibly could for his lamps. Nereus knew that, like Iris, he was viewed as only good for exploitation. And even though he was a freeman, he was also less likely to have food and clothing than Iris. Paul's direct descriptions of economic injustice would have resonated with Nereus, but there would have been more. For Nereus knew the Scriptures; he knew the stories of old. Nereus knew the Torah, and he knew the prophets, particularly the prophets that explained the plight of Israel in exile and promised hope of God's coming in salvation. And Nereus knew the psalms; they were his prayers day and night. Paul's many allusions to the psalms of lament, along with the great promises of restoration, were a litany of hope for Nereus. God would come and judge the arrogant and the wicked. God would come and defeat the gentile oppressors. God would come and lift up the poor, heal the sick, and restore creation. None of these hopes were lost when Nereus became a follower of Jesus. Indeed, they were intensified.

Resurrection and the Restoration of Justice

The underlying narrative of Israel's story, and particularly the overtones of economic justice, are also found in Paul's emphasis on the resurrection throughout this letter. Perhaps the best way to explore this theme is through the eyes of Nereus, one who was steeped in the Scriptures and who deeply longed for God's new act of salvation.

Nereus knew that in Israel's history and writings, resurrection language is intimately tied to establishing justice for those who suffer at the hands of the oppressor. Isaiah's eschatological vision of a feast of rich food and well-aged wines for all peoples also envisioned the defeat of death (Isa. 25:6–7). This is a hope in which all tears and disgrace will be wiped away (25:8), where the other ruthless nations (especially the Moabites) would be defeated (25:10–12), and where the poor and the needy would find shelter and shade (25:1–5). Similarly in Isaiah 26:19, God's promise that the dead shall rise occurs in the context of a plea for the inhabitants of the earth to learn justice (26:9). In Daniel 12:2–3 those who are faithful will rise to everlasting life, and those who oppressed them will rise to everlasting shame and contempt. The resurrection picture in Daniel 12 is part of a great reversal, found also in Daniel 7, where "the oppressors will be judged, and the righteous will receive the kingdom that is rightfully theirs."[57] Moreover, this coming great reversal "is basic to the biblical picture of God's justice" as seen in the Song of Mary (Luke 1:46–55) and the Song of Hannah (1 Sam. 2:7–9).[58] J. Richard Middleton demonstrates that on the basis of these texts, "'rising up' and 'standing' become synonyms for resurrection in the Bible."[59] Far from being limited to a hope for individual life after death, in Israel's eschatological vision the hope of resurrection signaled God's new act of restoration when the violent economic degradation imposed by gentile overlords would be overthrown by the new just rule of God. "The doctrine of resurrection is thus grounded in a vision of God's restorative justice."[60]

This hope for the resurrection of the righteous was one aspect of resurrection hope for a first-century Judean like Nereus. But there was also a tradition that called for God to "rise up" on behalf of those in need. This is nowhere more evident than in the psalms of lament that Nereus prayed regularly. Echoing the psalmists' pleas for God to bring salvation from enemies, whether the

57. J. Richard Middleton, *A New Heaven and a New Earth: Reclaiming Biblical Eschatology* (Grand Rapids: Baker Academic, 2014), 140. See also N. T. Wright, *The Resurrection of the Son of God* (Minneapolis: Fortress, 2003), 113–15.

58. Middleton, *New Heaven*, 113–15.

59. Middleton, *New Heaven*, 141. Moreover, the promise of resurrection for the tortured seven brothers (in 2 Macc. 7:6, 9, 11, 14, 20, 23, 29, 36) is contrasted with God's judgment on their oppressors, especially Antiochus Epiphanes (2 Macc. 7:17, 19, 31, 34–35). See also 4 Ezra 7:32–39.

60. Middleton, *New Heaven*, 154.

other nations (Pss. 9; 44; 68; 74; 102), their gods (Ps. 82), or those inside and outside Israel who are arrogant and wicked (Pss. 3; 10; 12; 17; 94), Nereus would call on God to "rise up!" And in these psalms, when God rises up, salvation comes for the poor, the needy, and the oppressed.[61] As Nereus prayed these psalms of lament, he would have hoped for God's defeat of the Roman overlords, including God's judgment on people like his employer and those who enabled his abusive practices. His prayers that God would rise up would be prayers for the establishment of God's kingdom and for the end of his own destitution and deprivation.[62]

When Nereus became a follower of Jesus, these two aspects of resurrection became one. In Jesus, God had risen up in judgment against oppressors to vindicate the "just who live by faithfulness," and as a result, the resurrection age of restorative justice had begun. As we imagine him, Nereus would joyfully have believed that in Messiah Jesus the prayers of the psalmists and the hopes of the prophets had been fulfilled. In Jesus, God had answered those prayers and "risen up" to inaugurate the new age of God's kingdom being realized on earth as it was in heaven. In this new age, enemies would be defeated, those who practiced injustice would be judged, Israel would be restored, the poor would have enough to eat, and the prisoners would be set free. All these hopes found their context and meaning in the longing for resurrection. When Paul, therefore, described the "good news" of God concerning his Messiah Jesus, who "was declared to be the Son of God with power according to the spirit of holiness by the resurrection from the dead" (Rom. 1:4), Nereus would have heard a breathtaking announcement of the fulfillment of his, and his people's, deepest hopes and longings. He would have heard that the good news of Isaiah, that God would reign and bring salvation and peace to those oppressed by injustice and violence (Isa. 52:7), had been fulfilled in the resurrection of Jesus. And, as we have seen, he would have heard all of this in stark contrast to the so-called good news of Caesar, a son of the gods through violence, oppression, and injustice. No wonder the

61. Pss. 9:9–11; 10:12, 17–18; 12:5; 68:5–6; 74:19, 21; 82:3–4; 94:6; 102:17, 20; 132:15.

62. There are, of course, many other intertestamental texts dating from before and during the time of Paul that support this reading of the resurrection. While biblical scholarship rightly reads New Testament texts with all the historical resources that provide access to the thought world of the time, we need to remember that most first-century Judeans would not have been aware of most of the texts we have access to. We have therefore limited ourselves to texts that we can be reasonably sure that Nereus was aware of, while acknowledging that other texts give us insight into the wider cultural consciousness around the topic. Some of the texts that support this reading are 1 En. 10:6–22; 62; 63:10; 103; 104; 108:11–15; Sib. Or. 4:179–92; 2 Bar. 50:1–51:6; 51:8–12.

apostle calls Nereus and all in the Christian communities in Rome to no longer "be conformed to this age, but be transformed by the renewal of your minds" (Rom. 12:2). They are no longer to be conformed to the deathly age of Nero because the age of new life, of restorative justice, had been inaugurated through the resurrection of Jesus!

Living as an exile at the heart of the empire, under the terribly crowded conditions of the tenement housing of Rome, with daily economic anxiety about having enough food to sustain life, and under constant threat and suspicion as a Judean, Nereus longed for the coming of God's kingdom, for enough food, for justice for the poor, for release from captivity. This is, of course, the longing for home. But Nereus knew that there was no going "back" home. The way home was forward. The way home was always the way of resurrection. This was the hope of the great homecoming. And this, Nereus recognized, was the promise of resurrection, fulfilled in Jesus and now on offer to all who would receive his homecoming gospel.

In his letter, Paul had helped it all come together for Nereus. Death and life, sin and salvation, exile and homecoming, injustice and justice—it all came together in the resurrection of Jesus! As Nereus listened to Paul's letter to the Romans, the story line of both the psalmists and prophets came to a deep moment of resolution. The resurrection hope that the hungry would be fed, the prisoners liberated, the wicked punished, and the earth set free from the power of the violent ones had dawned in Jesus! Over and over again, the apostle wrote of the resurrection of Jesus. Not only did this resurrection usher in the new age, but even more amazingly, those who hear this good news and are reconciled to God have also been raised with Christ (6:4–13; 8:11).

It all hangs on the resurrection. Paul wrote that the faithfulness of Abraham was "reckoned to him as justice" (*dikaiosynē*, 4:9, 22 NRSV alt.) because he believed the impossible promise that he "would inherit the earth" (4:13) and that the covenant God "gives life to the dead and calls to existence the things that do not exist" (4:17). So also is such a reckoning of justice granted to those "who believe in him who raised Jesus our Lord from the dead" (4:24). This provided Nereus with a radically deepened understanding of his own tradition in Abraham. But Paul wasn't finished unpacking the implications of the resurrection of Jesus.

There is no resurrection without death. Jesus "was handed over to death for our trespasses and was raised for our justification" (4:25), writes Paul. What happened to Jesus happens to those who put their faith in him. His story is our story. To be in Christ is to be brought into his story so that just as Christ died, was buried, and rose from the dead, so also do we.[63] For Nereus, there was something very familiar about the way in which Paul incorporated his readers into the story of salvation so that what happened in the past was taken up into the very identity of the present generation. This was a typically Judean way of understanding the relation of past events to the ongoing identity of the covenant people. What was breathtaking was how all of this was taken up into the story of Jesus and the identity of Christian believers in Rome.

"Do you not know that all of us who have been baptized into Christ Jesus were baptized into his death? Therefore we have been buried with him by baptism into death, so that, just as Christ was raised from the dead by the glory of the Father, so we too might walk in newness of life" (Rom. 6:3–4). The resurrection did not just happen to Jesus. Those who embrace his death, those who die to sin, are risen with Christ in order to realize resurrection hope in their everyday lives. Notice how Paul repeatedly identifies believers with the story of Jesus: we have "been buried *with him* in baptism" (6:4); "we have been united *with him* in a death like his" and "will certainly be united *with him* in a resurrection like his" (6:5); "our old self was crucified *with him*" (6:6); "if we have died *with Christ*, we believe that we will also live *with him*" (6:8). And while this resurrection life in Jesus has a dimension of eschatological longing and hope to it (if we "suffer *with him*," we will be "glorified *with him*" [8:17], which is why we "groan inwardly while we wait for adoption, the redemption of our bodies" [8:23]), Paul also insists that we are called to resurrection life *now*. We have died in Christ and we are risen in Christ to "newness of life" (6:4), no longer "enslaved to sin" (6:6) or under the "dominion of sin" (6:12, 14). But what does all of this mean if we put this call to resurrection life in terms of the resurrection hope of the prophets and psalmists? Would Nereus have recognized the resurrection hope that had sustained him all his life in what Paul was now arguing?

Paul sums up this section astoundingly by describing what resurrection means: if you have been brought from death to life, you no longer offer yourselves to sin as the weapons (or tools) of injustice (*adikia*), but rather you offer yourselves to God as weapons (or tools) of justice (*dikaiosynē*, 6:13). Nereus would have known what this meant. He had tried in his life not to be a weapon of injustice, not to be a pawn of the prince of darkness. But, preferring to keep his head down and avoid trouble, he had also not offered himself overtly as a tool of justice either.

63. We have addressed how the story of Jesus becomes the story of believers in Col. 2:8–3:4 in Brian J. Walsh and Sylvia C. Keesmaat, *Colossians Remixed: Subverting the Empire* (Downers Grove, IL: IVP Academic, 2004), 157–59.

As he reflected on Paul's language here, perhaps Nereus began to realize that in becoming part of this new community of Jesus followers, he had already begun to take steps toward a life where death no longer ruled over him. He had begun to teach new migrants to Rome how to work with clay, gentiles whom he would have avoided at all costs before. He had not only started to share stories of hope with a gentile slave woman; he had also eaten with her and begun to treat her with the respect worthy of a sister. He had begun to care for those even more destitute than himself, welcoming them and giving them honor. In short, he had begun to live as if God's kingdom had already come—and all are welcome.

Nereus stood in the rich tradition of the psalms and the prophets and believed that resurrection was all about justice. Unlike the individualism that has taken hold of most Christian piety since the Reformation, Nereus did not long for some sort of post-death heavenly bliss divorced from the call to this-worldly justice. So, being raised with Christ, the call to present his embodied life in the service of justice would have made total sense to Nereus. Embodied justice is, after all, what resurrection is all about. We wonder, however, if his conversations with Iris would have made him struggle with how Paul moved from speaking of presenting the "members" of our bodies as instruments of justice to employing the metaphor of "slaves of justice" (Rom. 6:17–19). Nereus's identity as a Judean was rooted in being liberated from slavery through the exodus, and one also didn't employ metaphors of slavery glibly in the presence of a woman like Iris, a slave in the empire. Admittedly, Paul acknowledged that he is "speaking in human terms because of the weakness of your flesh" (6:19 NRSV alt.), a weakness that makes this call to justice difficult to grasp. But maybe that is why he reached for the economic metaphor of slavery to make his point. You have been set free from slavery to injustice, set free from the rulers and powers of this age (8:38; 12:2), set free from the economics of empire and its false gospel of economic abundance at the expense of the poor and the rest of creation, precisely through the gospel of the risen one. And that resurrection is the inauguration of a new age, another kingdom, subject to the covenantal rule of a God of justice. Set free from the empire of greed and covetousness, we are called to become subjects of that kingdom of God, nothing less than "slaves of justice."

When Paul then moved from the metaphor of slaves to that of fruitfulness in Romans 7:4, Nereus was likely in more comfortable territory. Indeed, the metaphor of fruitfulness permeates Hebrew Scripture. After all, doesn't the biblical narrative begin with a Creator who plants a fruitful garden and calls the earth creature to "be fruitful and multiply" (Gen. 1:28)? And didn't Torah promise that covenantal obedience would be rewarded with fruitfulness in the land (Lev. 26:3–13), while idolatry would always result in the infertility and fruitlessness of life (Isa. 24:4–12; Hosea 4:1–3)? And wasn't the hope born of exile one of being fruitful and multiplying even at the heart of the empire (Jer. 29:4–7)? So it is no surprise that the prophets anticipated a return from exile in terms of a homecoming that would be blessed with renewed fruitfulness (Ezek. 36:8–12), and a covenant of peace in which "the trees of the field shall yield their fruit, and the earth shall yield its increase" (34:27). And in this return those who were enslaved will be rescued; "they shall no more be plunder for the nations," and "they shall live in safety, and no one shall make them afraid" (34:28). Indeed, God "will provide for them a splendid vegetation so that they shall no more be consumed with hunger in the land, and no longer suffer the insults of the nations" (34:29). This is a homecoming in fruitfulness and safety, a restoration of economic and ecological life to the shalom that was always the Creator's intention. This kind of creational fruitfulness and redressing of injustice was at the heart of the hope that Nereus learned from meditation on the law and the writings of Israel. Resurrection is for restored fruitfulness.[64]

So when Paul wrote that we now belong to Messiah Jesus, "who has been raised from the dead in order that we may bear fruit for God" (Rom. 7:4), Nereus knew what he was talking about. Through the resurrection of Jesus, he had been set free from his bondage to fruitless sin so that now he could bear the fruit of justice in his life.

Of course, Nereus was well aware that God's kingdom had not yet come in its fullness and that resurrection life still did not permeate his life or the lives of those around him. Like Paul in Romans 7, he was aware not only of sin in his own life but also that the weapons of injustice continued to beat down and destroy those who tried to live in the kingdom of life.[65] And so the promises in Romans 8 resonated with his longing: that the resurrection Spirit will one day raise him to new life (8:11), that there will be redemption for his body (8:23). But most of all Nereus would have trusted that the resurrection God of the Psalms and prophets,

64. In Phil. 1:11 Paul prays that the community will produce "the fruit of justice that comes through Messiah Jesus for the glory and praise of God" (our translation). Doing justice, then, is a way to give glory and praise to God. We have discussed the contrast of imperial fruitfulness and the way in which we meet this theme in the biblical story at further length in Walsh and Keesmaat, *Colossians Remixed*, chap. 4.

65. Tamez, *Amnesty of Grace*, 125, describes this dynamic in terms of "structures of social relations marked by sin—structures that are uncontrollable and that enslave all human beings." She also describes this as a "necrophilic system" (130).

the Lord who promised to vindicate the poor, the oppressed, the hungry, and the destitute, is the same resurrected Lord, Jesus, who sits at the right hand of God and intercedes for those in Nereus's community who suffer hardship, distress, persecution, famine, nakedness, peril, or sword (8:35). The love of the one who has risen up on behalf of the oppressed sustained him and surrounded him, for nothing could separate him from that love (8:35).

For Nereus to confess that Jesus is Lord and to believe that he rose from the dead means salvation (Rom. 10:9), not just in some sort of "spiritual" sense, but concretely in everyday socioeconomic and cultural life. For Nereus there would have been no division between spirituality and economics, or between salvation and politics. We miss the power of Paul's letter (and the rest of the Scriptures) if we impose such dualisms onto the text. Not only does salvation in Jesus disarm the imperial categories of shame (10:11); it also overthrows the religious and cultural divisions between Judeans and gentiles through a remarkable generosity of grace: for "everyone who calls on the name of the Lord shall be saved" (10:12–13). Moreover, this is the God who saves the poor and feeds the hungry, a God who promises the new kingdom of life everlasting (2:7; 5:18, 21; 6:22). Nereus would have heard these promises as a critique of the current oppressive economic structures where the greed and deceit of the wicked led to deprivation for so many, a system that, in the end, was a reign of death because it brought death to so many.[66] He would have heard a promise of economic justice in God's kingdom of life (5:17–21).

As we saw earlier in this book, the question is, Where do you live, where do you make your home? Or perhaps we could better put it, Who or what lives in you? Has the idolatrous spirit of injustice taken up residence in your life, or does the Spirit of Christ dwell in you? "But if Christ is in you, though the body is dead because of sin, the Spirit is life because of justice" (8:10 NRSV alt.). The Spirit is life because of justice. Without justice there is no life and there is no fruitfulness. "If the Spirit of him who raised Jesus from the dead dwells in you, he who raised Christ from the dead will give life to your mortal bodies also through his Spirit that dwells in you" (8:11). The question of salvation for Nereus, and for Paul, was always a matter of embodiment. If the Spirit of justice who raised Jesus from the dead takes up residence in our lives, if that Spirit is at home in our daily habits, our everyday choices and practices, then our lives will be an embodiment of justice. That's what resurrection is all about.

66. See Tamez, *Amnesty of Grace*, 130.

In his letter to the community of Jesus followers in Rome, therefore, Paul does not merely critique the oppressive economic practices of the empire; he also provides a vision of the defeat of the deathly economic ways of the empire, together with a vision of new life, resurrected life, for the community.

Home Economics in the Shadow of Empire

This vision of a life-giving praxis comes to a climax in Romans 12, where Paul outlines the way in which the community that follows Jesus will challenge the ethos of Rome. Paul's call to share in the needs of the saints and to extend hospitality to strangers (12:13), to weep with those who weep (12:15), and to not be haughty or conceited but rather to walk with the oppressed (12:16) undermines the relationships of patronage that hold imperial social relations together in a web of exploitation and control.[67] Rather than bestowing honor on those above them in the social hierarchy of the empire in order to court favor, while also accruing honor and indebtedness for oneself, Paul's resurrection community abandons all such self-honor by avoiding self-aggrandizement (12:3) and extending hospitality and honor to the stranger and the oppressed.

Furthermore, Paul's instructions concerning how the community is to relate to their enemies indicate that this community should not only practice a generous hospitality to those *within* their ranks but also extend this hospitality to those who act unjustly toward them. In other words, those who *enact* the kind of economic injustice that Paul has described throughout this letter are precisely those who are to experience the openhanded economic justice of this community: a generous welcome of food and drink is to be extended even to enemies. The alternative economic ethos of this community, therefore, doesn't just undermine the economic structures of patronage that shaped the empire; it also challenges the violence of the empire toward enemies, replacing vengeance with a love that is decidedly economic.

This vision of economic graciousness and love is reinforced by Paul's language of debt in Romans 1:14. Recall that Paul says that he is indebted (*opheiletēs*) to both Greeks and barbarians, to both wise and foolish. One could hardly imagine a more striking reversal of imperial notions of debt. In Paul's understanding, those who are clearly at the despised and shamed bottom of the imperial hierarchy

67. On the patronage system, see Andrew Wallace-Hadrill, ed., *Patronage in Ancient Society* (New York: Routledge, 1989).

of honor and debt are elevated to the same level as those at the top of the cultural system.

Paul picks up on this reversal in the language of debt in Romans 13.[68] In what appears to be a contradiction of the apostle's admonition in the previous chapter (12:10) to honor everyone in the community, Paul instructs the believers to "pay to all what is owed [*opheilas*], taxes to whom taxes are owed, revenue to whom revenue is owed, fear to whom fear is owed, honor to whom honor is owed" (13:7 our translation). On first reading this sounds like a reinscribing of the honor and debt system of the empire. But Paul then undermines the whole system anew in the very next verse: "Owe [*opheilete*] no one anything, except to love one another" (13:8). In the end, it is love, not taxes or revenue, or fear or honor, that binds together this community. The only debt under which we live is the debt of love, and that is a debt to all, regardless of cultural or economic status. It is such love that fulfills the law and the commandments. Living in covenantal love, this community maintains fidelity in sexual intimacy by not committing adultery, refraining from the violence of murder,[69] and embracing an economics of integrity by not stealing or taking advantage of the economically vulnerable. Moreover, they abandon all covetousness at the foundation of their economic lives (13:9). While greed, deceit, violence, and infidelity may be central to imperial economics, it is not to be so for the community that follows Jesus. Indeed, while the economy of the empire is about exploitation and the concentration of wealth among the elite minority, Paul identifies the heart of his economics of love by insisting that any law (whether Roman, Judean, or any other), and any commandment worth obeying, is "summed up in this word, 'Love your neighbor as yourself.' Love does no wrong to a neighbor; therefore, love is the fulfilling of the law" (13:9–10).

While gathering all law under the call of love has clear roots in the teaching of Jesus, the way in which Paul sums up these references to the Decalogue (Exod. 20:13–17; Deut. 5:17–21) with a quotation from Leviticus 19:18 ("Love your neighbor as yourself") is unparalleled in Jewish literature of the time.[70] The

68. We will address Paul's understanding of the state in Rom. 13 in chap. 8.

69. Murder is often economically motivated.

70. Citing Oda Wischmeyer, Jewett notes that "there are no citations at all from Lev. 19:18 in Jewish literature prior to Paul's letters." Jewett, *Romans*, 813. That the gospel tradition has Jesus making the very same reference to the Leviticus injunction (Matt. 20:19; Luke 10:27) doesn't undermine Jewett's (and Wischmeyer's) claim if we assume that Paul's letters are composed before the Gospels. But it could suggest that Paul's innovation is in fact dependent on the stories that he had been taught about Jesus.

apostle expands on this love of neighbor in Romans 13:10 with a double allusion, first to a psalm and then to the Lord's Supper.

Paul unpacks this call to love your neighbor as yourself by writing, "Love does no wrong to a neighbor" (Rom. 13:10). This is a clear echo of Psalm 15:3, which describes the blameless person with the very same words. Such a person, writes the psalmist, "does no evil to his neighbor."[71] This short psalm begins with the question of dwelling: "O Lord, who may abide in your tent? / Who may dwell on your holy hill?" (Ps. 15:1). Who can make home with the Holy One? What are the requirements of such a homemaking with God? And the answer is good neighbors. But the psalmist goes on to identify such homemaking neighborliness in ways that we have now come to expect in light of the economic allusions that we have found throughout the psalms that Paul quotes in his epistle to the Romans. The blameless speak the truth and there is no deceit in their hearts (Ps. 15:2). They do not slander, nor do they do evil (15:3). Rather than seeking their own benefit, they "stand by their oath even to their hurt" (15:4). And, of course, they engage in an economics of generosity and integrity because they "do not lend money at interest, and do not take a bribe against the innocent" (15:5). The echo of Psalm 15 in this pivotal text in Romans 13 carries these strong allusions to economic life within the household of God.

Until the advent of mass-produced and ready-made food, one of the central moments of a household gathering was, of course, the family meal. Home economics is about many things, but surely the production, preparation, and sharing of food is foundational to all homemaking. And it appears that Paul has in view nothing less than the family meal of the church in Romans 13:10. Curiously, the apostle begins and ends this verse, not with a generic love but with a specific love, indicated by the definite article. Robert Jewett translates the verse this way: "The agape does no evil to the neighbor; therefore the agape is law's fulfillment."[72] Jewett observes that by "repeating the definite article twice in this carefully constructed verse, Paul makes clear that the specific and distinctive form of love as experienced by the early house and tenement churches is the topic." Jewett continues, "The logical social corollary to 'the love' in this verse is the agape meal otherwise known as the love feast, the common meal shared by most sectors of the early church in connection with the Lord's Supper."[73]

71. Translation from Jewett, *Romans*, 814.
72. Jewett, *Romans*, 814. *Agapē* is the Greek word for love in this verse.
73. Jewett, *Romans*, 814.

If Jewett is right in reading Romans 13:10 as referring to the agape meals of the early church, then the implications are rather breathtaking. Such love feasts were modeled after the public meals known as *symposia* in Greco-Roman culture. These were gatherings for food, fellowship, and discussion. The symposia would have both mirrored and reinforced the social hierarchies and divisions of imperial society. Not only were these dinners reserved for men of similar socioeconomic status, thereby excluding women and slaves (except as servants for the event); even the seating arrangement was an indication of one's relative status or honor within the gathered community. But the Christian love feasts overturned the order of symposia in the empire by welcoming all to the table regardless of gender or socioeconomic status. So when Paul says that "the agape is law's fulfillment," he is making the audacious claim that in this meal of generous sharing, in this meal of retelling the story of Jesus, nothing less than a social revolution is happening. In *this* meal, not the violent and debaucherous meals of the empire (to which he will return presently), a new social order is established. If all law is subject to the law of love, then this meal disarms oppressive imperial law as it fulfills, in the midst of this diverse community of Jesus followers, the most profound goal of all law.

If this is true, then why did the apostle have to say that "the agape does no evil to the neighbor"? There are two possibilities that are not mutually exclusive. Perhaps some neighbors were in fact upset that their own family structures and loyalties were being undermined by these love feasts. As people became Christians and began to attend these feasts, it is possible that their nonattendance at their own household meals, or even at symposia for the few in the community who would have been invited to such gatherings, would have occasioned ill will among some concerning these Christian meals. But it is also possible, and more likely, that Paul is here anticipating the discussion of the next two chapters of his epistle. Paul's statement that the agape meal does no harm to the neighbor provides the basis for him to address the ways in which harm is in fact being done to Christian sisters and brothers during these meals. On occasion the ideal of love is far from being realized in the actual eating practices of the community, and this, Paul will argue, threatens both the integrity and the mission of the community. There are, if you will, family squabbles and dissension at the table.

Before proceeding to address the problems of eating in community, however, Paul reminds his hearers of what time it is and contrasts the ideal of the agape meal with the realities of feasting in the empire. The apostle reminds the community that in terms of God's timetable, the night is far gone and the day is near. Therefore, it is time to wake up and lay aside the deeds of darkness (13:11–12). Paul calls the community to put on the armor of light (13:12, recalling the language of bearing the weapons or instruments of justice in 6:13) and to live honorably (recognizing how he has so radically overthrown imperial notions of honor) as in the full light of day, not the hidden precincts of night (13:13). We can now see that Paul's injunction to no longer be conformed to the dictates of this age in 12:2 is rooted in the conviction that this age, this time, is coming to its close. The critical time, the "kairos moment" that is on them, is the end of the empire. Since time is up for the idolatrous empire, Paul says to no longer live by the dictates and the patterns of that empire, for the times they are a-changin'.

Paul does not leave things in general terms, however. He gets specific. If the Jesus followers in Rome are to live in the day, if they are to live into the kingdom of God in full understanding that the empire of Caesar has no eternal validity or endurance, and if the symbolic heart of their alternative community was found in a radically inclusive and revolutionary agape meal, then Paul insists that the community should be careful not to mimic the empire in their eating and partying together. "Let us live honorably as in the day, not in reveling and drunkenness, not in debauchery and licentiousness, not in quarreling and jealousy" (13:13). If this is a resurrection meal, a homecoming feast that anticipates the great eschatological banquet where the poor are fed, the homeless are housed, tears are wiped away, and there is an abundance of fruitfulness (Isa. 25:6–10; 65:13–19; Joel 2:15–26), then it must be in stark and liberating contrast to the meals of the empire. And that means that the kind of activities that characterized the symposia of the Roman elite must decidedly not be found in a Christian agape meal! The unrestrained sexual and alcoholic excess that was habitual in Roman banquets, and often depicted on murals of such banquets, has no place in the Christian community. Not only was such excess designed to showcase the wealth and honor of the host, but the exploitive and self-indulgent sexual debauchery of the symposia makes a mockery of the love, fidelity, compassion, and respect that is the very heart of the agape meal. Besides the joy of inclusion at the table, one of the things that Iris found so liberating about these agape meals was that she did not live in fear of being forced into sexual service at any point in the proceedings.

It is significant that the first four vices that Paul lists (reveling, drunkenness, debauchery, and licentiousness) are all in the plural form. These are repetitive and common behaviors at the symposia. But the last two vices are singular—namely, quarreling (or strife) and jealousy. There is a reference here to a partisanship, a taking of sides in a dispute within the community. Again, this was common enough at Greco-Roman symposia, and it could well have been this kind of behavior that was also in Paul's sights in his list of vices in 1:29–30, especially his references to envy, strife, gossip, slander, arrogance, and ruthlessness. "The early Christian revolution in the honor and shame system turned this tendency upside down, viewing 'strife' and 'dispute' as factors of the old age—the deeds of darkness—that eroded the equality of believers and destroyed the faith community."[74] And perhaps that is the real issue here. While Paul does not appear to be overly concerned about the Roman Christian agape meals being rampant with sexual immorality and drunken excess, it is clear from what follows in the next two chapters that he is deeply concerned about how strife, dispute, quarreling, and jealousy could indeed destroy this faith community and derail the mission of the kingdom of God.

It is, therefore, significant that Paul ends this chapter by contrasting a life cloaked in the imperial vices of sexual immorality, drunkenness, and communal strife with the call to "put on the Lord Jesus Christ, and make no provision for the flesh, to gratify its desires" (13:14). Returning to the unique formula "Lord Jesus Christ" from the very beginning of the letter (1:7), Paul places the issue squarely in the context of a conflict of sovereignties. Who (or what) will be the lord of this community's life? And how will that lordship be manifest in the way in which the community breaks bread together? If they have already abandoned the false lordship of Caesar for a crucified Savior; if they have already replaced the myths of Rome with the story of Israel, now fulfilled and reinterpreted in light of Messiah Jesus; if the Holy Spirit has taken up residence in their lives; if they have embraced a community ethic that dethrones the hierarchies of the empire, how then should they eat together? And should they do this in a way that is no longer fundamentally about the gratification of their own desires for wealth, honor, pleasure, and consumption?

Much indeed depends on dinner. Much depends on how you eat, with whom you eat, and what you eat. Eating is, of course, foundational to all of life. And where there is food, there are questions of justice, inclusion, and equality, and, perhaps most importantly, questions of identity. To eating, then, we now turn.

74. Jewett, *Romans*, 827.

7

Welcoming the Powerless

It should be no surprise that Paul's economic vision comes down to food. Where there is injustice, people go hungry. Where there is justice, people are fed. Not only are people fed; they also receive their sustenance in joyful community with others. If Paul's gospel is to be embodied in the lives of Jesus followers in Rome, it will be proven true at table fellowship. The whole anti-imperial agenda of this letter, together with its commitment to the formation of an alternative home at the heart of the empire, hangs on what happens when Jesus followers gather for the family dinner.

How Then Shall We Eat?

As we saw in chapter 2, questions of identity around eating and food are at the heart of the tensions between Nereus and Iris. While Iris experienced the sharing of meat at the agape meals to be a wonderful expression of the generosity and equality of those who followed Jesus, Nereus saw that same meat as a profound threat to the integrity of a community who followed the Messiah.[1] As we have seen, this isn't simply a matter of culinary preference but of the very identity of the early Christian community. And the tension is so thick, so fraught, and has so much destructive potential that Paul spends almost two chapters addressing it.[2]

1. See chap. 2, under "Nereus's Story."

2. It is important to note that the contrast between those who ate meat and those who abstained from meat was not necessarily along the gentile-Judean division. While all Judeans would likely have avoided pork, it is clear that vegetarianism was not a practice among all Judeans.

Indeed, the conflict within the house churches in Rome is a greater threat to the furthering of the gospel than anything that the empire itself can throw at these young followers of Jesus. If the gospel that Paul has been unpacking breaks through the imperial categories of shame and honor, then shaming anyone within the community undermines that gospel. If the apostle's purpose in writing is that there be mutual encouragement, a building up of the communities of Jesus in Rome (Rom. 1:12), then the tension at table fellowship that Paul addresses in Romans 14 and 15 serves to tear down precisely what the apostle is trying to build up. If Paul's gospel overthrew the imperial distinctions between Greek and barbarian, wise and foolish, gentile and Judean (1:14–16), then a new dichotomy of the powerful and weak would strip the gospel of the power of salvation that is its very heart. If Paul's argument from the beginning has been that we are in no position to pass judgment on each other, because we are all under the power of sin (2:1–11; 3:23) and all under the canopy of grace (3:24–26; 5:6–11), then any judgmentalism at the agape meal negates the gospel. If Paul has been proclaiming a gospel that consistently evokes an economics of generosity and justice, then reinscribing categories of the powerful and the weak flies in the face of such an economics. If this whole epistle has indeed been directed at homemaking in the heart of a domicidal empire, then conflicts at the table turn the family meal into a home-wrecking disaster. And if Paul's gospel has been all about faithfulness throughout this letter (1:17; 3:26; 3:30; 4:16; 5:1; 9:30), then the struggle around food at the table was ultimately a matter of breaking faith within the community and with the one whose faithfulness is our salvation.

If one thing was clear to most members of the house churches in Rome, it was that they were not welcome at the tables of the elite. Nereus was not invited to symposia, and Iris did not eat at the table with her master. The imperial table is always a table of exclusion. But Paul begins and ends his discussion of the economics of the agape meal with a call to radical hospitality, an inclusive welcome. "Welcome, in faithfulness, those who are weak, but not for the purpose of quarreling over opinions" (14:1 our translation). "Welcome one another, therefore, just as Christ has welcomed you, for the glory of God" (15:7). This is a welcome rooted in the very hospitality of Jesus, and whether God is glorified seems to hang

---

There was no standardized Jewish practice, as far as we can tell, that forbade the eating of all meat and the consumption of wine. See John D. Rosenblum, "Jewish Meals in Antiquity," in *Food in the Ancient World*, ed. John M. Wilkins and Shaun Hill (Oxford: Blackwell, 2006), 348–56. In addition, some God-fearing gentiles did not eat meat.

on whether the church engages in this kind of generous hospitality. If the very character of the community is manifest through loving one another in mutual affection (12:9), outdoing one another in showing honor (12:10), especially to those who are invariably dishonored and oppressed (12:16), then table fellowship in this community must be under the banner of welcome. Surely if this is a community that generously attends to the financial needs of its members and extends hospitality to strangers (12:13), then a failure to extend welcome to one another is a most fundamental failure. Tensions at the table, says Paul, are "works of darkness" (13:12) that make provision for the works of the flesh (13:14) and are unbecoming of those who know that "the night is far gone, the day is near" (13:12).

The meaning of this call to welcome is obscured, however, if we misunderstand the meaning of "weak" (*asthenounta*) at the beginning of Romans 14. It should be noted, first off, that although the usual translation of 14:1 is "Welcome those who are weak in faith," the Greek could be better translated "Welcome, in faithfulness, those who are weak."[3] Based on this translation, we shall assume that what is at issue, therefore, is not the validity or relative strength of the faith of these believers; in fact the subsequent argument made by Paul (which we will address below) undermines such a translation. Rather, the question is whether the faithfulness of Jesus Christ, the covenantal faithfulness that has been a recurring theme ringing throughout the letter, will be evident when the community gathers in the name of the faithful one.

The Greek word *astheneia* (translated as "weak" or "weakness") has a wide range of meaning. For instance, this word is used to describe the situation of those who come to Jesus with illnesses (usually translated "infirmities") in the Gospels. However, the word is also used for those who are economically vulnerable. Bruce Longenecker points out that in a number of places in Paul *astheneia* clearly includes those who are of a lower socioeconomic status. This is the meaning in 1 Corinthians 1:26–29, where the weak are contrasted with those who are wise, nobly born, and powerful.[4] Moreover, in 1 Corinthians 1:28 Paul says that such people are often despised, or treated with contempt, using the same verb

3. A. Katherine Grieb, *The Story of Romans: A Narrative Defense of God's Righteousness* (Louisville: Westminster John Knox, 2002), 129. The Greek is *ton de asthenounta tē pistei proslambanesthe*.

4. Bruce Longenecker, *Remember the Poor: Paul, Poverty, and the Greco-Roman World* (Grand Rapids: Eerdmans, 2010), 143. Longenecker indicates that they may be economically insecure because of actual physical weaknesses and vulnerabilities (143n21). In 1 Thess. 5:14 Paul encourages the believers to "encourage the fainthearted, help the weak [*antechesthe tōn asthenōn*], be patient with all of them."

(*exoutheneō*) that he employs in Romans 14:3 and 14:10. That is to say, how some people are being treated at the agape meal mirrors how people of lower social status are treated with contempt throughout the empire, a contempt that undermines the economic implications of the gospel that Paul preaches and has explicated in the letter to the Romans.[5]

So it is entirely possible that "the weak" in Romans 14 and 15 would have referred to those who were of a lower social status, those who were impoverished in the Roman community. Whatever their own reasons for abstaining from meat and wine (14:21), others in the community could have attributed such abstention to their poverty. Those others, who may themselves have come from situations where meat was unusual, could have experienced contempt for those believers "who don't know what is good for them" and who seem to be spurning the generosity of the community.[6]

Since the tensions in the community bear a striking resemblance to the socioeconomic divisions of the empire, it is not surprising that Paul seeks a resolution of these tensions by reminding the community of the identity of their Lord. If the community is still living under the economics of Caesar, then this situation will not be resolved without a return to their proper Lord. If the agape meal has been compromised and has begun to look like the symposia of the empire, then it is not surprising that the lordship of Jesus functions as a leitmotif throughout this passage. Indeed, Paul refers to Jesus as "Lord" no fewer than nine times in the first twelve verses of chapter 14, coming to the most intense concentration in 14:7–9: "We do not live to ourselves, and we do not die to ourselves. If we live, we live to the Lord, and if we die, we die to the Lord; so then, whether we live or whether we die, we are the Lord's. For to this end Christ died and lived again, so that he might be Lord of both the dead and the living." Let's put all of this in perspective, argues Paul. Whose are you? Who is the Lord before whom you bow the knee and give praise (14:11)? In whose story have you been incorporated? The story of Caesar or the story of the one who was crucified and raised from

5. In a similar vein, in 1 Cor. 9:22 Paul refers to his own ministry in this way: "To the weak I became weak, so that I might win the weak" (*egenomēn tois asthenesin asthenēs, hina tous astheneis kerdēsō*). As Longenecker points out, "Here Paul is using the term 'weak' to describe his self-imposed economic vulnerability." Longenecker, *Remember the Poor*, 143. This use of "the weak" to refer to the economically vulnerable—that is, the poor—is also found in Acts 20:35.

6. Peter Oakes, *Reading Romans at Pompeii: Paul's Letter at Ground Level* (London: SPCK, 2009), 86, 92–93, points out that hierarchy was present in all sectors of society, even within the lowest social strata. Hence even those who from the outside might seem to be equally impoverished would have interacted within an honor-shame dynamic.

the dead? If Christ is the Lord of all of life and even of death, how then should you eat together?[7]

Another way to put this is to ask, To whose household do we belong? If to Caesar's, then continue with meal practices that reflect his household and his economy. But if we belong to the household of Jesus, if Jesus is Lord, then our eating together must bear witness to the economy of the kingdom of God. And *household* is the right word. The welcome that Paul is talking about is explicitly a welcome into a home and to a common meal shared in that home.[8]

The motifs of household and lordship come together when the apostle writes, "Who are you to pass judgment on servants of another? It is before their own lord that they stand or fall. And they will be upheld, for the Lord is able to make them stand" (14:4). Whose household is this? Who is the host at this table? If Jesus is the Lord of this household, then only he can pass judgment on those in the household. And Paul has been careful in his use of terms here. Rather than referring to mere slaves or hired servants in the household (for which the term would be *doulos*), Paul uses the word *oiketēs*, "a household servant." The distinction is important. The term used here "denotes a normally inalienable member of the household, including slaves, who function almost as family members."[9] The point is that this is a family meal, and at this table all are equal and no one has the legitimate power to exclude anyone else. No one can take advantage of those who are more vulnerable to make them fall or stumble. If all members stand in grace (5:2) and it is the Lord of the household who has given them that standing, then any judgment that causes them to fall, that takes away their "standing" in the community, is a betrayal of that grace, a betrayal not just of that member but also of the Lord of grace.

Paul extends the metaphor explicitly to that of family a few verses later: "Why do you pass judgment on your brother or sister? Or you, why do you despise your brother and sister?" (14:10). While the "everything eaters" despise those who only eat vegetables, and the morally scrupulous "leaf eaters" pass judgment on the indiscriminate meat eaters (14:3), Paul here says that such judgments have no place among family members. If you have been adopted into the household of God and are joint heirs in Christ (8:16–17) and members one of another in

7. This is similar to Paul's argument about inequalities in eating at the Lord's Supper in 1 Cor. 11:17–34, where he reminds his hearers of the story of Jesus's crucifixion as the basis for their meal together.

8. Robert Jewett, *Romans: A Commentary*, Hermeneia (Minneapolis: Fortress, 2007), 835. Cf. Acts 18:27; 28:2; Philem. 17.

9. Jewett, *Romans*, 841.

one body (12:5), then do not replace the love of mutual affection (12:9) with the mutual exclusion and dismissal of a dysfunctional family.[10]

While Paul implicitly contrasts the body politic of the empire with the body of Christ in Romans 12, here he is insisting that the household of Jesus is radically different from the household of Caesar. The two households operate out of conflicting home economics. The economy of the empire is one of exclusion, status, and opulence for the very few, but the home economics of the kingdom is one of inclusion, mutuality, and equality. The household of Caesar imposes hegemonic order, while the household of Jesus embraces a diversity without judgment. Indeed, Paul offers a remarkable vision of freedom in this passage. Members of the household, subject to the same Lord, have the freedom to practice different diets as well as different calendars of special days as long as they do so "in honor of the Lord" and in thanksgiving (14:5–6). The unity of life under one Lord opens itself up to a rich variety of expression in belief and cultural practices. And to impose a uniformity of practice on such matters, Paul insists, by means of either judgment or contempt is to place a stumbling block before those who should be able to stand securely in the community on the basis of grace.

But this is a home economics that goes beyond a mere tolerance of difference. In light of what Paul has already said about genuine love and mutuality (12:9) and how love fulfills all law (13:8–10), he now goes on to write, "If your brother or sister is being injured by what you eat, you are no longer walking in love. Do not let what you eat cause the ruin of one for whom Christ died" (14:15). In other words, not only should the community abandon its quarreling and dissension about food, but those who have every good reason to eat certain things (perhaps even meat offered to idols), because "nothing is unclean in itself" (14:14), should

10. What is remarkable about this passage is the way in which subsequent interpreters have, with very few exceptions, interpreted Paul's words as a condemnation of those whom Paul describes as weak. So, for instance, N. T. Wright describes the weak as "people whose faith, though real, has not matured to the point where they understand its full implications" (Wright, "The Letter to the Romans: Introduction, Commentary, and Reflections," in *The New Interpreter's Bible*, vol. 10 [Nashville: Abingdon, 2002], 733). J. D. G. Dunn states that "to be 'weak in faith' is to fail to trust God completely" (Dunn, *Romans 9–16*, Word Biblical Commentary 38B [Dallas: Word, 1988], 798). See also Bruce J. Malina and John J. Pilch, *Social Science Commentary on the Letters of Paul* (Minneapolis: Fortress, 2006), 282: "The weak are simply locked up in their Torah based dreads and are unable to understand and follow the abrogation of Mosaic Torah requirements effected by Jesus' death and resurrection." Malina and Pilch also indicate that the weak are Judeans hoping to return to Judea.

Paul actually says that both those who abstain and those who don't are welcomed by God (Rom. 14:3), that they both stand before the judgment of God (14:4, 10), and that they all do what they do in honor of the Lord and with thanks (14:6). Paul has couched his argument in terms that indicate an understanding for the behavior of those who abstain *and* those who do not.

refrain from doing so if it causes harm to other members of the community. It is important to note here that the onus is put on those who eat everything to accommodate those who have a more scrupulous approach to their diet. That is to say, those who are described as "the weak" must be given priority in the community. And isn't that exactly what we would expect of a gospel that is preoccupied with justice for the socially and economically marginal?

Paul then brings it all together by proclaiming that "the kingdom of God is not food or drink but justice and peace and joy in the Holy Spirit" (14:17 NRSV alt.). And it is more likely that those who are identified as the weak, as those of a lower socioeconomic status, are more in need of justice than those who hold them in disdain. The question that Paul is struggling with in these chapters is the shape of food justice. Much depends on dinner. Who is invited to dinner? What is on the menu? And who is the host of this banquet? An agape meal is a feast of joy, but there is no joy at a table plagued with dissension, nor can there be joy in the face of injustice in the community.

Echoing his injunction to "live peaceably with all" (12:18), the apostle now calls the community to "pursue what makes for peace and for mutual upbuilding" (14:19). Just as he has portrayed the community as a household throughout this passage, now he uses a verb that has the building of a household, the shaping of a home together, in its purview. The English words *upbuilding* and *edification* carry with them the idea of a building, an edifice, and this is because they translate the Greek word *oikodomē*, from the root *oikos*, which is well translated as "home." As we have seen, the English words *economics* and *ecology* share the same root. So if the kingdom of God is a matter of justice, peace, and joy, and if the community is called to a shared life in the household of Jesus, then Paul's admonition to his hearers is to be busy with a life of building this household, engendering the peace and joy of this alternative home in the midst of the empire, and constructing together a life of faithfulness that is rooted in and radically reflects the justice of God.

That this justice is preferential toward the poorest members of the community is clear in the admonition given to those who have the most power. It isn't until the first verse of chapter 15 that we find Paul using the word *powerful* as a descriptor of some in the community. Rather than enjoining the "strong" to "put up with the failings of the weak" (NRSV), this verse is better translated as "We who are powerful (*dynatoi*) ought to bear the weakness (*asthenēmata*) of the powerless (*adynatōn*) and not to please ourselves."[11] The point is clear. Paul insists

11. The verb in this verse, "to bear" (*bastazein*), is the same as that used in Gal. 6:2: "Bear one another's burdens and so fulfill the law of Christ" (our translation; *Allēlōn ta barē*

that those who are *powerful*, a word with clear connotations of socioeconomic power and control, are to bear the weaknesses of the powerless. This supports a reading of the weak in chapter 14 as those who are poor, as well as reinforcing once again the parallels with chapter 12, where the community is called to an economic sharing for the needs of the saints, hospitality to the stranger (12:13), and a life of identification with the oppressed (12:16). In the words of Klaus Wengst, "This is a community oriented to the needs and distresses of its weakest members."[12] Jewett points out that Paul here reverses the ordinary structure of obligation: "Rather than the weaker being forced to submit to the strong as was typical in Greco-Roman culture, the powerful are here under obligation to 'bear/carry' (*bastazein*) the weakness of the powerless."[13] What else would be expected of those who follow the one who came to serve and not to be served? Rather than insulting the vulnerable in their midst, the powerful are called to follow the one on whom insult upon insult was laid (15:3).

So Paul repeats the call to welcome one another, "just as Christ has welcomed you, for the glory of God" (15:7). Of course, the corollary to this would be that in the absence of such welcome, in the perpetuation of economic oppression and dissension at the agape meal, God is not glorified. And if God is not glorified in the daily life of the Jesus followers in Rome, if the gospel is not manifest in the alternative way in which this community shares table fellowship, then might it be that the promises to the patriarchs remain unfulfilled (15:8) and that God will not be glorified among the nations (15:9–12)? The harmony that Paul is seeking in the house churches of Rome has both pastoral and evangelistic significance. Neither the gentiles nor anyone else will be attracted to come home to God in Jesus if that home is manifestly dysfunctional and perpetuates injustice in its midst.

But, says Paul, many throughout the empire have indeed come home to God in Jesus. Throughout the vast scope of Caesar's realm, the counter-imperial gospel

bastazete . . .). Some have suggested that Paul might be using this language of power sarcastically, as if to say, "This is what you so-called powerful ought really to be doing with your power." This certainly would fit in with Paul's use of this language elsewhere, particularly in Corinthians, where he clearly identifies himself with the weak and powerless rather than the powerful. See Beverly Roberts Gaventa, "Reading for the Subject: The Paradox of Power in Romans 14:1–15:6," *Journal of Theological Interpretation* 5, no. 1 (2011): 9n30, relying on Thomas Tobin, *Paul's Rhetoric in Its Contexts: The Argument of Romans* (Peabody, MA: Hendrickson, 2004), 409.

12. Klaus Wengst, *Humility: Solidarity of the Humiliated* (Minneapolis: Fortress, 1988), 47, speaking of Rom. 12:16.

13. Jewett, *Romans*, 877.

that Paul has been painstakingly explicating in this letter has been proclaimed, and now Paul intends to spread the good news beyond Rome to Spain (15:14–24). And one of the clear indications that the gospel has been proclaimed with the power of the Holy Spirit is that the gentiles "have been pleased to share their resources with the poor among the saints at Jerusalem" (15:26). Surely if gentile Christians throughout the empire were engaging in this kind of economic generosity toward Judeans in Jerusalem, then a similar generosity could be expected within the diverse community of Jesus followers in Rome. Throughout the empire the followers of Jesus are recognizing that they are "members one of another" (12:5) precisely by contributing "to the needs of the saints" (12:13). Let this example of the church throughout the empire be a witness to the sisters and brothers in Christ who live at its heart in Rome.

Betrayal and Economic Justice

So where do I sign up?

Excuse us, what did you say?

Where do I sign up?

What do you mean?

If this is all true, then where do I sign up? Where can I find something that might even begin to reflect the kind of economic vision that you have found in Romans? Frankly, this is all new to me, and it has been a bit of work to stick with your argument over the last two chapters. I've never heard Paul's letter interpreted in terms of economic justice before. The call to generosity in Romans 12 and the advice about welcoming one another in chapters 14 and 15 have always been presented to me as being about personal charity and how Jews and gentiles were supposed to get along. But you have argued that all of this is part of Paul's larger vision of God's justice, that somehow such a perspective was already hinted at way back at the beginning of the letter when he wrote, "The just shall live by faithfulness." I'd really like to get on board with a Christian faith that has real economic consequences in my daily life and maybe even in the life of my community, but I've also got this deep discomfort in the pit of my stomach. If this is all true, why didn't anyone tell me any of this before? If this vision of economic justice is integral to the gospel that Paul is proclaiming in the letter to the Romans, then how did that all get lost?

Well, that is a longer story than we can tell in this book, but remember Wendell Berry's caustic evaluation of things when he wrote that the church "has flown the flag and chanted the slogans of empire . . . [and] has admired Caesar and comforted him in his depredations and defaults."[14] We aren't going to rehearse the whole argument about the church losing its way when it became the official religion of the Roman Empire and an ally to the emperor of the day (Constantine). But if the economic vision that we find in Paul's letter to the Romans hangs on the question of lordship, then it certainly looks as if many North American Christians have bowed the knee to Caesar and to his predatory economy in their daily economic lives, while still confessing Jesus as Lord at church and in personal piety.

I guess I'm troubled by this because in my tradition we have always affirmed the authority of the Bible in the strongest possible terms. We learned in Sunday school that "all Scripture is inspired by God and is useful for teaching, for reproof, for correction, and for training in righteousness" (2 Tim. 3:16), but I never heard anything that reproved or corrected my economic assumptions or our day-to-day lives of thoughtless consumption. And since you are probably going to tell me that the word for righteousness *here is the same as the justice that Paul is talking about in Romans, then why wasn't my spiritual formation in the church one that led me to see that I was called to such justice, that such justice was at the heart of following Jesus?*

Your frustration is mirrored in so many people, especially young adults, that we have had the honor to teach over the years. The question "Why didn't anyone tell me this stuff?" implies a sense of betrayal. A sense that something had been kept hidden, that Christian faith had been watered down to personal piety married to social and cultural legitimacy. And this is a betrayal at so many levels. A betrayal of the young because they have been offered an insipid faith devoid of real sociocultural and economic significance. A betrayal of the text because it has been so domesticated. And, when it comes right down to it, a betrayal of the very one in whose faithfulness we are made just. This ends up being an apostasy dressed up in piety.

Sadly, this is nowhere more evident than in the reading of Paul's letter to the Romans. While the church has wielded this epistle as a sword within its own theological wars, the letter itself has been strangely (and paradoxically) rendered powerless in the real conflict that Paul names to be at the heart of the gospel of Christ. While the church has been preoccupied with the "justification" of the "sinner," it has lost the radical message of how in Jesus Christ those who are unjust are made to be just anew, equipped and empowered for lives of justice. To cite Elsa Tamez again, when Paul talks about justification, he is talking about

14. Wendell Berry, "Christianity and the Survival of Creation," in *Sex, Economy, Freedom and Community* (New York: Pantheon, 1993), 115. See also Wes Howard-Brook, *Empire Baptized: How the Church Embraced What Jesus Rejected* (Maryknoll, NY: Orbis, 2016).

how "God makes it possible for human beings to do justice. . . . The purpose of justification is to transform human beings into subjects who do justice, who rescue the truth that has been imprisoned in injustice."[15]

Wait, are you saying that a lot of talk about justification by faith has actually distracted us from the heart of the epistle?

Well, yes. That's why Paul's letter never corrected our economic assumptions or taught us the way of justice. That's why Paul's letter has so seldom actually accomplished what 2 Timothy 3:16 says is the purpose of Scripture. Look at how that sentence concludes: ". . . and for training in righteousness [or justice], so that everyone who belongs to God may be proficient [or complete], equipped for every good work" (2 Tim. 3:16–17). Reading Scripture isn't simply a matter of acquiring new information, together with some pious inspiration. Rather, a faithful reading of Scripture is to be nothing less than a training ground for lives of justice. If our reading of an ancient text like Romans doesn't deepen our lives and our habits in a way that makes us more proficient, more practically competent in lives of justice, then it isn't a reading of Scripture at all! The Spirit who inspires this text and who dwells in us, leading us on the path of justice and liberation, is simply absent if the reading doesn't shape us as agents of justice. We know that we have read Scripture and that we have read it well when this ancient text becomes alive, correcting and reproving the false ideologies that have taken us captive, liberating our imaginations, transforming our lives for a justice that becomes second nature to us in our day-to-day practices and habits. The Scriptures serve their purpose when they lead us to maturity, to the fullness of our human calling to bear the image of God in lives of justice, compassion, generosity, self-sacrifice, hospitality, and peace. And we have seen that justice for the most vulnerable is central to such a life in God's kingdom.

But justice for the most vulnerable hasn't been at the center of North American economics. Is the whole economic system that I've been raised with, the whole economic lifestyle that I've taken simply to be normal, my very way of life, fundamentally a matter of idolatry?

That's a very uncomfortable question to ask. And maybe one way to answer it is by asking a few more questions. Remember how Paul said that Abraham "would inherit the world . . . through the righteousness of faith" (Rom. 4:13)? Maybe a better way to put that is that he would inherit the world through faithful justice. Is that how it works? Who tends to inherit the land in our world?

15. Elsa Tamez, *The Amnesty of Grace: Justification by Faith from a Latin-American Perspective*, trans. Sharon H. Ringe (Nashville: Abingdon, 1993), 110.

Those who inherit the world tend to be the wealthiest 1 percent who pass down their wealth from one generation to another.

Faithful justice has nothing to do with it?

Not really.

You don't need to be an economist to know that those who get control of the world are those who deal in deception and injustice. And, of course, there's our privilege.

Our privilege?

Sure, our class, background, education, and race have set us up to "inherit the world" while so many other people are fundamentally disinherited. The fact that you are even reading this book suggests that you are ahead of the game.

It is interesting you should say that. I confess that I comfort myself by thinking that I could never end up sleeping in a ravine or over a heating vent downtown. I'll always have somewhere to go, even if I were to lose my job or my home. Either friends or family would take me in.

That comfort comes from your social capital, your privilege. But what if you didn't have that kind of privileged community surrounding you? It isn't hard to see that the desperate poverty in the African American community is an ongoing consequence of a slave economy that was at the very foundation of the United States, or that the social problems in the Indigenous community are the result of colonialism.

The problem is that even when I see someone like Iggy asking for money, or someone sleeping on a hot-air vent, I don't know what to do about it. And now you are saying that the problem is deeper than one person's bad choices and laziness. That's scary because if poverty is the result of bad choices made by the poor themselves, then it isn't my responsibility to do anything more than offer the kindness of a meal.

And now the kindness of a meal doesn't seem like enough.

Not if the comforts of my life and my stable income and my security are the result of benefiting from an unjust economy.

Economics and Worldview Revisited

Let's unpack this a little more. Remember the way in which we surmised how a global capitalist narrative would answer the five worldview questions back in chapter 3?

Give me a break. That's four chapters back!

Good point. Well, we think it might be helpful to consider for a minute how those answers to the worldview questions from chapter 3 would contrast with how we might imagine answering those questions from the perspective of Paul's letter to the Romans. We'll try to do this in such a way that we briefly recap those other answers as well, just in case you don't remember them.

Where are we? In contrast to a worldview where everything has a price, Paul's vision is of a world rooted in and sustained and redeemed by grace. This is a world not of price, commodity, and exploitation but of radical gift. Far from the passive, inert, and mute object of human domination, this is a creation that is eloquent in bearing witness to the very nature of God's steadfast love, justice, compassion, and faithfulness. While both Marx and Locke said that "nature" had no value unless it was transformed by human labor into economic products, Paul's economic vision is rooted in a belief that the creation is called into being through the love of the Creator and is endowed with deep value as a creature of the Creator.

Who are we? In contrast to *Homo autonomous*, humans are created in the image of God, subject to the rule of God, and called to lives of faithfulness, justice, compassion, service, and love. And rather than being *Homo economicus*, realizing our freedom most fully in an economic power that satisfies our consumptive self-indulgence, human beings are called, elected, and chosen for "glory." But this is not the empty glory of empire. This is the glory of a life fully lived in the image of God. The human creature's glory is manifest precisely in lives of careful, fruitful, and loving servanthood. While our capitalist selves grasp at life through our possessions and wealth, followers of Jesus have died in Christ and now live in Christ as slaves of justice, taking all the resources and gifts of our lives and dedicating them to seeking justice. Rather than sacrificing the poor to the machinations of the Market, or the richly diverse and eloquent creation to the requirements of global capitalism, we offer ourselves as living sacrifices to the one who brings a kingdom of justice.

What's wrong? Creation groans, injustice reigns, idolatry deforms the image of God, and we have been taken captive by a sexuality and an economics of violence and exploitation. While capitalism tells us that what's wrong is anything that inhibits human economic freedom, anything that puts constraints on the Market and those who benefit the most from its operation, Paul says that what is wrong is that no one is just, no one is faithful. What's wrong is poverty, persecution, violence, and exclusion. What's wrong is the misdirection of human freedom and the disordering of human desire.[16] Life is under the grip of an imperial

16. See Daniel M. Bell Jr., *The Economy of Desire: Christianity and Capitalism in a Postmodern World* (Grand Rapids: Baker Academic, 2012), esp. chaps. 5–7.

imagination, subject to a false Lord, and we seek salvation in idols within an imperial narrative of deceit.

What's the remedy? In the face of faithlessness, there is a faithful one. In the face of injustice, there is one whose faithfulness brings justice. In the shadow of the empire and its impostor of a lord and savior, the Lord Jesus Christ has come to establish his kingdom of justice, joy, and peace. The lament of the poor resonates with the groaning of all creation and the very Spirit of God. But this is a lament and a longing for nothing less than a new creation, the redemption of bodies held captive by injustice, a redemption accomplished on an imperial cross by Jesus. The empire of violence and inequity, together with its economics of death, is overturned, dethroned, and disarmed in the resurrection of Jesus. In this resurrection, justice reigns anew and the building of a home of fruitfulness and welcome has begun. This is a home built on the foundation of justice. In this home economics there is one law that surpasses all other law, one law that fulfills all debt and obligation, one law that is the criterion by which all law, all economic systems, all economic practices are judged, and that is the law of love.

If this exercise in answering the first four worldview questions at all makes sense, if this is a way that both summarizes what we have learned of Paul's economic vision of life and places that vision of life in dissonance with the dominant worldview of global capitalism, then how do we answer the fifth worldview question?

The question about time, right?

Correct. We will need to answer this crucial question in careful contrast and conversation with other answers that are presently on offer.

Okay, I'm listening.

What Time Is It? Repentance and Secession

What time is it? As we saw in chapter 3, a variety of voices offer conflicting answers to this question at this moment in the history of global capitalism. Post-9/11 there were some who said that it was time for the United States to step up to its global responsibility. It was time for the American Empire, the *Pax Americana*. In the absence of any other superpower, it was time for the United States to wield its power and influence to rid the world of the forces of terror, together with any other obstacles to economic freedom in the unrestricted operation of the Market. The American Empire is an intensification of global capitalism wherein the military and political power of the United States is put at the service of unfettered capitalism.

But the promise of the "American dream" turned into a nightmare for so many in the disappearance of jobs (often to offshore producers), the draining of the economy in military expenditures (it is expensive to police the world in never-ending wars against terror!), the erosion of investments, and the loss of homes in the crash of 2008. And so greed turned to fear and the *Pax Americana* was replaced by a nationalist cry to "Make America Great Again." Eduardo Galeano notes that "along with greed, fear has always been the most active engine of the system that used to be called capitalism." The fear of unemployment, of losing your investments, your house, your pension. The fear of all your debts coming due and being unable to pay. The fear of destitution. Galeano continues, "Fear, father of a large family, also begets hatred."[17] The hatred of the illegal immigrant, the foreigner, the politicians who have taken your money in taxes and allowed your economic security and prosperity to be squandered. And so the disenfranchised and angry white middle and working classes revolted in the 2016 US election by embracing the virulent antipolitics of division and the hatred of a demagogue.[18] Scapegoating, violence, nationalism, racism, misogyny, and xenophobia all gathered under the banner of "Make America Great Again." From this perspective, what time is it? It's time to lay aside political correctness and even civility, discard any remainders of a political order that would restrain the rich for the sake of the poor, abandon all vestiges of economic or environmental policy that might keep corporate greed in check, expel all illegal immigrants, close the borders, and embrace a strong man who will lead the nation back to its greatness. Ironically, while none of this resonates with the kind of passion for economic justice that we see in the prophets, Jesus, or Paul, white evangelicals flocked to the "Make America Great Again" agenda and embraced this politics of hate.

So if neither the *Pax Americana* nor the mantra "Make America Great Again" is faithful to the gospel of Jesus Christ, what time is it?

Could it be time to repent? I don't know if I think that a whole nation can repent, but surely now should be a time of repentance for the church. I'm still thinking about that Wendell Berry quote, and it seems to me that talk of the American Empire or the language of making America great again is "chanting the slogans of empire" and sacrificing the

17. Eduardo Galeano, *Upside Down: A Primer for the Looking-Glass World*, trans. Mark Fried (New York: Holt, 2000), 170.

18. See Juan Cole, "Why the White Working Class Rebelled: Neo-liberalism Is Killing Them (Literally)," *The Guardian*, November 9, 2016.

gospel before the kind of idolatry that Paul has been attacking all along. And when I think of how you used the word apostasy *a moment ago, a deep sadness overcomes me.*

When the anger of betrayal gives way to grief, then we know that we are on a path to healing. But we still need to do something with that grief.

What I want to do with my grief is to repent. That's hard to say, but it feels even harder to do. I mean, I'm not totally sure I know what it would mean to repent of empire.

Maybe Wendell Berry can continue to be helpful to us. Here is the opening stanza from his iconic poem "The Mad Farmer, Flying the Flag of Rough Branch, Secedes from the Union."

> From the union of power and money,
> from the union of power and secrecy,
> from the union of government and science,
> from the union of government and art,
> from the union of science and money,
> from the union of ambition and ignorance,
> from the union of genius and war,
> from the union of outer space and inner vacuity,
> the Mad Farmer quietly walks away.[19]

What time is it? It is time to secede from empire. This is what is required if we are to renounce idolatry in our lives. "Where power and science are united with money, ambition is driven by ignorance, and human genius is employed in service of war, there is only one option, says Berry: walk quietly away. From such unions we must secede. But secede to what or whom?"[20] Berry replies:

> From the union of self-gratification and annihilation,
> secede into the care for one another
> and for the good gifts of Heaven and Earth.

What time is it? It is time to secede, Berry counsels, *from* a self-gratification that inevitably results in annihilation *into* a life of care for one another and for the good gifts of creation.

Let's unpack this a little more. First, we need to come to grips with the fact that the kind of self-gratification that is at the heart of all empire, including the

19. Wendell Berry, "The Mad Farmer, Flying the Flag of Rough Branch, Secedes from the Union," in *The Selected Poems of Wendell Berry* (Washington, DC: Counterpoint, 1998), 162–63.

20. Brian J. Walsh and Sylvia Keesmaat, *Colossians Remixed: Subverting the Empire* (Downers Grove, IL: IVP Academic, 2004), 159.

imperial economics of late capitalism, is always an economics and a way of life on the path of annihilation. Empires always fall prey to the temptation of overreach. Not only does the imperialism of something like the *Pax Americana* require vast resources to sustain its expansionism and military protection of its own interests (which are, by definition, global), but the consumptive insatiability of an imperial economics will always outstretch the carrying capacity of its territory and peoples.[21] Simply stated, unfettered economic growth poses a grave threat to the very inhabitability of the planet.[22]

Wendell Berry draws a contrast between the present economy that safeguards the "rights of profit" through the "private exploitation of public wealth and health," and "the economy of community" that safeguards "the protection of gifts."[23] If the rights of profit are at the foundation of an economy, then not only will all public resources (air, water, minerals, land, etc.) be privatized for corporate profit, but such profit-making can know no limit. By contrast, if one thing is clear in an economics of gift, rooted in a vision of creational wholeness, it is that an economy of unlimited growth is on a disastrous collision course with the reality of creational limits. And while Rome's economic overreach resulted in the kind of ecological collapse that we discussed in chapter 5, the ideology of economic growth in the modern world was accelerated by a technological revolution that dwarfs Rome's imperial economy. Moreover, the fossil fuel consumption that has driven the modern economy has also accelerated global ecological damage, most extremely evident in the reality of climate breakdown. Recalling Naomi Klein's

21. The classic argument of imperial overreach in the modern world is Paul Kennedy's *The Rise and Fall of the Great Powers: Economic Change and Military Conflict from 1500 to 2000* (New York: Fontana, 1990). While not uncritical of Kennedy, Geir Lundestad discerns the decline of the American Empire in the economic overreach of its military expenditures. When taxes are decreased in order to benefit the rich, but military expenditures dramatically increase in order to fund imperial expansion, the only possible result will be sky-rocketing national debt. And so the economic question becomes, How long can the world's biggest borrower remain the world's leading power? Or, as Lundestad puts it, "Others ask what kind of superpower the United States would be when it spends more on interest payments than on defense, a condition that is likely to occur in a few years' time" (Geir Lundestand, *The Rise and Decline of the American "Empire": Power and Its Limits in Comparative Perspective* [Oxford: Oxford University Press, 2012], 149). For a neo-Marxist take on Kennedy's thesis, see David Harvey, *The New Imperialism* (Oxford: Oxford University Press, 2003), chap. 2. See also Jared Diamond, *Collapse: How Societies Choose to Fail or Succeed*, 2nd ed. (New York: Penguin, 2011).

22. See Steven Bouma-Prediger and Brian J. Walsh, *Beyond Homelessness: Christian Faith in a Culture of Displacement* (Grand Rapids: Eerdmans, 2008), chap. 5.

23. Berry, *Sex, Economy, Freedom and Community*, 138; Walter Brueggemann, "Reflections on Biblical Understandings of Poverty," in *A Social Reading of the Old Testament: Prophetic Approaches to Israel's Prophetic Life*, ed. Patrick J. Miller (Minneapolis: Fortress, 1994), 276, draws a similar contrast between a royal/urban and a prophetic/covenantal economics in the Hebrew Scriptures.

observation that climate change requires the contraction of humanity's use of resources, while our economic system demands unfettered expansion, she says we face a stark choice: "Allow climate disruption to change everything about our world, or change pretty much everything about our economy to avoid that fate."[24]

I think that is why we have so many people who deny climate change out there. They have to question the science because if climate change is true, then this will have an impact on the way they live and the way the economy runs.

Precisely. Klein puts it this way: "It is always easier to deny reality than to allow our worldview to be shattered."[25] As we have seen, the idea of a "contraction" of our use of natural resources, especially fossil fuels, together with the contraction of the economy that would result, is simply unthinkable to most of us. Decades ago, Robert Heilbroner noted that "expansion has always been considered as inseparable from capitalism," and "conversely, a 'stationary,' non-expanding capitalism has always been considered either as a prelude to its collapse or as a betrayal of its historic purpose."[26] Within the worldview of global capitalism, the idea of slowing down our consumption and acquisition is a betrayal of our very identity and destiny. In terms of the ideology of American exceptionalism, this is a failure of nothing less than the American dream.[27]

24. Naomi Klein, *This Changes Everything: Capitalism versus the Climate* (Toronto: Knopf Canada, 2014), 22. See also Bill McKibben, *Deep Economy: The Wealth of Communities and the Durable Future* (New York: Holt, 2007), chap. 1.

25. Klein, *This Changes Everything*, 37. Commenting on the ideological resistance to climate change, Klein writes, "Changing the earth's climate in ways that will be chaotic and disastrous is easier to accept than the prospect of changing the fundamental, growth-based, profit-seeking logic of capitalism" (81).

26. Robert Heilbroner, *An Inquiry into the Human Prospect* (New York: Norton, 1974), 83.

27. In our living memory, the only president of the United States who could have imagined an American way of life characterized by consumer restraint was Jimmy Carter. In his famous speech on July 15, 1979, Carter called the nation to abandon the worship of "self-indulgence and consumption," with its mistaken understanding of a quantitative freedom realized in the never-ending quest for more. In its place, he offered an alternative vision, rooted, he believed, in core American values. This would be a path of qualitative freedom that would require consumer restraint and settling for less. It was a prophetic moment in US history. Sadly, Carter was wrong. There are no such values of common care at the heart of the United States, and Ronald Reagan's stunning defeat of Carter in the 1980 election demonstrated what subsequent history has proven: there is no United States apart from an ideology of self-interest within a narrative of ever-accelerating economic growth. The text of this speech can be found online at http://www.presidency.ucsb.edu/ws/?pid=32596. On Carter's speech, see Andrew J. Bacevich, *The Limits of Power: The End of American Exceptionalism* (New York: Holt, 2008), 32–37. For a critique of Barak Obama's failure to question this American ideology of economic growth, see the postscript in Brian J. Walsh, *Subversive Christianity: Imaging God in a Dangerous Time*, 2nd ed. (Eugene, OR: Wipf & Stock, 2014), 97–124.

It is, therefore, not surprising that those who pay the closest attention to the crisis of climate change, together with the failures of our economic system to produce anything approaching a sustainable equity in the world, call for nothing less than a new worldview to replace the discredited and disastrous vision of life that has brought us to this place of rising economic inequality and ecological crisis. What is needed is not a few adjustments to the economic systems in which we live, but nothing less than a comprehensive worldview shift. Klein says that for anything to really change, "a worldview will need to rise to the fore that sees nature, other nations, and our own neighbors not as adversaries, but rather as partners in a grand project of mutual reinvention."[28] And as we have seen, worldviews are always rooted in stories. What we need, says Klein, is "a different story," because the one we are living in is killing us and the planet.[29]

But where can we find this "different story"? I get that repentance requires abandoning the worldview of capitalism because it is the union of "self-gratification and annihilation," as Berry put it. But where do we go from there?

An Economy of Care

Well, look again at Berry. With a deeply biblical (indeed, Pauline) imagination, he counsels that we "secede into the care for one another / and for the good gifts of Heaven and Earth." There it is again, an economy of gift. What time is it? It is time for an economy of care.

Care *seems to me to be kind of a weak term.*

Not when you consider the rapacious carelessness of economic injustice and creational desecration. Recall the placelessness of an ecologically destructive economics that we critiqued in chapter 5. An ever-expanding economy that protects the rights of profit will always be a displaced economy. Because the criterion of economic success is limited to profit, any place can be sacrificed for the sake of making a profit. An economy of care is an emplaced economy, one that knows its place, respects the limits of place, and seeks the regenerative health of its place and its inhabitants. Randy Woodley describes this in Indigenous terms as the Harmony Way.[30]

28. Klein, *This Changes Everything*, 23. Cf. Lester R. Brown, who argues that we need "a shift in our worldview, in how we think about the relationship between the earth and the economy." Brown, *Eco-Economy: Building an Economy for the Earth* (New York: Norton, 2001), 6.

29. Naomi Klein, *No Is Not Enough: Resisting the New Shock Politics and Winning the World We Need* (Toronto: Knopf, 2017), 8.

30. Randy S. Woodley, *Shalom and the Community of Creation: An Indigenous Vision* (Grand Rapids: Eerdmans, 2012), 111–36, 151–56.

In chapter 5 you talked about how ecological homemaking could not happen apart from knowing and loving your "place." Are you now expanding that ecological argument to the economy?

That is exactly what we are doing. If Paul is right when he says that we are to "owe no one anything, except to love one another," because "love is the fulfilling of all law" (Rom. 13:8, 10), then we need to ask what economic love looks like, both in our personal lives and in the very economic structures in which we live. If economy is best understood in terms of how we carefully shape the world that we have received as radical gift so that it becomes a home, a household of love, then what kind of an economy are we looking for?

Again Naomi Klein is helpful. She writes about the need "for a shift from a system based on endless taking—from the earth and from one another—to a culture based on caretaking, the principle that when we take, we also take care and give back."[31] This is a call to replace "an economy built on destruction with an economy built on love."[32] What time is it? It is time for an economy of love, an economy of care. While Klein might be shocked to hear it, this kind of sounds like Paul.

Bob Goudzwaard and Harry de Lange have proposed an economic perspective that resonates deeply with the biblical vision we have uncovered in Paul's epistle to the Romans. What happens if we take seriously the homemaking character of economic life and place "care" at the foundation of economics? They write, "In an economy of care, economic needs or ends include more than the output of production can satisfy. They also include what human culture needs to survive: the level of care required for the environment to remain fertile; the amount of care needed to sustain communities so that people's care for each other will acquire continuity and tradition; and adequate care for employment opportunities and the quality of work."[33]

An economy that *begins* with care reverses the relationship between economic growth and care for the vulnerable by prioritizing justice over narrowly conceived notions of economic efficiency. This is an economy rooted in an economics of enough, in contrast to an insatiable economics of more. This is an economy "that considers justice, compassion, community, good work and ecological responsibility as points of departure for economic life, not as (necessary) afterthoughts."[34]

31. Klein, *No Is Not Enough*, 241.

32. Klein, *No Is Not Enough*, 241.

33. Bob Goudzwaard and Harry de Lange, *Beyond Poverty and Affluence: Toward a Canadian Economy of Care*, trans. Mark Vander Vennen (Toronto: University of Toronto Press, 1994), 87.

34. Bouma-Prediger and Walsh, *Beyond Homelessness*, 144.

Or perhaps we need to use the language of hospitality and generosity, as Paul does in Romans. Such hospitality and generosity were central to the community life practiced by Indigenous peoples before colonization. So central was this generosity that the ritual redistribution of wealth, called a *potlatch*, or "giveaway," was practiced at key points in one's life. Such practices were so threatening to the economic narrative of the colonizers that they were outlawed. But these core practices of hospitality and generosity are still central in Indigenous communities today.[35] This is best described as an economics of gift and welcome.

Let there be no mistake—this is indeed nothing less than a full-scale paradigm shift in economic life. If we are going to take seriously Paul's creational vision and prioritizing of economic justice in the face of imperial economics, then we will need to embrace an economics of gift in the face of an economics of acquisitive grasping. Rather than an abstract theology of capital growth, we will practice an economic homemaking rooted in real places. This will be a local economics in contrast to global capitalism. It will privilege propriety and frugality over self-indulgent consumption. The arrogance and violence of economic mastery will be replaced by a humble economics that seeks peace in the service of the most vulnerable. An economy of care protects common resources as the foundation of the economic household over against the exploitation of those resources for private gain. In sharp contrast to a "virtual economy" that is little more than financial transactions around the world in which capital produces more capital, an economics of care will be measured in the fruitfulness of real people in real places producing real economic goods and services in community with one another.[36] And while the consumerism of global capitalism is an economics of ignorance where the consumer knows little about where the products come from, how their savings, mutual funds, or pension plans were invested, or whose lives and what places were sacrificed to bring about this economic benefit, an economy of care, rooted in affection and love, refuses to abdicate its responsibility to know and to make economic choices on the basis of such knowledge.[37]

What does this look like on the ground?

35. Woodley, *Shalom*, 151–56.

36. Galeano wryly comments that in the virtual economy "money is more fertile when it makes love to itself." Galeano, *Upside Down*, 166.

37. Wendell Berry, "Two Economies," in *What Matters: Economics for a Renewed Commonwealth* (Berkeley: Counterpoint, 2010), 115–38.

Well, that is where the imaginative fun begins. Our friend Joe Mihevc is a long-standing city councilor in Toronto. He once had a campaign sign with pictures illustrating the diversity of his part of the city, with these words below:

> Politics is dreaming a society,
> then building it together.
> Vote Joe Mihevc

What kind of society and economy would we build if we had the kind of dreams that we meet in the economic vision we have been exploring here? This is not the place for a full-blown socioeconomic platform, but surely a biblically inspired imagination would suggest at least some of the following.

We need an economy in which there is a guaranteed basic annual income so that all people have access to economic stability.[38] And this likely means that there should be a maximum annual income as well. From a biblical perspective of economic justice, disparity of wealth invariably indicates the presence of injustice and exploitation in a society. As impossible as it might seem in our present economic context, Christians need to advocate for a cap on how rich anyone really should be allowed to become. No economic shalom can come from dramatic wealth disparity in society.

Short of a guaranteed basic annual income, an economy of care will prioritize economic justice for the poorest members of the community through living minimum wages and universal health care. Where those with the least money end up with the least opportunity for education, we need more programs of educational justice. We need to invest in schools for all kids but especially for the disadvantaged. And to make higher education accessible to all, we need to increase tuition support for those with the lowest income, if not going the extra step and abolishing tuition altogether.[39]

An economy of care is a home economics. But there is little chance of such an economics in the face of real homelessness. And since it is clear that private enterprise will never produce affordable housing because the profit margins are

38. The Basic Income Canada Network has an excellent website (www.basicincomecanada.org) with a wealth of resources on basic income, including academic articles, podcasts, case studies, and educational resources.

39. These are not utopian suggestions. Of developed nations, only the United States does not have universal health care. Countries that offer free post-secondary education include Turkey, Argentina, Denmark, Norway, Iceland, Finland, Estonia, Sweden, Brazil, Sri Lanka, Mauritius, France, Greece, Germany, Malta, Scotland, and Trinidad and Tobago.

too small, we need to institute planning policies that require developers to build affordable housing in every project proposed for approval.[40] Private enterprise needs to be held responsible for public good. And we need government policies that will support and encourage alternative models of housing like cohousing and co-ops.

Bringing together home economics and care for the most vulnerable means that such an economy will prioritize respect for housing in Indigenous communities. No more homes will be destroyed by hydroelectric dams and tar sands, and adequate funding will be made available for clean water, insulated housing, and culturally appropriate dwellings on reserves.

Further, since an economy of care is an economy of place, we need to see policies that protect places, protect the environment, not as extrinsic restrictions on economic development but as central to a home economics. This planet is our home and the home of countless other species created out of the overflowing love, wisdom, and generosity of the Creator. There is no human economy apart from the broader economy of creation. So we need to build an economy that is ecologically sustainable and regenerative. We should be investing in renewable energy. Here is a growth industry that produces jobs while also seeking to alleviate the damage that fossil fuel extraction and consumption has wrought in our fragile home. We should be moving from a carbon-intensive to a clean energy economy. Such a clean energy economy would also include a complete rethinking of how we engage in agriculture. Rather than continuing with industrial methods of agriculture that release enormous amounts of carbon into the air through the use of fertilizers, pesticides, and grain-based feed for all cattle, we need to return to traditional and Indigenous ways of growing and grazing that not only hold carbon but also build resilience and fertility.[41] This is another area where we need to learn to listen to the elders who have lived on the land for thousands of years.[42]

40. For example, in New York City; Washington, DC; and Amsterdam all developers must build one-third social housing, one-third affordable housing, and one-third market-rate housing.

41. See Eric Toensmeier, *The Carbon Farming Solution: A Global Toolkit of Perennial Crops and Regenerative Agriculture Practices for Climate Change Mitigation and Food Security* (White River Junction, VT: Chelsea Green, 2016); and Paul Hawken, ed., *Drawdown: The Most Comprehensive Plan Ever Proposed to Reverse Global Warming* (New York: Penguin, 2017). The drawdown project measures and models the top one hundred solutions that could begin to reduce greenhouse gases, otherwise known as drawdown. With a breadth of focus on buildings and cities, energy, food, land use, materials, transport, and women and girls, the project included over seventy researchers from twenty-two countries. All of the technical reports and guidelines can be found at www.drawdown.org.

42. Woodley, *Shalom*, 147.

When someone like Naomi Klein gets to dreaming about this kind of regenerative economy, she talks about "comprehensive policies and programs that make low-carbon choices easy and convenient for everyone." She continues:

> Most of all, these policies need to be fair, so that the people already struggling to cover the basics are not being asked to make additional sacrifice to offset the excess consumption of the rich. That means cheap public transit and clean light rail accessible to all; affordable, energy-efficient housing along those transit lines; cities planned for high-density living; bike lanes in which riders aren't asked to risk their lives to get to work; land management that discourages sprawl and encourages local, low-energy forms of agriculture; urban design that clusters essential services like schools and health care along transit routes and in pedestrian-friendly areas; programs that require manufacturers to be responsible for electronic waste they produce, and to radically reduce built-in redundancies and obsolescences.[43]

And this is just a start. Rooting their proposals in an economy and ethos of care, Klein and a collective of advocates, dreamers, and leaders from various sectors and communities in Canada have produced something called "The Leap Manifesto."[44] At the very foundation of any proposal for an economy of care in our time and place, they argue, there must be a recognition of and respect for "the inherent rights and title of the original caretakers of this land." And so the Manifesto acknowledges the harm done to the Indigenous communities of Canada and the need both to respectfully learn from those with the longest and deepest tradition of caretaking in this place and to prioritize reparations and reconciliation with First Nations in any economic, political, and social development in this country. There can be no economic justice in Canada without economic justice and renewed opportunity for First Nations.

As a fossil fuel–free economic vision, the Manifesto calls for a cessation of all infrastructure building for the fossil fuel industry. No more pipelines. Indeed, the Manifesto calls for an energy democracy in which local communities take more control of their energy resources. This is a localization of energy policy that strips the multinational energy giants of their power over resources and people's lives. Moving away from a fossil fuel–based transportation system preoccupied with the automobile and the massive infrastructure needed for cars, the Manifesto calls for high-speed rail systems powered by renewables and affordable public transit.

43. Klein, *This Changes Everything*, 91.

44. The manifesto can be found as the postscript in Klein, *No Is Not Enough*, 267–71, and at https://leapmanifesto.org.

Agribusiness structures that require transporting goods over long distances need to be discouraged in favor of a more localized and ecologically based agricultural system. Trade deals "that interfere with attempts to build local economies, regulate corporations, and stop damaging extractive projects" must be dismantled.[45]

And, of course, all this would require restructuring how subsidies and taxation work. So the Manifesto calls for an end to fossil fuel subsidies, while introducing the taxation of financial transactions, higher corporate tax rates and income tax on the wealthy, and a progressive carbon tax.

This is just a sampling of the agenda that is promoted in "The Leap Manifesto." These are people who know that something is desperately wrong with our economy and have taken an approach rooted in an economics of care that we find deeply resonant with what we imagine a Pauline ethic of economic justice might look like today. They end the Manifesto with these words: "And so we call on all those seeking political office to seize this opportunity and embrace the urgent need for transformation. This is our sacred duty to those this country harmed in the past, to those suffering needlessly in the present and to all who have a right to a bright and safe future."[46] A "sacred duty," they say. This is not cheap religious language. There is something decidedly post-secular about all of this. The secular worldview has run its course, and thoughtful folks are looking beyond the confines of secularity for an alternative worldview, a new story. And while they will find that story in various places, not least in the Indigenous worldview that colonialism so violently tried to eradicate, they know that the ideal of self-interested autonomy embedded in the narrative of economic progress has proven to be a dead end economically, ecologically, socially, and, for so many, literally. They seek a regenerative economics of life in the shadow of this culture of death. We think that Christians should join these neighbors in standing against the forces of exclusion, violence, racism, greed, and injustice.

There's a sad irony to all of this, isn't there?

What do you mean?

Here you are calling us to take sides with non-Christians who have a better understanding of economic justice than so many Christians do. I begin to wonder who is evangelizing whom.

The question really boils down to this: Where are we seeing initiatives that resonate deeply with a biblical vision of justice? And it is with those groups that we will find allies.

45. "Leap Manifesto," in Klein, *No Is Not Enough*, 269–70.
46. "Leap Manifesto," in Klein, *No Is Not Enough*, 271.

Ways of Engagement

Although I want to agree with all of this, I have two problems with what you have outlined. The first is that everything you have just said here requires governmental interventions. Although such interventions are possible in many countries, and I know that some of these things are being explored in Canada, it is also clear that to many people in Canada and the United States, most of these policies seem unlikely to ever be implemented. What advice do you have for those of us working at a grassroots level? How do we demonstrate an economics of care in our own lives and communities?

What if we began with a commitment to our places? We have talked about an emplaced economics and a localized economy. These themes are embraced by the Transition Movement, an initiative concerned about both place and local economy, particularly the renewal of local economy. Some places have actually created a local currency that keeps money circulating within their communities.

A local currency?

The most common model is for a number of businesses in a community to commit to honoring a common local currency. Shoppers can pay with that currency at the designated establishments. Those who use the currency are committed to keeping their shopping dollars local. In Britain there are a number of well-known local currencies; the Totnes Pound is perhaps the best known.[47] Other people are asking how local communities can create better relationships with local food producers, thereby lessening economic dependence on agribusinesses as well as supporting farmers in their own community.

Are you saying that going to the farmer's market is an act of economic subversion?

It can be. Or joining a Community Shared Agriculture program.[48] But these things are out of reach for many people. Teaching people how to grow food, establishing gardens in schoolyards, enabling community gardens in food deserts and underserviced parts of town—these things start to level the playing field, creating an economics of enough around food systems.

47. See www.totnespound.org. Other local currencies are the Brixton Pound (http://brixtonpound.org), the Kawartha Loonie (in Peterborough, Ontario: http://transitiontownpeterborough.ca/Kawartha-Loon-Exchange), the Calgary Dollar (www.calgarydollars.ca); Ithaca Hours (www.ithacahours.com); and the Ithaca Dollar (digital only: http://ithacash.com/#home). A variation on this are timebanks, where services are shared without a currency: https://timebanks.org/more-about-timebanking/.

48. In Community Shared Agriculture (CSA), buyers prepay for a weekly or monthly box of food from a farm, thereby helping the farmer with upfront costs and sharing in the risks and benefits of the growing season. CSA boxes can include vegetables, herbs, flowers, and even meat.

It seems to me that you are just repeating what you said about food sovereignty in chapter 5.

That's because food, land, and economics are always interconnected. But we should add that food sovereignty is just a start. Transition movements are also localizing the economy around clothing by teaching people how to repurpose old clothes and sew new ones, and around transport by showing people how to repair bicycles and strengthening local transport options, including bike-share programs. Some places hold ReSkilling events to show people how to repair a wide variety of items from toasters to computers.[49]

But these things don't really involve money. So how can they strengthen the local economy?

Every time we repair something, or have someone local fix something, or buy from a local independent business, we keep money circulating within our community. We are withholding our proxy that would otherwise go to a corporation; we are withholding dollars that would otherwise go outside our community, usually for the destruction of another community. And we are building relationships with others in our community. When we do these things, we are engaging in acts of secession.

I guess my problem with secession is that it seems so, well, insular. I mean, we've created a global economy that has forced Indigenous peoples around the world off their land so they have to work in factories and in cash-crop farming. This provides them with an income, even if it is meager. Are you suggesting that we refuse to buy the products that give those people their livelihoods? Isn't this just abandoning them to poverty?

No. Buying those products abandons them to poverty. Local community has already been destroyed by the larger corporations, and if we continue to buy their products, we just put the stamp of approval on the continued destruction

49. A local social enterprise that teaches bike repair in our part of the world is New Hope Community Bikes in Hamilton, Ontario (www.newhopecommunitybikes.com), and Switchback Cyclery in Toronto (www.switchbackcyclery.ca) offers the opportunity for a collaborative bike build. An example of a community initiative that helps people learn to repair a wide variety of items is the Fixers Collective in Ithaca, New York (http://ithacareuse.org/fixers/), which has regular hours for people to drop in and learn to fix a wide variety of items. The Denver Tool Library (http://denvertoollibrary.org) not only offers space to fix things, including bikes, but also lends out tools. For other examples of communities engaged in these kinds of events, see Rob Hopkins, *The Transition Handbook: From Oil Dependency to Local Resilience* (White River Junction, VT: Chelsea Green, 2008); and Rob Hopkins, *The Transition Companion: Making Your Community More Resilient in Uncertain Times* (White River Junction, VT: Chelsea Green, 2011). Almost every issue of *Permaculture* magazine (www.permaculture.co.uk) has a story about initiatives such as these.

of local economies around the world. To think local is to work for the health of *all* communities on a local level, both nearby and far away. So the question then becomes, How can we support those local communities? One way is by being careful about the products we use. Does the coffee we buy impoverish someone else's community? Or are we buying fair trade, so that the profits actually benefit the community from which the coffee comes? What about our clothes? If we are not buying secondhand, do we try to buy fair-trade clothes when we buy new?[50]

Wait a minute. Do you have any idea how expensive this is? Fair trade coffee, chocolate, and clothes are luxury items for most people.

For some people, yes. So maybe this is where we practice the restraint we talked about in the last chapter. Maybe we own fewer clothes. Maybe we buy new jeans that are made in Canada and sold by small independent stores in our local communities, but we limit the number we own. What if we all limited ourselves to fewer clothes? What if we ate less chocolate and drank less coffee?

Now you are starting to cut into my comfort levels. Drink less coffee?

You are reminding us of the old saying "Everyone wants the kingdom to come, but no one wants to give up their coffee."

Wait, wasn't that saying about the revolution and doing dishes?

Well, yes, but we've come up with a few variations.[51] Let us ask this: Are these things *really* too expensive? While for some of our friends these options are economically impossible, the reality is that many of the people we know have enough disposable income to afford a cell phone, lattes, and beer in the pub with friends. Many of them would *say* that fair-trade products are too expensive, but their spending habits betray them. We are not saying this to be judgmental but rather to flag something we have noticed over and over. We know people with *investments* who consider themselves poor and think fair trade is too expensive.

With investments? Well, that certainly wouldn't be me. But that does raise another question. Say that I did have money to invest, how could that be done without becoming enmeshed in this oppressive economic system?

We've talked about this at more length elsewhere.[52] Let us just say here that to our mind the whole idea of money being used solely to make money is fun-

50. See Sally Blundell, *The No-Nonsense Guide to Fair Trade*, 3rd ed. (Toronto: New Internationalist, 2013).

51. Another is "Everyone wants to save the planet, but no one wants to empty the sawdust toilets."

52. See Sylvia C. Keesmaat and Brian J. Walsh, "Outside of a Small Circle of Friends: Jesus and the Justice of God," in *Jesus, Paul, and the People of God: A Theological Dialogue with N. T. Wright*, ed. Nicholas Perrin and Richard B. Hays (Downers Grove, IL: IVP Academic, 2011), 66–89.

damentally unbiblical. That is why charging interest is equated with injustice in the biblical text.[53] However, should you decide to have investments, at the very least search for places to invest your money that contribute to the well-being of the most vulnerable and the building of community. For instance, affordable housing projects often need loans in order to do the preliminary work necessary to apply for funding.[54] Or, going back to your local community, are there people looking for low- or no-interest loans to enable them to begin a business or social enterprise?[55]

No interest loans! How on earth are we supposed to save anything for retirement if we can't put money in a retirement savings plan that pays interest? While a lot of what you are saying about local economy seem difficult, this seems entirely unrealistic!

Given our current assumptions about economics, you are right. But have you stopped to think why this is so? Maybe if we had a community that practiced the radical generosity described in Romans, we wouldn't have so much anxiety about our economic future. An economics of radical trust in God's provision is a Sabbath economics, an economics of generosity and welcome.[56]

I can't even imagine what that would look like.

53. See Exod. 22:25; Lev. 25:35–37; Deut. 23:19; Ps. 15:5; Ezek. 18:5–18. In "Outside of a Small Circle of Friends," we interpret Luke 19:11–27 as condemning the charging of interest as well. See Wright, *Jesus, Paul, and the People of God*, 66–89.

54. One such organization in Canada is Indwell, which provides affordable housing and community for vulnerable adults: www.indwell.ca.

55. The idea of community microloans was pioneered by the Grameen bank in Bangledesh. The idea has spread around the world, with a number of local currencies tying microloans into their organizations. The Local Investing Resource Center provides a listing of all local investment opportunities in the United States: www.local-investing.com. Online the most well-known organization for microloans is Kiva: www.kiva.org.

56. On Sabbath economics, see Sylvia C. Keesmaat, "Sabbath and Jubilee: Radical Alternatives for Being Human," in *Making a New Beginning: Biblical Reflections on Jubilee* (Toronto: Canadian Ecumenical Jubilee Initiative, 1998), 15–23; Ched Myers, *The Biblical Vision of Sabbath Economics* (Washington, DC: Tell the World Press, 2001); Woodley, *Shalom and the Community of Creation*, also describes Jubilee economics as part of an Indigenous vision. See also Michael Schut, ed., *Money and Faith: The Search for Enough* (Denver: Morehouse Education Resources, 2008), which includes essays on various aspects of money and Christian discipleship, along with a study guide for groups who are struggling with these issues, and a detailed bibliography for further reading with sections on "Fair-Trade and Micro-lending," "The Corporation," and "Investments, Consumption and the Individual." See also Byron Borger, "Reading for a Global Perspective," in *Do Justice: A Social Justice Road Map*, ed. Kirstin Vander Giessen-Reitsma (Three Rivers, MI: *culture is not optional, 2008), 69–79. This annotated bibliography, by one of the most well-read Christian authors in the United States, is a wealth of information and helpful sources. *Do Justice* is available from www.heartsandmindsbooks.com.

There are resources available to help think this through, from Bible studies to "Household Covenants" that provide guidance on faithful economic life.[57] But why not begin where Paul begins? Extend hospitality. Extend it even to strangers. In a world that is becoming more and more hostile to the stranger, could you see yourself inviting strangers who are in real need to your table or your community's table? This is what happens at Sanctuary, the community with which we began this book. Meals are offered with open arms to everyone. Everyone is invited to help cook, and everyone eats together (there are no "staff" and "clients" in this community).[58] Or, if you really want to go out on a limb, provide full hospitality; provide shelter for those who need it.

How would I find strangers who need shelter? I confess that I would worry about my safety.

Right now in some countries there is a program that matches up people who need shelter with those willing to host them. Elderly people, young people, and many in between find a place to stay, some short-term, some long-term. Sometimes friendships are formed.[59] We have a colleague who found himself unexpectedly hosting seven Syrian refugees a few months ago. The agency knew that he had a hospitable home, and so they called him. It isn't hard to find people who need hospitality. Just open your eyes and look. But you don't need to do this in your home. In Canada, churches, mosques, and synagogues provide shelter for the homeless through Out of the Cold programs. Often these are rolling shelter programs where a different place of worship provides shelter each night of the week.

But if hospitality is too difficult for you or your community, start with a meal. You don't even have to do this at your home. Find a community meal program. Begin to eat with people who don't have access to food; hear their stories. Soon you will know their needs, and you may decide to help them meet those needs. It might not be monetary. Perhaps they need a ride to the doctor occasionally. Or childcare. Or someone who can write an official-sounding letter. Before you know it, you will find that an economics of generosity has begun to shape you. Paul describes this as making your way with the oppressed.[60]

57. See Ched Myers and Matthew Colwell, *Sabbath Economics: Household Practices* (Washington: Tell the World Press, 2007), and the excellent website of Christian economic reflection put together by the Australian organization Manna Gum: www.mannagum.org.au. Of special interest might be the downloadable PDF of a seven-week Household Covenant Bible Study: http://www.mannagum.org.au/faith_and_economy/the_household_covenant.

58. Information about Sanctuary can be found at http://sanctuarytoronto.ca.

59. In Britain this program is called Nightstop UK: https://www.nightstop.org.uk.

60. An example of how this dynamic works can be found in Bruce Longenecker's *The Lost Letters of Pergamum: A Story from the New Testament World*, 2nd ed. (Grand Rapids: Baker Academic,

I don't quite see how this answers my question about saving for retirement.

If you begin to walk this path of generosity and hospitality, of learning from those who have nothing, we suspect that two things will happen. On the one hand, you will realize how much you really have. The need of the person directly in front of you will become more important than your hypothetical future need. And on the other hand, you may decide that your money is better "invested" in the needs of others in the present than being "invested" for your own needs in the future.

The way you phrase that almost makes it sound like investing in a retirement plan is a form of hoarding.

Perhaps it is a matter of perspective. Do you remember the parable of the man who had such a great grain harvest that he built bigger barns to store the grain and all his other stuff? It is clear that he saw this as his retirement fund—he told himself that he had lots of equity set aside for many years and he could enjoy his retirement: relax, eat, drink, and be merry (Luke 12:19)! But it is clear that Jesus views this as hoarding. In fact, Jesus describes this man as greedy, using the same word that Paul does in his list of economic sins in Romans 1:29 (*pleonexias*). Contrast this man with Zacchaeus, who shared his wealth. He no longer had retirement money, but he was returned to his community.[61]

Let me get this straight. You are telling me to "invest in community" for my retirement plan.

Yes we are. And we suggest that the easiest, simplest way to do so is to practice the kind of economic sharing that the followers of Jesus engaged in at their meals together. Find a community where you can welcome and eat with those you wouldn't normally eat with. Find a community that will welcome *you*! Share your stories and hear the stories of others. Share your needs and hear about the needs of others. Share your resources and discover what resources others have to offer you.

That would be a little beyond my comfort level.

We are increasingly convinced that neither Paul nor Jesus cared much about helping us find our comfort levels. God's kingdom is not about making life comfortable for any of us. It is about the far more radical vision of justice and shalom,

2016), an excellent glimpse into the lives of a first-century community of Jesus followers and their care for one another.

61. The salvation that comes to Zacchaeus, Jesus says, means that he too is a son of Abraham—that is, he was restored to the community (Luke 19:9). Of course, in our society we don't build bigger barns. We rent storage lockers.

a vision that will push the boundaries, a vision that will make some of us decidedly *uncomfortable.*

Speaking of pushing the boundaries reminds me of one last question.

Let's hear it.

Let's say that I am convinced by the last three chapters. I'm convinced that Paul really is concerned with the ecological damage of his own time and that his lament and his creational vision spoke to those problems in the Roman Empire. I'm convinced that there really is a strong emphasis on economic justice to be discerned in his letter to the Romans. And I'm even convinced that all of this means that we need to respond to our own environmental crises and economic problems with something like a Pauline vision.

That's a lot of being convinced, and we doubt that we've been that successful in our argument with many of our readers by this point in the book.

Maybe not, but let's say that I am convinced and maybe some of your other readers are too. We hadn't seen these kinds of ecological and economic concerns on the surface of Paul's letter to the Romans. These things weren't self-evident in our reading of the letter, but the discussion of the last three chapters has convinced some of us that Paul really does have something like this ecological and economic vision.

And this gives rise to a new question.

Yes. What about the state? What about politics? Even if we do begin to practice a local economics of care, in the end we can't deal with either the environmental or economic issues that you have addressed without talking about the role of the state in all of this.

Fair enough.

Many of your proposals require political action, policy change, and advocacy. Others assume a state that at the very least permits certain kinds of community and local action.

That's true.

And that is where the problem begins when it comes to reading the letter to the Romans.

How so?

Your interpretation may have shown us something that was lying just under the surface of Paul's letter, but isn't a pretty conservative view of the state right on the surface of something like Romans 13? If what you are saying is true, then we can't be quietly passive when it comes to the state, especially if our governments are actively working against the vision of the kingdom that you are describing. But when Paul explicitly talks about the state, isn't he arguing that Christians are to be good law-abiding citizens? We pray for our rulers and obey them. We don't rock the boat.

Somehow I'm thinking that there is going to be a lot of boat-rocking going on if we take seriously what you have argued in the last three chapters. So that's my question. What about the state?

That's a good question and certainly a necessary question in light of Romans 13 and its traditional interpretations. And it will require a chapter of its own.

8

The *Pax Romana* and the Gospel of Peace

The letter to the Romans has been counter-imperial from the beginning. From the very first words, "Paul, a slave of Jesus Christ," it has been on a trajectory of disarming the empire. The gospel of the empire, the lordship of the emperor, the salvation that the empire has to offer, the empire's claims to justice and piety, together with imperial notions of peace, law, and justice—all of this has been undermined, turned on its head, and ultimately disarmed by the gospel that Paul proclaims in his letter to Jesus followers who reside at the heart of the empire.

Just as our fictional characters, Iris and Nereus, had to struggle with the meaning of Paul's letter in the context of life in first-century Rome, so we also have engaged the Epistle to the Romans in our own twenty-first-century imperial context. How do we hear this letter speak a word of hope to us in the face of the conflicting stories and worldviews of our own time? If Paul is indeed seeking to engender an alternative experience of home for the Christian communities in a city that could never, ultimately, be home to his hearers, then does his letter help us to shape home together in our world where the foundations of homemaking are being destroyed and where so many have been rendered homeless, displaced, and exiled? If Paul calls the Roman Christians to join in the lament of creation, indeed the same lament of God the Holy Spirit, in the face of imperial destruction and despoliation, then what does that lament look like in the face of the ecological crises of our own times? How does the story that Paul narrates in his understanding of the gospel shape us in our own places, our watersheds, our land? And if it is true that "Paul's letter burns with the incendiary proclamation of God's justice, and with a searing critique of the injustice (*adikia*) of those who smother and suppress the truth,"[1] and that such injustice is invariably manifest in economic oppression, then what does Paul have to say to us about the institutionalized economic inequities of our own time?

You see, once you start down the path of disarming the empire, once you begin to see that justice is at the "revolutionary" heart of the epistle to the Romans, it is no longer possible to domesticate this powerful letter by means of a pietistic interpretation preoccupied with individual salvation or personal righteousness.[2]

And, as we have seen, there is no escaping the political implications of this letter in either its original context or a faithful reading today. Indeed, Paul begins and concludes his letter by speaking of "the obedience of the nations," and while we tend to read this in terms of the inclusion of gentiles in the family of God, that misses the broader political meaning of what Paul is saying. When Paul writes in his opening sentence that he has received "grace and apostleship to bring about the obedience of faith among the nations" (1:5 NRSV alt.), he intentionally places his gospel on a political collision course with Rome, precisely because such obedience of all nations was already the prerogative and agenda of the empire. Paul then bookends his epistle by returning to this notion of the obedience of the nations at the end of the letter, where he concludes his argument by claiming that the gospel of Christ is nothing less than a fulfillment of Isaiah's prophecy:

> The root of Jesse shall come,
> the one who rises to rule the nations;
> in him the nations shall hope. (Rom. 15:12 NRSV alt., quoting Isa. 11:10)

1. Neil Elliott, *The Arrogance of Nations: Reading Romans in the Shadow of Empire* (Minneapolis: Fortress, 2008), 6.

2. It is no surprise that Latin American liberation theology was far ahead of North American and European interpretation of Romans. Already in 1971, José Porfirio Miranda argued that justice was the "revolutionary and unprecedented core" of Paul's message. And long before the "New Perspective" on Paul, Miranda argued that "Paul's gospel has nothing to do with the interpretation which for centuries has been given to it in terms of individual salvation. It deals with the justice which the world and peoples and society, implicitly but anxiously, have been awaiting." José Porfirio Miranda, *Marx and the Bible: A Critique of the Philosophy of Oppression*, trans. John Eagleson (1971; repr., Maryknoll, NY: Orbis, 1974), 179. Similarly, see Elsa Tamez, *The Amnesty of Grace: Justification from a Latin-American Perspective*, trans. Sharon H. Ringe (Nashville: Abingdon, 1993).

The "explosive political implications" of this are unmistakable.[3] The proper sovereign and Lord of the nations is not the emperor but the very messianic Lord whom Paul proclaims. Subject to *this* Lord, the nations will have hope rather than the faux benevolence of the empire. Not surprisingly, the wider context of the Isaiah citation is all about justice for the poor, equity for the impoverished, judgment on the unjust, and the restoration of all creation.[4]

Paul repeats the theme of obedience one more time and makes it clear that this was the heart of his epistle all along: "For I will not venture to speak of anything except what Christ has accomplished through me to win the obedience of the nations, by word and deed, . . . by the power of the Spirit of God" (Rom. 15:18 NRSV alt.). The political implications of such a gospel are indeed incendiary, revolutionary, and explosive, subverting the sovereignty of any power that does not acknowledge the life-giving rule of Jesus. Rather than challenging such false powers who bring death through injustice (5:17, 21; 6:13), the church has often engaged in political accommodation. This has been most apparent when those who wield political authority are willing to be called "Christian." In fact, it is particularly when governments call themselves Christian while engaging in oppressive and violent behavior that Romans 13:1–7 is appealed to as the summation of Paul's political ethic.[5] For example, under the rule of Hitler this passage was used to legitimate allegiance to the Nazi regime, with Bonhoeffer and the Barmen Declaration providing perhaps the best-known challenges to this reading. Similarly, under the apartheid regime in South Africa, Allan Boesak described how Romans 13 was used as a stick to demand his obedience to the state.[6] The same appeal to Romans 13 was used by church leaders in Rwanda to justify their uncritical support of a genocidal government.[7] And in the United States it

3. N. T. Wright, "The Letter to the Romans: Introduction, Commentary, and Reflections," in *The New Interpreter's Bible*, vol. 10 (Nashville: Abingdon, 2002), 748.

4. Isa. 11:1–10. Wright evocatively suggests, "Paul, we may suppose, has had this verse [Isa. 11:10] in mind throughout the whole letter, waiting to produce it as the final move in his entire argument." Wright, "Letter to the Romans," 748.

5. Much of what follows is reworked from Sylvia C. Keesmaat, "If Your Enemy Is Hungry: Love and Subversive Politics in Romans 12–13," in *Character Ethics and the New Testament: Moral Dimensions of Scripture*, ed. Robert L. Brawley (Louisville: Westminster John Knox, 2007), 141–58. Used with permission.

6. Allan A. Boesak, "What Belongs to Caesar: Once Again Romans 13," in *When Prayer Makes News*, ed. Allan A. Boesak and Charles Villa-Vicencio (Philadelphia: Westminster, 1986), 138.

7. See Roger W. Bower, "Genocide in Rwanda 1994—An Anglican Perspective," in *Genocide in Rwanda: Complicity of the Churches*, ed. Carol Rittner, John K. Roth, and Wendy Whitworth (St. Paul, MN: Aegis, 2004), 41; David P. Gushee, "Why the Churches Were Complicit," in Rittner, Roth, and Whitworth, *Genocide in Rwanda*, 263.

doesn't matter how weak the evidence for war or how despicable the character of the commander in chief, Christians (especially white, evangelical Christians) continue to use Romans 13 as a tool of ideological legitimation.

Rather than the gospel disarming the empire, the empire has effectively domesticated the gospel. For much too long we have read Paul's comments on the state and its authority in Romans 13:1–7 in a way that has stripped the letter to the Romans of its political bite precisely by interpreting these seven verses out of context of the letter as a whole. In this chapter we will begin by offering a reading of Romans 13:1–7 within the larger context of Romans 12 and 13:8–14 in order to demonstrate that Paul is proclaiming nothing less than a political ethic that undermines the political authority of Rome. Paul disarms the empire in the only way possible, by calling the church to a unilateral act of disarmament in the face of a violent regime. The gospel of peace meets the *Pax Romana*. We will then offer another targum on the entirety of Romans 12 and 13 wherein the gospel of peace addresses the Christian community living in the shadow of the *Pax Americana* of more recent years.

Imperial Persecution

Discussions of Romans 13 in the context of the community to which Paul addressed the letter often highlight the need for a beleaguered community to practice political quietism. Most commonly, the context is considered to be a possible tax revolt, and, as the argument goes, the Christian community in Rome is encouraged not to participate in such resistance to imperial rule.[8]

However, as we have seen in the previous chapter, the larger context of the letter to the Romans indicates that Paul's hearers had experienced persecution at the hands of Roman authorities. Such persecution lies behind Paul's discussion of suffering in Romans 5:3–5, as well as in Romans 8, with its references to "oppression, distress, persecution, peril, and sword" (8:35 our translation), together with "death," "rulers," and "powers" (8:38). This suggests that the suffering that Paul is referring to had something to do with the rulers who had the power to wield the sword in Rome, and who had already introduced oppression, distress, persecution, peril, and sword into the Judean community there.[9]

8. See Christopher Bryan, *Render to Caesar: Jesus, the Early Church and the Roman Superpower* (Oxford: Oxford University Press, 2005), 78–82; Wright, "Letter to the Romans," 721.

9. Ernst Käsemann also suggests that "*machaira* [sword; 8:35] perhaps means concretely execution." *Commentary on Romans*, trans. and ed. Geoffrey Bromiley (Grand Rapids: Eerdmans, 1980),

Additional, more allusive evidence can be adduced. Like those who protest the injustice of empire in the psalms, Paul portrays Christian believers as those who cry "Abba! Father!" (Rom. 8:15). In the story of Israel, this cry to God as father is a cry for redemption out of suffering. The Greek word that Paul uses for this cry, *krazomen*, is found frequently in lament psalms to describe those crying out to God in the midst of their oppression. Most notably, it occurs in a number of those psalms that are explicitly quoted by Paul in Romans.[10] And, as we saw in chapter 5, the groans of those living in the shadow of empire are reflected in Romans 8 in the groaning of creation (8:22), the groaning of believers (8:23), and the groaning of God's very Spirit (8:26). This language of groaning originated in Israel's first experience of empire and was repeatedly used when Israel found itself suffering under imperial control during its history.[11]

In addition, the context for the intercession of the Spirit in Romans 8:26–27 is described thus by Paul: "The Spirit helps us in our weakness [*astheneia*]" (8:26). As Michael Barré has convincingly argued, based on the Septuagint and intertestamental usage, Paul uses *astheneia* to refer to persecutions, which are interpreted as being part of the eschatological ordeal.[12] This evidence from Romans 8 is augmented by the language of our passage, where the call to "bless those who persecute you" (12:14) clearly assumes that this community is facing persecution. So our first observation about the context of Paul's counsel to the Roman community about the state is that the *Pax Romana* was seriously overrated. To a persecuted community, what the Romans called "peace" looked a lot more like violent repression.

But more needs to be said about context. We need to remember who has written this passage. Mark Nanos puts it most succinctly:

> The traditional interpretations have not successfully accounted for the fact that this letter was addressed to Rome during the reign of Nero by a Jewish man whose worldview was thoroughly informed by the prophetic writings and who

249. So also Robert Jewett, *Romans: A Commentary*, Hermeneia (Minneapolis: Fortress, 2007), 547, 795. J. G. D. Dunn, *Romans 9–16*, Word Bible Commentaries 38B (Dallas: Word, 1988), 505, points out that *diōgmos* ("persecution"; 8:35) always refers to persecution for religious reasons.

10. Pss. 18:6, 41 (17:7, 42 LXX); 32:3 (31:3 LXX); 69:3 (68:4 LXX). See also Pss. 4:3; 17:6; 22:5; 28:1–2; 31:22; 55:16; 61:2 (60:3 LXX); 88:1, 9, 13.

11. See, e.g., Exod. 2:23–24; Judg. 2:18; Pss. 31:10; 38:9–10; Isa. 24:7; 30:15; Lam. 1:18, 21–22; Ezek. 21:11–12; 1 Macc. 1:26; 3 Macc. 1:18. For more on the background of the language of groaning in Israel's Scriptures, see Sylvia C. Keesmaat, *Paul and His Story: (Re)Interpreting the Exodus Tradition* (Sheffield: Sheffield Academic Press, 1999), 107–10.

12. Michael Barré, "Paul as 'Eschatalogic Person': A New Look at 2 Corinthians 11:29," *Catholic Biblical Quarterly* 37 (1975): 510–12; Keesmaat, *Paul and His Story*, 120–22.

> had, along with his whole generation, seen the continual destruction of their people and interests under the tyrannical reigns of Herod and the Roman rulers (how could one involved in declaring the Jesus crucified by Romans as King of the Jews be assumed to be so naive as to ascribe Roman authority, ostensibly without caveat, to the ordering of God?). It is in this context that the wealth of apocalyptic literature of this period was born with many veiled references to Rome as "Babylon."[13]

This is a letter written by a Judean man well aware of brutality and violence at the heart of the Roman Empire. We have seen that this Judean man is deeply rooted in the justice traditions of Israel. He is a follower of Jesus, crucified under duly authorized Roman officials.[14] He has written a letter to those who live at the heart of this empire, to those who have experienced persecution at the hands of this empire. This is the context of chapters 12 and 13 of Romans. At the end of a very detailed argument in which Paul outlines his hopes for salvation for both Judean and gentile, indeed a salvation that results in the obedience of the nations, these chapters flesh out the shape of the new community in Christ. If we are to understand the nuances of what Paul says (and doesn't say) in these chapters, we need to take seriously the context in which they were written.

Challenging the "New Age" of the Empire

We need to begin by noting that the whole of Romans 12 and 13 is framed by an apocalyptic context.[15] Paul begins by calling the community in Rome to not be conformed to "this age" (12:2 our translation). This language recalls the apocalyptic ordering of this world into this age, with all its moral corruption and political oppression, and the age to come, when God's kingdom will once again ensure healing, food, justice, and peace for all God's people. Romans 13 ends with the assurance that the new age is dawning, contrasting the night that is far gone with the day that is at hand (13:12), thereby evoking the texts of both promise and judgment concerning the day of the Lord. Such texts served in times of political oppression to remind God's people that, contrary to all appearances, God is the one who ultimately reigns; God is the one who controls

13. Mark D. Nanos, *The Mystery of Romans: The Jewish Context of Paul's Letter* (Minneapolis: Fortress, 1996), 290.

14. After writing Romans, Paul himself would become a political prisoner at the hands of the state, arrested for proclaiming "another Sovereign, another reign, and another justice." Tamez, *Amnesty of Grace*, 57.

15. So also Wright, "Letter to the Romans," 701.

the story of the nations. This framing, therefore, sets the passage in a context where the power of Rome is already undermined. In contrast to the present age, with its persecution, its need for the sword, its evil and enmity, the Christian community in Rome lives in light of a new kingdom, where justice, peace, and joy are the rule (Rom. 14:17). As we shall see, such a subversion becomes more prominent in 13:1.

Apocalyptic language flourished particularly in times of political oppression. The highly charged language of this age and the age to come was often accompanied by vivid symbolism that gave those on the underside of history a vision of deeper realities that were hidden from their oppressors. For the Roman community, therefore, Paul's reminder of their eschatological hope means, as we shall see, that they are able to share a communal life that would normally be counterintuitive for those who live at the heart of an empire like Rome, but which makes perfect sense if they are truly followers of a crucified Messiah.

In addition, the reference to "this age" also evokes the "new age" that Augustus inaugurated many years before and that was undergoing a revival at the time of Nero. "No less than in Augustus' day, the 'gospel' of the emperor's accession proclaimed the restoration of a 'golden age,' not only for the Roman people but for all peoples fortunate enough to be brought beneath the benevolent wings of empire."[16] Paul's language here clearly judges this new imperial age in light of the coming kingdom of God's rule, where justice and peace are brought not by imperial rule but by a crucified Messiah. As a result, Paul begins this section not only with a clear allusion to God's control over history but also with a call to the community in Rome to remember who shapes their communal life together and to reject the new age of the empire and all that it stands for.

A Transformed Body Politic

The whole of this passage is also framed by the controlling metaphor of the body. Just as "gospel" (*euangelion*) was freighted with imperial meaning, so also "body" (*sōma*) was employed as a term to refer to the body politic of the empire.[17] But

16. Neil Elliott, "Paul and the Politics of Empire," in *Paul and Politics: Ekklesia, Israel, Imperium, Interpretation; Essays in Honor of Krister Stendahl*, ed. Richard A. Horsely (Harrisburg, PA: Trinity Press International, 2000), 37. On the new age inaugurated by Augustus, see Paul Zanker, *The Power of Images in the Age of Augustus*, trans. Alan Shapiro (Ann Arbor: University of Michigan Press, 1990), chap. 5.

17. Richard A. Horsley, *1 Corinthians* (Nashville: Abingdon, 1988), 171, lists the following sources for the analogy between the body and the city-state: Marcus Aurelius, *Meditations*

Paul's language is, again, a challenge to the Roman body politic. While the body over which Caesar is head functions only if all the members inhabit their correct sphere in the hierarchy of imperial order, Paul describes the Roman Christian community as the body of Christ, which functions only if its members share the gifts that God has given them.[18] These gifts have nothing to do, however, with wealth or social standing and everything to do with prophecy, service, teaching, generosity, assistance, and acts of mercy.[19]

In an imperial body politic, moreover, where one was required to make sacrifices to the emperor and be willing to sacrifice one's body to the needs of the empire, Paul calls for the Roman Christians to present their bodies as a holy and acceptable sacrifice to God, their "reasonable worship."[20] On the one hand, as Katherine Grieb points out, this is a "military metaphor of putting the members of one's body at the disposal of one's lord," a metaphor, moreover, which Paul uses at length in his description of the baptized in Romans 6:12–23.[21] On the other hand, this is the cultic language of sacrifice. In both instances, the political overtones are clear for the Roman community. No longer do they make sacrifice to the empire; no longer do they consider themselves part of a body politic for which they would sacrifice their very selves. Rather, they are one body in Christ and are to put on *the* Lord, Jesus the Messiah (13:14). So the passage ends by highlighting the name of the Lord they worship, not Caesar but Jesus.[22]

2.1; 7.13; Epictetus, *Dissertationes* 2.10.3–4; Seneca, *Epistulae morales* 95.52; Livy, *History of Rome* 2.32. In the last instance, the fable of the body was used by the senators to try to make the plebeians repent of their plans of mutiny. It thus functioned as a means of ensuring that the ruled classes continued to fulfill their civic duties to the state. Wright, "Letter to the Romans," 710, also lists Plato, *Republic* 462c–d; Plutarch, *Aratus* 24.5; *Marcius Coriolanus* 6.2–4.

18. See Halvor Moxnes, "The Quest for Honor and the Unity of the Community in Romans 12 and in the Orations of Dio Chrysostom," in *Paul in His Hellenistic Context*, ed. Troels Engberg-Pederson (Edinburgh: T&T Clark, 1994), 225.

19. Paul engages in a similar contrast in 1 Cor. 11:17–12:31. As Bruce Winter says, "Paul thereby overthrew centuries of Roman self-definition based on class with this counter-cultural self-evaluation based on God-given gifts that were meant to benefit others or contribute to their needs." Bruce Winter, "Roman Law and Society in Romans 12–15," in *Rome in the Bible and the Early Church*, ed. Peter Oakes (Grand Rapids: Baker Academic, 2002), 79.

20. On the contrast between the "reasonable worship" that Paul mentions here and the debauchery and excess of Roman worship, which Paul criticizes in Rom. 1:18–32, see Elliott, "Paul and the Politics of Empire," 39.

21. A. Katherine Grieb, *The Story of Romans: A Narrative Defense of God's Righteousness* (Louisville: Westminster John Knox, 2002), 118.

22. On the political nature of the term *Christianoi*, which was applied to followers of Jesus (e.g., in Acts 11:26), see Winter, "Roman Law," 70–74.

Undermining the Honor System

Further, Paul calls this community to reject the honor/shame dynamics that drive both the patron-client system and the pattern of civic benefaction in the empire. The patron-client relationship, with its promise of benefit from the patron in exchange for the honor and praise of the clients, functioned as a powerful means of social cohesion and control in Roman society. This dynamic, which permeated personal relationships, also operated on a macro level: the emperor was the ultimate patron, bestowing his benefits on those who honored him.[23] Subverting the complex system of relations based on status and honor that formed the building blocks for the patron-client relationship, Paul counsels each member of the community not to think of themselves more highly than they ought (12:3). This is counterintuitive in a society where one was to think as highly of oneself as was possible, and in such a way that others would also be inclined to reinforce that status. In contrast, Paul calls the community to love one another with familial affection and to outdo one another in *showing* honor, not *receiving* it (12:10). And to make sure that they grasp how counter-imperial this showing of honor is to be, he adds, "Do not be haughty, but associate with the lowly" (12:16)—perhaps better translated as "walk with the oppressed." The honor they are to show one another is not the honor that is due to those who already have status; this is honor that is to be shown to the lowly, to those who traditionally deserve no honor in Roman society.[24] "It appears that Paul's exhortation 'not to think too highly' is directed not to an individual character trait, but to a total system of relations between individuals of unequal status."[25] Throughout these verses the contrast between the empire of Rome, built on honor and privilege, and the kingdom of the Messiah, which raises up the lowly and is built on service, is unmistakable. As we shall see, this contrast permeates all of Romans 12 and 13.

Imperial Violence or Blessing Our Enemies?

Paul describes the shape of this new body politic in Romans 12:14–21 in ways that appear to undermine the description of the Roman state in 13:1–7. Through

23. On Caesar as the highest patron, see Andrew Wallace-Hadrill, "Patronage in Roman Society," in Andrew Wallace-Hadrill, ed., *Patronage in Ancient Society* (New York: Routledge, 1989), 84.

24. This is, of course, exactly what Paul argues in 1 Cor. 12, a passage with extensive parallels to Rom. 12.

25. Moxnes, "Quest for Honor," 222. In this article, Moxnes thoroughly explores the context of *hybris* in Greek and Hellenistic philosophy and literature.

a series of exhortations Paul contrasts the behavior of this body of Christ not only with Roman society but also with the traditional hopes of Israel. This is evident in 12:14 where Paul says, "Bless those who persecute you; bless and do not curse them."

As we have seen, throughout Romans Paul frequently quotes and echoes many psalms of lament. But he employs these psalms in a way that turns them on their heads. While such psalms frequently called for the violent overthrow of God's enemies as evidence of God's justice and faithfulness to God's people, Paul evokes the justice of God for the inclusion of the nations and the salvation of the oppressors, rather than their violent demise. Far from reinforcing the call for retribution in these psalms, Paul describes a community modeled on a different kind of messiah: Jesus, who by suffering death became more than a conqueror and who calls the community to a similar ethic.[26] In Romans 12:14 we see a call to be a community, therefore, that rejects a "justice" achieved by the might of the sword and the defeat of enemies, and subversively seeks blessing even for those who are the perpetrators of oppression. This amounts to a disarming of Roman injustice.[27]

Some have argued that Paul's language a few verses later suggests that a violent vengeance may in fact be due to enemies: "Beloved, never avenge yourselves, but leave room for the wrath of God; for it is written, 'Vengeance is mine, I will repay, says the Lord.'" But then Paul continues: "No, 'if your enemies are hungry, feed them; if they are thirsty, give them something to drink; for by doing this you will heap burning coals on their heads'" (12:19–20). Let's look more closely at these verses in their context so that we can see clearly the contrast between the *Pax Romana* and the peace of Christ.

The Old Testament background of these verses is illuminating. Romans 12:20 quite closely follows Proverbs 25:21–22:

> If your enemies are hungry, give them bread to eat;
> and if they are thirsty, give them water to drink;
> for you will heap coals of fire on their heads,
> and the Lord will reward you.

A few verses earlier in Proverbs 25 we find this exhortation: "With patience a ruler may be persuaded, / and a soft tongue can break bones" (25:15). And a few

26. Rom. 8:37; 15:3.

27. See Sylvia C. Keesmaat, "Crucified Lord or Conquering Saviour: Whose Story of Salvation?," *Horizons in Biblical Theology* 26, no. 2 (2004): 69–93.

verses later we find this: "It is not good to eat much honey, / or to seek honor on top of honor" (25:27). These thematic echoes with Romans 12:10 ("outdo one another in showing honor") and 12:21 ("Do not be overcome by evil, but overcome evil with good") suggest that the whole of Proverbs 25 was whispering around the edges of Paul's thought. Proverbs 25 counsels patience with a ruler who is presumably used to doing his persuading with a sword in a clearly political context. Such a political context, we suggest, is also in Paul's sights here. Similarly, Proverbs condemns precisely the kind of status-seeking that was evident in Roman society and that Paul explicitly challenges.[28]

A second possible Old Testament referent for this passage is the story of Elisha and the Aramean army in 2 Kings 6:8–23.[29] You may recall the story: After God has struck the Aramean army blind, Elisha leads them to the king of Israel inside Samaria. When the Lord opens their eyes, the king of Israel asks Elisha, "Father, shall I kill them? Shall I kill them?" (6:21). Elisha replies, "No! Did you capture with your sword and your bow those whom you want to kill? Set food and water before them so that they may eat and drink; and let them go to their master." The story concludes, "So he prepared for them a great feast; after they ate and drank, he sent them on their way, and they went to their master" (6:22–23).

A few things are notable about this story. First of all, not only could this army be considered an enemy to Elisha personally—after all, the only reason they were in Israel was to capture Elisha at the command of their king—but they were also political enemies of Israel. They were trying to capture Elisha because he kept betraying the location of the Aramean army to the Israelites. Here food and drink are given to enemies in a decidedly political context. And the result is political as well, for "the Arameans no longer came raiding into the land of Israel" (2 Kings 6:23). The result of such actions is peace. Peace without the blood of the sword.

The other startling thing about this passage is Elisha's response to the king who wants to kill the soldiers. Elisha says, "Did you capture with your sword and bow those whom you want to kill?" (2 Kings 6:21). The implied answer, of course,

28. Marva Dawn appeals to the Egyptian provenance of these verses in Proverbs as a way to clarify the meaning of the clause "for by doing this you will heap burning coals on their heads." Apparently bearing hot coals on one's head was a symbol of repentance; hence kindness toward the enemy could be a way to bring the enemy to repentance. As we shall see below, this coheres well with a possible allusion to 2 Kings 6 in these verses. Marva Dawn, *Truly the Community: Romans 12 and How to Be the Church* (Grand Rapids: Eerdmans, 1992), 283. See also Jewett, *Romans*, 777. Cf. Gordon Zerbe, "Paul's Ethic of Nonretaliation and Peace," in *The Love of Enemy and Nonretaliation in the New Testament*, ed. Willard M. Swartley (Louisville: Westminster John Knox, 1992), 196.

29. See Grieb, *Story of Romans*, 122.

is "No, God captured them." And the implication is that God is the one who will now kill these enemies. Contrary to expectation, however, God, after restoring their sight, does not kill them. Instead, the man of God prepares a great feast, sets before them food and drink, and sends them home. The message is clear: while the impulse of the king of Israel is to destroy the enemy, God's way is to provide food and drink. And it is God's way that brings peace.

If this story is read as a background to Romans 12:19–20, then the political overtones of this passage become clear. In a context of warfare, God chooses paradoxically generous means to relate to his enemies and bring peace. In addition, the "vengeance" of God is revealed to be deeply subversive of any violent retaliation, for God's vengeance does not mirror the violence of the empire. This may be the force of Paul's "No!" in verse 20. In contrast to what is written about the vengeance of God, Paul is saying, "No, that's not the way it is. Enemies are not regarded as enemies but welcomed with hospitality." This is, of course, consistent with Paul's argument in Romans 5:8–10: "But God proves his love for us in that *while we were still sinners* Christ died for us. Much more surely then, now that we have been justified by his blood, will we be saved through him from the wrath of God. For if *while we were enemies*, we were reconciled to God through the death of his Son, much more surely, having been reconciled, will we be saved by his life."

Richard Hays offers this commentary: "How does God treat enemies? Rather than killing them, Paul declares, he gives his son to die for them. . . . It is evident, then, that those whose lives are reshaped in Christ must deal with enemies in the same way that God in Christ dealt with enemies."[30] And, as the Elisha story makes clear, God's way of dealing with enemies has consistently been the unexpected path of love, from early on in Israel's story right up to the death of Jesus.[31] In Romans 12 Paul draws out the implications of Jesus's death for the sake of his enemies: the Roman community is called to be a blessing for those who persecute them.

Rejecting the Imperial Path of Peace through Conquest

Throughout Romans, Paul offers a gospel of peace not through imperial conquest but through messianic suffering. And we have seen that this comes to its most eloquent expression in Romans 8, where God's response to the suffering

30. Richard B. Hays, *The Moral Vision of the New Testament: Community, Cross, New Creation; A Contemporary Introduction to New Testament Ethics* (San Francisco: HarperSanFrancisco, 1996), 330.

31. We are not arguing that this is the *only* way of dealing with enemies in Israel's Scriptures; it is, however, the thematic strand that both Jesus and Paul affirm and develop.

community is not revenge on their enemies but rather a relentless solidarity in their suffering in the groaning of the Spirit (8:26) and in the death of the Son (8:32). Moreover, in Romans 8:37 this solidarity results in the community being "more than conquerors."[32] The whole dynamic of this passage rejects the traditional categories about who is victim and who is conquered. The Messiah who died and was raised is the one in the position of authority at the right hand of God, and those who suffer are not the conquered ones but are more than, indeed above, the conquerors. Paul is rejecting the imperial categories of victory, categories beloved by both Israel and Rome, and is replacing them with the path of suffering love. The way to respond to the violence of the empire is to bear it and, in that bearing, to reveal that one is part of the family of Jesus (8:17, 29) and therefore one of those who cannot be separated from God's love. It is such love, such "relentless solidarity," that enables the Roman Christians to bear the suffering that they experience at the hands of their persecutors.[33]

In this light it is not surprising that the Christian community in Rome is to "live peaceably with all" (12:18) and "not repay anyone evil for evil" (12:17). In this way the community will "not be conquered by evil, but conquer evil with good" (12:21 our translation), and peace will be the result. Again, Paul subverts the language of the conqueror by robbing it of its violent force. The *Pax Romana* was considered by Rome to be one of its greatest achievements. Roman peace, however, was secured by the violent oppression of its enemies and the brutal suppression of those who resisted its rule. This contrast is heightened by Paul's use of the verb "to conquer" in 12:21. Language of conquering the enemy was used in association with Victoria, the goddess of Victory. For the Romans, peace came only through Victory.[34] For Paul, however, evil was overcome not by military victory; it was, rather, disarmed when conquered by good.

By the end of Romans 12, therefore, Paul has outlined very tangible ways that this community should embody the peace that comes through the Messiah, Jesus. One of those ways is by ending the divisions created by the hierarchies rooted in status, honor, and shame, divisions that governed even low-status relationships. This in itself was likely to draw negative attention to the community. But

32. The rest of this paragraph is dependent on Sylvia Keesmaat, "The Psalms in Romans and Galatians," in *The Psalms in the New Testament*, ed. Steve Moyise and Maarten J. Menken (New York: T&T Clark, 2004), 151–52.

33. The importance of the "relentless solidarity" of God in transforming the darkness is discussed by Walter Brueggemann, *The Message of the Psalms: A Theological Commentary* (Minneapolis: Augsburg, 1984), 12.

34. Jewett, *Romans*, 779.

these groups of Jesus followers were also called to practice a radical form of hospitality—not a hospitality designed to bolster up their own status and honor, but rather a hospitality that moved beyond the boundaries of the household to embrace the oppressed stranger and even the enemy, the oppressor. Just as God disarmed and reconciled enmity on the cross (Rom. 5:10), so this community is to disarm evil, by conquering it with generous hospitality, the sharing of food and drink with the enemy. This was a path to peace alien to Rome. This contrast between how the body of Christ and the body politic of Rome achieve peace is heightened further in Romans 13:1–7.

Demythologizing the Divine Authority of Rome

It is striking that the vocabulary of Romans 13:1 ("Let every person be subject [*hypotassesthō*] to the governing authorities") echoes that of Colossians 3:18 ("Wives, be subject [*hypotassesthe*] to your husbands") and Ephesians 5:21 ("Be subject [*hypotassomenoi*] to one another"). Both of these passages in Colossians and Ephesians can be shown to have elements that undermine the authoritarian patriarchal structures that formed the backbone of the social structure of ancient Roman society.[35] This passage contains a similar dynamic. Paul's call to subjection first of all suggests the need to submit to one's place in an existing hierarchy.[36] Second, as the passage continues, it becomes clear that such subjection is ambiguous. The very next sentence echoes a recurrent apocalyptic theme—namely, that the governing authorities have their power only because it has been given by God. Even in times of oppression, such assertions are a way of insisting that although it appears that the (often evil) empire has control, it is really God who is sovereign; it is God who really has power (e.g., Dan. 2:21). From the outset, Paul undermines the self-appointed divine authority of Rome. It is neither Rome's virtue nor Rome's gods that bestow authority on Rome. All authority is rooted in the God of Jesus Christ—the very God that Rome rejects in its persecution of Judeans and Christians alike. Far from providing divine sanction for Rome's rule,

35. On Colossians see Brian J. Walsh and Sylvia C. Keesmaat, *Colossians Remixed: Subverting the Empire* (Downers Grove, IL: IVP Academic, 2004), chap. 11. According to Philip H. Towner, this passage has all the marks of the household code tradition. Philip H. Towner, "Romans 13:1–7 and Paul's Missiological Perspective: A Call to Political Quietism or Transformation?," in *Romans and the People of God: Essays in Honor of Gordon D. Fee*, ed. Sven K. Soderlund and N. T. Wright (Grand Rapids: Eerdmans, 1999), 159.

36. According to Wright, "The word has echoes of military formation: one must take one's place in the appropriate rank." Wright, "Letter to the Romans," 720.

this is a relativization of imperial authority. As a result, "Romans 13 constitutes a severe demotion of arrogant and self-divinizing rulers. It is an undermining of totalitarianism, not a reinforcement of it."[37]

Luise Schottroff situates this passage in the context of loyalty tests demanded by the empire. Even though Christians would assert their loyalty to the governing authorities, this does not mean that they were willing to worship the imperial gods or bow the knee to Caesar.[38] She points out that "in the case of conflict . . . Romans 13:1–7 was insufficient in the eyes of the Roman authorities, because at that point a positive recognition of the Roman gods was demanded. If one considers the context of the Roman policy of religion, Romans 13:1–7 loses its apparently singular character and becomes a link in the long chain of declarations of loyalty of subjugated peoples toward Rome."[39] Paul *seems* to be advocating subjection to Rome in this passage. However, in rooting Rome's authority in the higher authority of God, he undermines the authority of the empire at the outset. As Jewett puts it, "The sacred canopy of the Roman gods has been replaced."[40] Or, in the vernacular, the emperor has no clothes.

The Body Politic of Jesus Meets the Sword of the Empire

Paul also makes it clear in his description of the imperial state that it is entirely different from both the body politic of the Christian community and its own self-perception. You see, it is one thing for Paul to contrast a political regime of

37. Wright, "Letter to the Romans," 719.

38. Luise Schottroff, "'Give to Caesar What Belongs to Caesar and to God What Belongs to God': A Theological Response of the Early Christian Church to Its Social and Political Environment," in Swartley, *Love of Enemy*, 228–29.

39. Schottroff, "'Give to Caesar,'" 229.

40. Robert Jewett, "Response: Exegetical Support from Romans and Other Letters," in *Paul and Politics: Ekklesia, Israel, Imperium, Interpretation*, ed. Richard A. Horsley (Harrisburg, PA: Trinity Press International, 2000), 65. Jewett, *Romans*, 790, says,

> That the Roman authorities were ordained by the God and Father of Jesus Christ turns the entire Roman civic cult on its head, exposing its suppression of the truth. Its involvement in the martyrdom of Christ, crucified under Pontius Pilate, cannot have been forgotten by the readers of chapter 13 who knew from firsthand experience of the Edict of Claudius the hollowness of Rome's claim to have established a benign rule of law. The critique of the law in all its forms in the first eight chapters of this letter cannot have been forgotten, which explains why the proudest institution of the *Pax Romana*, the rule of law, goes unmentioned here. Nothing remains of the claim in Roman propaganda that its law-enforcement system was redemptive, producing a kind of messianic peace under the rule of the gods Justitia and Clementia. Christ alone is the fulfillment of the law (10:4), not the emperor or the Roman gods. . . . Submission to the governmental authorities is therefore an expression of respect not for the authorities themselves, but for the crucified deity who stands behind them.

fear, wrath, violence, and bloodshed with a community of love, blessing, care, and nonviolence rooted in Jesus Christ, but we need to remember that Nero took pride in the fact that he had not won his empire by the sword, and that under his rule the golden age of Augustus had been renewed. In Nero's self-understanding and official propaganda, this was a time of unprecedented peace. Indeed, under Nero the sword was supposed to become "a quaint relic of bygone days."[41] Paul, the Judeans of Rome, and the Christian community knew differently. The imperial sword was not idle; it continued to pierce the bodies of those who would not submit to Nero's body politic. In the face of such imperial propaganda, Paul's words in Romans 13:1–7 "betray a sobering caution. The imperial sword is *not* idle: it continues to threaten destruction and bloodshed."[42]

Similarly, this is a rule that demands "fear" (13:3–4) and is described as executing wrath (13:4) by means of the sword. As Elliott notes, the imperial powers linked persuasion and force as the twin agents of consent.[43] In addition, Judeans such as Philo were adept at seeming to give lip service to the honor due to rulers, but they did so in a way that betrayed their real allegiance. Elliott points to a passage in which Philo describes how the Judeans in the Alexandrian marketplace "quickly make way 'for the ruler, and for beasts beneath the yoke.'" Elliott continues, "Of course, Philo protests that the motive is different. 'With rulers, we act out of respect [*timē*]; to beasts beneath the yoke, we act on account of fear [*phobos*], so we suffer no serious injury from them.'"[44] We need to note the sarcasm. Philo here compares harsh rulers to deadly animals. He says that one "gives way out of honor to the rulers, but out of fear to the beasts. . . . But [Philo's] Jewish readers would quite well have understood that the reason Philo gave way to each was the same, because he knew that if he did not he would be crushed."[45]

Further, while Paul appears to be paying lip service to the goodness of the Roman state, the vocabulary he uses, and the context in which his discussion

41. Neil Elliott, "Romans 13:1–7 in the Context of Imperial Propaganda," in *Paul and Empire: Religion and Power in Roman Imperial Society*, ed. Richard A. Horsely (Harrisburg, PA: Trinity Press International, 1997), 203. Elliott quotes a number of sources that demonstrate this point: Calpurnius Siculus, *Eclogue* 1.45–65; *Einsiedeln Eclogues* 25–31 (both taken from J. Wright and Arnold M. Duff, eds., *Minor Latin Poets*, LCC [Cambridge, MA: Harvard University Press, 1954]); and Seneca, *De Clementia* 1.2–4; 11.3; 13.5. See also Elliott, *Arrogance of Nations*, 155–56.

42. Elliott, "Romans 13:1–7," 203.

43. Elliott, "Romans 13:1–7," 198.

44. Elliott, "Romans 13:1–7," 200. *Phobos* (fear), is used by Paul to describe the state in Rom. 13:3 and 13:4; both *timē* (usually translated as "honor") and *phobos* (translated as "respect" in the NRSV) are found in 13:7.

45. E. R. Goodenough, *An Introduction to Philo Judeaus*, 57, quoted in Elliott, "Romans 13:1–7," 200–201.

occurs, heightens the difference between the body that he evokes in Romans 12 and the body politic that he describes in chapter 13: one is characterized by love, hospitality to the stranger, blessing of persecutors, peace, and the rejection of vengeance; the other is to be obeyed out of fear of the sword.

Paul's rhetoric here is certainly less than enthusiastic in his call for submission to the state. He does not even try to be as nuanced as Philo. Live in fear and be afraid, he says (13:3–4). And well we should live in fear of a regime that bears the sword (v. 4). And yes, give taxes to whom taxes are due, revenue to whom revenue is due. Why? Because you are also wise to give fear to whom fear is due and "honor" to whom "honor is due" (13:7). We should have our eyes wide open and be fearful of the state that wields such violent authority. And when Paul says "honor," we suggest that that word should be in quotation marks. Give imperial "honor" to those who demand such honor, while at the same time associating with the oppressed, with those who have no honor in this regime. Here and throughout this whole discourse on the authorities, you need to hear the irony. You see, when the straightforward meaning of a text is implausible, and when an incredibly intelligent author seems to be blatantly contradicting himself, then "that is one of the signals that may alert the reader or audience to the presence of irony."[46]

Beyond Fear and Honor to Love

This irony is heightened in the contrast between 13:7 and 13:8: "Pay to all what is owed them: taxes to whom taxes are owed, tolls to whom tolls are owed, fear to whom fear is owed, and honor to whom honor is owed. Owe no one anything, except to love one another, for the who one loves the other has fulfilled the law" (our translation). On the one hand, Paul tells the community to fulfill their obligations; on the other hand, in a blatant contradiction of what he has just said, he makes it clear that the only real obligation is to love one another. In the face of a state that demands as its right taxes, tolls, fear, and honor, Paul has been describing a community where the only law is love.

The radical character of this verse should not be lost: whether or not taxes, tolls, fear, and honor are owed to Rome (and the only one that is clearly owed to Rome is fear, according to the previous verses), what this community ultimately owes to Rome is love. Such love is the only obligation of those who serve another

46. T. L. Carter, "The Irony of Romans 13," *Novum Testamentum* 46, no. 3 (2004): 209–28, here 213.

Lord, the messianic Lord Jesus (13:4). From the calls to bless your persecutors (12:14) and feed your enemies when they are hungry or thirsty (12:21) to this call to love even the empire whose violence is so deeply present in the community, Paul ends up, not surprisingly, echoing the call of Jesus in the Gospels to love your enemies (Matt. 5:44; Luke 6:22–28). Such a calling has deep roots in the Scriptures, most clearly in Jeremiah's letter to the exiles, who are called to "seek the welfare of the city" in the heart of the empire that has made them captive (Jer. 29:7).

The irony, of course, is that such love is the only thing that ultimately undermines the violence and fear that the empire inflicts. Such love enables the community to bring healing and hope for those who suffer most at the hands of a violent imperial system. And it is precisely this love that reveals the community to be the body of the crucified Messiah, whose crucifixion brought reconciliation for his enemies (Rom. 5:10).

Notice also that Paul frames such love as the fulfilling of the law (13:8, 10). Hovering above Romans 13:1–7 was the imperial sword, swift to ensure that Roman law was obeyed. The fear of that sword is real. Accordingly, don't be naive about the violence of the state, Paul tells these Christians. Handle the state with care, he counsels. Some authorities really should be feared. But don't allow such fear to be the last word on the way you comport yourself in this world. Rather, Paul writes, "owe no one anything, except to love one another; for the one who loves another has fulfilled the law" (13:8). Paul subjects the whole Roman socio-legal system to another law that is decidedly Judean and not Roman. In three short verses (13:8–10), most of which is a quotation from the Ten Commandments, Paul undermines the very foundations of Roman law with its system of honor and shame, obligation and debt, and judges all law by the law of love. If love is the fulfilling of the law, then any laws that call us to anything short of love, or that would legitimate the oppression of others, are judged by the law of love as null and void. If Paul's readers hadn't caught the irony of how he was negotiating the relationship of Jesus followers and the Roman imperial order in 13:1–7, then his shifting of the discussion to the law of love in the next verses should have made it abundantly clear.

We are perhaps surprised by this move, but we should have expected it. Hasn't Paul just overthrown this imperial system by calling the community to a life of mutual honor, with a special emphasis on associating with the lowly, associating with those to whom one has no debt? And hasn't he already demonstrated his disregard for the status quo at the very beginning of his epistle when he writes that he is indebted to the uneducated foolish and to uncivilized barbarians (1:14)? These are people for whom an educated citizen like Paul would have had no obligation at all! Hasn't he given notice that a system of honor and shame has no hold on him when he so boldly claims that he is "not ashamed" of the gospel that is born of the shameful Judeans and their crucified Messiah (1:16)? So it is not surprising at all that Paul follows up his rather ironic invocation of obedience to the laws of the empire—laws that are all about obligation and being in debt to others—by relativizing the whole system with a reference to another law.

Another law, one that undermines Roman law. One that passes judgment on all law, especially laws that hold the seal of Nero. One that is decidedly Jewish. All Paul had to do was cite the commandments against adultery, murder, stealing, and coveting, and everyone would know that the imperial household, indeed the whole edifice of the *Pax Romana*, would come crumbling down. There was no *Pax Romana*, no imperial household in Paul's memory, that was not erected on sexual immorality, violence, theft, and greed.

Knowing the Time

And then, as if to dismiss the imperial order once and for all, the apostle concludes this discourse about the shape of the Christian community and how it should comport itself in the empire, with a devastating discernment of the time. "Besides this, you know what time it is" (13:11). You know that "the night is far gone, the day is near" (13:12). You know that while Nero's poets have declared the dawning of the new Augustan age, an age of peace and virtue, an age of benevolence and security, the truth is something very different. You know that this too is an age of darkness, that this too is an age stuck in the night. So don't be conformed to this age (12:2). Live as if you are in the day, not the night. And embrace an "honor" worthy of the name. Don't mimic the empire in a life of excess filled with sexual license, violence, and insatiable consumption (13:13). The emperor masquerades as the epitome of virtue, but we know better. So "put on the Lord Jesus Christ"; subject your lives to this liberating Lord, not that imperial impostor. And make "no provision for the flesh" (13:14), Paul counsels, but "present your bodies as a living sacrifice, holy and acceptable to God, which is your spiritual worship" (12:1). Paul calls this young Christian community living at the heart of the empire not to be *of* the empire. They live at the center of the body politic of Rome, but this is a body of "flesh." "But you are not in the flesh; you are in the Spirit, since the Spirit of God dwells in you" (8:9). While the empire is a culture of death because of injustice (1:18–32), "the Spirit is life because of justice" (8:10 NRSV alt.). They live in Rome, but they "dwell" in the Spirit (8:9–11).

A Targum for a Time Such as This

So how about us? If we grasp the radical character of the charter that Paul sketches for the Christian community in Romans 12 and abandon a quietist reading of Romans 13 by catching the irony and the subversion of what Paul is arguing here, then how might Paul's vision shape our political imaginations?

What would Paul say? If Paul were writing to us, living in the shadow of empire, what would he say? In the wake of a dangerous shift in world politics toward nationalism, identity politics, racism, and xenophobia, how might Paul respond? As the blood is daily cleaned from the streets, nightclubs, churches, and mosques; as yet another unarmed black man in the United States is shot by the police or another Indigenous young man is shot in Canada by a settler and there are no convictions; as Indigenous young people continue to take their own lives; as thousands of refugees drown in the Mediterranean every year seeking safety in Europe . . . is there any way that we can move from Paul's ancient letter to the followers of Jesus in Rome to address our own imperial context?

While we have seen that the whole letter to the Romans is constantly engaging the imperial context of Rome, with clear implications for the praxis of the Christian communities at the heart of the empire, it is also fair to say that Paul specifically and intentionally turns his attention to the daily practices of these communities in these two chapters of the epistle. So what happens if we attempt to hear Paul's sociopolitical vision, specifically in Romans 12 and 13, speaking directly into a world such as ours? What might these chapters of the letter have sounded like if they were written not two thousand years ago but in our own political context of violence, nationalism, greed, climate breakdown, and increasing inequality?

So we return to the imaginative practice of targum that we introduced in chapter 1 of this book. When rabbis would stand up to read the Torah to Diaspora synagogue congregations throughout the Roman Empire, they would have to translate because Hebrew had already been lost for so many Judeans. But they never translated straight. They did not understand meaning to be conveyed through exact and literal translation (that is a modern notion of translation). No, that would have been too reductionist for them. Rather, they believed that the Torah was a living word, still speaking into every new situation. So their translations were also interpretations of the ancient text, an updating of the text, an attempt to allow the Torah to speak anew and fresh to a covenant people far from their homeland, living as strangers in a foreign land. Are we not in a decidedly analogous situation? We have an ancient text that we have been struggling to understand, sometimes trying to free it from the shackles of dogmatic interpretation, and we desperately want to hear this text speak a word of liberation into our own lives. Such a fresh hearing of this text requires an exercise in interpretive imagination. So we turn again to the genre of targum.

Remember that a targum is invariably longer than the original text. It has to be, because it needs to explicate a lot of what would have been implicit in the original writing. What might have been easily grasped by the first hearers is often lost on a later audience. And a targum also needs to bring the ancient text into conversation and perhaps conflict with later historical, cultural, political, and economic realities. Moreover, this particular targum, coming three-quarters of the way through a sixteen-chapter epistle, also needs to spend some time hearing what Paul is saying in light of all that has come before. In other words, the targum needs to take the time to unpack something of what Paul means when he says "therefore" at the beginning of our passage.

Here, then, is a possible way to hear Paul addressing our present sociopolitical context. Might Paul's social charter for the ancient Christian community at the heart of the empire look something like this in the early decades of the twenty-first century? We offer this targum to you as if it were still in the voice of the apostle.[47]

Romans 12:1–13:14 Targum

Therefore . . . (12:1)

Therefore, sisters and brothers, friends in Christ,

> if it is true that Jesus the Messiah is Lord,
> and that no other leader,
> or nation, or ethnic identity,
> or institution, or system of economics,
> or political structure can demand your ultimate allegiance;
>
> if it is true that the gospel of Jesus is truer, more radical,

47. This targum has been developed in various contexts over the past fifteen years but came to something close to its present form when Brian spoke at a conference on "Faith and the Politics of Enemy Love" at Meadowvale Christian Reformed Church in Mississauga, Ontario, on February 4, 2017.

and more transforming
than any other grand narrative
or worldview on offer;

if it is true that this gospel has the power
to disarm all legitimations of violence,
to overthrow all scapegoating, all ethnic exclusion,
through the loving and inclusive embrace of Jesus;

if it is true that this is a gospel of radical justice,
rooted in the faithfulness of Messiah Jesus,
calling forth a covenantal faithfulness of those who will follow him,
who will bow the knee or pledge allegiance to no other god;

if it is true that while we were enemies
God reconciled us, made us whole,
through the death and resurrection of Jesus,
that Jesus embodied enemy love on a cross
and broke the deathly power of injustice by breaking open the
imperial grave;

if it is true that in this resurrection life
we are called to abandon all injustice
and present our bodies, every dimension of our lives,
as servants, instruments, tools, even slaves, of justice
regardless of the cost;

if it is true that God is taking a homeless
and divided people at the heart of the empire
and calling them to be family,
to make a home of welcoming hospitality together
in the face of generations of enmity;

if it is true that this restoring mercy of God
extends to all creation,
still longing for redemption in the face of ecological devastation,
crying out under the burden of climate breakdown,
waiting for the children of God to abandon an economics of
extraction
and to take up a loving and regenerative relationship with creation;

if it is true that nothing can separate us
from the love of God in Messiah Jesus, our only rightful Lord;

neither death nor life,
neither persecution nor the surveillance mechanisms of the state,
neither violence nor unemployment
neither deportation nor imprisonment,
neither ridicule nor terrorism;

if it is true that in a post-truth world
the depths and riches and wisdom and knowledge of God are
unsearchable;
and if it is true that in a world of Market supremacy
that glorifies brash displays of gold-plated opulence
we stubbornly confess that all things are from God,
through God, and to God,
and that all true glory is God's and God's alone;

if all of this is true . . .

then I urge you with everything that I have,
I appeal to you,
I call out to you,
in response to this radical, life-transforming good news of Jesus,

to offer up your bodies,
not simply your piety and your devotional life,
but your very bodies;

to offer up your bodies,
not your Twitter account, nor your online signature,
but your bodies put on the line for the sake of the gospel;

to offer up your bodies,
not your armchair punditry,
but the totality of your embodied existence;

indeed, to offer up your bodies,
the body of Christ,
the body politic of the incarnate Word,
assembling here and there in cells of resistance,
gathering to be formed in subversive discipleship,
coming to worship the One who liberates in the face of oppression,
the One who embodies justice and calls us to
lives of his inclusive and costly justice;

. . . offer up your bodies as nothing less than a living sacrifice.

While you know that your whole economy is rooted in self-interest,
and you have heard from the most recent emperor
that we are to put our own interests and the interests of the nation first,
I call you to sacrifice those interests.

We are not called to sacrifice the most vulnerable in our world.
We are not called to sacrifice compassion
    through the closing of our doors to the most marginal.
We are not called to sacrifice creational care
    through the quick extraction, movement, sale, and use of fossil fuels.
We are not called to sacrifice truth
    for the sake of deceitful lies.
We are not called to sacrifice neighborliness
    on the altar of ethnic and racial scapegoating.
We are not called to sacrifice generosity
    before the false god of the Market
    for the sake of the enrichment of the 1 percent.
We are not called to sacrifice justice
    in the name of a violent patriotic nationalism.

No, my friends, if there is to be a sacrifice,
then, following the crucified One, we are it.

Indeed, without a discipleship of living sacrifice,
    we make a mockery of the cross,
    cheapen the riches and depths of God's mercy,
    domesticate and tame the radicalism of the gospel,
    and tragically miss the meaning of the "therefore"
    with which we have begun.

Living sacrifice.
That is the only appropriate response
to the all-encompassing mercy of God.

Living sacrifice.
That is the shape of true holiness.

Living sacrifice.
That is a life acceptable to God, true to the call of the gospel.

And that, my friends, is spiritual worship.
That's right, bodies offered as living sacrifices
    is the heart of spiritual worship,

while bodies conformed to the consumptive patterns of this world
can never be living sacrifices.

And if we are talking about spiritual worship,
the question becomes, "Which spirit?"

Bodies held in the self-interested grip of the spirit of this world,
bodies enamored with ostentatious displays of wealth,
bodies preoccupied with images of success,
bodies driven to rage against the bodies of others,
bodies of insatiable consumption
are all bodies making the wrong sacrifices to the wrong gods.
They are not holy and pleasing to God,
and they are not very good candidates for living sacrifices.

Transformed, Not Conformed (12:2)

So don't be conformed to the empire, my friends,
but be transformed by the kingdom.
Do not have minds conformed to the reigning ideologies,
but experience, in this praxis of living sacrifice,
nothing less than the renewing of your minds.
Your imaginations no longer held captive,
but set free, renewed, and liberated.

Renewed minds,
liberated imaginations,
for a restored creation,
for a discerning resistance,
for lives of justice,
for subversive hospitality,
for radical peacemaking.

Renewed minds,
imaginations no longer shaped by the dead-end narratives
of progress, colonialism, civilization,
but transformed by the grand story of redemption.

Renewed minds,
rooted in the story of Jesus, not the president,
the story of creation, not our nation,
the story of love, not self-interest.

With embodied lives of sacrificial love,
a gospel spirituality permeating all of life,
and liberated imaginations,
we will be a people of discernment,
  seeing just beyond the range of normal sight,
  understanding the path ahead in these dark times,
  discerning God's will in the midst of the crisis,
  knowing what side we are on and who our allies are.

That, dear friends, is what knowing the "will of God" is all about.
So this is no time to limit God's will to the piety of our personal lives.
We need to know what is good, acceptable, and perfect
in the face of the depraved, blasphemous,
and profane times that we are living in.

But not alone, friends, not alone.

The Body Politic of Christ (*12:3*)

This call for bodies offered up in gratitude is a call to *a body*.

  There are no bodies offered as living sacrifices
    without the body of Christ;
  there is no spiritual worship
    without a renewed community in Christ;
  there are no transformed minds
    without a faithful community rooted in the Word of God;
  there is no discernment of God's good, pleasing, and perfect will
    without the church.

And let's be clear that when I now say "body,"
I am talking about the body of Christ,
itself a body politic.

A body politic embodying a story
in conflict with the dominant story of our age.
We are a body politic
in contrast to the body politic of the empire.

Let there be no mistake:
when we talk about the body of Christ,
this is a clear provocation in the face of the empire.
When we invite others into this body of Christ,

we are calling them out of their embeddedness in the empire.
We are members of the body of Christ,
not the body politic of our time;
and Jesus is our Lord and Savior,
not Caesar or any of his contemporary doubles.

This stuff is not about "me and Jesus."
This is not limited to "my personal relationship to Jesus."
This is not about a solitary spirituality.
This is not limited to individual salvation.
And it certainly isn't about Jesus bringing you financial prosperity!

No.
In the face of rampant individualism and a narrowly personalistic piety,
I call you back to the body.

We are members one of another.

From Identity Politics to Gift and Community (12:4–5)

In the face of an identity politics that wants to separate us from one another,
the body of Christ consists of a beautifully diverse and inclusive membership.
In the face of the fragmentation and divisiveness of our times,
we are "re-membered," made whole and one, through our membership in this body.

So if you want to find some sense of identity,
some sense of your uniqueness, or even your "individuality,"
then discern, with humility, what your place of service is in that body.

Indeed, you only have life in your membership,
and you only have membership
in terms of the service that you provide to the body.

A leg that is not exercised in carrying a body will atrophy and die.
A lung that no longer can receive oxygen for the body will die.
A liver that no longer serves the body will die.

So let there be no illusion, my friends;
a body offered up as a living sacrifice to God
that does not find its place in service of the body of Christ,
in service of this alternative body politic,
is a body that will die.

This is no solitary spirituality that I am talking about.
That is too simple, too tame, too easily co-opted.
No, this is a call to community;
this is a call to the body of Christ.

So, in sober judgment, not haughtiness,
in sober judgment,
  neither prideful overestimation
  nor the false humility of "I'll let someone else handle this,"
in sober judgment
  and in the midst of the community
  as members one of another,
discern the gifts that you have received
  from the God of grace,
  the God of gift.

These gifts are gifts of grace.
They are gifts to a body,
  for the health of the body,
  for the growth of the body,
  for the body to fulfill its calling in the world
  as nothing less than the body of Christ.

In this time of divisiveness, we need to be members of the body.
In this time of crisis, we need all the gifts that we bring
to be placed in service of the body of Christ,
not the dominant body politic of our time.

And God has not left us without gifts for such a time as this.

Subversive Gifts in the Face of Empire (*12:6–8*)

Prophecy,
service,
teaching,
encouraging,
giving,
leading,
and compassion.

These are gifts that build up the body,
  mind-transforming gifts,
  gifts that sustain a community of nonconformity,

gifts that shape an alternative body politic,
gifts that engender a generous community of inclusion,
gifts that empower resistance,
gifts that equip us to be subversives in the empire.

You see . . .

There are no transformed minds without
the *prophetic* ministry of discerning God's Word
addressing our ever-changing situation.
We need prophetic discernment that cuts through ideology
and rhetorical smoke screens
so we can wisely discern the times.

There is no living sacrifice without
a *serving* ministry in our midst and in our world.
The body of Christ needs to be a discipleship school of service,
especially to those most hurt and marginalized
by the regime of exclusion.

There is no antidote to the deceit and lies of the empire without
radically truthful, profound, and persistent *teaching* of the way of Jesus.
We need to reclaim and reimagine what teaching biblical faith looks like
if our imaginations are to be liberated.

There will be no sustaining of a community in these times without
a ministry of *encouragement* in the face of discouragement,
anxiety, and despair.
We will judge the health of the body by how well we foster a community
of gratitude and mutuality.

There will be no creating of a generous spaciousness
against the grain of our times without
folks gifted with and demonstrating
that kind of radical *generosity* in our midst.[48]
In the face of a self-interested culture of greed and inequity,
we will engender a community of generosity of our money,
our time, our hearts, our lives.

There is no subversive and liberating direction for the body of Christ without
diligent and visionary *leadership*.

48. We intentionally allude to the Generous Space communities with whom we are allied; see www.generousspace.ca.

While the world seems increasingly drawn
to the bravado of strong, bullying leaders
basking in their own power and arrogance,
we will follow and raise up servant leaders of quiet humility,
who will lead in the way of the cross.

And there is no hope for this body experiencing violent
persecution and intimidation without
a joyful ministry of *compassion*
in the face of the deepest and most painful trials
that the body might experience.
In the face of harshness,
in the absence of the basics of civility,
we will be a people of compassion,
embracing the pain of our neighbors,
sharing their sorrow so we can be agents of hope.

These are the gifts of the body,
and without these gifts this body doesn't have a chance.
Without these gifts the body of Christ is reduced to
an anachronistic society of piety at best,
or a handmaiden of empire at worst.

So let me get specific.

The Specifics of Love (*12:9–13*)

Let's begin by getting beyond a pious sentimentality of love.
If love is genuine,
if love is really willing to go the distance for the beloved,
if love is to be more than a secondhand emotion,
then to deeply love we must learn how to hate what is evil.

That means that love requires the naming of names.
Love does not play nice.
There is too much at stake for that.

If we are to love in a time of hate,
then we need to paradoxically hate that hate
and name it for what it is.

If we are going to love women,
we must hate misogyny.

If are going to love our Muslim neighbors,
we must hate Islamophobia.

If we are going to love the Indigenous peoples of this land,
we must hate colonialism, its persistent wound,
and the way that we remain the beneficiaries of colonial systems.

If we are going to love our LGBTQ+ siblings,
we must hate homophobia and transphobia.

If we are going to love those of different ethnicities than our own,
we must hate racism.

If we are going to love the voices of our neighbors,
we must hate systems that disenfranchise voters.

If we are going to love generosity and equality,
we must hate economic structures that willingly sacrifice the poor
and a caste system that enriches the very few at the expense of the very many.

If we are going to love those who suffer displacement and injustice,
then we must hate the geopolitical and economic-military forces
that render whole peoples homeless and refugees.

If we are going to love kindness,
then we must hate forces of violence and torture,
whether they be ISIS, CSIS, or the CIA.[49]

If we love our creational home,
then we must hate ways of living that cause its rape and destruction.

You see, my friends, if love is genuine,
then we must hate what is evil
and hold fast to what is good.

And to do that we will need to be diligent in discerning the good.
That's why we need *prophets* and *teachers* in our midst.

But it isn't really all that complicated.
Counter-imperial love hates what is evil and holds fast to what is good
by loving one another in mutual affection
and outdoing one another in showing honor.

49. ISIS is the acronym for the Islamic State, who is waging a war of terror in the Middle East and who engages in acts of terrorism in other countries. CSIS stands for the Canadian Security and Intelligence Services, and the CIA is the Central Intelligence Agency of the United States. All three have admitted complicity in violence and torture.

The love that is manifest in the body
is a profound antidote to the discord and hatred
that has taken a demonic hold on our culture.
And while the competitiveness of a capitalist culture
amounts to little more than a war of all against all,
including a war on the very creational foundations of life,
we are called to a competition that subverts this culture.

While everything around us calls us
to honor those who are the most powerful,
to pay homage to the "honorable member" from such and such,
"his worship, the mayor," or "your worship," the judge in court,
and certainly to give honor to those who hold the highest
positions of state (especially when they come down golden escalators!),
the body of Christ sees all of this as nonsense.

The body of Christ is all about outdoing one another in showing honor,
especially to those who are most dishonored in society.

Associate with the lowly.
Walk with the oppressed.
Give preference to the voices of the poor.
Replace exploitation with affection.

While the forces around you will wear you down
and tell you in so many ways that resistance is futile,
do not lag in zeal, don't give in,
hold each other up,
be a community of spiritual vitality against the odds.
You will need to exercise the gift of *encouragement*
as if your life depends on it,
because your life does depend on it.

Yes, I know that this is a path of suffering.
This isn't the easy way in these times.
But Jesus did call us to a cross, didn't he?
So remember who is your Lord.
Remember the path that he took.
Let the hope of his resurrection,
the hope of his coming kingdom,
sustain you.
God has given you *leaders* who will show you the way.

And let this hope, facing this suffering,
animate your prayers.

Never give up praying, friends.
Without prayer, we're done for.

Remember *generosity*.
Care for the needs of the community,
but don't stop there.
Extend hospitality,
to strangers as well.

If the powers that be will replace the open hand
with a closed fist raised in salute,
then you must be an open-handed people,
not only to those in your communities
but also to those "outside,"
providing homes to those whose families have kicked them out,
offering hospitality to those who have no community,
sanctuary for those who fear deportation,
welcome for those who would be banned,
refuge for those who are targeted and profiled.

The Politics of Peace (*12:14–21*)

And if that way of living brings persecution,
if online trolls, vigilantes in the neighborhood,
or the security apparatus of the state should come down hard on you,
then invite them in for coffee,
invite them to the potluck dinner,
ask them to share their story with you.
I know that this is dangerous.
It may be that they will murder you
while you pray.
But it is better to bless them,
to open the hand to them,
so that they might be ashamed of their hatred
and perhaps converted to the way of love.

We are all about hating evil,
but we are called to the hard work of loving evildoers.
And since we are all about blessing,
we do not call down curses on our enemies.

So we are a people who know how to party,
rejoicing with those who rejoice;
while also acquainted with grief and lament,
weeping with those who weep.

There may be more weeping for a while.
We may find ourselves at the side of the refugee,
  separated from family, fearing deportation.
We may find ourselves with another mom
  lamenting a lost son.
And we will likely spend a lot of time in hospital rooms,
  by hospice beds,
  at funerals,
  on the streets,
weeping with those who weep,
exercising the gift of *compassion*.

For those brief glimpses of shalom, however,
  those times of joy,
  those moments of healing,
  those times of reawakened hope,
we will put on parties of liberation,
dancing with our hands outstretched,
singing, "There's a city, across a river,
  and it's shining from within.
  People are dancing on the ramparts
  beckoning to you, come on in,
  to the city of refuge."[50]

And we're looking to build that city.
That's why we are seeking the peace of the city.
That's why we look not for conflict but for harmony,
  on our streets,
  in our workplaces,
  in the halls of power.

Like the *Pax Romana* before it, the *Pax Americana*
was always a fraud.
And as its facade falls off,

50. To quote again from the thematic anthem of the Sanctuary Community in Toronto: Red Rain, "City of Refuge," on *A Night at Grace's*, Red Rain, 2006. Used by permission.

as the ugly face of empire is revealed,
the violence will escalate.

In the face of such violence,
we embrace the gospel of peace,
the reconciliation of enemies,
the disarming of the empire
as it collapses all around us.

We're not claiming to be wiser than we are.
We're not claiming to have all the answers.
We are just trying to make our way with the vulnerable,
just trying to walk with the oppressed,
whether that means showing up to witness
when the immigration officers arrive,
or walking Palestinian children to school,
or gathering at Standing Rock,
or joining with the people of Grassy Narrows,
or sponsoring a refugee family,
or being part of a circle of support,
or just helping the single mom down the street
with free childcare
and a meal.
All we are trying to do is be present with those who need us.
Maybe that is the only answer we have for the injustice around us:
help bear it.[51]

51. The American Friends Service Committee runs a program that accompanies and documents undocumented immigrants' interactions with authorities, in addition to providing support and legal help. For more on this program and the Sanctuary program in general, see www.afsc.org. Tucson-based Mariposas Sin Fronteras supports LGBTQ+ refugees and immigrants (www.mariposassinfronteras.org). The FaithAction ID program in Greensboro, North Carolina, which provides identification for undocumented immigrants, arose out of an initiative run by FaithAction International House and Greensboro Law Enforcement (www.faithaction.org). For more on Sanctuary, see *YES!* The Sanctuary Issue 82 (Summer 2017): www.yesmagazine.org; and Dhana Addanki, "Safe House," *Sojourners* 46, no. 10 (November 2017): 26–30. Christian Peacemaker Teams Palestine accompanies Palestinian children to and from school to protect them from Israeli settler violence (www.cptpalestine.com). Standing Rock became a flashpoint for the Standing Rock Sioux protests against the Dakota Access Pipeline, which poses a threat to their water sources; see www.standwithstandingrock.net. The Ojibway people of Grassy Narrows have been dealing with mercury poisoning from a paper mill in their water for over fifty years; see www.freegrassy.net. Circles of Support and Accountability, a program of the Mennonite Central Committee of Canada, seeks to form support and accountability groups around released prisoners convicted of sexual offences; see https://mcccanada.ca/learn/more/circles-support-accountability-cosa.

And we sure aren't looking for payback.
That path only leads to more misery, more pain.
The justice that we seek has nothing to do with such vengeance.
Indeed, if there is to be any kind of retribution in this life
or the next, then it's up to God and its none of our business.

Yes, yes, I know the old line,
"'Vengeance is mine, I will repay,' says Lord."

But that's not the way we have learned from Jesus.
Rather, if your enemies are hungry, then feed them,
and if they are thirsty, give them something to drink.

Again, it's a matter of not repaying evil with evil.
It's a matter of disarming your enemy.

Isn't there a better chance that your enemies
will cease being enemies if you invite them to a feast,
if you rain down food on them,
if you come to them in their need,
if you offer them the grace of common humanity,
rather than raining down bombs on their villages,
rather than "taking them out" with drones that kill in stealth,
rather than seeking to eradicate them from the face of the earth?

I know, I know, this sounds naive.
But here is a truth to hold on to in a post-truth world.
Here is a truth that Jesus embodied in his life
   and most profoundly in his death.
Here is a truth that gets about as close to rock-bottom certainty
as you will ever find:

   Evil never overcomes evil.
   Violence never ever ends violence.

And "when you ingest the poison of violence
   even in a just cause,
   it corrupts, deforms and perverts you."[52]

So, dear friends, in these violent times,
in the face of enemies who will seek to overwhelm you,
remember this:
   Do not be overcome by evil, but overcome evil with good.

52. Chris Hedges, *Death of the Liberal Class* (Toronto: Vintage Canada, 2011), 198.

You see,
goodness is stronger than evil,
love is stronger than hate.
Light is stronger than darkness,
truth is stronger than lies.
Peace is stronger than war,
reconciliation surpasses revenge.
And generous hospitality
disarms enmity.

Watch Your Back around the State (*13:1–7*)

Now I know what you are thinking.

I can already hear the question:
What about the state?
I can already hear the objection:
Aren't we called to be a law-abiding people?

I know too well how you have interpreted my words on this matter,
I know that somehow I have been interpreted to say
that all Christians should obey the ruling authorities,
regardless of how violent, unjust, and cruel those authorities might be.

Really?

Do you think that I could call for such a radically alternative body politic,
as I have just done,
and then in the very next breath somehow call for blind obedience
to the regime of the empire?

How could I call for total obedience to Lord Jesus
and also require such obedience to Lord Caesar or any other regime?

How could I call for blessing our enemies at one moment
and then require obedience to the war machine of the state in the next?

Or perhaps I should put the question to you.

How could you have ever read what I said in Romans 13
apart from what I had just written in Romans 12
and indeed in the whole letter?

How could you ever interpret my words as legitimating the rule of the empire,
when it was the empire that persecuted our people and put our Lord on a cross?

And how could you ever have read my words about the state
apart from how deeply rooted I am in both the Torah and the prophets?
Haven't I been quoting these texts throughout my letter to you?

So listen up.

Yes, if we are to be the alternative body politic that I am talking about,
then we have to seriously consider
our relationship with the ruling authorities.

And here is my word to you.

Listen closely to what I am saying.

The state has no self-appointed divine authority.
Saying "God bless America" is presumptuous
and "America First" is blasphemy.
All authority is rooted in the God of Messiah Jesus,
the very God that the empire rejects in its embrace of idolatry.
While the state might appear to be in control,
all the power that it seems to have is only temporary.

Ironically, the state's power is granted by the very God
its actions betray.
The gods it really serves
have no power,
no authority,
no ability to bring life.

Submitting all governmental rule to the sovereignty of God,
we demote arrogant and totalitarian rulers.
But knowing that these are violent regimes,
we urge caution:
watch your back around the state.

While we grant no ultimate authority to the state,
because God is the final authority,
we are wise to be careful around the state.

The state does, after all, bear the sword.
It may present itself as a benevolent force of law and order,
but the Taser guns come out pretty quick,
along with the stun grenades, tear gas,
and finally lethal force,

especially if you are black or Latino,
undocumented or Indigenous.

So if you get on the wrong side of the regime,
fear is a healthy response.

I know this seems to be contrary
to the subversive ethic that I've been talking about.
If we are called to be living sacrifices,
then why not take that as far as it will go,
and let ourselves be sacrificed before the violent state?

I'm suggesting you choose your battles.
For some of us protest, resistance, and defiance
are not only possible but necessary.
But others should have a healthy fear for those to whom fear is owed.

Be careful with the authorities.
Don't mess with the Homeland Security folks if you can help it.
Don't cheaply bring the attention of the RCMP, the FBI, or ICE to your community.[53]
This is no game.
Don't expose your vulnerable neighbors unnecessarily.
Some folks really should be feared,
but don't allow such fear to be the last word
on the way you comport yourself in this world.

And even though I have insisted that we are to walk with the oppressed,
and that we are to turn all notions of honor and prestige on their head
by bestowing honor on those deemed shameful by the regime,
give "honor" to those who think that they are at the top of the heap.

You need to notice the quotation marks.
Notice the irony.
Notice the nudge nudge, wink wink.

Those "at the top" might in fact be undeserving,
yet we honor them anyway.

Outdoing one another in showing honor
means honoring the underserving,

53. RCMP stand for the Royal Canadian Mounted Police; FBI stand for Federal Investigation Bureau (United States); and ICE stands for Immigration and Customs Enforcement (United States).

both in society's eyes
and in your own.
But even this is not the last word, for while I've urged you
to show respect to those who are due such respect,
and even to show "honor" to those who think they are owed such honor,
remember this:

> Owe no one anything except to love one another,
> for the one who loves the other has fulfilled the law.

Law, Love, and Civil Disobedience (*13:8–10*)

Not only do we need to relativize all authority,
subjecting it to the God of Jesus the Messiah,
so also do we need to relativize all law,
    all judicial rulings,
    all constitutions,
    all executive orders,
by subjecting all law to the law of love.

There is another law that is above all law.
There is another law that passes judgment on all law
regardless of which imperial seal that law bears.

According to this law, the only thing that we
most profoundly owe to one another is love.

And to make sure that no one misses the reference,
let me locate this law of love in the radical tradition of Torah.

The commandments, "You shall not commit adultery;
You shall not murder;
You shall not steal;
You shall not covet,"
and all other commandments,
all other laws that would be worthy of obedience,
are summed up in this word,
"Love your neighbor as yourself;
love does no wrong to a neighbor;
therefore love is the fulfilling of the law."

This is how the gospel of Jesus undermines
the very foundations of all worldly systems of law.
All laws are judged by this law of love.

If love is the fulfilling of the law,
then any laws that call us to anything short of love,
any laws that make us obligated to some at the expense of others,
any laws that would legitimate the oppression of others,
are judged by the law of love as null and void.

The law of love not only judges all other law;
it also calls us to civil disobedience against laws
that contravene the law of love.

Maybe that means setting up a blockade against a pipeline,
or protesting a travel ban on Muslims,
or demanding that children
not be taken from their parents at the border.

If you need it to be any more specific,
then look again at those injunctions against
adultery, murder, stealing, and coveting.

While I may have had in mind the imperial regime of Nero
when I first wrote those words—
Nero's insatiable sexual appetite,
his household of blood and murder,
his economy of theft and pillage,
his empire of insatiable greed and expansion—
things haven't really changed that much, have they?

Yes, you have a system of law,
but it doesn't seem to protect women from misogynistic violence,
it doesn't stop Indigenous land from being stolen,
it doesn't inhibit state sanctioned murder,
it doesn't stop the vulnerable from being deported,
it provides legal sanction
for the theft of public resources for private gain,
and it serves to protect covetousness and greed as virtues,
not crimes.
It is, in short, a law that results in death,
not life.

Discerning the Times (13:11–14)

But what else would you expect?
I mean, you know what time it is, don't you?

You know that "the times they are a-changin',"
you know that "the night is far gone and the day is near."

You know that time is up for this imperial house of cards.
You know that while we have heard all the bravado
of a new age, a new day,
of renewed strength, renewed greatness,
the truth is something very different.

You know that this too is an age of darkness,
this too is an age stuck in the night.

But you also know that this age is coming to an end.
It is darkest just before the dawn,
but the dawn is coming.

That's what this whole story of Jesus has been all about.
That's what time it really is.

It is time for the "creatures of the dark in disarray"
to "fall before the morning light."[54]
It is time for this endless night to give way to dawn.

What time is it?
It's time to wake up.
Wake up from our culturally imposed slumber.
Wake up to what God is up to in transforming our world.
Wake up to live in the full light of the coming kingdom.

What time is it?
It is time to put aside the works of darkness.
But if you are going to do that, my friends,
then you'll need the "armor of light";
you'll need to clothe yourselves in this light,
because the forces of darkness will try to hold you down
with a strong arm up their sleeve.

What time is it?
It is time to put on the Lord Jesus Christ.
That is what it means to wear the "armor of light."
It is time to be dressed in Christ,
to be transformed as the body of Christ,

54. Bruce Cockburn, "Santiago Dawn," track 7 on *World of Wonders*, High Romance Music Inc., 1985.

to be precisely the kind of subversive body politic
that we've been talking about.

This is no time for petty quarrels and dissension.
This is no time for the body of Christ to mimic
the debauchery of the empire.
This is no time for us to fall prey to sexual license
or a cynical drunkenness to numb our pain.
This is no time to be distracted by empty entertainment.

No, my friends,
the night is far gone, the day is near,
so live in the day.

Time is up for the oppressive laws of the state,
so obey the law of love.
Time is up for the empire,
so live in the kingdom.
Time is already up for the newly inaugurated regime,
so put on the Lord Jesus Christ.

The night is far gone, the day is near,
and I know, dear friends, I know,
that it sure doesn't feel that way most of the time.

I know that for many of us it feels like the night is endless,
and there is no day in sight,
no slight glimmer of dawn on the horizon,
not even the morning star is visible to you.

I know that even the morning star can be hidden
in the clouds of despair and sadness,
blocked by the overcast of deep darkness.

But if you can see just beyond the range of normal sight,
if you can see with the eyes of faith,
if your imagination has been set free,
if your minds have been renewed,
if you can discern the times . . .
you will see against the grain of the times,
against the imperial evidence amassed against you;
you will see that the night is indeed far gone
and the day is near.

So, living in faith
and embracing the politics of love,
let us say to the darkness, "We beg to differ,"[55]
and live as in the day.

55. Mary Jo Leddy, *Say to the Darkness, We Beg to Differ* (Toronto: Lester & Orpen Dennys, 1990).

234-3375 (TTY: 1-800-234-3375).

ملحوظة: إذا كنت تتحدث اذكر اللغة، فإن خدمات المساعدة اللغوية تتوافر لك بالمجان. اتصل برقم 1-3375-234-800 (رقم هاتف الصم والبكم: 1-3375-234-800).

PAUNAWA: Kung nagsasalita ka ng Tagalog, maaari kang gumamit ng mga serbisyo ng tulong sa wika nang walang bayad. Tumawag sa 1-800-234-3375 (TTY: 1-800-234-3375).

သတိျပဳရန္ - အကယ္၍ သင္သည္ ျမန္မာစကား ကို ေျပာပါက၊ ဘာသာစကား အကူအညီ၊ အခမဲ့၊ သင့္အတြက္ စီစဥ္ေဆာင္ရြက္ေပးပါမည္။ ဖုန္းနံပါတ္ 1-800-234-3375 (TTY: 1-800-234-3375) သို႔ ေခၚဆိုပါ။

ATTENTION : Si vous parlez français, des services d'aide linguistique vous sont proposés gratuitement. Appelez le 1-800-234-3375 (TTY: 1-800-234-3375).

注意事項：日本語を話される場合、無料の言語支援をご利用いただけます。1-800-234-3375 (TTY: 1-800-234-3375) まで、お電話にてご連絡ください。

ВНИМАНИЕ: Если вы говорите на русском языке, то вам доступны бесплатные услуги перевода. Звоните 1-800-234-3375 (телетайп: 1-800-234-3375).

LUS CEEV: Yog tias koj hais lus Hmoob, cov kev pab txog lus, muaj kev pab dawb rau koj. Hu rau 1-800-234-3375 (TTY: 1-800-234-3375)..

توجه: اگر به زبان فارسی گفتگو می کنید، تسهیلات زبانی بصورت رایگان برای شما فراهم می باشد. با (TTY: 1-800-234-3375) 1-800-234-3375 تماس بگیرید.

KUMBUKA: Ikiwa unazungumza Kiswahili, unaweza kupata, huduma za lugha, bila malipo. Piga simu 1-800-234-3375 (TTY: 1-800-234-3375).

This letter is final notice from Delta Dental of Kansas that your **premium payment** to purchase individual coverage **was not** received. Your coverage will terminate effective the last day of the month for which payment was timely received if no action is taken. Call us at 800.234.3375 with any questions.

Sincerely,

W + K Repair
Washington
844 385
1/2 4[illegible]

Finance Department
Delta Dental of Kansas

DELTA DENTAL OF KANSAS
1619 N. Waterfront Parkway
P.O. Box 789769
Wichita, KS 67278-9769

Main Telephone:	316-264-1099	800-733-5823	Fax: 316-462-3393
Customer Service:	316-264-4511	800-234-3375	Fax: 316-462-3392
Marketing & Sales:	316-264-8413	800-264-9462	Fax: 316-462-3329
Eligibility & Enrollment:	316-264-4511	800-234-3375	Fax: 316-462-3394

9

Imperial Sexuality and Covenantal Faithfulness

We often begin seminars and courses with our "attract/repel" question. We ask participants to share with us what attracts them to the Bible and what repels them. What do they love, value, and cherish about this collection of ancient texts, and what do they find difficult, troublesome, even repulsive? Sometimes people are taken aback by the second part of the question. Are we allowed to be repulsed by the Bible? And are we really allowed to say so in public, especially in a Christian setting? Often enough people share that being given permission to voice their discomfort, doubts, and struggles with the Bible is itself a very liberating thing. They've had a deep aversion to something in this book for years but have never felt that they were allowed to openly say so.

Gossip and the Elephant in the Room

We have asked this question about the Bible in general and about Romans in particular. On one such occasion the question elicited these three responses of attraction:

- "I love Romans 5:8: 'God proves his love for us in that while we were sinners Christ died for us.' There is such comfort in that. It sums up the whole gospel for me."
- "I so appreciate the honesty of the struggle in Romans 7. That conflict is me all over."

- "During hard times in my life, I have taken great comfort knowing that 'all things work together for good for those who love God' (Rom. 8:28)."

When people began to name dimensions of Romans that repelled them, some of these things came up:

- "I have to admit that while there are bits that I really like, I find myself lost in the argument. I just don't get it. Why does he have to be so convoluted?"
- "Romans 9–11. Not only do I not quite follow the argument, but I have a sinking feeling that my Jewish friends would really be offended."
- "What Paul has to say about the state in Romans 13 sure doesn't fit with my politics."

And then, as if it were the elephant in the room that no one had named yet, someone said, "The last section of Romans 1."

We pushed the question: "Oh, you have some problems with Romans 1?"

"Yes," came the reply. "I find what Paul says there to be harsh and, well, pretty offensive to much of what I believe."

The elephant had been acknowledged but not yet named. So we pushed further. "We totally agree. We too have a hard time thinking that people who gossip are worthy of death."

Confused laughter. So we kept pushing. "And insolence. Really, who among us here would have survived our adolescence if insolence is punishable by death? What would this mean for youth ministry? We agree with you. That stuff at the end of chapter 1 really is problematic!"

More chuckling. And then, looking surprised and incredulous, we said, "Oh, wait a minute. That isn't the bit of chapter 1 that you are talking about, is it? You mean those two verses about homosexuality!"

The contrived confusion became the occasion to make an important point about how we deal with these troublesome two verses in our reading of Paul in the context of the contemporary church's struggles with homosexuality. No one in that room—not one person, we suggested—actually believes *everything* that Paul wrote in this passage to the churches in Rome. There may have been someone present who believed that the death penalty is the just punishment for murder. But gossiping and insolence? How about haughtiness, boasting, and being rebellious to your parents? Surely these are serious human vices. And as we have seen, these are deathly forces in human communal, economic, ecological, and political life. But are they worthy of death? Isn't that what the apostle has said?

Or let's take covetousness. We live in a culture and an economy that is founded on covetousness. Without covetousness, without greed and consumptive desire, our whole economy would collapse. As the character Gordon Gekko so memorably put it in the film *Wall Street*, "Greed is good."

You get our point. Of the twenty-one vices and sinful activities that Paul names at the end of Romans 1, only murder is illegal in North America, though many of these vices and behaviors could well lead to illegal activity. There is no legal sanction in our society against being wicked per se—or against covetousness; or against harboring malicious thoughts and intentions; or against envy, personal strife, deceit, craftiness, gossiping, insolence, haughtiness, boastfulness, rebellion toward parents, foolishness, faithlessness, heartlessness, or ruthlessness; or even against hating God. You can do all these things without breaking the law, and you certainly do not deserve death because you do these things. In fact, you can even be the president of the United States while manifesting most of these vices!

It seems to us that there is an astounding double standard in how these verses are read. It isn't just a matter of whether we think that these vices are worthy of death, but a matter of how we so easily appeal to verses 26–27 to condemn certain sexual sins, while maintaining an incredibly cavalier attitude toward greed, envy, quarreling, slander, arrogance, and boasting, just to name a few. What is that about? How does it make any sense to have abrasive preaching against homosexuality, even calling for death for homosexuals, in churches that embrace a prosperity gospel that embodies greed, covetousness, boasting, and arrogance? Paul says that the people who do these things—all these things, including greed, slander, arrogance, and boasting—deserve to die. Why are we concerned about sexuality but not about the kind of economics that ruins lives, debases creation, and deals in death?

Of course, it works both ways. Our respondent who said that he had a hard time with the end of Romans 1 was referring to the texts purportedly about homosexuality, but he wasn't as equally disturbed by how gossips are worthy of death. So let's simply be honest and say that no one agrees with everything that Paul is saying here. Some might choose to gloss over the economic nature of the vices listed, while others will need to either "agree to disagree" with Paul's comments on homosexuality or find a way to better understand Paul in his own context. Either way, we will need to continue the hard work of interpreting this passage. We have already offered some interpretation of the list of vices; it is now time to turn our attention to the difficult matter of how we interpret Romans 1:26–27 in its context in the letter, the biblical story as a whole, the ancient world, and in relation to our own struggles around the inclusion of gay and lesbian brothers and sisters in the body of Christ.[1]

We hope that by now it is clear that we read Paul's counter-imperial epistle to the heart of the Roman Empire as a life-giving and authoritative word that speaks into our own imperial context. And while we all need to admit candidly that no one agrees with everything that the apostle writes here, it would be foolish, impious, and arrogant to dismiss Paul's words as simply out of touch with contemporary life. Such a dismissal is too easy, too cheap. No, we need to struggle with the apostle and wrestle with this letter until it blesses us, even if we should find ourselves limping after the contest.

Paul means what he says here, even if he seems to be a little over the top. Indeed, he means what he says here, even if the whole thing is a setup. And a setup it is.[2] You see, though some of the addressees of this letter were listening to Paul's all-out attack on the vices of gentile life in the empire and quietly saying, "Amen, brother Paul, you preach it, because we sure don't live that way," Paul was also setting up those self-righteous members of the community for a profound judgment in the very next sentence: "Therefore you have no excuse, whoever you are, when you judge others; for in passing judgment on another you condemn yourself, because you, the judge, are doing the very same things" (2:1). And he says this as if it were a fait accompli. No real argument, just that in the very act of judging others we demonstrate our own guilt. So whatever we do with this passage, if we somehow find it judging other people but not ourselves, then we are seriously missing the point. Attending to the context of this last section of Romans 1 in light of what Paul is about to do in the next chapter, we are cautioned against too quickly hearing

1. We understand that there is a much wider range of human sexualities than can be limited to the homosexual/heterosexual distinction. The acronym LGBTQ+ has itself been subject to change and expansion within the queer community. Even the term *queer* is not universally accepted within this broad community. For the purposes of this book, however, we are limiting ourselves to the two poles of the Kinsey scale; namely, heterosexual (straight) and homosexual (gay and lesbian). This is not to deny the range of sexual experiences and identities but to limit our engagement with the letter to the Romans to the question of homosexuality because that is the issue that this text is used to address. We assume that there will be implications of our interpretation of Paul for bisexual, transgender, genderqueer people, and others, but we will not be drawing out those implications in this book since that would take us too far from Romans.

2. Richard B. Hays refers to this as Paul's "homiletical sting operation." Richard B. Hays, *The Moral Vision of the New Testament: Community, Cross, New Creation; A Contemporary Introduction to New Testament Ethics* (San Francisco: HarperSanFrancisco, 1996), 389.

this depiction of sinfulness as about anyone other than ourselves. Paul's whole homemaking agenda in this epistle is to break down all self-righteous "us/them" polarities. And part of the genius of this letter is that it is addressed to the whole community and presumably would have been read in the presence of people on both sides of the Judean/gentile division. In terms of our narrative in chapter 2, both Nereus and Iris are addressed in this letter, and the meaning of the epistle needs to be interpreted in the midst of the divided community.

Since it is easiest to maintain an "us/them" polarity if "they" are not present, we think that it is unconscionable to have a discussion of the meaning of Romans 1:26–27 as if gay and lesbian friends are not in the room. Indeed, it is very unlikely that the room will be full of straight people. But we would push this even further. We are not sure that anyone can speak with sensitivity, care, respect, and insight about what Paul may or may not be saying about these matters if they do not have friendships with people who identify themselves as gay. To make any interpretive pronouncements outside of real relationships is in deep tension with the tone and intent of Paul's letter to the Romans as a whole and 1:26–2:1 in particular.[3]

Sadly, so much of the debate around homosexuality in the global church isn't just devoid of real face-to-face conversation and friendship; it is characterized by nothing less than violent repulsion. And Romans 1:26–2:1 should cause us to stop and think more deeply about what is going on. Here's what we need to face up to: those Christians in the world who advocate for the criminalization of homosexuality, and even in some extreme cases the death penalty, are, by the terms of Paul's text, themselves worthy of death. Their malice and slander, together with their heartless and ruthless stance toward gay and lesbian people in the community, are, by the very terms of this text, worthy of death. Why? Because these are death-dealing attitudes and practices. Paul says that people who do such things are worthy of death because the attitudes and practices he is describing here are nothing less than a way of death. While Paul is striving to engender a sense of a common home in Jesus for this community, these attitudes invariably murder community, destroy families, do violence to others, and strip the community of any foundation for a healthy homemaking together. Such a reading beats Paul's

3. Stephen E. Fowl puts it this way: "Christians have no reason to think they understand how the Holy Spirit weighs in on the issue of homosexuality until they welcome homosexuals into their homes and sit down and eat with them." *Engaging Scripture: A Model for Theological Interpretation* (Oxford: Blackwell, 1998), 122. This is true, of course, but reading Fowl twenty years later, we are struck by how anachronistic and perhaps even patronizing this sounds today. His point was radical at the time, but now sounds like it is rooted in an "us/them" dynamic that is alien and offensive to many of us (Fowl included, we assume) in 2018.

homemaking and peacemaking text into a weapon of violence and home-breaking. Again, we need to disarm Romans.

Paul is not spinning abstract, timeless, and objective theological principles in these verses or in the rest of his letter. He is addressing a real community that is deeply divided. And he is seeking to find a way that will allow people across the Judean/gentile divide to see each other as sisters and brothers, to understand that in sin they are equal and in grace they are called to a life of hospitable justice together. And so we stand with a host of other writers and visionaries who call for a generous, gracious, and honest conversation about what Paul is talking about and how it speaks a word of judgment and a word of hope into our sexual lives.[4]

The Church and My Lesbian Friend

Um, can I interrupt?

Of course you can. We were wondering what happened to you.

Well, I guess that I've been waiting for you to address that elephant in the room. I'm really upset and confused about this debate. I'm worried for my church. And while I understand why the issue of sexuality is such a hot issue in the church, I've got to admit that I find so much of the debate to be . . . well, hateful. I get it that people are serious about defending what they believe to be true and biblical, but somehow this defending of the "truth" has become offensive to me and is insensitive and hurtful to a lot of my friends.

So this isn't an abstract issue for you. It's personal.

Yes, it is personal. And while I've got a number of gay friends, there is one person in particular whom I really care about.

Why don't you tell us about your friend.

My friend grew up in an evangelical church in a very committed Christian family.[5] *She attended Christian summer camps when she was growing up, and most of her friends were Christians. When she was fourteen, she started to wonder why she wasn't really*

4. Among many examples, see Wendy VanderWal-Gritter, *Generous Spaciousness: Responding to Gay Christians in the Church* (Grand Rapids: Brazos, 2014); James Brownson, *Bible, Gender, Sexuality: Reframing the Church's Debate on Same-Sex Relationships* (Grand Rapids: Eerdmans, 2013); Justin Lee, *Torn: Rescuing the Gospel from the Gays-versus-Christians Debate* (New York: Jericho Books, 2012); and David Myers and Letha Dawson Scanzoni, *What God Has Joined Together? A Christian Case for Gay Marriage* (San Francisco: HarperSanFrancisco, 2005).

5. This story is a composite of the stories of various people that we know. We have also drawn on the thoughtful and compelling description of the struggle of one evangelical with his gay orientation. See Lee, *Torn*.

attracted to guys. Instead, she had a crush on a girl that she knew. And she knew this was wrong. So she fought against it. She tried to become more interested in guys. As she got older, she went for counseling and tried various therapies to make her interested in guys. She spent years trying to be straight. And of course, all this time she was scared to death of what her parents would say if they found out. She was scared to death of what her church would say if they found out. She lived in fear not only of rejection but of eternal damnation as well.

She was depressed and afraid that sometimes she wondered whether it might not be better to kill herself, but that seemed like a worse sin even than being gay. And she couldn't bring herself to do it.

Finally, she realized that there was no way that she was going to be straight. So she decided to accept the fact that she was gay and try to live a faithful life as a Christian who is gay.

How has that been going for her?

At first, not so well. She decided to tell her parents, and they were surprisingly accepting, as long as she was committed to being celibate. At her church, the few people she told were not so accepting. She was asked to no longer teach Sunday school, and she felt totally weird when she went to the young adult fellowship group. And she was no longer allowed to work at the Christian camp that had been so important to her.[6] *So she didn't really fit into any world that she knew. She didn't fit into the gay club scene, and she didn't fit into her church. Her friends were getting married and having kids, but she was alone. And she was really lonely.*

Then she found a church that welcomed gay and lesbian members. She found a place where she could be at home. She began to teach Sunday school again (her evangelical background had given her a great knowledge of the Bible!) and volunteer in their lunch program for homeless people in the neighborhood. After a year she met another woman there, and eventually they were married. Now they have a little boy. The thing is this: my friend is in a committed, faithful marriage; she is a parent who is raising her son to love Jesus; she is not only active in her church but also a powerful Christian witness in her community. She doesn't seem to be morally degenerate, or an abomination, or even the reason that marriage is being undermined in our society. Deep in my heart, I think that she is actually one of the finest Christians that I know. But at the back of my mind I have those nagging thoughts that this is all wrong.

6. On these dynamics in at least one Christian camp that we have been involved with over the years, see Kristy Woudstra, "One Pioneer and the Fight for LGBTQ Inclusion at a Beloved Summer Camp," *Huffington Post*, March 9, 2017, http://www.huffingtonpost.ca/2017/03/09/one pioneer-camp-gay-inclusion_n_15122628.html.

Why do you think that is?

Well, it's because of what the Bible says. There are texts that explicitly say that my friend's life is wrong.

Clobber Texts

You mean texts like Romans 1:26–27?

Yes, along with a few other passages. You know, the story of Sodom and Gomorrah, the laws prohibiting a man lying with a man, and those two other texts from Paul against homosexuality.[7] *But Romans seems to be the most important because it is the clearest, and it also includes lesbians in the condemnation. That doesn't happen anywhere else.*

Well, let's start with that point. Why do you think that of the six texts that talk about same-sex intercourse, five are only about men? What is it about the culture in which these texts were written that make men the focus?

I guess the fact that they were written two thousand years ago.

So they were written in a patriarchal culture, where sex was embedded with power.

Even in our world male sexuality is deeply rooted in power. You just have to read the news to see that sex is not only used by men as a weapon in war but is increasingly used to humiliate and demean, even at the highest levels of power in our supposedly "equal" society.

This kind of humiliation is at the heart of some of these "clobber texts." For instance, the men of the city of Sodom in Genesis 19 were not gay men looking for a good time. They were men who were interested in humiliating and demeaning the strangers who had come to their town. And the fact that Lot offers up his virgin daughters to them suggests that he knew they weren't looking for gay sex: they were looking for violent and abusive control.

As an aside, have you ever wondered why Lot's despicable offer to send his daughters out to a bunch of gang rapists gets rather less airtime than the issue of homosexuality in our discussions? Why don't the leaders of our churches consider that to be a deeply troublesome part of this story?[8] In Judges 19 we have a similar story where the violence is heightened. There the concubine of the visiting Levite

7. Gen. 19:1–29; Lev. 18:22; 20:13; 1 Cor. 6:9–11; 1 Tim. 1:10.

8. Holly Joan Toensing notes that "given the gendered notions of appropriate and inappropriate uses of bodies, the message is more likely 'It's better to rape these females than these males.'" Holly Joan Toensing, "Women of Sodom and Gomorrah: Collateral Damage in the War against Homosexuality?," *Journal of Feminist Studies in Religion* 21, no. 2 (2005): 71.

is pushed out to satisfy the violent demands of the men of the city. She is gang raped all night long and dumped on the doorstep in the morning in an act of derision: if you come to our town, here is what will happen to your possessions. Clearly these were not men looking for other men to satisfy their sexual desire; they were men looking to engage in an act of violent humiliation. That story escalates into more and more violence, particularly against women. You can read the disturbing tale in Judges 19–21.

In the story of Sodom, Abraham had just engaged in a desperate process of negotiation for the salvation of the city. After the angel-men visitors tell Abraham the good news of a son to be born to barren Sarah, God tells him of the destruction about to fall on Sodom for its grave sin. And that is when the amazing bargaining session between Abraham and God begins. "What if there were fifty righteous people in the city?" Abraham asks. "Would you spare the city on behalf of those fifty?" God takes the bait. "Yes, for fifty, I'll spare the city." But this is only the beginning of the negotiations. Abraham pushes it further: from forty-five to forty to thirty to twenty and finally to ten righteous people. If there were only ten righteous people, would God spare the city? Yes, but that is as low as Abraham dares to press the bargain.[9]

The angel-men go to Sodom to see if they might find those ten righteous people. They are welcomed into the home of Lot, and then the trouble begins. The men of the city, perhaps already distrustful of the newcomer Lot and his family, want to "know" these visitors more intimately. The rest of the violent story then unfolds. There are no such ten righteous people in Sodom.

Are you saying that the story of Sodom isn't really about homosexuality?

Right. It is about shaming the stranger through gang rape and violence. Interestingly enough, when later biblical passages talk about Sodom, they never mention homosexuality. Here is what Ezekiel says about Sodom: "This was the guilt of your sister Sodom: she and her daughters had pride, excess of food, and prosperous ease, but did not aid the poor and needy" (Ezek. 16:49).[10] It is pretty hard to help the poor and needy if your attitude toward strangers is a violent one. And, as we have seen in chapter 6, pride, affluence, and well-fed stomachs are often combined with injustice and violence.

9. Gen. 18:22–33. Whether God would have gone lower if Abraham had the audacity to ask is an open question.

10. The two times that Jesus is recorded mentioning Sodom, they are both in the context of the sin of inhospitality to strangers, with no reference to homosexuality at all. See Matt. 10:14–15; Luke 10:10–12.

In Jude 7 Sodom and Gomorrah are condemned for sexual immorality and going after other flesh—a good description of gang rape. In fact, the use of *sarkos heteras* in Jude 7 emphasizes that this is different flesh, not defined by sameness. Some suggest this may refer to the angelic flesh of the visitors or to the fact that they were strangers.[11] At any rate, homosexuality does not seem to be in the sights of Jude either.

Okay, well none of this applies to my friend. Not only would she never engage in any kind of sexual violence; she also shows a gracious hospitality in her life, especially with our poorest neighbors. She's the opposite of that gang in Sodom. But what about those other passages? Doesn't Paul explicitly name homosexuals as excluded from the kingdom of God?

No. Some *translators* have excluded "homosexuals" from the kingdom of God, not Paul. A lot of ink has been spilled over what Paul means in 1 Corinthians 6:9–10 and 1 Timothy 1:9–10, and we don't want to let this discussion take us too far from his letter to the Romans, but a couple brief comments might be helpful. Essentially the issue is how to translate two Greek words: *malakoi* (in 1 Cor. 6:9) and *arsenokoitai* (in both passages). A cursory glance at various English translations will show that there is no universal agreement on the translation of these words but that they are individually and sometimes together often translated with reference to homosexuality.[12] The NRSV translation of these words in 1 Corinthians 6:9–10 can be representative for this discussion: "Do not be deceived! Fornicators, idolaters, adulterers, male prostitutes [*malakoi*], sodomites [*arsenokoitai*] . . . none of these will inherit the kingdom of God." While the translation of *malakoi* as "male prostitutes" has some merit, the use of the English word *sodomite* is deeply problematic. The root of the word is, of course, Sodom, but the meaning that it has in English is "one who engages in anal sex." It is clear from our discussion above that the central sin of Sodom wasn't anal sex per se but gang rape and the transgression of the sacred requirements of hospitality. By using the ill-conceived English term *sodomy*, the translators end up stacking the translation against homosexuality.

Then what do these two terms mean?

It isn't easy to say. *Malakoi* carries with it a sense of someone who is soft, lazy, self-indulgent, and given to decadent living. That much is pretty clear from any lexicon. *Arsenokoitai* seems to be a word coined by the apostle that brings together

11. James E. Miller, "A Response to Robert Gagnon on 'The Old Testament and Homosexuality,'" *Zeitschrift für die Altentestamentliche Wissenschaft* 119 (2007): 88. Miller also cites rabbinic references that interpreted the sin of Sodom as injustice and abuse of the poor and stranger.

12. Myers and Scanzoni offer a helpful chart, "Table 1. Variations in Translation among Bible Versions," for various renderings of these words. Myers and Scanzoni, *What God Has Joined Together*, 96.

the unusual combination of the words for "male" (*arsēn*) and "bed" (*koitē*). Since the same words appear in the Greek translation of Leviticus 18:22 ("You shall not lie with a man as with a woman; it is an abomination"), might Paul have simply put them together into a new compound word?

So wouldn't that be a clear reference to homosexuality?

Well, it is a clear reference to some sort of homoerotic act. The question is, what kind? Indeed, this question will be central to our discussion of Romans 1:26–27. There seems to be scholarly consensus that the Leviticus text is referring to cultic prostitution.[13]

So what does Paul mean by these terms in Corinthians and Timothy?

While there is no way to be totally certain, we think that both the historical context and the combination of *arsenokoitai* with *malakoi* in the 1 Corinthians reference suggest that Paul is talking about some form of pederasty here, some form of sexual predation on prepubescent boys. The *malakoi*, the "soft ones," are likely the boys who were used for sexual pleasure by the *arsenokoitai*.[14] So translating *malakoi* as "male prostitute" might have some merit, though not all these boys were paid for their services. But if they *were* male prostitutes, then this gives an even more disturbing overtone to the meaning of *arsenokoitai*. In 1 Timothy 1:10 *arsenokoitai* appears in a list between "fornicators" and "slave traders" (NRSV), or "whoremongers" and "men stealers" (RSV), suggesting that these are men who delight in unbridled sexuality and will even stoop to enslaving little boys into prostitution to fulfill their desires while also filling their pocketbooks.

So these texts don't seem to apply to my friend either.

Not at all.

Sex in the Empire (Rom. 1:26–27)

But things seem different when we get back to Romans. "For this reason God gave them up to degrading passions. Their women exchanged natural intercourse for unnatural, and in the same way also the men, giving up natural intercourse with women, were

13. Even those on the conservative side of the debate acknowledge that temple prostitution is the likely context for the Levitical decrees. See Robert Gagnon, *The Bible and Homosexual Practice: Texts and Hermeneutics* (Nashville: Abingdon, 2001), 130.

14. Cf. Victor Paul Furnish, "The Bible and Homosexuality: Reading the Texts in Context," in *Homosexuality in the Church: Both Sides of the Debate*, ed. Jeffrey S. Siker (Louisville: Westminster John Knox, 1994), 24; and Richard B. Hays, *First Corinthians*, Interpretation (Louisville: Westminster John Knox, 1997), 97.

consumed with passion for one another" (*1:26–27a*)*. That's the passage that I struggle with in relation to my friend. It seems to me to be very clear.*

Perhaps we need to start where we start with any other interpretation of the Bible: with the differences between our context and the context in which the text was written. For instance, when we talk about the clear depictions of tax collectors as sinners in the gospel accounts, we put that in its context. We describe how tax collectors collaborated with the occupying Roman forces and how those taxes impoverished the people of Galilee and Judea. If we are doing responsible reading, we are careful to distinguish those tax collectors from the people today who work for Revenue Canada or the Internal Revenue Service in the United States. This attention to context and the difference between ancient and contemporary context is part of the task of interpretation.

So we need to ask whether what we're talking about is the same as what Paul was talking about. Right?

Yes.

Then maybe the question is whether something like same-sex orientation would ever have arisen in the ancient world. Was this something that would have made sense in biblical times?

In biblical times the idea of same-sex orientation would not have made any sense. The assumption was that men were attracted to women and vice versa. This was considered the natural order of things. The idea of having a sexual orientation toward people of the same sex was unknown because any notion of sexual orientation was unknown.[15] That doesn't mean that there wasn't homoerotic sex going on. Temple prostitution was a common place for that. In the Roman world, the world of Paul, the sexual abuse of boys, slaves, and freedmen was widespread and accepted.

But haven't some people argued that same-sex orientation was known in Paul's time? I've heard of appeals to Plato and to some Roman satirists that say committed gay relationships were known of and approved.[16]

The examples given don't really fit the argument. Sometimes Plato, Xenophon, and Aristotle are referred to, but it is hard to base an argument on Roman practice in the first century using documents written by Greek writers a full four

15. Though Hays takes a more conservative view on these matters than we do, he nonetheless acknowledges that "neither Paul nor anyone else in antiquity had a concept of 'sexual orientation.'" Hays, *Moral Vision*, 388.

16. Cf. Mark D. Smith, "Ancient Bisexuality and the Interpretation of Romans 1:26–27," *Journal of the American Academy of Religion* 64, no. 2 (1996): 223–56. N. T. Wright makes a similar appeal to Plato in *Romans, Part 1: Chapter 1–8*, Paul for Everyone (Louisville: Westminster John Knox, 2004), 22.

centuries before Paul.[17] Martial, a satirist who was Paul's contemporary, wrote witty epigrams in which it is clear that pederasty was both well accepted and common among his audience. Indeed, he refers to pederasty as often as heterosexuality in his epigrams. Homoeroticism makes infrequent appearances in his poems and invariably in a negative light. "There is no ambiguity in sexual ethics for Martial and his buying public, for pederasty is merely another aspect of social life but homosexuality between adult males is an aberration, the butt of humor and scorn."[18] Now here's the curious thing: while sex between consenting adult men was not culturally acceptable in Paul's time, pederasty was.[19]

So if Paul wasn't talking about homosexual orientation, what was he talking about? What were the contexts in which same-sex intercourse would have occurred?

Maybe we should answer that by remembering the context of Romans 1. We have discussed at some length the imperial context of this letter written to Christians who lived at the heart of the Roman Empire. They were surrounded by the stories, lifestyle, imagery, and symbols of the empire. At the outset of his letter Paul quotes from Habakkuk 2:4: the righteous will live by faith (or faithfulness). As we have seen, this insight comes to Habakkuk in the midst of a rhetorical attack on the imperial idolatry of the Chaldeans. It is not surprising that Paul's thought in the first chapter of his epistle similarly moves to a critique of the idolatry and injustice of the empire in which he finds himself. As part of that critique, Paul argues that idolatry leads to a certain kind of violent consumption that results in an abusive sexuality and an economics of greed rooted in deceit and unfaithfulness.

17. James E. Miller, "Response: Pederasty and Romans 1:27; A Response to Mark Smith," *Journal of the American Academy of Religion* 65, no. 4 (1997): 861.

18. Miller, "Response: Pederasty and Romans 1:27," 862.

19. Miller, "Response: Pederasty and Romans 1:27," 863. Miller appeals to Amy Richler for corroborating evidence in Amy Richler, *The Garden of Priapus* (Oxford: Oxford University Press, 1992), 220–26. Miller also helpfully outlines the ways in which sexual assumptions differ between our time and the first century:

> In the Roman empire pederasty was accepted, and homosexuality between adults of either sex was despised. Today pederasty is clearly the more despised practice of the two. In the Roman Empire anal intercourse (pederastic or heterosexual) was considered relatively normal, and oral intercourse was under a great stigma (Richlin: 25–26, 69), where today the situation is largely reversed. In our culture marital fidelity is usually considered reciprocal, but in the Roman Empire it certainly was not, among Jews as well as Gentiles. Then the male was relatively free, but the female restricted. Also in the Roman Empire slaves of either gender were considered the sexual property of their master . . . , a situation that is illegal, unethical, and relatively rare in our culture since the abolition of slavery in the nineteenth-century. ("Pederasty and Romans 1:27," 864)

Regarding slavery and Roman sexual practices, Miller references Moses I. Finley, *Ancient Slavery and Modern Ideology* (New York: Viking, 1980), 95–96; and Eva Cantarella, *Bisexuality in the Ancient World* (New Haven: Yale University Press, 1992), 101–4.

We have also argued that, from the salutation on, Paul is engaging in a counter-imperial rhetoric. N. T. Wright comments that "the whole introduction of the letter contains so many apparently counter-imperial signals that I find it impossible to doubt that both Paul and his first hearers and readers—in Rome, of all places!—would have picked up the message loud and clear."[20] In the last three chapters we have argued that the list of vices in Romans 1:28–32 is an extension of Paul's counter-imperial perspective right into the political and economic life of Rome. It would only stand to reason, then, that there is something imperial about the sexuality that Paul is addressing in 1:26–27.

In what way?

Let's begin by remembering that this critique of the empire is rooted in Paul's understanding of idolatry. Precisely because they exchanged the glory of the immortal God for images resembling a mortal human being (read: Caesar) or other creatures (read: all the gods of Rome and Greece) (Rom. 1:23), "God gave them up in the lusts of their hearts to impurity, to the degrading of their bodies among themselves" (1:24). Because in idolatry they abandoned their call to bear God's image in faithfulness, "God gave them up to degrading passions" (1:26); "God gave them up to a debased mind and to things that should not be done" (1:28).[21]

Also, it is important to note that this passage begins with a contrast. We read Romans 1:17 as saying that the justice of God is revealed through the covenantal faithfulness of the Messiah and calls forth our faithfulness in response, because those who are just will live by faithfulness. Then, contrasting the faithfulness of the just with idolatrous injustice, Paul declares, "For the wrath of God is revealed from heaven against all ungodliness [impiety] and injustice of those who by their injustice suppress the truth" (1:18 NRSV alt.). This wrath "is revealed." There is an assumption here that anyone with eyes to see can see God's wrath already manifest in the midst of the idolatrous lives of those who practice injustice. Anyone can see where all of this leads. Anyone can see that God has "given them up" to the distorted sexuality of degraded passions (1:26–27). And anyone can see

20. N. T. Wright, *Paul in Fresh Perspective* (Minneapolis: Fortress, 2005), 76.

21. N. T. Wright detects here a consistent echo to Ps. 81:11–12. Writing of Israel's stubborn penchant for idolatry, the psalmist writes,

> But my people did not listen to my voice;
>   Israel would not submit to me.
> So I gave them over to their stubborn hearts,
>   to follow their own counsels.

Wright comments, "Thus, again, Paul's surface text describes paganism, but the subtext quietly includes Israel in the indictment." "The Letter to the Romans: Introduction, Commentary, and Reflections," in *The New Interpreter's Bible*, vol. 10 (Nashville: Abingdon, 2002), 433.

that God has "given them up" to a debased mind and a life that is characterized by injustice, covetousness, murder, deceit, invention of evil, rebellion toward parents, and ruthlessness, to name only some of the vices in Paul's list (1:28–32).

Paul assumes that anyone *can see* and *has seen* that idolatry and ingratitude to God will invariably descend into sexual debauchery and an unrestrained ruthlessness and violence in everyday life! But *where* would Paul's readers have seen such a clear and pervasive outworking of the wrath of God? Where would they see people whom God has "given up" to the excesses of insatiable sexuality, together with the kind of violent injustice that he here depicts? Neil Elliott answers: in this depiction of degraded humanity, "Paul intends his hearers to recognize definite allusions to none other than *the Caesars themselves.*" Elliott continues, "No others could serve Paul's argument so effectively by offering, in their own persons, a fitting lesson on the inevitability with which divine punishment follows horrendous crimes." Indeed, "we can read every phrase in this passage as an accurate catalog of misdeeds of one or another recent member of the Julio-Claudian dynasty."[22] Given the counter-imperial rhetoric of the whole opening chapter of Paul's epistle, it should come as no surprise that Paul has the imperial household in view in this depiction of what he will later call "the wages of sin" (6:23).

When you say "the Roman imperial household," do you mean that Paul is referring to some of those crazy emperors like Caligula and Claudius and Nero?

Well, what do you know about those emperors?

Not all that much, really. But the popular history that I've read and seen shows them all as devious, power-hungry crazies.

That about sums it up. Caligula (37–41 CE), also known as Gaius, had his predecessor (Tiberius) murdered and then shortly into his reign declared himself a god. He was ruthless in how he treated anyone whom he perceived to be a threat, executing or forcing suicide on countless people during his reign. In his narrative on the life of Caligula, Suetonius writes of his extravagances, not least in matters of sexuality. Boasting of incest with his sisters, he was a known sexual predator, raping "almost every woman of rank in Rome," even a bride on her wedding day.[23] He would also take female guests from a dinner party, rape them in another room, and then return to comment on their performance. Suetonius also writes of Caligula's sexual escapades with various men, acting as both the passive and active partner. James Brownson writes, "Finally, a military officer

22. Neil Elliott, *The Arrogance of Nations: Reading Romans in the Shadow of Empire* (Minneapolis: Fortress, 2008), 79, 82.

23. Suetonius, *Gaius* 36. Cited in Elliott, *Arrogance of Nations*, 80.

whom he had sexually humiliated joined a conspiracy to murder him, which they did less than four years into his reign. Suetonius records that Gaius [Caligula] was stabbed through the genitals when he was murdered. One wonders whether we can hear an echo of this gruesome story in Paul's comments in Romans 1:27: 'Men committed shameless acts with men and received in their own person the due penalty for their error.'"[24]

When Caligula was succeeded by Claudius (41–54 CE), things didn't get much better, especially in terms of a rule of extreme violence from which members of his own family were not exempt. As we have seen from the story of Caligula, those who live by violence and deceit invariably breed a violence and deceit that rebounds on themselves. Claudius was poisoned by his wife Agrippina so that her son, Nero, could become emperor (54–69 CE).

Wasn't Nero the emperor when Paul was writing to the Romans?

Yes. Paul wrote his letter to the Romans during the early years of Nero's reign. Standing in the ignoble tradition of the caesars before him, Nero both raped his younger brother, Britannicus, and, offended by a joke and worried about the possible threat that the boy might pose to his rule, had him murdered within months of Nero's ascension to the throne.[25] His own mother, Agrippina, would come to a similar fate some years later. And the decadent debauchery of his later years was already in evidence in the youthful excesses of the young emperor. Wandering the streets with a gang of youths (and at times a security detail at a discreet distance), Nero would look for violent fun and unrestricted pleasure, which included beating, stealing from, and sexually molesting passersby. Like Caligula before him, Nero was notorious for his riotous parties, often in the open for all to see. Indeed, it seemed that everywhere he went, there was a party complete with both promiscuous and humiliating sexual acts. In one case, the spectacle ends when Nero is sexually mastered by a man that he has "married."[26]

A man that he has "married"? This brings us back to homosexuality. Isn't this exactly what Paul is getting at when he talks about men committing "shameless acts with men"?

Well, no. Paul is condemning the sexual violence and excess that Nero and the other emperors engaged in, including the deliberate use of oral and anal sex to overturn the "natural order" of things and to deliberately demean someone.

24. Brownson, *Bible, Gender, Sexuality*, 13.

25. Edward Champlin, *Nero* (Cambridge, MA: Harvard University Press, 2003), 165 (rape) and 151 (murder).

26. Champlin, *Nero*, 160.

This is getting a little embarrassing, but I've got to ask. It takes two to perform either oral or anal sex acts, but it was only demeaning for one of them?

Yes, that is correct. To penetrate another person anally or to have someone else perform oral sex on you was to be in a position of superiority over that person. To flip it around, as it were, is to be submissive, either receiving an aggressive sexual penetration or performing the embarrassing act of oral sex. Such submission was seen as humiliating.

Okay, but even with those qualifications, this whole story is still about homosexuality, and that is precisely what Paul is attacking in this passage, right?

That depends. What do you mean by "homosexuality"?

Well, someone like my friend who is attracted to other women. She is a homosexual, or a lesbian, because she can only find fulfillment in an intimate relationship with someone of her own gender.

And that is *not* what Paul is talking about. As we have argued above, Paul would have had no idea of anything like a homosexual orientation. In ancient Roman understandings of sexuality, there was sexual desire and that desire could take on any of a number of expressions, but what we today understand to be a sexual "orientation" was simply unheard of. The ancient world "did not conceive of what we today call homosexual orientation, a natural erotic preference for others of the same gender, as distinct from heterosexual orientation."[27] Various kinds of homoerotic practices there surely were, but nothing that clearly parallels what we are talking about with the term *homosexual*.

But Nero was "married" to this other man. So this was a homosexual marriage, right?

No. Nero had a number of liaisons that he called "marriages" happening at the same time. Two were with men, but it is clear that these are not matters of homosexual marriage per se, nor can they be used to argue that homosexual marriage was known at the time of Paul.[28] The first was a form of street theater intended to

27. Elliott, *Arrogance of Nations*, 78. Noting that "scholars of ancient sexuality have been emphasizing for more than twenty years that modern categories of sexuality [especially *homosexuality*] do not match those of the ancient world," Sandra Boehringer argues that we should not "look back to the ancient world for a category that has existed for scarcely more than one hundred and twenty years." Sandra Boehringer, "Female Homoeroticism," in *A Companion to Greek and Roman Sexualities*, ed. Thomas K. Hubbard (Oxford: Blackwell, 2015), 150. Contra Bernadette Brooten, *Love between Women: Early Christian Responses to Female Homoeroticism* (Chicago: University of Chicago Press, 1996).

28. Contra Wright, *Romans, Part 1*, 22. Thomas K. Hubbard's essay "Peer Homosexuality" makes no reference to homosexual marriage in either ancient Greek or Roman culture (Hubbard, *Greek and Roman Sexualities*, 128–49). Indeed, every reference to marriage in this important collection of essays assumes a heterosexual union in which procreation is crucial.

shock by overturning expectations, and the second was a replacement for Nero's lamented late wife.[29] In this case, he looked first for a woman to take her place, but none resembled her sufficiently, so he settled for a castrated boy instead. Even this act of castration suggests he doesn't want a man; he wants a woman.

So when Paul described men who "committed shameless acts with men and received in their own persons the due penalty for their error," people in Rome would not have thought of any kind of homosexual marriage, but of the kinds of unequal and oppressive sexual behavior witnessed in pederasty, and the homoerotic excesses seen in the imperial household during their own time. Take a look at Nero's court! Look at how he flaunts in public his sexual degradations! Look at this out-of-control sexual licentiousness!

But they didn't have to look even that far. As our story of Iris illustrates, the exploitive sexuality of the imperial rulers was mirrored in the exploitive sexuality of the regular household, where the paterfamilias, the master, had sexual rights over not only his wife but also all of his slaves, both male and female.[30] Moreover, when a dinner party was held, the slaves of the household were made sexually available for the dinner guests—this was part of their duties. It was also the case that masters often sexually used both their female and their male slaves; and occasionally their male slaves were made to dress like women, for the sexual enjoyment of their dinner guests. In short, this was a society where sexual abuse of boys and slaves of both genders was widespread and usual.

When Paul wrote in Romans 1:27 about men giving up natural relations with women and committing shameless acts with men, this is what his hearers would have thought of. Nothing even remotely like a homosexual orientation or a committed same-sex relationship would have been in Paul's mind.

Well, that does make sense in relation to verse 27, but what about verse 26? You are talking about men who are acting in abusive ways to their wives, slaves, and little boys, but what about Paul's comments about women acting in ways that are against nature? The pattern of Roman society was that men had these rights to the bodies of others, not that women had these rights.

Jeramy Townsley has convincingly argued that these verses reflect the idolatrous sexual practices of the goddess religions, where women would engage in

29. On both of these "marriages," see Champlin, *Nero*, 167. It should also be noted that both of these incidents took place *after* the time of Paul's letter to the Romans.

30. See Margaret Y. MacDonald, "Slavery, Sexuality, and House Churches: A Reassessment of Colossians 3.18–4.1 in Light of New Research on the Roman Family," *New Testament Studies* 53 (2007): 94–113.

oral or anal sex with men and castrated male priests would be available for anal penetration.[31] All of these acts were considered to be "against nature."[32]

When you say "goddess religions," do you mean goddesses like Artemis? I seem to recall that there was a conflict between Paul and the priests of the Artemis temple in Ephesus.[33]

Artemis, Cybele/Attis, Aphrodite/Venus, Demeter, and Astarte: all of these goddesses had temples in most large cities where Paul grew up and traveled. And it is clear from Acts 19 that Paul's preaching was seen to be in such conflict with the religious practices and worship of the goddess Artemis that a riot broke out. There were a few different goddess religions that the early Christians were in conflict with, and the language of Romans 1:26 points to those contexts as well. Rather than a reference to lesbianism, which was rarely described in the ancient world, and usually in satire, the context of temple prostitution was widespread and widely known in Rome, and it was vehemently opposed by the church fathers for centuries.[34]

Let me be very clear here. Are you saying that when Paul describes women acting against nature, he isn't referring to women having sex with women but rather to women engaging in acts that are "against nature" with men?

Exactly. And in the ancient world the language of "against nature" is used for a whole host of sexual acts that women and men do with each other. Although it *can* refer to men who not only have intercourse with women but also abuse boys and other men,[35] the very first references to Romans 1:26 in the patristic

31. Jeramy Townsley, "Paul, the Goddess Religion, Queer Sects," *Journal of Biblical* Literature 130, no. 4 (2011): 707–28.

32. To get a sense of how culturally particular notions of "against nature" are, consider two things. First, in 1 Cor. 11:14 the apostle argues that it is "against nature" for men to have long hair and women to have short hair. Very few Christian communities today believe that this argument from nature is binding on Christians' hair lengths. Second and more shocking is that in the ancient world performing oral sex or receiving anal sex was considered to be against nature, but the institution of pederasty was not. Being used as a boy sexual partner was a necessity in the life of a slave and a duty to a young freedman. Today, while some Christians might think that anal sex is "against nature," few would have the same repulsion to oral sex. We would assume, however, that all Christians consider pedophilia to be a grave crime.

33. Acts 19:21–41.

34. Jeramy Townsley, "Queer Sects in Patristic Commentaries on Romans 1:26–27: Goddess Cults, Free Will, and 'Sex Contrary to Nature?,'" *Journal of the American Academy of Religion* 81, no. 1 (2013): 58–61. Miller lists eight references to female sexuality in classical sources, some of which emphasize women who take on the attributes of a male. In two instances female homosexuality is discussed in the context of a violation of adultery laws. James E. Miller, "The Practices of Rom. 1:26: Homosexual or Heterosexual?," *Novum Testamentum* 37, no. 1 (1995): 5.

35. Hays, *Moral Vision*, 387, rather disingenuously indicates that *para physin* (against nature) "is very frequently used (in the absence of convenient Greek words for 'heterosexual' and 'homosexual') as a way of distinguishing between heterosexual and homosexual behavior." A look

literature show that the church fathers didn't interpret this verse as referring to same-sex intercourse.[36] They interpreted it as referring to the goddess religions.[37] It wasn't until the late fourth century that this verse was first interpreted as referring to same-sex relations between women, and when that interpretation was introduced, it had to be argued for.[38]

Creation, God, and Sex

That's pretty significant. If some of the earliest interpreters of this letter didn't think that it referred to same-sex acts between women, it is unlikely that Paul's audience did either. But what about the way in which the whole passage, including the attack on idolatry, is rooted in creation? Doesn't this show that Paul is criticizing homosexuality because it breaks the creation order of marriage as the relationship between a man and a woman?[39]

Let's look closely at what Paul says and does not say about creation. "For the wrath of God is revealed from heaven against all ungodliness and injustice of those who by their injustice suppress the truth. For what can be known about God is plain to them, because God has shown it to them. Ever since the creation

at his endnotes (p. 405), however, indicates that his references (Dio Chrysostom, *Discourse* 7.135, 151–52; Plutarch, *Dialogue on Love*, 751C, E; Josephus, *Against Apion* 2.199; Philo, *On the Special Laws* 3.37–43; *On the Life of Abraham* 133–41) are referring to those with unnatural lusts, who indulge themselves with both men and women. In some cases, certain pederastic practices are in view. While it is clear that *para physin* could be used to portray a wide variety of sexual practices, both heterosexual and homoerotic, that were condemned at this time, it is quite the stretch to suggest that the term refers to "homosexual" behavior per se. Both Ambrosiaster and Augustine use "against nature" to refer to sexual relations between a man and a woman. This would have included anal and possibly oral sex. Theodore de Bruyn, "Ambrosiaster's Interpretation of Romans 1:26–27," *Vigiliae Christianae* 65 (2001): 469, 472. See also Miller, "Practices of Rom. 1:26," 8–11, on unnatural heterosexual intercourse in the classical sources.

36. De Bruyn, "Ambrosiaster's Interpretation," 468–69.

37. According to Townsley, "Queer Sects in Patristic Commentaries," 58–60, both Rom. 1:26 and 1:27 were seen as referring to the goddess cults. The church fathers he cites are Hippolytus in *Refutation of All Heresies* 5.2 (222–235 CE), Athanasius in *Against the Pagans* (335–337 CE; referring to cult prostitution by women and male castration), Chrysostom's *Homily on Romans* (early 390s CE in Antioch, where Townsley notes that the Greek used, *arrenōn mania*, is often translated as "homosexuality," although the same language occurs in Chrysostom's commentary on Ps. 115 to refer to the sexual rituals of the Roman festivals to the gods). Temple prostitution and male castration were in Chrysostom's sights as well. Pelagius, in his *Commentary on Romans*, takes "the degrading of their bodies" to refer to the ritual use of brands and burns (p. 63). Idolatry is also in the sights of Origen (pp. 67 and 68).

38. De Bruyn, "Ambrosiaster's Interpretation," 469–70, 477–77.

39. E.g., Hays, *Moral Vision*, 388; and Wright, *Romans, Part 1*, 20–22; Wright, "Letter to the Romans," 433–34.

of the world his eternal power and divine nature, invisible though they are, have been understood and seen through the things he has made" (Rom. 1:18–20 NRSV alt.).

Let's begin by noting that the truth that is being suppressed here is not a truth about creation, or even a truth about humanity, and certainly not a truth about male/female complementarity. The truth is the truth about *God* that has been revealed *through* creation. The emphasis here is on God, not on creation order or even the creation narratives.[40] And the apostle keeps the emphasis on God as he continues: "Though they knew God, they did not honor him as God" (1:21); "they exchanged the glory of the immortal God for images" (1:23); "they exchanged the truth about God for a lie and worshiped and served the creature rather than the Creator" (1:25). Idolatry is what happens when humans who are created in the image of God refuse to image that Creator, and idolatry bears the bad fruit that Paul is about to describe, beginning with human sexual life but then proceeding to vices that tear apart the fabric of social and economic life through their promotion of injustice (1:28–32).

So then, if what is being suppressed here is what we know about God from creation, then we need to ask what that means. What does Paul say can be known about God through creation, through the things that God has made?

Um, his eternal power and divine nature?

And how are these things relevant to human sexuality?

I guess that because we know something of God's nature and because we are created in the image of God, then our lives should reflect that nature.

And is there a male/female binary in the nature of God?

I've never thought about that. Paul doesn't say that there is in this passage.

Then we need to think more deeply about the nature of God as we meet this God through creation. If we seek a biblical background to what Paul is getting at here, we will find more fruitful literary allusions in the Psalms than in Genesis 1–3.[41] Doesn't Psalm 19:1–4 proclaim that creation is revelatory? Doesn't this psalm's reference to a voice being heard where there is no voice, to words pouring forth where there are no words, have a striking resemblance to Paul's notion of

40. Commenting on Rom. 1:18–32, Joseph A. Fitzmyer argues, "The alleged echoes of the Adam stories in Genesis are simply nonexistent." *Romans*, Anchor Bible Commentary (New York: Doubleday, 1992), 274.

41. While Wright argues that Gen. 1–3 lies behind Rom. 1:18–32, especially 1:26–27 (*Romans, Part 1*, 21; "Letter to the Romans," 433–34), he also notes that Paul evokes Ps. 71 in Rom. 1:16 and that Rom. 1:24–27 clearly echoes Ps. 81:12. See Wright, "Letter to the Romans," 424, 433.

that which is invisible being seen (Rom. 1:20)?[42] And doesn't the psalmist confess that creation is eloquent, proclaiming the very glory of God that Paul says is exchanged in idolatry (1:23)?[43] And what is that glory? What does creation reveal about the divine nature? Consider Psalm 33:4–5:

> For the word of the Lord is upright,
> and all his work is done in faithfulness.
> He loves righteousness and justice;
> the earth is full of the steadfast love of the LORD.[44]

The earth is full of the covenantal love of the Creator. Creation is saturated by and overflows in that love. The very "word" through which "the heavens were made" (33:6), through which "all the earth . . . came to be . . . and . . . stood firm" (33:8–9), is an upright word, and the creation that it has wrought bears witness to the Creator's righteousness and justice. Indeed, the very justice of God that is revealed in the gospel (Rom. 1:16) is an echo of the justice to which all creation is an eloquent witness. Moreover, Psalm 98, which Paul echoes in Romans 1:16–17, describes not only the salvation, justice, and truthfulness of God (Ps. 98:2–3) but also the way in which the seas and the sea creatures, the earth and the creatures who live there, the floods and the hills rejoice in God's justice and salvation (98:7–8).[45] No wonder Paul says that such a creationally revealed truth about God is repressed through injustice.

In Psalm 145 we meet one of the most common refrains in the Hebrew Scriptures that describe God:

> The Lord is gracious and merciful,
> slow to anger and abounding in steadfast love. (v. 8)

42. Fitzmyer, *Romans*, 280. Cf. Wis. 13:1–9; Job 12:7–12. The revelatory power of creation is, of course, also a central theme in Wisdom literature. "For the wise, God is known most basically in and through the experience of creation. That is, wisdom is so built into the infrastructure of the creation that God's character and purposes for the world can be reasonably, if not fully, discernible to human probing and reflection." Terence E. Fretheim, *God and the World in the Old Testament: A Relational Theology of Creation* (Nashville: Abingdon, 2005), 219.

43. Note that Paul references this very psalm in Rom. 1:18.

44. Cf. Pss. 119:64; 136:4–9. Parallel to the revelatory character of creation is creation's praise, bearing witness and in response to God's justice, righteousness, and truth. Cf. Pss. 96; 98.

45. Sylvia Keesmaat, "The Psalms in Romans and Galatians," in *The Psalms in the New Testament*, ed. Steve Moyise and Maarten J. Menken (New York: T&T Clark, 2004), 142–43. Keesmaat also notes that Ps. 106:20 is echoed in Rom. 1:23.

This is the divine nature: gracious, merciful, and overflowing in steadfast love. And in the imagination of the psalmist, this steadfast love permeates all of creation:

> The Lord is good to all,
> and his compassion is over all that he has made.
> All your works shall give thanks to you, O Lord,
> and all your faithful shall bless you. (vv. 9–10)

Notice the repetition of "all." The Lord is good to *all*, his compassion is over *all that he has made*, *all your works* give thanks, and *all your faithful* shall bless you. Not only is all of creation saturated with the love of God, so also, the psalmist confesses, compassion goes all the way down. As all creation looks to God for "their food in due season" (v. 15), God opens his hands, "satisfying the desire of *every living thing*" (v. 16), and that is why the psalmist sings:

> The Lord is just in all his ways,
> and kind in all his doings.
> The Lord is near to all who call on him,
> to all who call on him in truth. (vv. 17–18)

"Ever since the creation of the world," wrote Paul, God's "eternal power and divine nature . . . have been understood and seen through the things he has made" (Rom. 1:20). And it is clear from the poetry of Israel that the creation reveals the divine nature to be characterized by faithfulness, justice, and covenantal love. And this, it would seem, is what humanity is blind to in their idolatry. By rooting his lament about idolatry in the context of what creation reveals about God, Paul is not making a point about the creational normativity of heterosexuality. Rather, he is alluding to the most foundational criteria by which imperial sexuality will be judged in 1:26–27. Paul is attacking erotic practices that transgress what is known about God from the very creation of the world, not what is known about human gender identity and reproduction. Sexual lives that are steeped in infidelity, injustice, and insatiable consumption are brought under judgment because they fall so short of our calling to image God in faithfulness, justice, and love.

That's exactly what I see in my friend's marriage. Faithfulness, justice, and love!

Yes, and if Paul's point here is not concerned with heteronormativity per se but with the calling to image God in every aspect of our lives, including our sexual lives, then it seems to us that we have a strong biblical foundation for affirming same-sex marriage. If the fundamental criteria are faithfulness, justice, and covenantal love, then we can responsibly affirm and encourage monogamous same-sex marriage as not just faithful to the covenantal story in which we live but also more deeply, faithful to the very character of God as revealed for all to see in creation. It is this Creator God whom we are called to image in all of our lives, not least in our sexuality.[46] When we exchange our glory as God's image bearers and follow graven images, it is impossible for us to image the God of faithfulness, justice, and love in our sexual lives, regardless of our sexual orientation. And at least some of the idolatrous rituals that Paul knew of were directly connected to the sexual degradation that he is attacking.

But there's more. Insofar as cultural liturgy shapes wider society,[47] the exploitive sexual rituals found in various religious contexts would have been reflected in the practices of the household. What people learn in liturgy, they practice in the home. And so we see a violent and predatory sexuality of exploitation and consumption practiced not just in the imperial household but throughout all of Roman society. The sexual exploitation of women, slaves (of either gender), boys, and temple prostitutes is legitimated by the cultic practices of the empire. Combine that with a hierarchical social structure and the public example of the emperor and the aristocratic classes, and it is not surprising that the degradation of human sexuality is rampant throughout the body politic.

So you aren't just talking about certain acts that were abusive and exploitive, but about a whole worldview that legitimated abusive sexual practices?

Yes, and as we have seen in the lives of the caesars, in the list of vices in 1:28–31, and in Israel's prophets, degrading and violent sexuality is always linked to an exploitive and predatory economics. Just as Iris would have recognized this kind of behavior in her master, Nereus would have been repulsed by it in his employer and clients.

Targum on Romans 1 Revisited

Remember that "targum" on Romans 1 that you shared in the first chapter?

Yes.

46. There is, of course, much more going on in Rom. 1 than can be discussed in this chapter. Engaging the moral argument of 1:24–27 vis-à-vis lust and desire, purity and impurity, honor and shame, and what is and is not "against nature," Brownson offers a nuanced and carefully constructed argument that this text cannot be used to argue against same-sex marriage. Brownson, *Bible, Gender, Sexuality*, part 3.

47. On liturgies (cultural and cultic) shaping societal life, see James K. A. Smith, *Desiring the Kingdom: Worship, Worldview, and Cultural Formation* (Grand Rapids: Baker Academic, 2009); and Walter Brueggemann, *Israel's Praise: Doxology against Idolatry and Ideology* (Philadelphia: Fortress, 1988).

Well it ended at 1:25, and while I didn't mention it at the time, I was wondering why you didn't keep going into the next couple of verses. I confess that I was torn at the time about this. On the one hand, I really wanted you to keep going because I wanted to know how all of this would be played out in terms of my friend. On the other hand, I guess that I thought it was a bit of a cop-out that you stopped where you did. You know what I mean? You took the counter-imperial themes and applied them to our contemporary economic context but then stopped short of taking on homosexuality. So I'm wondering, what would that targum look like if you continued it to the end of the chapter?

Let's try that out. We'll pick it up at 1:24 and run it through to 2:1, where the "sting operation" makes its turn. Here goes:

Romans 1:24–2:1 Targum

We are called to live in the truth,
we are called to embody truth in our lives,
but we have traded in the truth for a lie.
Our imaginations have been taken captive;
we can hardly dream of what life outside the grip of idolatry
would look like;
we can scarcely imagine a life that isn't enslaved to consumption;
we can't even begin to get our heads around justice and
righteousness;
generosity and contentment are alien to us,
and an economics of enough is impossible to conceive,
let alone live.
And it is all so empty,
it is all so foolish,
it is all so senseless.
We have crawled into bed with idols
and not known the Lord.
We have bent the knee to idolatry
and not worshiped the Creator,
who is blessed forever. (Amen.)
Having embraced an insatiable idolatry of greed,
having been taken captive by an idolatry of consumption,
our desires are perverted,
our passions run wild,
and we are lost in a sexual fantasyland that is deathly.

Having suppressed what all creation declares about the nature of God,
  having blinded ourselves to the Creator's
    steadfast love,
    faithfulness,
    and justice,
  we now bear the image of our idols in lives of
    voracious lust,
    self-serving infidelity,
    and sexual violence.
Our young women package themselves as sexual products
  ready for consumption.
Our young men take and conquer,
  racking up one sexual exploit after another.
Our sexuality is divorced from covenantal intimacy
  and reduced to cheap carnal entertainment.
But this is not why God created us as sexual beings.
  All of this is a betrayal of who we are called to be.
  The image of God is perverted by such sexual idolatry.
And remember, idols are insatiable.
  They always require sacrifice, they are never satisfied,
  and they have a terrible appetite for children.
  There is no idolatry apart from child sacrifice.
  This is the devastating truth of our culture.
Yes, idols are insatiable.
  They always require sacrifice and they are never satisfied.
  They heap up the bodies of others,
  consumed with a gluttonous sexual hunger.
  Faithful intimacy, commitment, and sexual dignity
  are all placed on their altars.
This is a predatory culture;
  children are the most vulnerable victims,
  even as we are victimized in our own predations.
This is the bitter fruit of idolatry.
  This is the sexuality of empire.
So it is no surprise that the God who gives us up to insatiable lust,
  and who gives us up to perverted desire,
  also gives us up to a debased vision of life,
    a mind of debauchery.
That's what happens when you refuse to know God
  because you are too busy screwing with idols!

But make no mistake!
Such idolatrous copulation bears the bad fruit
of a deeply distorted life,
full of evil longing,
greed, hatred,
envy, death,
breaking community and destroying families,
arrogance, insolent disrespect,
foolishness, infidelity,
and a ruthlessness that is born of a heart
that has turned its back on love.
All of this . . .
this imagination,
this worldview,
this cultural practice,
this way of life,
. . . all of this is in service of a culture of death.
So don't be surprised if this culture dies,
and don't be surprised that this way of life will kill you,
even as you applaud and cheer everyone who lives this way.
And let's be clear.
I'm not talking about "them"
somehow in contrast to "us."
No, my friends, we're all in this mess together.
I'm talking about you.
I'm talking about me.

I'm Talking About You!

Does that get at what we've been talking about?

Yes, that brings it all together. And I guess that while all of this is still pretty new to me, I've got to admit that I'm relieved that your targum says that we are all in this together, and does not target the gay community in its critique.

Not explicitly, but let's also admit that the insatiable sexual fantasyland that is named in the targum is tragically as alive and well in the gay community as it is among straight folks. Those who argue that sexual debauchery is part and parcel of empire, especially in its decline, are undoubtedly right. But this debauchery is no respecter of sexual orientation.[48] When the targum ends with "we're all in this

48. Contra N. T. Wright, "Communion and *Koinonia*: Pauline Perspectives on Tolerance and Boundaries," in *Pauline Perspectives: Essays on Paul, 1978–2013* (London: SPCK, 2013), 267.

mess together," we mean all of us. Consumer capitalism, the commodification of all life, and rampant individualism all function as the ideological ground and legitimation of a cultural ethos of sexual promiscuity and exploitation, regardless of sexual orientation.[49] Paul is judging a sexual ethic that is found throughout our culture. Look again at Paul's language. Where in our culture do you see the "degrading of . . . bodies" (Rom. 1:24), the reduction of bodies to items to be consumed or exploited?

Well, I guess pornography is the obvious example, because there women's bodies are reduced to objects of desire outside of any relationship. But most advertising is just "pornography lite." And the reduction of bodies to sexual ideals begins already in kids' movies. Disney movies begin the whole cycle with their thin, big-breasted women with big eyes and long hair. They all look exactly the same, just with different hair—and now skin—color. And I don't think I even have to mention Barbie dolls.

The distorted sexuality of our culture *seems* to begin innocently enough with movies and advertising and results in abusive pornography.

I've been surprised in the last two years to discover that not only is pornography addiction now talked about in my church but at least one leader has also admitted to having such an addiction.

We have noticed this as well. When we talk about Romans 1:26–27 in churches, people speak to us afterward about how it isn't homosexuality that is the threat to marriage and faithfulness in our sexual lives; it is pornography. And these people speak out of their own struggles with this kind of exploitive sexuality and their own experiences of healing in support groups.

But Paul is talking about more than just the degrading of bodies. As we have shown, he is talking about an abusive and violent sexuality that assaults children, rapes slaves, whether they are men or women, and considers such slaves to be objects for the sexual pleasure of others.

At first when you were describing what was acceptable in first-century Rome, I was feeling increasingly uncomfortable; I felt glad that I live in less sexually violent times. But then I thought about that a bit. Even though child abuse is against the law, child

49. And when we say that we are "all" in this mess together, we include all Christians as well. "There is no point in getting all morally absolute about sexual promiscuity if Christians are screwing around with the same consumerist way of life as everyone else." Brian J. Walsh and Sylvia C. Keesmaat, *Colossians Remixed: Subverting the Empire* (Downers Grove, IL: IVP Academic, 2005), 162. Indeed, recent statistics indicate that pornography viewing rates are higher in conservative Christian communities than in the population in general. See Adam Alter, *Irresistible: The Rise of Addictive Technology and the Business of Keeping Us Hooked* (New York: Penguin, 2017), 265.

pornography charges are laid in my community on a regular basis. Children in schools "act out" with other kids the sexual abuse that they experience at home.[50] *And, as a woman, I am very careful about not drinking at parties because I know that women who drink are likely to be raped—and judged for having allowed that to happen.*[51]

At the heart of this is a mind-set of greed and consumption that views all sexual desire as legitimate and sexual promiscuity as a good time. And really, how could it be different in a culture in which desire and greed are virtues and consumption is our calling? But we know that this is a distortion of our real calling to be creatures of faithfulness and covenantal love.

Which brings me back to my friend. While she is in this "mess" of living in a consumer-capitalist society just like you and I are, I am still relieved to learn that Paul isn't talking about her sexuality or most of her life in this passage. She is not an idolater but a deeply faithful follower of Jesus. She strives to live a life of justice, and I'd be hard pressed to think of anyone who is more faithful than she is. She does not engage in any kind of violent and promiscuous sexual activity but is married in a committed monogamous relationship. Together, with their little boy, my friend and her wife are making a home together.

That is such a simple and beautiful way to put it: they are making a home together. Notice that the kind of practices that Paul is critiquing here are all home-breaking ways of life. From the out-and-out murder of family members to lives of greed and covetousness, slander, gossip, insolence, ruthlessness, and unrestrained sexual pleasure, these are all home-breaking vices. There is

50. We were shocked when our daughters, who were in their teens at the time, had to deal with explicit verbal and physical sexual harassment at a community youth program. What shocked us was that the perpetrator was eleven years old.

51. When we first wrote this section, women who had been raped at Brigham Young University were protesting the university's processes that resulted in the punishment of rape victims for having violated the university's honor code. See Maria L. La Ganga and Dan Hernandez, "'You're a Sinner': How a Mormon University Shames Rape Victims," *The Guardian*, April 30, 2016, https://www.theguardian.com/world/2016/apr/30/mormon-rape-victims-shame-brigham-young-university. Since then the school has offered amnesty to sexual assault victims so that they won't be punished for honor code violations. However, victims may still face expulsion if their bishop determines that they did not abide by church standards; in one case the sexual assault was deemed "irrelevant" by the bishop and the student was punished for being intoxicated. See Erin Alberty, "Her Mormon College Upheld Her Sex-Assault Complaint—But Kicked Her Out Anyway," *Salt Lake Tribune*, https://www.sltrib.com/news/2018/08/05/her-mormon-college-upheld/.

Other high-profile cases of women who have been raped while intoxicated include that of perpetrator Bröck Turner, who received a six-month sentence, widely thought to be so light because he is a white athlete. His father thought that even six months was too harsh for what he called "twenty minutes of action." See Elle Hunt, "'20 Minutes of Action': Father Defends Son Convicted of Sexual Assault," *The Guardian*, June, 6, 2016, https://www.theguardian.com/us-news/2016/jun/06/father-stanford-university-student-brock-turner-sexual-assault-statement.

no justice or faithfulness in this way of life. And where there is no justice and faithfulness, there is no home. Just as Paul is concerned with shaping the diverse communities of Jesus followers into a home in his letter to the Romans, so also your friend and her family are seeking to be homemakers in their church and their community.

I know, and it is so hard to see her living out the gospel so faithfully, only to continue to receive the scorn of so many in the Christian community. And while this discussion of Romans 1 is really helpful to me, I'm still left with the despairing feeling that nothing is going to change. My friend and your friends are still going to face condemnation and rejection in the church. Even if you can offer an alternative interpretation of these two verses in Paul's letter, that isn't going to change anything. They're still going to say, over and over again, "The Bible condemns homosexuality, and so must we!"

If Bible-believing people won't abandon their homophobia even when good exegesis shows that it is groundless, then maybe the problem is in their view of the Bible.

I also think that part of the problem is their view of gay and lesbian people. There is a lot of stereotyping going on.

That too. Let's take those two issues and explore them further. First, what is the real role of biblical authority in this whole conversation? And second, how do we rightly discern the healing and redemptive work of the Spirit in the lives of people who have been viewed for so long as unlikely candidates for such Spirit-led renewal?

Biblical Authority Revisited

That first question has certainly been nagging at me for some time now, and it is only heightened from our conversation. If the so-called clobber texts in the Bible do not legitimate an all-out rejection of what today we know as the orientation of homosexuality, then how does the Bible speak into our situation? How is the Bible an authoritative word in our discussions of homosexuality, or anything else, for that matter?

Perhaps one way to answer that question is to ask how the Bible is authoritative in general in our lives. How does it function authoritatively?

Sometimes it seems to me as though biblical authority is appealed to only when the church wants to beat someone up. I sometimes feel as though every time I open the Bible, I get punched in the face by the absolute.

So biblical authority in your experience means exclusion and shutting people down?

Most often, that's the way it seems. But that is in tension with how I experience God. When I look at God and how God exercises authority in the Bible, it isn't like that at all. When God acts with authority, things are created and given life, the oppressed are set free, hearts that were hard as stone are replaced with hearts of flesh, and the desert becomes a place where food and water are free for the taking.

Some would say that you have too rosy a picture of God here and that you are overlooking that God's authority is also for judgment. Paul is clear that some things need to be judged. God's wrath is revealed against a way of life that is distorted and unjust.

But throughout the biblical story, God's judgment is always in service of redemption. God judges ways of death in order to open up new paths of life. Pharaoh is judged so that the people can be liberated from the oppression of his empire; Israel is judged and sent into exile so that the poor and the widow and the land can be set free (Lev. 18:28); Jesus judges evil spirits so that people can be healed. The flip side of God's judgment is always redemption. And, of course, judgment is never the whole story. In the wilderness, with the golden calf, Moses talks God into abandoning judgment for forgiveness (Exod. 32–34). In Hosea 11:8–9 God abandons judgment and says he will not come in anger (because he is God, not a human!). And on the cross judgment is replaced with forgiveness—not just in Jesus's words ("Father, forgive them; for they know not what they do" [Luke 23:34 RSV]) but also in the very act of Jesus's death itself (Rom. 5:6–11).

Well that's ironic. The Bible is a book committed to forgiveness and life, but when it comes to the question of homosexuality, it ends up being reduced to a book of condemnation and death. I've even heard the Bible quoted in support of imposing capital punishment on gays! And maybe even more tragically (if that is possible), people like my friend have contemplated taking their own lives because of how this book has been used against them. I sometimes think that because the Bible has become a text of death, not a text of life, so many gay and lesbian people who grew up Christian abandon faith altogether when they leave home.

We hear you. Why attempt to live out a story of death? And interestingly, this was also a significant concern for some of the earliest biblical interpreters. The earliest Jewish interpreters of the Torah were concerned that the biblical text remain a living text; this meant that it constantly had to be reinterpreted in faithful ways in new cultural contexts. If it was just being repeated as it had been in the past, then it was a text that no longer had a living word for the present.[52]

52. On this dynamic, see Michael Fishbane, "Inner-Biblical Exegesis: Types and Strategies of Interpretation in Ancient Israel," in *The Garments of Torah: Essays in Biblical Hermeneutics*

I can see how your targum tries to do that. But more broadly, how would we do this today? How can the authority of the Bible function as a living word in the face of changing historical circumstances? Is there a way to think of biblical authority that would be more helpful in addressing these questions of sexuality?

How about if we read the biblical story as a drama?

What do you mean?

Well, the biblical story can be compared to a six-act play. Act 1 is the creation of a good world. Act 2 is the distortion of that world by sin. Act 3 is the calling of Israel to be a blessing to this fallen world. Act 4 is the coming of Jesus, where sin is decisively dealt with. Act 5, scene 1, is the day of Pentecost when the Holy Spirit was poured out on the new covenant community, and the following scenes in the Acts of the Apostles and the Epistles tell the story of the early church, where the life, death, and resurrection of Jesus are grappled with and lived out in the lives of the first Christian communities. Further scenes unfold, from the apostolic era, through the patristic period, and so on, to the present. Act 6 is the coming consummation, when Jesus will return and we will join him on the new earth at the resurrection of the dead. Of course, act 6 hasn't happened yet. So this is an unfinished drama, and we are *in* act 5.[53]

(Bloomington: Indiana University Press), 3–18; and Sylvia C. Keesmaat, *Paul and His Story: (Re) Interpreting the Exodus Tradition* (Sheffield: Sheffield Academic Press, 1999), 22–31.

53. This understanding of biblical authority in terms of an unfinished drama is, of course, indebted to N. T. Wright, "How Can the Bible Be Authoritative?," *Vox Evangelica* 21 (1991): 7–32, which is further developed in his *The New Testament and the People of God* (Minneapolis: Fortress, 1992), 139–44. We follow the innovation of J. Richard Middleton and Brian J. Walsh in adding a sixth act to the model in order to create a little more discontinuity between the history of the church (act 5) and the consummation of all things in the return of Christ (act 6).

For another suggestive modification of Wright's proposal, see Samuel Wells, *Improvisation: The Drama of Christian Ethics* (Grand Rapids: Brazos, 2004). Wells employs such a model of unfinished drama to address the question of LGBTQ+ identity in *How Then Shall We Live? Christian Engagement with Contemporary Issues* (London: Canterbury Press, 2016), 99–115.

It is, of course, not lost on us that the more controversial thing about our adoption of Wright's model is not the adaptation of a sixth act but in how we employ the same model to come to a very different perspective within contemporary Christian debates about homosexuality from that of our friend Tom Wright. (See Brian J. Walsh, "Sex, Scripture and Improvisation" in *One God, One People, One Future: Essays in Honour of N.T. Wright*, ed. John Anthony Dunne and Eric Lewellen [London: SPCK, 2018], 287–315.) We actually see this as part of the genius and fruitfulness of the model itself. People of faith, struggling to be faithful innovators and improvisers, prayerfully discerning the way of the Spirit at a different place in the unfinished drama, do not always agree on what faithful innovation looks like. There is nothing new about such disagreement. The New Testament is full of it. Below we will discuss a biblical model of how the early church, and by extension the contemporary church, can faithfully proceed in the midst of such profound disagreements.

Now, if this is the story in which we live, then we need to discern in the Holy Spirit where we are in this unfolding drama. And if we are to live out this play in our new cultural context, then we can't just repeat what came before, as if we are in act 3 or act 4. Indeed, when it comes to the questions of homosexuality, it is very important that we learn from that earlier scene when Paul wrote his letter to the Romans. But fidelity to Paul and to the story in which we are called to live will not be found in simply repeating what Paul said, even assuming that we have properly understood him. This unfinished drama of redemption is moved forward through innovative improvisation that is faithful to where the story has come from and discerns where the Spirit is leading the church in the unfolding of the story in different historical contexts. Securely rooted in the biblical text, including Paul's epistle to the Romans, we need the courage of creative imagination to chart innovative, yet faithful, paths forward.

Did you say "innovative improvisation"?

Yes, that's exactly what we are called to do. We are in an unfinished drama, and there is no clear script telling us what to do about a whole host of things, homosexuality included.

But "improvisation" sounds like we're just making it up as we go! I may be tired of being punched in the face by the absolute, but I'm also pretty scared of relativism.

Any good actor or musician will tell you that improvisation is never a matter of "anything goes." Rather, improvisation is always a disciplined freedom. Jeremy Begbie describes the improvisatory relationship as "'giving space' to the other through alert attentiveness, listening in patient silence, contributing to the growth of others by 'making the best' of what is received from them such that they are encouraged to continue participating."[54] Note that giving space to the other is a necessary "constraint" of improvisation. By carefully listening to the voice of others in this "act 5" performance of Christian faith, we are always in a dynamic of change and innovation.

But we can't be so innovative that we are no longer a part of this story.

Exactly. Innovation and faithfulness must always go together. Fidelity to the story without innovation results in a dead orthodoxy unable to respond creatively to an ever-changing sociohistorical context. On the flip side of this, innovation without fidelity can result in what Walter Brueggemann calls a "deeper relativizing which gives up everything for a moment of [contemporary] relevance."[55] A

54. Jeremy Begbie, *Theology, Music, and Time* (Cambridge: Cambridge University Press, 2000), 206.

55. Walter Brueggemann, *The Creative Word* (Philadelphia: Fortress, 1982), 7.

lot of the debate throughout the history of the church has been precisely about what this faithfulness looks like.[56]

If the history of the church begins with Pentecost, then maybe we could say that the debates in the history of the church have often been about discerning where the Spirit is leading.

Yes, that would be a good way to put it.

Discerning the Spirit

Then that brings me back to the question of how people can't recognize the working of the Spirit in my friend's life. I think that they have actually been blinded by the Bible, or at least blinded by their interpretation of the Bible, so that it is impossible for them to see that my out-of-the-closet lesbian sister is leading a Spirit-filled life. In fact, she will testify that once she came out of the closet and affirmed her own identity as a lesbian woman, her relationship with Jesus was reignited and she was on the path of Christian discipleship in a more powerful and exciting way than she had ever experienced before. But none of that makes any sense to so many members of her family and her former Christian community.

Kind of like gentile converts in the earliest days of the church.

How so?

Well, it made just as little sense to the disciples of Jesus that gentiles were being converted to the Messiah and being filled with the Holy Spirit as it does to so many "Bible-believing" Christians today to see that same Spirit at work in the lives of gay Christians who are following Jesus in lives of integrity and in committed gay marriage.

So how do we get beyond this impasse? Even if we accept a more dynamic view of biblical authority, how do we get to a point where people can discern the work of the Spirit in the gay community and accept these brothers and sisters into the full life of the church?

It won't be easy, but maybe the same way that gentiles were admitted into the full life of the early church.

Are you talking about that big meeting in Jerusalem to discuss gentiles and circumcision?[57]

56. While we are only focusing on homosexuality in this chapter, there have been, of course, all kinds of other examples in the history of the church. For a profound discussion of how the church engaged the Bible around four other issues that were controversial at one time or another, see Willard Swartley, *Slavery, Sabbath, War, and Women: Case Studies in Biblical Interpretation* (Scottdale, PA: Herald Press, 1983). Another issue, about which there seems to be little debate anymore, is whether divorced people can remarry.

57. Acts 15:1–29.

Yes, and while big meetings might not be so fruitful today in discerning the Spirit, there are some important lessons to be learned from the council in Jerusalem about how the church discerns the Spirit in a way that is faithful yet innovative.

It is a very interesting story because it deals with an issue much like the one we are discussing.[58] The story begins with an angel appearing to a centurion named Cornelius. He is told that his prayers and generosity to the poor have risen up to God, and that he should send for someone called Peter. While his servants are on the way, Peter has a vision where a sheet full of unclean food is lowered. A voice from heaven commands that he eat, and he responds that he has never eaten anything unclean. The voice responds with these words: "What God has made clean, you must not call profane" (Acts 10:15). Now Peter is clearly puzzled by this vision. What could it mean? While he is trying to figure it out, the delegation from Cornelius arrives. Peter goes with them to Cornelius's house. And there he realizes that the vision from God means that he should not call anyone profane or unclean (*koinon ē akatharton*; 10:28). This is quite the hermeneutical jump. We might think that since God showed Peter *food*, that means that Peter can now eat all kinds of food, including that which is normally only allowed to be eaten by the gentiles. But it is clear that Peter sees God's revelation applying to *people*, to the gentiles. We don't really catch the radical nature of this story because we are gentiles. We think, "Of course gentiles are not unclean!" But for Judeans in the ancient world, gentiles were seen as the height of godless immorality. They were considered to be idolaters who were sexually immoral and promiscuous. In fact, Paul's description in Romans 1 mirrors standard Judean descriptions of gentiles (cf. Wis. 14:22–31). If you want to know what Judeans thought of gentiles, read Romans 1:18–31.

The insult of all insults was that gentiles were considered to be unclean. They were repulsive and somehow morally contagious. And that uncleanness had everything to do with the uncircumcision of the male reproductive organ. Sound like any group you know these days? Do you know of a whole group of people who are viewed as unclean because of their sexuality?

Yes, I see that disturbing analogy.

58. Our exegesis here follows that of Sylvia C. Keesmaat, "Welcoming in the Gentiles: A Biblical Model for Decision Making," in Dunn and Ambidge, *Living Together in the Church*, 30–49. For similar treatments of this passage in relation to the question of homosexuality and the church, see also Luke Timothy Johnson, *Scripture and Discernment: Decision Making in the Church* (Nashville: Abingdon, 1996), 60–108; and Stephen E. Fowl, *Engaging Scripture: A Model for Theological Interpretation* (Oxford: Blackwell, 1998), 101–27.

So when Peter decided to baptize Cornelius and the other gentile believers without insisting that they be circumcised, this was an extremely contentious thing. So contentious that other Christian leaders came from Judea to challenge the practice and to insist that circumcision was necessary in order to be saved (Acts 15:1). Which is how Paul and Barnabas and Peter found themselves part of a larger meeting of apostles and elders in Jerusalem. The Christian Pharisees who were arguing that new believers had to be circumcised and keep the law of Moses (15:5) had the Scriptures on their side (cf. Exod. 12:43–49). There was absolutely no biblical precedent for welcoming gentiles into the covenant community without them being circumcised and following Torah. There was no scriptural text that overturned this requirement. Even those texts in Isaiah that spoke about welcoming in the gentiles never went so far as to say, "And they won't need to be circumcised."[59] Not even Jesus had ever suggested anything different from this tradition. Orthodoxy on this matter was clear.

What is interesting is that, while Acts tells us that there was considerable debate about this matter of orthodoxy and inclusion (15:7), the narrator doesn't bother to recount the arguments and counterarguments. Rather, we are told that after all the theological jockeying had taken place, Peter stood up and offered his own position on the matter. He begins by telling them the story of how gentiles had indeed been receiving the gospel and were becoming believers. Having seen all of this with his own eyes, Peter then offered this conclusion: "And God, who knows the human heart, testified to them by giving them the Holy Spirit, just as he did to us; and in cleansing their hearts by faith he has made no distinction between them and us" (Acts 15:8–9). The unclean are clean because they have received the Holy Spirit and live in faithfulness to the Messiah. The God who knows the heart and who promises renewed hearts in the new covenant community bears witness to these gentiles![60] The us/them polarity is overthrown in Jesus! For Peter, and the others, this was a world-changing moment. He then immediately saw the implication of all this: "Now therefore why are you putting God to the test by placing on the neck of the disciples a yoke that neither our ancestor nor we have been able to bear?" (Acts 15:10). This is a stunning conclusion. Knowing that we Judeans have been unable to keep Torah, why would we now impose that on these disciples (notice his term here) who have received the Holy Spirit?

59. Johnson points out the theological weight and respectability of the Pharisees' position in *Scripture and Discernment*, 101.

60. On God knowing the heart, see Pss. 44:21; 51:10. On the new heart of the new covenant, see Jer. 31:33; 32:38–40.

You would think that this pronouncement would have got the theological debate raging all over again, but instead it silenced the endless debate and opened the door for more testimonies. If what Peter was saying was to be taken seriously, then the only way to proceed was by hearing more stories of what the Spirit was doing among the gentiles. And so Paul and Barnabas tell more stories. When they are finished, James makes a decision by appealing to Amos's vision of the return from exile and the rebuilding of "the dwelling of David . . . / so that all peoples may seek the Lord— / even all the Gentiles over whom my name has been called" (Acts 15:16–17, quoting Amos 9:11–12). Isn't it curious that while this text says nothing about whether gentiles should be circumcised or not, it does envision a dwelling place, a home that is welcoming to all, including "unclean" gentiles?

So what was James's decision based on?

It appears to have been based on the experience of God's work in the lives of these new believers, rather than on what the law said. But it was in complete agreement with the way the gospel had been unfolding in the lives of Jesus's followers. In fact, if you read the Gospel of Luke, there is this ever-widening circle that included more and more unlikely people as the story goes on: the shepherds were unlikely bearers of the good news; the Samaritan is used as an example of faithfulness in Luke 10; the messianic banquet is to include the poor, the crippled, the lame, and the blind (Luke 14). And as Luke continues the story into the Acts of the Apostles, the circle continues to widen with the baptism of the Ethiopian eunuch (Acts 8:26–39) and the welcome of the centurion Cornelius (Acts 10). And then in light of all these other moments in the story, there is this decision.[61]

Are you saying that James hadn't just discerned what was happening with the gentiles and the Holy Spirit at this particular moment but that he was looking at the whole story of what had happened in Jesus?

He acted in faithfulness to the ever-widening circle of the gospel.

We could almost say that James and the rest of the community engaged in a process of faithful improvisation. While there was no simple and definitive biblical directive regarding the terms by which gentiles could enter the community, it was clear that this unfinished drama would have to include the gentiles if it were to proceed. And then, in light of the testimony of trusted members of the community about what the Spirit was doing in the lives of these new believers at that time and in that place, they discerned a path forward of radical inclusion.

61. On this dynamic of an expanding inclusiveness in Luke's telling of the story of Jesus and the early church, see Arlo Duba, "Disrupted by Luke-Acts," *Theology Today* 68, no. 2 (2011): 116–22.

I have two questions. First, how wide is the circle? Is everyone welcomed in, or are there still some criteria of inclusion and exclusion? And second, how would this work in the church today?

The circle is as wide as the redemptive movement of the Holy Spirit. The circle is as wide as those who bear witness to Jesus through lives of faithfulness, justice, and love. The circle is as wide as those who have abandoned idolatry and been renewed in the image of God through the power of the Holy Spirit. But that is also where we meet the limit to the circle, the place of self-exclusion. While circumcision is not a requirement of membership in the Christian community, rejecting idolatry is. So some stipulations were set. As gentiles, and especially as gentiles who were not required to follow Torah and be circumcised, these believers would have been tarred by faithful Judeans with the same brush as unbelieving gentiles. The polemic reflected in the first chapter of Romans would have applied to all gentiles; if they did not worship the living God, they could not be anything but idolatrous and hence immoral. And James's decision addressed precisely this question of morality by instructing them to abstain from things polluted by or sacrificed to idols, and from sexual immorality, and "from whatever has been strangled and from blood" (Acts 15:20, 29).

In fact, all three of these stipulations revolved around the issue of idolatry. Gentile believers were being asked to put off precisely those things that are central to a life of idol worship in the Roman Empire. Just as in Romans 1, which sees idolatry at the root of the depravity of life in the empire—sexual immorality, slander and gossip, envy and covetousness, deceit and unfaithfulness—so the Jerusalem Council discerned that rejecting idolatry needed to be named as the central stipulation for gentiles to continue on the path of Christian discipleship.

Instructed to stay clear of anything that has been sacrificed to idols, gentile converts are called to a quiet secession from pretty much all civic celebrations in the empire. The *porneia* (sexual immorality) that is prohibited has a wide variety of overtones: adultery, sex for hire, pederasty, temple prostitution. All these ways of behaving betray a sexuality rooted in the idolatrous practices of the empire. Gentile followers of Jesus are called to a higher standard of sexual fidelity. And meat that was butchered in pagan temples as a sacrifice to the gods was invariably strangled and the blood had not been drained from the carcass. This too must be avoided so as not to be polluted with idolatry.

That's it? That is all that is required of these converts?

Abandoning idolatry isn't a radical enough requirement? These are stipulations that prove to be very difficult to negotiate in the life of the early church, and they take up a large amount of space in the rest of the New Testament. After all, once you set the contours for how and what we eat, how we participate or not in public life, and then throw in our sex lives, you've got most of life covered. And it isn't all done and settled at the Jerusalem Council. The debate about food and idolatry continues to be a matter of "no small dissension" (15:2) in the rest of the New Testament, not least in Paul's letter to the Romans.

Wait, if they continued to debate these issues, does that mean that these rules were not binding in the end? Isn't Paul still debating whether they can eat meat offered to idols in his letter to the Corinthians?

Not only idol meat. The Corinthians seemed to have some issues about sexual morality as well.[62] Even after setting these parameters, it becomes clear that the churches to whom Paul was writing were still debating issues around what was sexually moral and what kind of eating constituted idolatry. There was no unity on these issues in the churches. As we have seen, there was no agreement on what food people could eat even in the Roman assemblies.

But at least there seems to be agreement about abusive and violent sexuality being wrong.

Perhaps. But even on that issue there are some things that Paul doesn't address. For instance, Paul nowhere forbids using one's slave for sex. A slave like Iris might have heard such a condemnation in Paul's language, but there is no evidence that a master would have heard the same condemnation. After all, if slaves were property, then it was a master's right to use them sexually.[63]

So a Christian master might have still sexually abused his slaves?

We don't really know. However, because Paul twice says that in Christ there is no longer slave or free (Gal. 3:28 and Col. 3:11), and because he tells masters to treat their slaves justly and with equality (Col. 4:1),[64] we suspect that would have forbidden the sexual use of slaves by their masters, though he never states this explicitly in his letters.[65] Our point is that, even though the Jerusalem Council

62. On meat offered to idols, see 1 Cor. 8–10; on sexual morality, see 1 Cor. 5–7.

63. Two excellent articles that explore the complexity of this issue are Carolyn Osiek, "Female Slaves, *Porneia*, and the Limits of Obedience," in *Early Christian Families in Context: An Interdisciplinary Dialogue*, ed. David L. Balch and Carolyn Osiek (Grand Rapids: Eerdmans, 2003), 255–74; and Margaret Y. MacDonald, "Slavery, Sexuality, and House Churches: A Reassessment of Colossians 3:18–4:1 in Light of New Research on the Roman Family," *New Testament Studies* 53 (2007): 94–113.

64. The Greek is *dikaion* and *isotēta*. The latter refers to the equality of different social groups in Roman law.

65. See Walsh and Keesmaat, *Colossians Remixed*, 202–12; see also MacDonald, "Slavery, Sexuality, and House Churches," 108–12.

imposed certain stipulations, it is not clear that these were uniformly accepted in early Christian communities. There was considerable diversity in discerning what faithful discipleship looked like.

Okay, I get that. I can see that there was considerable debate on these issues. But there must have been some unity about what it looked like to be a follower of Jesus. I guess my question is whether there were more positive expectations of gentile believers, and Judean ones as well, for that matter.

Of course there were. The Jerusalem Council was an early and foundational deliberation about inclusion and exclusion, but it had a negative focus. A party of the church was trying to keep certain folks out unless they conformed to certain practices, and the Council gathered to lift those restrictions and set out the most basic stipulations for membership, though we have seen that those were themselves radical stipulations. The rest of the New Testament begins to unpack in more profound and mature ways what faithful Christian discipleship looks like. To return to the notion of an ongoing drama, if the Jerusalem Council was something like act 5, scene 8, then we would expect and hope that what happens in later scenes will have moved the narrative further to deeper levels of insight and complexity.[66]

We see that kind of deepening of Christian faith, understanding, and practice in the way Paul will later describe the fruit of the Spirit in Galatians 5:22–23. What does it mean to abandon an idolatrous life full of injustice, insolence, murder, strife, deceit, covetousness, faithlessness, ruthlessness, and envy? How about bearing the fruit of the Spirit? Wouldn't love, joy, peace, patience, kindness, generosity, faithfulness, gentleness, and self-control bear witness to a restored life in Christ that is no longer distorted by idolatry?[67] And isn't Paul doing something just like this in Romans 12 when he calls the Christians in Rome to no longer conform to this age but to be transformed by the liberating of their minds from idolatry? Isn't this why he calls them to live out a counter-imperial community ethic of love, mutual affection and honor, generosity, solidarity with the oppressed, and peacemaking? All of this is how the apostle continues this

66. However, like the story of Israel in act 3, or even the story of Jesus and the disciples in act 4, there have been and will continue to be various dead ends, misdirections, and moments of devastating faithlessness throughout act 5 when the story gets stuck and needs to be seriously redirected to get back on course. This is one of the reasons that we have adopted a sixth act in our model.

67. We have written at some length on how the virtues that Paul unpacks in Col. 3:12–17 are also a charter for a counter-imperial Christian community both in the ancient Roman Empire and in our contemporary context; see Walsh and Keesmaat, *Colossians Remixed*, chap. 10.

process of faithful improvisation, forging Christian identity and witness at the heart of the empire.

Maybe we need to come to my second question. How does all of this work today? What can we learn from the Jerusalem Council and all that happened in those earlier scenes in act 5 that will give us insight and direction to address the confusion around sexuality in our communities? Does this story actually help us today in discerning how this unfinished drama should continue to unfold? What does this story teach us about how to be a church that is faithful to Jesus, biblical, loving, and redemptive in relation to gay sisters and brothers in Christ?

We think that the answer might be found in stories. The improvisatory move that they made regarding the inclusion of gentiles was rooted in an attentive listening to the stories of what the Spirit was doing among the gentiles. But notice that the gentiles were not in fact in the room speaking in their own defense. At that stage of things, they needed trustworthy allies, members of the Christian community who had spiritual stature and integrity, to bear witness on their behalf. Maybe that is something you are called to do for your friend.

That's a little scary. I mean, then I would have to come out of the closet myself as supportive of her. And if I defended her in public, there would definitely be negative backlash.

And you don't think you could handle that?

I don't know. People can be so hateful on this issue. But I guess if Paul calls us to walk with the oppressed in Romans 12, that would also mean being willing to take some of the hatred that is directed toward my friend.

As our lesbian sisters and gay brothers tell their stories, more straight folk need to voice support and help to create safe environments in which these stories can be heard. Without the stories, without testimonies bearing witness to what the Spirit is doing in our midst, there will be no change. We need to hear stories of Christ-shaped lives in which the fruit of the Spirit is evident. You have told us about your friend and her life of faithfulness. Let us tell you about a few of our gay and lesbian friends.

Marj is a nurse who retired early to spend her days binding up the wounds of the many homeless people who come through her church doors each day. Both Jim and Amy have patiently taught young children the stories of the Bible each week in Sunday school. Daniel was a widely respected crown attorney who nurtured our church youth group as they navigated what it meant to be faithful Christians in the difficult terrain of urban adolescence. Cynthia left a successful career in engineering to start up a bike shop that trains street-involved men and women in bicycle repair and customer service. Melodie hangs out with homeless folks and helps them express themselves through art. Billy has the gift of healing and an amazingly generous spirit. Amy's prayers during worship invariably bring together the deepest longings of the community. Danice puts her musical skill and pastoral wisdom to work in her care for LGBTQ+ youth. Beth is one of the finest preachers we know. Mark works with intellectually disabled adults. Karen and Heather are a lovely example of what faithful, committed love looks like. Chris has quietly held many fractious children through many a Eucharist. Abigail's academic gifts are exercised consistently in the service of her church. Fred volunteers on the board of his local social justice group, and Jack, a teacher, stuffs envelopes as a volunteer at the same place. John's choices of songs that are theologically rich and biblically faithful rival the best sermon on a Sunday morning. Megan is a street nurse who has spent late nights in freezing weather at a pop-up safe injection site saving the lives of addicts at the height of the Fentanyl crisis in Toronto. Susan cares for the sick, comforts the broken, buries the dead, and advocates for the vulnerable. We could go on and on. Most of these sisters and brothers are in deeply committed, monogamous relationships. Some of them are married.

"For as in one body we have many members, . . . so we, who are many, are one body in Christ, and individually we are members one of another," writes Paul (Rom. 12:4–6). But the body cannot be whole if it constantly casts off different members. That is what has been happening to faithful, Spirit-led gay Christians for much too long. And that body, continues Paul, is a body of gifts: prophecy, ministry, teaching, exhortation, generosity, leadership, and compassion. In our community, these gifts have been given to us in gay brothers and lesbian sisters for the upbuilding of the body of Christ. Who are we to deny the gifts of God? As we write this, we are astounded by the stories, overwhelmed by the blessing, and deeply humbled that these people are in our lives and our community. Is our experience unusual? For some yes, for others no. It all depends, we suspect, on what kind of people are welcomed around the table of the Lord. It all depends on how we discern the Spirit and improvise faithfully in the midst of this unfinished drama of Christian faith.

So here's the question. What would happen if we listened closely to the stories of these and countless other gay and lesbian Christians? What happens if, like the Jerusalem Council, we put aside the theological debate just long enough to respectfully and humbly hear these stories and get to know these brothers and sisters? Might it be that we would begin to see, in the daily lives of these friends, nothing less than the Spirit of God doing a beautiful work in our midst? Might we even see in their committed relationships nothing less than a sexuality that has profoundly rejected the idolatrous, predatory, and consumptive eroticism of our age and embraced the faithfulness, justice, and love that creation tells us is the very nature of God? And if we receive the testimony of the Holy Spirit through the lives of these friends, might that also open to us new readings of Scripture and new paths of fidelity as we discern the way forward? Might we see committed Christian homosexual relationships not as a threat to marriage but as a witness to its restoration?

Those are deeply moving questions. As you told those stories of your gay and lesbian friends, I found my eyes tearing up.

Maybe that's because there has been so much sorrow in your life and in the life of your friend over these issues.

That is certainly part of it. But I think there is more. You see, I grew up in a world where there was so much promiscuity, such enormous expectations to be sexually active in my early teens, such a high incidence of sexual assault and even sexual abuse in the lives of my friends, that when you describe people who are living deeply committed, faithful lives, it seems like this is a vision of the new earth.

So your tears are tears of longing?

Yes, they are tears that long for more stories like this, more stories of covenantal relationships that display such deep honor and joy. You have described people who bear the image of God in their lives and show a welcome for the stranger and the lost. Isn't that how you have described Paul's call to us in the letter to the Romans? I'm crying because this sort of community seems so impossible in so much of my life. And yet you have just given me a glimpse of where I might find it, you have given me a glimpse of what we hope for.

According to Paul, what we hope for is always a source of deep joy and of deep sorrow. And it is to that hope we now turn.

10

Salvation, Lament, and Hope

Salvation Revisited

It was the neon light that caught his eye. Every time he rode by on the Keele Street bus, he'd glance east down St. Clair and look at it. If it was malfunctioning, he knew. It was a sign that held both attraction and repulsion; that is to say, it both resonated deeply within him and made him uneasy, maybe even scared. You see, it was clear that there were folks behind that sign who knew something, something that he had just come to know deeply in his own life. Yet he had a hunch that he would nonetheless feel uncomfortable if he were to walk into that building.

The sign proclaimed one strong message in bright neon lights for everyone in that rough, meatpacker, working-class neighborhood to see:

J E S U S
    A
    V
    E
    S

"Jesus saves." Undoubtedly a text like Romans 10 would have come easily off the tongues of the folks in that church: "If you confess with your lips that Jesus is Lord and believe in your heart that God raised him from the dead, you will be saved" (10:9). "For, 'Everyone who calls on the name of the Lord shall be saved'" (Rom. 10:13, quoting Joel 2:32).

Brian was sixteen years old and had, during that momentous year of his life, decided to follow Jesus. And the language that was used for that transformation in his life was that of salvation. He was "saved." And he was okay with that language, because he really did feel as if he had been saved. Something radical had happened to him; there had been a total turnaround in his life. He had been walking one way and found that to follow Jesus his life had to go in another direction, a direction he was overjoyed to take.[1]

But here's the weird thing. Brian knew that this "saved" language had a certain meaning among most of his new Christian friends, and while he didn't dispute that meaning, it was never really at the heart of what the idea of being saved meant to him. You see, Brian didn't come to follow Jesus because he felt that he was a hopeless sinner "in the hands of an angry God" (as Jonathan Edwards put it). Sure, he knew that he was a sinner, and he knew that there wasn't any way forward in his life without forgiveness, but that wasn't the overwhelming reason that he came to follow Jesus. So that wasn't really what resonated with him when he thought of being saved.

The question is, if you're going to be saved, then what do you think that you need to be saved *from*? For Brian, as a sixteen-year-old kid from the suburbs of Toronto, what he needed to be saved from wasn't an angry God; he didn't even believe in God, so whether God was angry or not wasn't really an issue. No, what he needed to be saved from was a life of meaninglessness: a monotonous life of suburban boredom and emptiness; a life of climbing the corporate ladder to who-knew-where; a lonely life of deep, deep brokenness; and, truth be known, a life without a father who loved him. From all of that, he needed salvation. Or maybe we could say that he needed to be saved from a secular narrative that had no moral depth, couldn't sustain him in a life of joy, and seemed to be at a historical and cultural dead end. And while he couldn't have put it that way at the time, he is now pretty sure that something like this was what was really going on. At the heart of it, Brian was looking for home. A home that neither his absent father nor his broken family provided, and that could not be found in the empty suburban secularism in which he lived. He needed to be saved from the homelessness that he felt so deeply in his own soul and in the culture in which he had been raised. If this was what was on offer from a Jesus who "saved," then Brian was eager to get on board.

Of course, this isn't likely what the folks behind the "Jesus Saves" sign had in mind. Nor was it what was in the mind of a listener who once questioned us

1. This is not a fictional narrative; it is the actual conversion story of Brian Walsh. While it would be natural to tell this story in the first person, as Brian has in other places, since two of us wrote this section, we have put it in the third person.

as we spoke on Romans and empire at a conference. We had spent a fair bit of time unpacking Romans 1 in terms of how Paul was writing a counter-imperial letter to the heart of the empire. We had demonstrated how Paul's language was consistently undermining and disarming the imperial ideology of Rome, that Paul was offering an alternative gospel to the imperial proclamations of Caesar. And then a man raised his hand with a question. "What do you mean by the 'gospel'"?

It was clear from the way he put the question that this wasn't a question at all. This was a test. He had heard us talk about the gospel in terms that he was uncomfortable with and decided that he would test our orthodoxy with a simple, straightforward question. So we replied, "The gospel is the good news that in Jesus Christ the kingdom of God has come and that the empire of Caesar will inevitably fall."

He pushed it further. "And how would someone accept this gospel?"

"Get on board, little children."

"And why would we need this gospel?"

"Because we're f***ed."

"What did you say?"

"We're f***ed."

"What about sin?"

"That's what we mean."

As you can imagine, our interlocutor wasn't satisfied with our quick answers. So he pushed us further to explain what we meant by the gospel, sin, salvation, and—for good measure—homosexuality. If he reads this book, we hope that he will find a fuller answer to these questions than we could provide in that interaction, but the heart of the matter really was salvation.

And he was right. The heart of the matter *is* salvation. And one of the reasons that we replied to his questions in such a forceful way was because we knew that there were a lot of people in that room suffering from Post-Evangelical Traumatic Stress Disorder (PETSD). These folks had been spiritually and emotionally traumatized by precisely the kind of language, spirituality, and evangelical culture that lay behind our questioner's interrogation. This kind of evangelicalism had pushed many of them to the brink of abandoning Christian faith. These questions and the inquisitorial tone in which they were presented reawakened all the bad memories of an oppressive past. Just as gunfire can be a trigger for those who suffer post-traumatic stress disorder because of past experiences of violence, we sensed that a number of people in that session were being retraumatized by this line of questioning. Our forceful pushback to our interlocutor was out of

pastoral concern for the mostly young adults all around him. We felt that it was necessary to break the spell of his rhetoric with abrasive language that might in fact be liberating for so many in the room. Our f-bomb was an intervention that sought to interrupt a traumatic and paralyzing memory in the lives of those suffering from PETSD. The liberating work we might have accomplished in our counter-imperial exegesis of Romans was threatened by the very nature and tone of the questions this man was asking.

We suspect that many of our readers resonate with the notion of PETSD. If someone asks, "Are you saved?" you respond with embarrassed silence, anger, or an anxiety attack. This may have been one of the reasons why so many of you have had such a hard time with Paul and with his letter to the Romans. If you have got this far in reading a book dedicated to this letter, we are incredibly grateful and humbled. But there is no way to get around the language of salvation. We can only deal with the spiritual trauma that so many of us experience with this language by facing it head-on and seeking to understand salvation in a way that is healing and liberating. If we are going to disarm Romans, then we will need to disarm the language of salvation of its exclusionary judgmentalism. There is no other way to be healed of our PETSD.

Here's the question: What is Paul talking about when he uses the language of salvation? We suspect that he would profoundly agree that "Jesus Saves" but wouldn't likely have any idea what modern Christians mean when they talk this way. Nor, we suspect, would our fictional characters Nereus and Iris have any idea what most Christians are talking about when they employ the language of salvation.

Let's begin with Nereus. When Nereus prays the psalms of lament, when he cries out to God because God's people are being shamed, the nations are mocking, and the unjust are plotting ways to stick it to the innocent, he is asking for something specific: for God to come and overthrow the pagan nation that has enslaved his people and restore justice and wholeness to creation. This is what salvation looks like. It has nothing to do with an eternal home in heaven or the release of the guilty conscience of his soul. No, for Nereus, standing as he did in the deep traditions of Torah and the prophets, and acquainted with the grief of the psalms of lament, salvation is a matter of justice for his people, especially the poor. If there is to be a homecoming for Nereus, it is a decidedly this-worldly homecoming. For Nereus salvation was tangible. His tradition was clear: when God came in salvation, there would be an end to injustice and suffering. Pagan oppressors would be overthrown, and God's people would be saved and set free from those who had subjected them. So when Paul began to write about his "great sorrow and unceasing anguish" (Rom. 9:2) over his fellow Judeans who had not embraced the Messiah, Nereus would have shared that anguish and confusion. Where is God, if the story ends this way?[2] If the story of salvation ends with Israel no longer in the story, then how is this a story of salvation at all? Like Paul, Nereus lived with the tension of God's salvation revealed and enacted in the death and resurrection of Jesus, alongside the absence of that salvation in the historical realities of his people. Not only had they not embraced the Messiah; their oppression had not been overturned by the justice of God.

Now recall Iris. She also wanted an end to injustice and suffering. An end to a system where her children could be taken away, an end to her slavery, which forced her to do things that she considered shameful, even when she tried to be virtuous. For Iris, freedom from bondage was at the heart of salvation. In Iris's ears, Paul's letter spoke to the deep suffering that she experienced in her life, particularly as a slave.

Even though Iris and Nereus, as gentile and Judean, slave and free, would have heard different things, some parts of the letter would have spoken to both of them. If they had in some later meeting discussed their responses to this letter, they might have come to this conclusion:

> We could both see our own suffering in Paul's words, particularly when he referred to the distress, hardship, persecution, famine, nakedness, peril, and even the Roman sword that hangs over our heads.[3] When Paul talked about the empire's rule of death, as opposed to the imperial rule of justice that comes through Messiah Jesus, well, that made so much sense.We could both see how the rule of Caesar brought death to so many: death to those who were conquered, death to those who worked in the fields and built the roads, death to those who worked in the mines, death to slaves who were beaten by their masters, death to the children starving on the streets while one more temple was built to honor Rome, and yes, death to so many Judeans in their homeland.

For both Iris and Nereus salvation meant an end to *the imperial rule of death*.[4] It meant resurrection, and it meant life: life for those who were enslaved, life for those who were hungry, life for the poor who were naked, life for those who were

2. Such a question is always at the heart of lament. See Scott A. Ellington, *Risking Truth: Reshaping the World through Prayers of Lament*, Princeton Theological Monograph Series (Eugene, OR: Pickwick, 2008), 87–88.

3. Rom. 8:35.

4. Our translation of "the dominion of death" in Rom. 5:14–17.

dying because of the economic and political violence of the empire. When Paul said that they would be saved if they confessed that Jesus was Lord and that God had raised him from the dead, that made perfect sense. There is another Lord, whose kingdom is justice and peace and joy (Rom. 14:17). This Lord is the one who brings life because he has conquered death. *Of course* confessing this Lord and believing that he brings life would mean salvation! And, as we saw in chapter 3 of this book, for both Nereus and Iris, such salvation had everything to do with the restoration of home.

Let's look a little more closely at Paul's language. Paul's proclamation that salvation is received when we confess Jesus as Lord comes within a context that is something of a romp through the Law, Prophets, and Writings of Israel's Scriptures. While Romans 9–11 evokes and quotes Israel's Scriptures at great length, if we look just at Romans 10, we will see that Paul moves from Deuteronomy to Isaiah, on to Joel, back to Isaiah two more times, then drops in on Psalm 19, returns to Deuteronomy, and then, for good measure, finishes with a flourish of Isaiah one more time.

All these texts, with the exception of Psalm 19, have one thing in common. They are all addressing the reality of exile and the longing for return. They are all addressing moments in the story of Israel that either predict exile as the necessary consequence for breaking covenant with God or speak words of hope about a return from that exile. These texts are all addressing, if you will, the reality of losing one's home and the promise of and hope for a return to that home. They are all addressing homelessness and homecoming. And, along the way, they are also describing the character of that home, how one gets home, and who is welcome home. Salvation and homecoming are inseparable.

The invitation of Deuteronomy 30:12–14 (quoted in Rom. 10:6–8) is to a covenantal homemaking through listening and obeying the word of God that is as near as your breath and now embodied in our midst in the resurrected Lord Jesus. Confess this Lord, Paul says, and the salvation of covenantal homemaking in the face of the home-wrecking power of sin and death is yours. Referencing Isaiah 28:16 (in Rom. 10:11) Paul assures us that "no one who believes in him will be put to shame." The context of Isaiah's good news is an oracle about the end of exile. Similarly, when Joel says that those who call on the Lord will be saved (Joel 2:32, quoted in Rom. 10:13), that salvation is from the captivity of exile. So also the one who brings "good news" (Isa. 52:7, quoted in Rom. 10:15) is proclaiming the end of exile. Salvation is about coming home out of exile.

Of course, this is all so difficult to believe. No wonder Isaiah asks, "Who has believed our message?" (Isa. 53:1, quoted in Rom. 10:16). It is hard to believe a promise is fulfilled when the fulfillment doesn't look like anything that you have expected. Yes, Israel wanted homecoming, but surely this is *their* homecoming; these were, after all, *their* promises, *their* covenant, *their* righteousness. So what are all these gentiles doing here? How can this be a homecoming if the house is full of strangers? And Paul answers from Deuteronomy 32:21 (quoted in Rom. 10:19) and Isaiah 65:1 (quoted in Rom. 10:20), again to say that the homecoming of God was always a homecoming for the nations, the promises were always for the whole world, and even those who were not looking for this homecoming are invited home. In Isaiah 65 this is a homecoming vision that entails nothing less than new heavens and a new earth. No wonder that Paul refers to Psalm 19:4 (in Rom. 10:18). The voice of God, spoken from the very stars of heaven, this word of God echoing through all creation, "has gone out to all the earth," to the very ends of the world! The call home goes all the way down. The call home is a call to all creation and to all nations.

And that call took on flesh in Jesus Christ. He is the end of the story; he is where the story has always been going; he is the fulfillment of God's homemaking promises. So "if you confess with your lips that Jesus is Lord and believe in your heart that God raised him from the dead, you will be saved." Saved from homelessness, whether at the heart of the empire or as despised Judeans at its margins, through confession that Jesus, not Caesar, is Lord.

Echoing back to the very first lines of the epistle (Rom. 1:4), Paul says that the confession that Jesus is Lord is inseparable from believing that he has been raised from the dead (10:9). In that resurrection, the home-breaking powers of death are vanquished, and the door is open anew for homemaking in the kingdom of God. In that resurrection, and in this confession, a new covenant community is born and the return from exile is fulfilled. And so we return to that sign from Brian's youth.

Jesus saves! . . . from homelessness.

Jesus saves! . . . from home-breaking.

Jesus saves! . . . from all false and inhospitable constructions of home.

But we, like Israel, continue to sabotage our own homecoming. So Paul ends with God's word to Isaiah 65:2 (quoted in 10:21): "All day long I have held out my hands to a disobedient and contrary people." All day long God holds out hands to welcome us home. All day long God holds that door open. All day long, with tear-filled eyes, God calls, cries, whispers, "Come home, come home." This is God's longing for home. This is the pathos of God. This is where God's lament echoes our own.

Lament Revisited

When we grounded this book in a specific situation of lament, we did so because we believe that Paul's larger vision of new creation, inaugurated in Jesus and bearing fruit in the communities that followed him, also begins in that pathos. As Walter Brueggemann has indicated, a prophetic imagination that intends to bring transformation with new symbols of hope needs to begin by articulating the depths of the darkness. It is impossible to imagine newness without acknowledging the pain and grief that are the result of violence and sin.[5] Paul, we believe, begins where the prophets begin, and indeed where the whole biblical story begins, with the pain and grief of the communities to whom he is writing.

So it is no surprise that Paul's description of salvation occurs right at the heart of chapters 9–11, where the apostle reveals the depth of his grief over his own people. Paul begins Romans 9 by talking about his great sorrow and unceasing anguish (9:2), echoing the anguish of both Jeremiah and Hosea as they struggle with God's love, turmoil, and pain for a faithless people.[6] Again and again in these chapters, as Paul tells the story of the people of Israel, we glimpse the struggle that is found throughout the prophetic texts, the struggle of a God who is bound to a people who have refused to walk in the ways of the covenant, who have refused to do justice, love kindness, and walk humbly with their God (Mic. 6:8).

This struggle has been present since the beginning of the letter to the Romans. When Paul describes God's wrath revealed against the unjust and the ungodly in Romans 1:18, we find ourselves in a story line that describes the tension between, on the one hand, God's judgment on the people of Israel and, on the other hand, God's compassion for God's people. This story line is revisited again and again in the epistle. The wrath of Romans 1 gives way in Romans 2:4–5 to the kindness, patience, and forbearance of God. In Romans 3:3–4 and 3:21–26 the unfaithfulness of the people is met with the faithfulness, grace, justice, and patience of God. God's passing over of sins is emphasized in 3:25, and the grace of the promise is outlined in 4:16–25. Romans 5 describes God's love for sinners and enemies (5:8–10) and the free gift of grace and eternal life (5:15–21). Romans 7 and 8 describe how even slaves to sin are not condemned but set free (8:1–2), ending with the assertion that *nothing* that anyone can do on earth or in heaven can get in the way of God's love (8:35–39).

5. Walter Brueggemann, *Prophetic Imagination* (Philadelphia: Fortress, 1978). See also his "The Costly Loss of Lament," *Journal for the Study of the Old Testament* 36 (1986): 57–71.

6. Jeremiah and Hosea are quoted or echoed in Rom. 1:23; 9:25, 26; and 11:27.

In these first eight chapters, Paul constantly moves back and forth between judgment and forgiveness, humankind's injustice and God's faithfulness, humankind's sin and God's love. In so doing he is moving in the world of the prophets, who described the pathos of God in just this way: in the midst of grieving the loss of a faithful partner, God continues to wrestle with the possibility of a new thing. Scott Ellington puts it this way: "Yahweh is finally a reluctant spouse who despite extreme provocation, cannot bring himself to sign the divorce papers."[7] The result of such reluctance, such a desire to stay in relationship, no matter what, is that God bears the pain of the relationship. God mourns and weeps the loss of the relationship, and yet endures and lingers in the anguish of this relationship.[8] Even though God might respond in silence or anger initially, God's compassion and love are too great to let anger ever be the last word.[9]

In chapters 9–11 Paul explores this dynamic more explicitly. In the face of injustice, in the face of turning away, in the face of unbelief, God will come with a new word, banishing ungodliness and forgiving sin (11:27). Throughout the twists and turns of these chapters, Paul returns again and again to the underlying theme of Romans 8, reminding those in the community of Rome of God's love, compassion, patience, longing for salvation, grace, kindness, and unending desire to welcome back those who have been cut off.[10]

In the prophets it is this commitment to stay within the bonds of the covenant that enables God to envision a different ending to the story. In the same way it is the deep desire of God to act out of compassion and for salvation that enables the new vision of Romans where all of Israel will be shown mercy and be saved (11:26, 31), where there will be a new covenant when God takes away their sins because they are beloved.

Paul's telling of this story portrays exactly the same struggle, passion, and hope that is found in the prophets on whom he draws. And in so doing he reveals the deep pathos at the heart of God, God's aching desire to be in right relationship with God's people, and through them with the world. This is why God continues to suffer for creation and for the people that God has called. And while Paul will

7. Ellington, *Risking Truth*, 135.

8. See Isa. 8:18–9:3. See also Ellington, *Risking Truth*, 47–52, 133–43; and Kathleen M. O'Connor, *Jeremiah: Pain and Promise* (Minneapolis: Fortress, 2012), 61–64.

9. Hosea 11:5–9. It is worth repeating what Fretheim says: "Grief is always what the Godward side of judgment looks like." *The Suffering of God: An Old Testament Perspective* (Philadelphia: Fortress, 1989), 112.

10. Love (9:13, 25); compassion (9:15, 16; 11:30–32); patience (9:22); desire for salvation (10:1, 9, 10, 13; 11:11, 14, 26); grace (11:5, 6); kindness (11:22); desire to welcome back those who have been cut off (11:23–32).

expend many words in this epistle to plumb the depths of that pathos and the salvation that is born of such suffering, at the heart of that lament he admits that there are few if any words at all to adequately express these experiences.

So as we near the end of a book of many, many words, we too confess that sometimes there is simply nothing to say. Sometimes words are too easy, too cheap. Sometimes words are just the chatter to cover up the silence. When Iggy died, we sat with the community in silence. When Frenchy remembered his friend, he sat at the edge of the party and wept. You see, when it gets to the deepest places of our lives, when we plumb the depths of our most powerful (indeed, most overpowering) experiences, longings, emotions, desires, and hopes, we find that there are very few words indeed.

Maybe that is why we stumble around so much in our prayers. We just can't find the words. It's not simply a matter of no longer being comfortable with the formulas of past pieties (although it may well be that), but more profoundly it is that those deepest longings seem somehow inarticulate. We find ourselves reduced to inarticulate groans, moaning, sighing, weeping, and sometimes just sitting before God in silence because we just don't know what to say. We are at a loss for words, and we find ourselves overcome with a profound sense of longing, a deep experience of waiting, waiting, and waiting some more, and we can't find the words to even name that waiting. We suspect that anyone with PETSD knows what we are talking about.

Paul seems to understand this loss of words, even though he was so elegant and expansive in his own use of words. And when it all comes to a head at the very middle of this expansive letter, he writes that the inarticulate longing and waiting that characterizes so much of our lives is in tune with the very heart of creation and resonates with the very heart of God.

All of creation, Paul writes, waits with eager longing (Rom. 8:22). All of creation is longing for redemption. All of creation is groaning as with birth pangs for the restoration of all things, not least the restoration of human beings as faithful homemakers in this good creation (8:23). All of creation waits. Waiting goes all the way down. So we are not alone in our waiting. We are in tune with the very nature of things. Indeed, our groaning, our lament, is evidence that the Spirit of God is at work within us (8:23). The Spirit who has taken up residence in us, who dwells in us, making home in our lives (8:9–11), is the very Spirit who sets us free from slavery and makes us heirs of Christ in the homecoming of God (8:12–17). But if we are heirs with Christ, writes Paul, then we will suffer with Christ (8:17). We suffer in that tragic gap between vision and reality. We experience the woundedness of the world, the bite of oppression, the lament of creation, the longing for redemption embodied in everyday social, political, and economic life, all the more acutely because of our experience of Christ.

But there is more. Paul also insists that God the Holy Spirit groans with all of creation, and groans with all of humanity in the travails of childbirth, in the labor pains of the new creation (Rom. 8:26). Pathos goes all the way down, all the way up, and all the way through and around and within. We're all in this together.

Then Paul takes this a step further. Not only does the Spirit groan in the travails of childbirth with us; those groans are sighs too deep for words. This is quite stunning. You see, the Holy Spirit cannot take our inarticulate prayers and translate them into words for God, because the Holy Spirit is just as much at a loss for words as we are. The brooding Spirit over the face of the deep is still brooding, is still about to give birth, but like all women in the throes of contractions, the Spirit isn't all that articulate in her groaning. These are sighs too deep for words. And, Paul assures us, God can interpret the groaning of the Spirit. God can understand the mind of the Spirit, because the Spirit is groaning on behalf of us. And God knows those deepest longings, God knows what we wait for, because God shares those longings and God is waiting for the same thing as we are.

So we find ourselves so often at a loss for words. We find ourselves struggling to pray, struggling to voice our pain, our despair, our deep confusion. We end up speechless. All that we have is our tears, our sighs and groans. And then someone breaks through it all with a cheerful citation of the next verse in Romans 8. "We know that all things work together for good for those who love God, who are called according to his purpose" (8:28). That ever happen to you? Have you noticed how often Christians appeal to this verse in the most desperate of circumstances?

A young father is tragically killed in a car accident, leaving behind a young widow and an infant son, and someone says, "Michael is with the Lord now. He is in a better place." Really? Some kind of postmortem bliss "with the Lord" is better than a life lived to its fullness as a dad and a husband?

A child is diagnosed with a terminal illness. "God is going to use this in a wonderful and powerful way." Well, maybe we'd just prefer that God didn't play games with the life of this beloved child.

Our brother Iggy, like so many First Nations folks on the streets of our urban centers, dies an untimely death from the sheer weight and burden of the life that he has led. "God has a purpose in all things, and this is all part of his plan," we are told. And we wonder whether we really want to believe in such a divine determinism.

You can predict when this verse is going to be brought out to trump all lament. You know that if the situation is desperate, it won't take too long before someone reaches for Romans 8:28 to bring comfort, while also silencing our inarticulate groaning. The irony is thick. Precisely when we have nothing to say, we blithely quote Paul only two verses away from where he has told us that the Spirit herself has only inarticulate sighs and is at a deep, deep loss for words. The Spirit may be at a loss for words, but we'll not be left speechless. So we grab hold of a spirituality that in effect sugarcoats the tragedies in which we live.

It is true that Paul writes, "We know that all things work together for good for those who love God," but surely this is not to dismiss or disregard the real pain and suffering that we face. Surely we have seen by now that Paul is no author of cover-up. This letter to the Romans is born of pathos, acquainted with grief. And chapter 8 of the epistle is full of pain and suffering. We suffer with Christ, Paul writes. And while he will want to place this suffering in the perspective of what he calls "the glory about to be revealed to us" (8:18), we have seen that such a suffering resonates with a groaning throughout all of creation that reaches right into the very heart and being of God the Holy Spirit. Paul speaks of a waiting and longing for redemption precisely because he knows that our present reality is so far from such redemption. He speaks of a hope that is not seen (8:24–25), precisely because there is no hope to be cheaply found in the mangled body of a young husband and father, in the lifeless body of a little Syrian refugee boy on the Turkish shore, in disease that debilitates, and in depression that leaves us paralyzed.

Paul isn't offering us determinism here. He is giving us a glimpse into the heart and purposes of God. We are saved in hope, he has just written. Hope for what? Hope that love wins. Hope that goodness is stronger than evil. Hope that we will be conformed to the image of Christ. Hope that we will come to full hamanity in Christ, that we will bear the image of God in our lives. Hope that humanity and all creation will come to the fulfillment of our calling. Hope that we will be a people not of shame but of restored glory. This is the hope that has been woven throughout this epistle.

And this leads us to a rereading of this famous verse about all things being for good. It isn't just that we have employed Romans 8:28 as a panacea to all evil that befalls us. We've actually misread it altogether. Indeed, we have been happily seduced by a mistranslation. There is good reason, from closely looking at the tense of the Greek in this verse, to question the usual translations. It is not

> We know that all things work together for good for those who love God, who are called according to his purpose. (NRSV)

or

> We know that in all things God works for the good of those who love him, who have been called according to his purpose. (NIV)

but rather

> We know that in all things God works for good *with those* who love God and are called to his purpose.[11]

Do you see the difference?

Paul is not saying, "Cheer up, God's got it all under control, even if it doesn't look that way." No, Paul is saying that in the face of the suffering, pain, brokenness, and labor pains of creation; in the face of such deep, deep longing, inarticulate sighs and groaning; in the face of being rendered utterly wordless, followers of Jesus don't grasp for cheap words and easy comfort but get busy in paths of redemption. We get busy with the purposes to which we have been called. Those who love God are those who embrace their calling to tend creation, who have a vision of life in the face of death, and who claim redemption even against the evidence. In Paul's worldview those who love God are renewed in the image of God, they live with an aching longing for his kingdom, and they suffer with Christ.

God works for good *with those* who love God and are called to his purpose. Whether we are planting a community garden or seeking a reduction in fossil fuel extraction, sponsoring a refugee family or seeking deeper reconciliation with the First Nations, building community or holding vigil at the side of the dying, sharing our own resources or advocating for economic redistribution, in these and in so many other ways, we are working with God to bring all things together for good in the face of unspeakable evil. We may be speechless, but we are not paralyzed. We may have nothing to say, but that doesn't mean we have nothing to do.

Paul goes on: "Those whom he foreknew he also predestined to be conformed to the image of his Son, in order that he might be the firstborn within a large family" (8:29). Don't get hung up on later theological debates about predestination

11. See Robert Jewett, *Romans: A Commentary*, Hermeneia (Minneapolis: Fortress, 2007), 527.

here. That's not the point. God's foreknowledge is more a matter of loving us before we were born than it is a statement of God's omniscience. And God's predestination here is that we be conformed to the image of his Son. Do you want to know God's purpose for your life? Then be like Jesus! That is God's purpose. That is how we are restored to what we were always called to be, the image of God. We are not predestined to violence, to death, to tragic brokenness. That is the debilitating heresy of pious determinism. Rather, we are predestined to be conformed to the image of Jesus. We are predestined and called, and we find our deepest meaning and fulfillment by being invited into the family of Jesus and living as members of that family.

And this, Paul says, is our glory. It all comes down to glory. In our idolatry we exchanged the glory of God and our call to bear God's image for worthless and foolish graven images (1:23). Paul writes that we suffer with Christ so that we may also be glorified with him (8:17). He dares to say that the sufferings of this present time are not worth comparing with the glory about to be revealed to us (8:18). The creation will obtain the freedom of the glory of the children of God (8:21). Those whom God justified he also glorified (8:30). This glory is the kingdom of God that overthrows the kingdom of death. This glory is the homecoming of God's children as loving and caring homemakers. And this glory is manifest when the weighty presence of God takes up residence in lives of restored justice. This is the glory that we meet when God's purposes are fulfilled and love wins. When we are working toward such glory, when we are living out our lives as restored bearers of the image of God, indeed the image of the suffering Christ, then we are working with one another and with God toward the redemption of all of life, the transformation of all things into the "good" that was first pronounced on all of creation (Gen. 1:4, 10, 12, 18, 21, 25, 31).

Paul's vision does not cover up the real evil that creates such pain in our lives. Indeed, he ends this chapter by naming many of the evils that attack the people of God. After asking, "Who will separate us from the love of Christ?" (8:35), Paul names the candidates for such a separation: the hardship of economic oppression, the distress of life in crisis, the persecution of the powerless by those who wield the might of the state and the economy, famine wrought by ecological breakdown and market manipulation, the nakedness of those who produce our clothing, the peril of those who work in substandard conditions, and, finally, the sword, the oppressive coercion of the state. Surely these are real evils, real threats. As we have seen throughout this discussion of Paul's epistle, he does not shrink from naming names. But in the face of all this, he confesses that nothing can "separate us from the love of God in Christ Jesus our Lord" (8:39). This is no cheap piety. This is no cover-up. This is a rallying cry of resistance. This is the heart of a counter-imperial hope.

Hope Revisited[12]

The importance of a God who engages in lament with God's people cannot be overestimated. For, at bottom, the practice of lament is the practice of *truth-telling*, the practice of naming the injustice, naming the pain, naming the horror that violence and lies create.[13] God is unremittingly the God of truth-telling; that is why God is in such pain as a witness to the terror that human beings continually inflict on one another and the world. And it is because God is committed to naming the suffering that God is able to envision a future beyond such suffering. God's very self desires reconciliation, healing, forgiveness. The overwhelming confessions of God's compassion and forgiveness mean that God needs to name the sorrow so that it can be dealt with, healed, borne, forgiven. This is what creates both the pain of death at the heart of God and the possibility of resurrection.

As those who image this God, such truth-telling is our calling as well. That is why, early on in this book, we described the pathos of the community in Rome, outlining what life was like for a slave and a subsistence laborer. Unless we are willing to name the injustice of sexual abuse, economic oppression, human trafficking, an honor system that brings shame to slaves and Judeans, and the exclusion of the stranger, we have no way of understanding either the word of hope that the gospel brought into these situations of pain or the radical nature of Paul's language in Romans. When Paul condemns violent sexual abuse of boys and temple prostitutes (1:26–27), and the injustice, arrogance, greed, death dealing, lies, and ruthlessness of the Roman economic system (1:29–31), he is talking about something specific. When Paul describes those who are self-seeking and ignore the truth for injustice (2:8); when he describes the deceivers, whose mouths deliver death, and who bring bloodshed, ruin, and misery because they

12. The following section is dependent on Sylvia C. Keesmaat, "Walking with the Oppressed: Lament and New-Creational Hope," in *One God, One People, One Future: Essays in Honour of N.T. Wright*, ed. John Anthony Dunne and Eric Lewellen (London: SPCK, 2018), 388–417.

13. Soong-Chan Rah discusses the importance of lament and truth-telling in relation to the realities of racial injustice in the United States. Soong-Chan Rah, *Prophetic Lament: A Call for Justice in Troubled Times* (Downers Grove, IL: IVP, 2015), 44–59. See also Joshua Beckett, "Lament in Three Movements: The Implications of Psalm 13 for Justice and Reconciliation," *Journal of Spiritual Formation and Soul Care* 9, no. 2 (2016): 209.

do not know the way of peace (3:13–17); when he talks about the imperial rule of death and sin that works for injustice (5:17 and 6:12), the original recipients of this letter would have heard Paul naming the sexual abuse they experienced; the economic violence that made them hungry, homeless, and enslaved; the lies that made such a system possible; and the misery and ruin that Roman colonialism visited on other peoples. Paul wasn't talking about sin or injustice in general. He was naming the experience of those to whom he wrote, those who lived in Rome in the middle of the first century CE.

Walter Brueggemann calls this the "*critique of ideology*" that enables the "*public expression of pain*."[14] Without such a critique, the depth of the suffering of the community is not acknowledged, and the need for far-reaching healing is never envisioned. Because Paul was naming the pain and violence that shaped the lives of so many in this community, and because their suffering shaped his writing, his vision for what this community was called to be in the image of the Son was truly radical and healing. As we have seen, in Romans 12–15 Paul describes a community that overturns the social structures that made possible the honor/shame system. It is hard to maintain the boundaries of honor when you are practicing love and mutual affection and trying to show more honor than you receive (12:10). It is hard to practice an economics of ruthless greed and lying arrogance if you are not thinking of yourself more highly than you ought (12:3), while contributing to the needs of others in the community, extending hospitality to strangers (12:13), avoiding haughtiness, and walking with the oppressed (12:16). It is hard to sexually abuse your slaves if you are acting in genuine love and mutual affection, hating evil, and holding fast to what is good (12:9). It is hard to inflict violence on your neighbor when you are blessing those who persecute you (12:14), weeping with those who weep (12:14), and providing food and drink to your enemy (12:20). It is hard to continue to treat others with arrogance and injustice when you are welcoming the powerless to your table and doing so because Christ welcomed you (15:1–7).

Therefore, when Paul tells us to "walk with the oppressed" (12:16 our translation), he is doing so partly because it is precisely the oppressed, those who mourn, who can teach us what the Christian walk looks like.[15] It is they who can help us

14. Walter Brueggemann, "Unity and Dynamic in the Isaiah Tradition," *Journal for the Study of the Old Testament* 29 (1984): 89–107, here 97.

15. In relation to Isa. 31:8–9, O'Connor describes how in the prophets "the feeble and vulnerable, the lowly and the wounded—will become the center of new life." Similarly, she says, "Although they [the forgotten, the disabled, and the vulnerable] are the lowest in the society, they will be the beating heart of the new community." O'Connor, *Jeremiah*, 105, 106.

to name the pain and the grief that is required for the "normal" functioning of a violent culture. That is why we began this book with the story of our friend Iggy and why we have always kept the attempted genocide of the Indigenous peoples within view of our interpretation of Romans. It is those who still bear the trauma of the residential schools who show us the violent outcome of the colonialism that shapes Western culture. It is those who are unable to find homes or living-wage jobs who show us how our economic system grinds down those who don't start ahead of the game in middle-class families. It is those who have had their housing destroyed to make way for a more gentrified neighborhood who show us the hopelessness and homelessness that our socioeconomic system breeds for the poor. It is those who have been jailed without bail, or even shot to death, for a traffic violation who show us the injustice that white privilege makes possible. It is those who have had their lands contaminated by the mines that produce cell phone components who show us the violence that our lives inflict on the earth. It is those who have been displaced by famine and war who show us the environmental toll that our constant consumption places on the livelihoods of the poor. It is those in the LGBTQ+ community who show us how the exclusion practiced by our churches is nothing less than a covenant with death. It is only when we share in the suffering of these people that we truly understand the need for repentance, that we truly understand the sins for which we must ask forgiveness.[16] Only those who have suffered from the dominion of death can show us how life-giving the dominion of justice really is (Rom. 5:21). Without the leadership of those who mourn, how can we possibly understand the suffering of those for whom the promise of new creation is truly gospel, good news, salvation? Without the leadership of those who mourn, how can we possibly understand the pathos of a crucified God? Without entering into their lament, how can we presume to live in a hope that is anything more than sentimental optimism?

Brueggemann emphasizes that the *critique of ideology* and *the embrace of pain* make possible the *embrace of newness* and *the release of social imagination*.[17] This dynamic roots the possibility of imagining a new creation in the critique of ideology. That is to say, unless injustice is named, unless sin is described on the ground in Paul's context and our own, there is no possibility of acknowledging the suffering and pain it has created. And unless that suffering is embraced and lamented, no

16. See further Rah, *Prophetic Lament*, 89–97; Katherine Moloney, "Weeping, Warning, and Woe in Revelation 18: The Role of Lament in Establishing Collective Responsibility and Enabling Collective Repentance," *Expository Times* 127, no. 7 (2016): 320.

17. Brueggemann, "Unity and Dynamic," 99–102.

vision of hope for the future can even be imagined. As Brueggemann has evocatively put it, "Only grief permits newness."[18] Hope is always born of lament. This is the dynamic of truth-telling that is led by a community that mourns. It is the dynamic not just of the prophets but also of the letter to the Romans. Perhaps it would even be accurate to say that *because* it is the dynamic of the prophets, it is the dynamic of Romans, written by an apostle who was steeped in the prophetic tradition. In Romans Paul begins with the critique of ideology (Rom. 1–7), moves to the embrace of pain (Rom. 8–11), and then outlines a vision of an alternative future that challenges the ruling ideology and worldview (Rom. 12–16).

Hope apart from lament is ideology. Paul writes, "For in hope we were saved. Now hope that is seen is not hope. For who hopes for what is seen? But if we hope for what we do not see, we wait for it with patience" (Rom. 8:24–25). It is in the tension between what is seen and unseen, between the undeniably painful reality in which we live and the vision of a coming restoration of all things, that hope is born. But just as Paul moves beyond generalities when describing the reality of human sinfulness, so also does the hope that animates his letter to the Romans have a specific sociocultural and historical shape.

In a world where status and honor legitimated the shaming and denigration of the poor and slaves, Paul called this community not only to welcome all but to offer dignity and respect to those who had never experienced it (Rom. 12:10, 16). Can we also envision communities where the homeless, those with mental illness, and those with intellectual disabilities are treated with dignity and respect?

In a world where economic divisions were clearly maintained and households were in competition with one another, Paul called this community not only to practice a sharing economy in their communities but also to welcome the stranger (Rom. 12:13). Can we envision a world where we ensure that no one has too much and all have enough, and where no one is attacked on the streets or deported because of their skin color, accent, gender identity, or sexual orientation?

In a world where the enemy is vilified, Paul calls for generous blessing and hospitality for those who have wronged us (Rom. 12:14, 20). Can we imagine a world where we offer political aid rather than aggressive revenge, where our churches preach forgiveness rather than militancy, where offenders are welcomed and supported rather than excluded?

In a world where the pain of the suffering was denied and ignored because it was considered collateral damage in the good ordering of society, Paul called

18. Walter Brueggemann, *The Hopeful Imagination: Prophetic Voices in Exile* (Philadelphia: Fortress, 1986), 41. See also Brueggemann, "Unity and Dynamic," 94–102.

this community to weep with those who weep and to walk with the oppressed (Rom. 12:15–16). Can we envision a world where the voices of the suffering are allowed to subvert the ideology of militarism and consumption that dominates our imagination? Can we imagine a world where those of us with privilege sacrifice that privilege in order to enter into the suffering of others, of creation, of God?

It is clear that Paul could envision such a world, and this is a world that we want to live in too. This is the kind of hope that Paul calls us to. If we truly walk with the oppressed and allow ourselves to be led by those who mourn, perhaps we will find ourselves, with Iris and Nereus, not only imagining the new creation but living in such a way that others too will recognize it when it arrives.

Scripture Index

Old Testament

Genesis

Exodus

Leviticus

Deuteronomy

Judges

Proverbs

Ecclesiastes

Isaiah

Jeremiah

Lamentations

Ezekiel

1 Corinthians

2 Corinthians

Galatians

Ephesians

Philippians

Colossians

1 Thessalonians

1 Timothy

2 Timothy

Philemon

Jude

Revelation

General Index